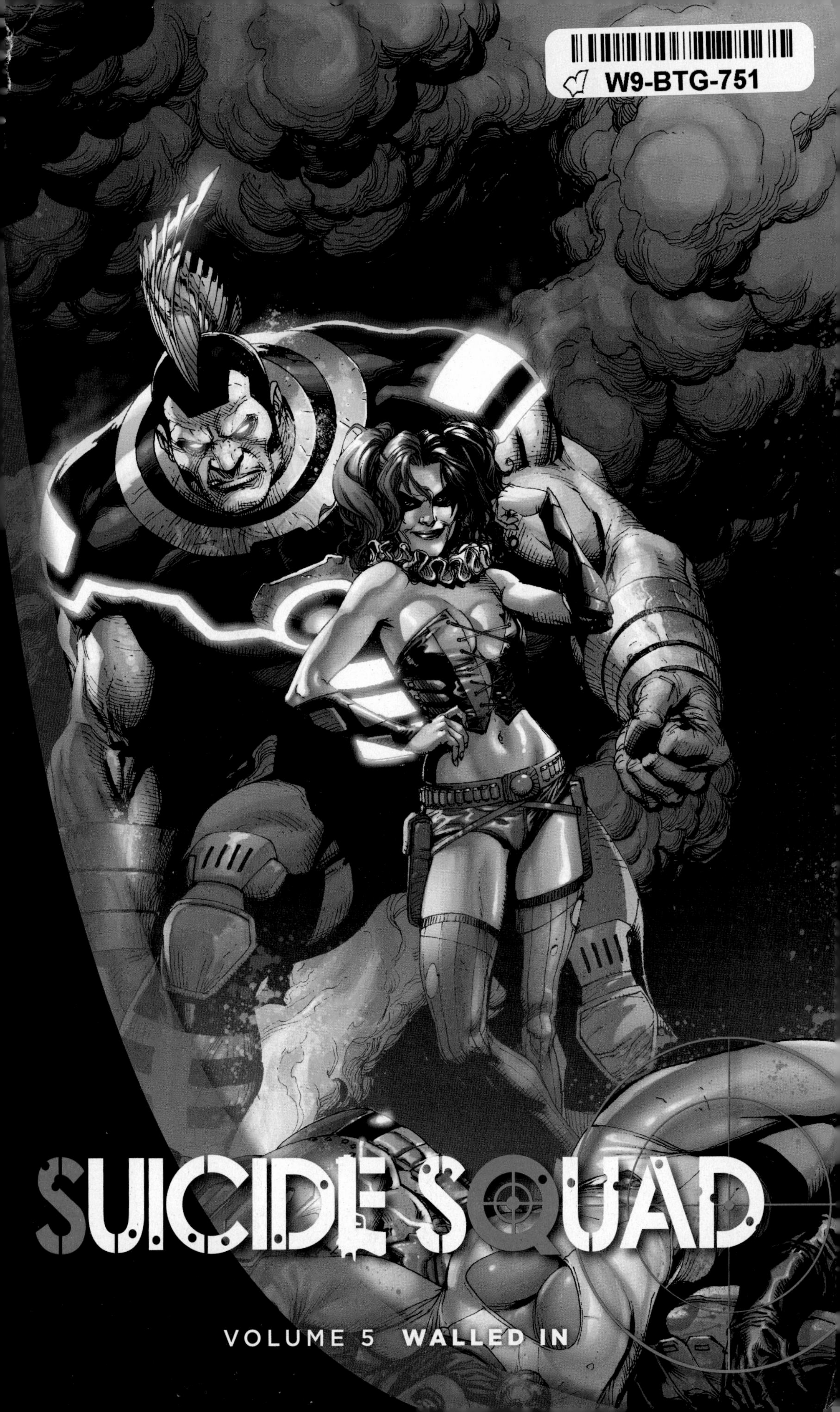

SUICIDE SQUAD

VOLUME 5 **WALLED IN**

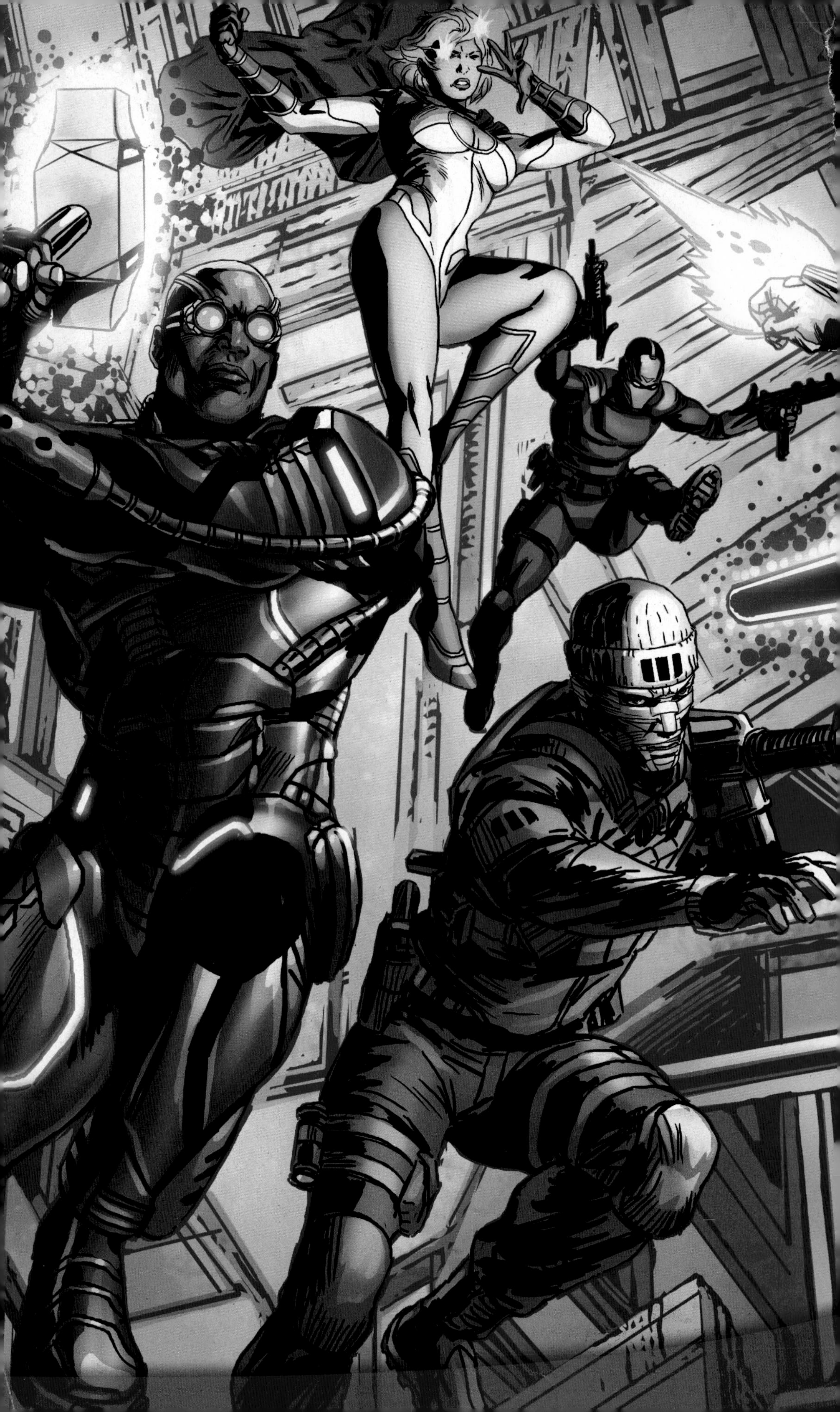

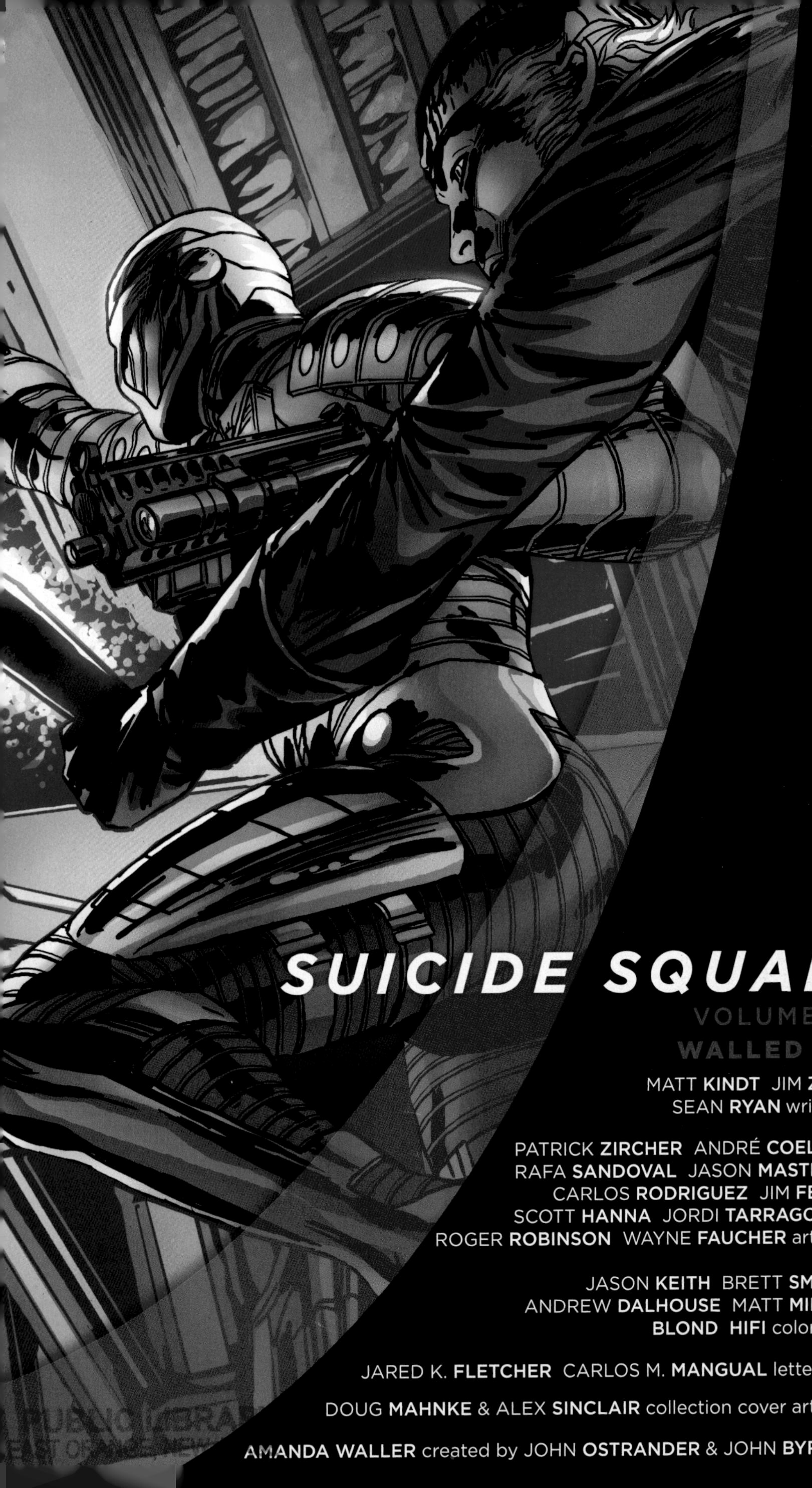

SUICIDE SQUAD

VOLUME 5
WALLED IN

MATT **KINDT** JIM **ZUB**
SEAN **RYAN** writers

PATRICK **ZIRCHER** ANDRÉ **COELHO**
RAFA **SANDOVAL** JASON **MASTERS**
CARLOS **RODRIGUEZ** JIM **FERN**
SCOTT **HANNA** JORDI **TARRAGONA**
ROGER **ROBINSON** WAYNE **FAUCHER** artists

JASON **KEITH** BRETT **SMITH**
ANDREW **DALHOUSE** MATT **MILLA**
BLOND **HIFI** colorists

JARED K. **FLETCHER** CARLOS M. **MANGUAL** letterers

DOUG **MAHNKE** & ALEX **SINCLAIR** collection cover artists

AMANDA WALLER created by JOHN **OSTRANDER** & JOHN **BYRNE**

SU1
v. 5

BRIAN CUNNINGHAM WIL MOSS Editors – Original Series HARVEY RICHARDS Associate Editor – Original Series
KATE DURRÉ Assistant Editor – Original Series JEB WOODARD Group Editor – Collected Editions LIZ ERICKSON Editor – Collected Edition
STEVE COOK Design Director – Books ROBBIE BIEDERMAN Publication Design

BOB HARRAS Senior VP – Editor-in-Chief, DC Comics

DIANE NELSON President DAN DIDIO and JIM LEE Co-Publishers
GEOFF JOHNS Chief Creative Officer AMIT DESAI Senior VP – Marketing & Global Franchise Management
NAIRI GARDINER Senior VP – Finance SAM ADES VP – Digital Marketing BOBBIE CHASE VP – Talent Development
MARK CHIARELLO Senior VP – Art, Design & Collected Editions JOHN CUNNINGHAM VP – Content Strategy
ANNE DEPIES VP – Strategy Planning & Reporting DON FALLETTI VP – Manufacturing Operations
LAWRENCE GANEM VP – Editorial Administration & Talent Relations ALISON GILL Senior VP – Manufacturing & Operations
HANK KANALZ Senior VP – Editorial Strategy & Administration JAY KOGAN VP – Legal Affairs
DEREK MADDALENA Senior VP – Sales & Business Development JACK MAHAN VP – Business Affairs
DAN MIRON VP – Sales Planning & Trade Development NICK NAPOLITANO VP – Manufacturing Administration
CAROL ROEDER VP – Marketing EDDIE SCANNELL VP – Mass Account & Digital Sales
COURTNEY SIMMONS Senior VP – Publicity & Communications JIM (SKI) SOKOLOWSKI VP – Comic Book Specialty & Newsstand Sales
SANDY YI Senior VP – Global Franchise Management

SUICIDE SQUAD VOLUME 5: WALLED IN

DC Comics, 2900 W. Alameda Avenue, Burbank, CA 91505
Printed by Transcontinental Interglobe Beauceville, Canada. 3/18/16. Fourth Printing.
ISBN: 978-1-4012-5012-6

Library of Congress Cataloging-in-Publication Data

Kindt, Matt, author.
Suicide Squad. Volume 5 / Matt Kindt, Patrick Zircher.
pages cm. — (The New 52!)
ISBN 978-1-4012-5012-6 (paperback)
1. Graphic novels. I. Zircher, Patrick, illustrator. II. Title.
PN6728.S825K56 2014
741.5'973—dc23
2014015071

16.99
7/29/16
DS

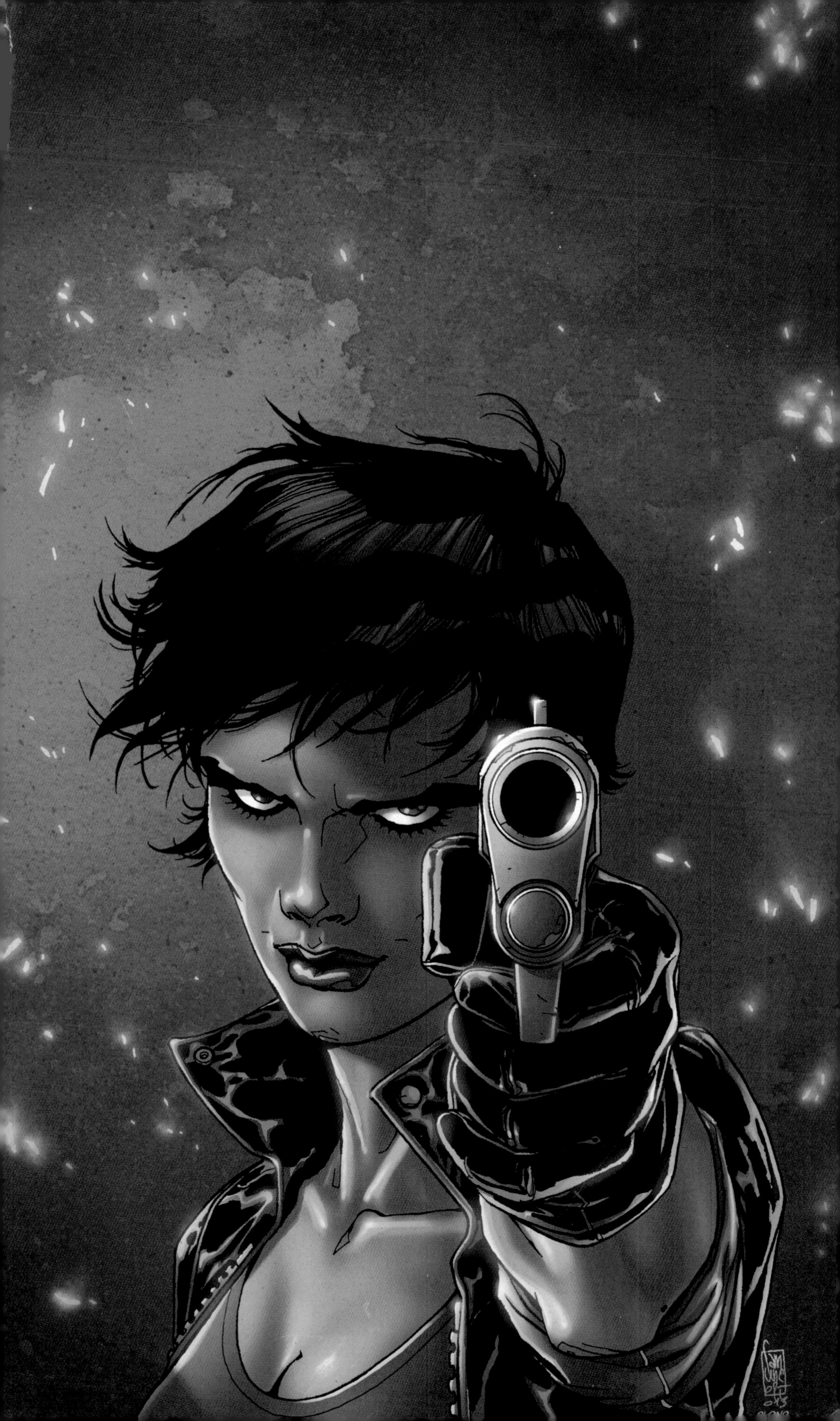

SACRIFICES IN THE STORM

JIM ZUB writer **ANDRÉ COELHO** penciller **SCOTT HANNA** inker **ANDREW DALHOUSE** colorist **CARLOS M. MANGUAL** letterer
cover by **GIUSEPPE CAMUNCOLI** and **BLOND**

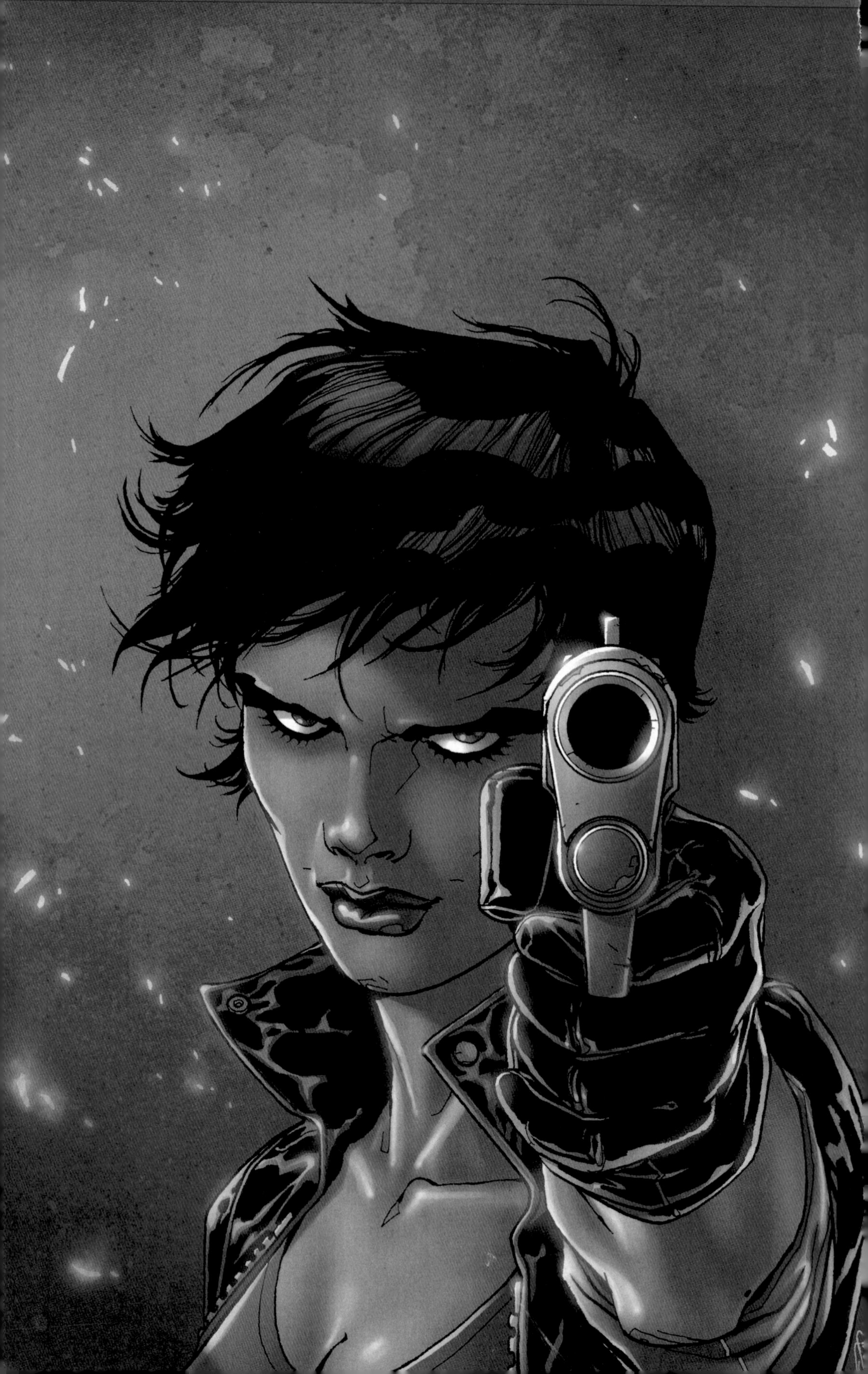

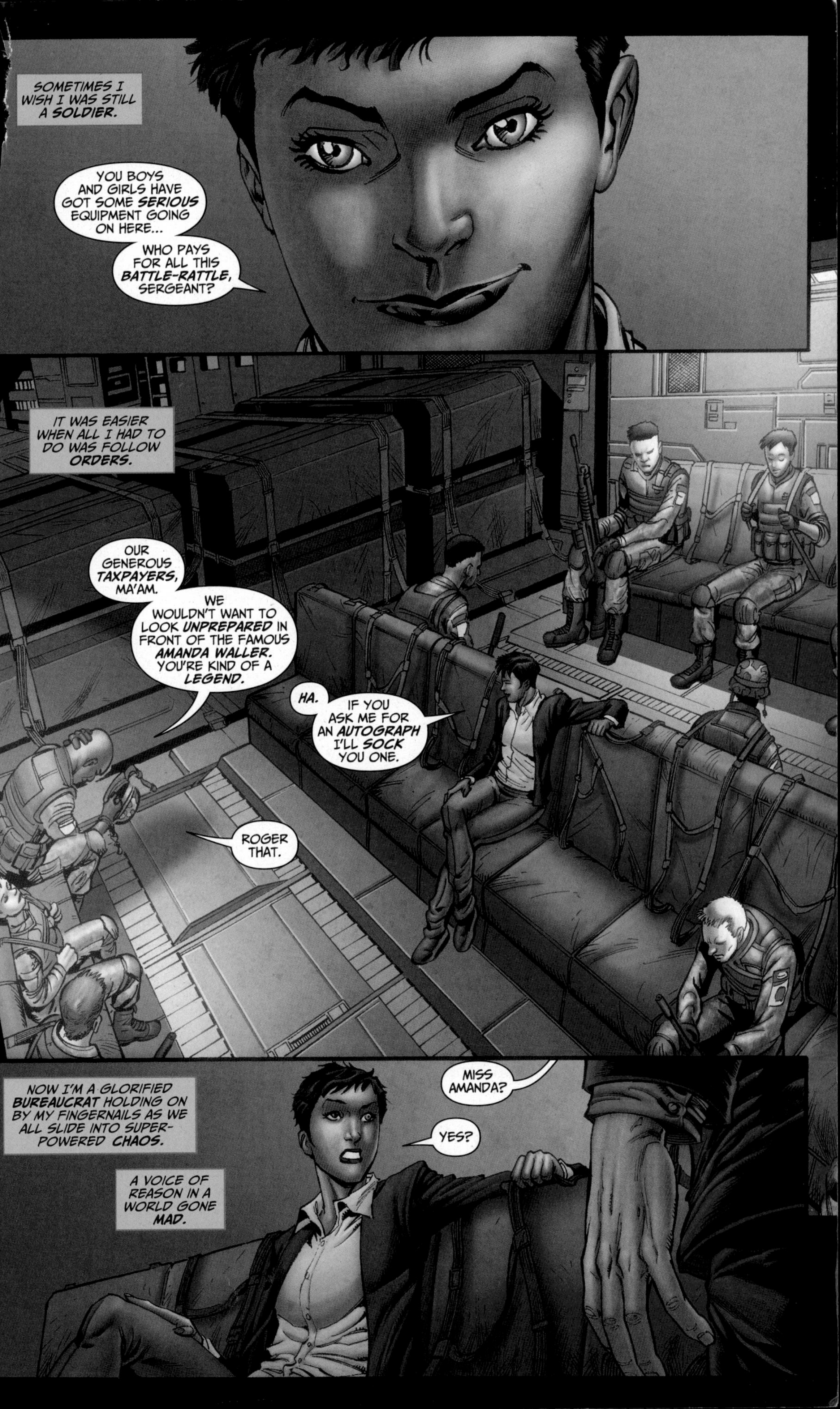

SOMETIMES I WISH I WAS STILL A SOLDIER.
YOU BOYS AND GIRLS HAVE GOT SOME SERIOUS EQUIPMENT GOING ON HERE...
WHO PAYS FOR ALL THIS BATTLE-RATTLE, SERGEANT?
IT WAS EASIER WHEN ALL I HAD TO DO WAS FOLLOW ORDERS.
OUR GENEROUS TAXPAYERS, MA'AM.
WE WOULDN'T WANT TO LOOK UNPREPARED IN FRONT OF THE FAMOUS AMANDA WALLER. YOU'RE KIND OF A LEGEND.
HA.
IF YOU ASK ME FOR AN AUTOGRAPH I'LL SOCK YOU ONE.
ROGER THAT.
NOW I'M A GLORIFIED BUREAUCRAT HOLDING ON BY MY FINGERNAILS AS WE ALL SLIDE INTO SUPER-POWERED CHAOS.
MISS AMANDA?
YES?
A VOICE OF REASON IN A WORLD GONE MAD.

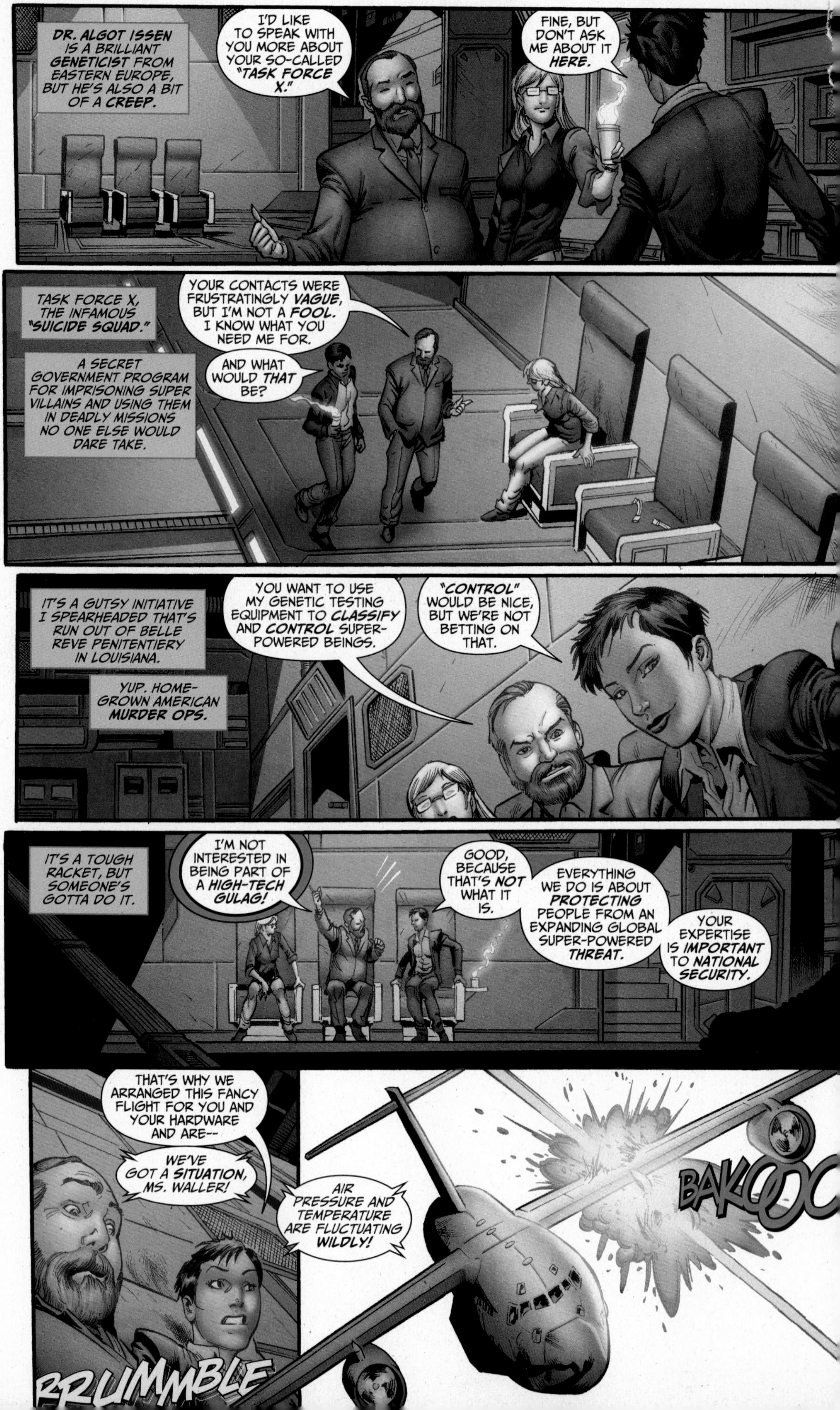

DR. ALGOT ISSEN IS A BRILLIANT GENETICIST FROM EASTERN EUROPE, BUT HE'S ALSO A BIT OF A CREEP.
I'D LIKE TO SPEAK WITH YOU MORE ABOUT YOUR SO-CALLED "TASK FORCE X."
FINE, BUT DON'T ASK ME ABOUT IT HERE.
TASK FORCE X, THE INFAMOUS "SUICIDE SQUAD."
A SECRET GOVERNMENT PROGRAM FOR IMPRISONING SUPER VILLAINS AND USING THEM IN DEADLY MISSIONS NO ONE ELSE WOULD DARE TAKE.
YOUR CONTACTS WERE FRUSTRATINGLY VAGUE, BUT I'M NOT A FOOL. I KNOW WHAT YOU NEED ME FOR.
AND WHAT WOULD THAT BE?
IT'S A GUTSY INITIATIVE I SPEARHEADED THAT'S RUN OUT OF BELLE REVE PENITENTIERY IN LOUISIANA.
YUP. HOME-GROWN AMERICAN MURDER OPS.
YOU WANT TO USE MY GENETIC TESTING EQUIPMENT TO CLASSIFY AND CONTROL SUPER-POWERED BEINGS.
"CONTROL" WOULD BE NICE, BUT WE'RE NOT BETTING ON THAT.
IT'S A TOUGH RACKET, BUT SOMEONE'S GOTTA DO IT.
I'M NOT INTERESTED IN BEING PART OF A HIGH-TECH GULAG!
GOOD, BECAUSE THAT'S NOT WHAT IT IS.
EVERYTHING WE DO IS ABOUT PROTECTING PEOPLE FROM AN EXPANDING GLOBAL SUPER-POWERED THREAT.
YOUR EXPERTISE IS IMPORTANT TO NATIONAL SECURITY.
THAT'S WHY WE ARRANGED THIS FANCY FLIGHT FOR YOU AND YOUR HARDWARE AND ARE--
WE'VE GOT A SITUATION, MS. WALLER!
AIR PRESSURE AND TEMPERATURE ARE FLUCTUATING WILDLY!
BAKOOOC
RRUMMBLE

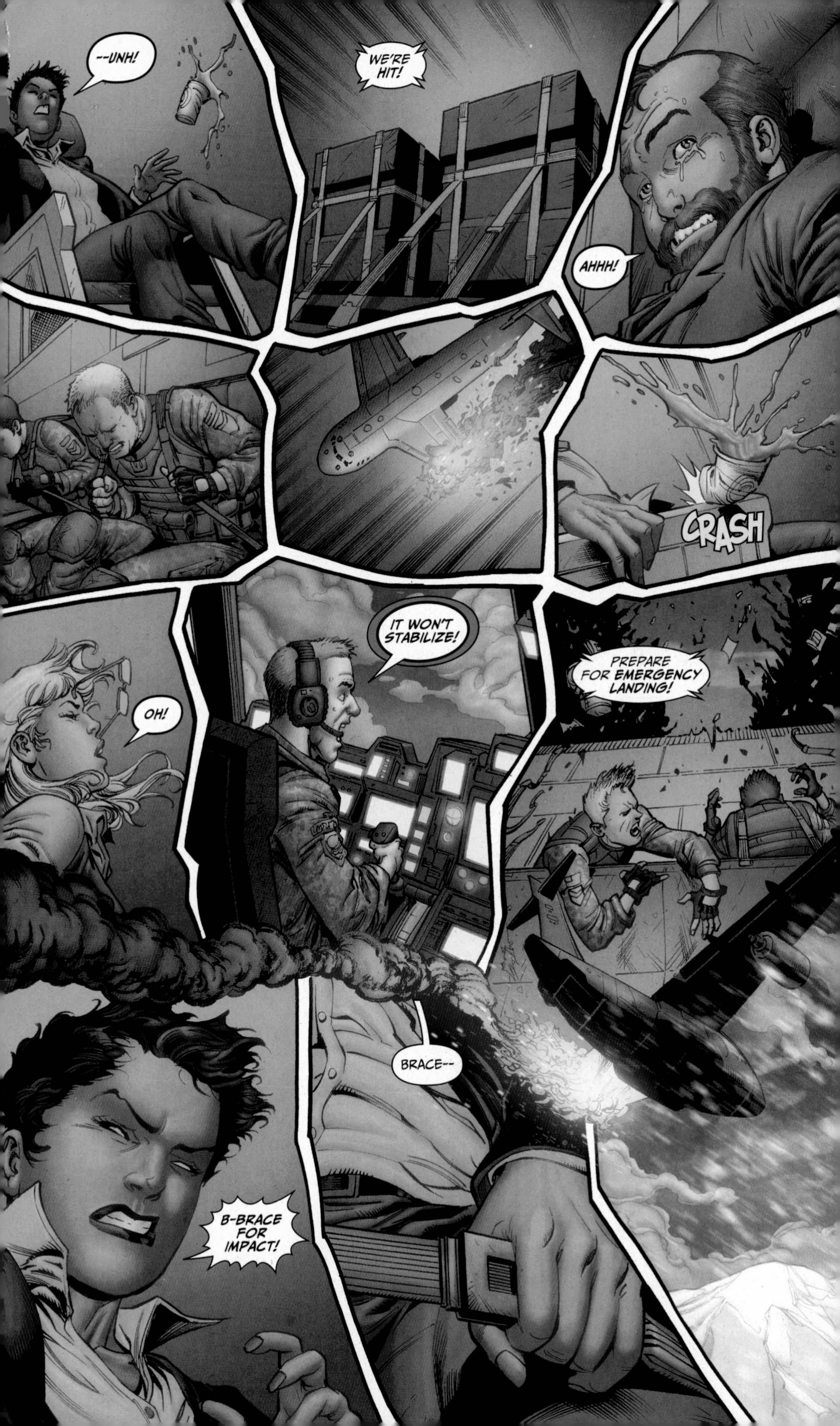
--UNH!
WE'RE HIT!
AHHH!
CRASH
IT WON'T STABILIZE!
PREPARE FOR EMERGENCY LANDING!
OH!
BRACE--
B-BRACE FOR IMPACT!

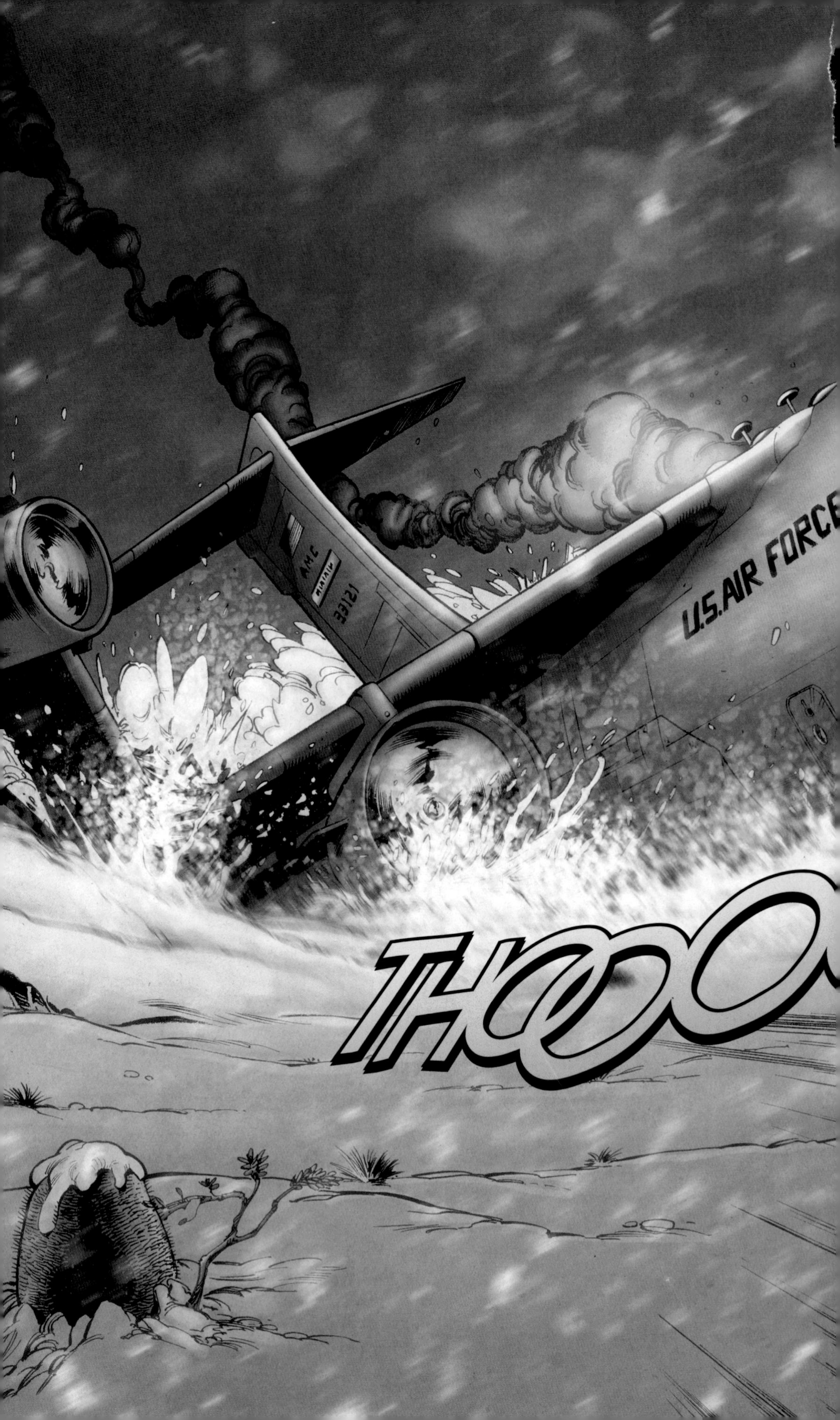

U.S. AIR FORCE
THOO

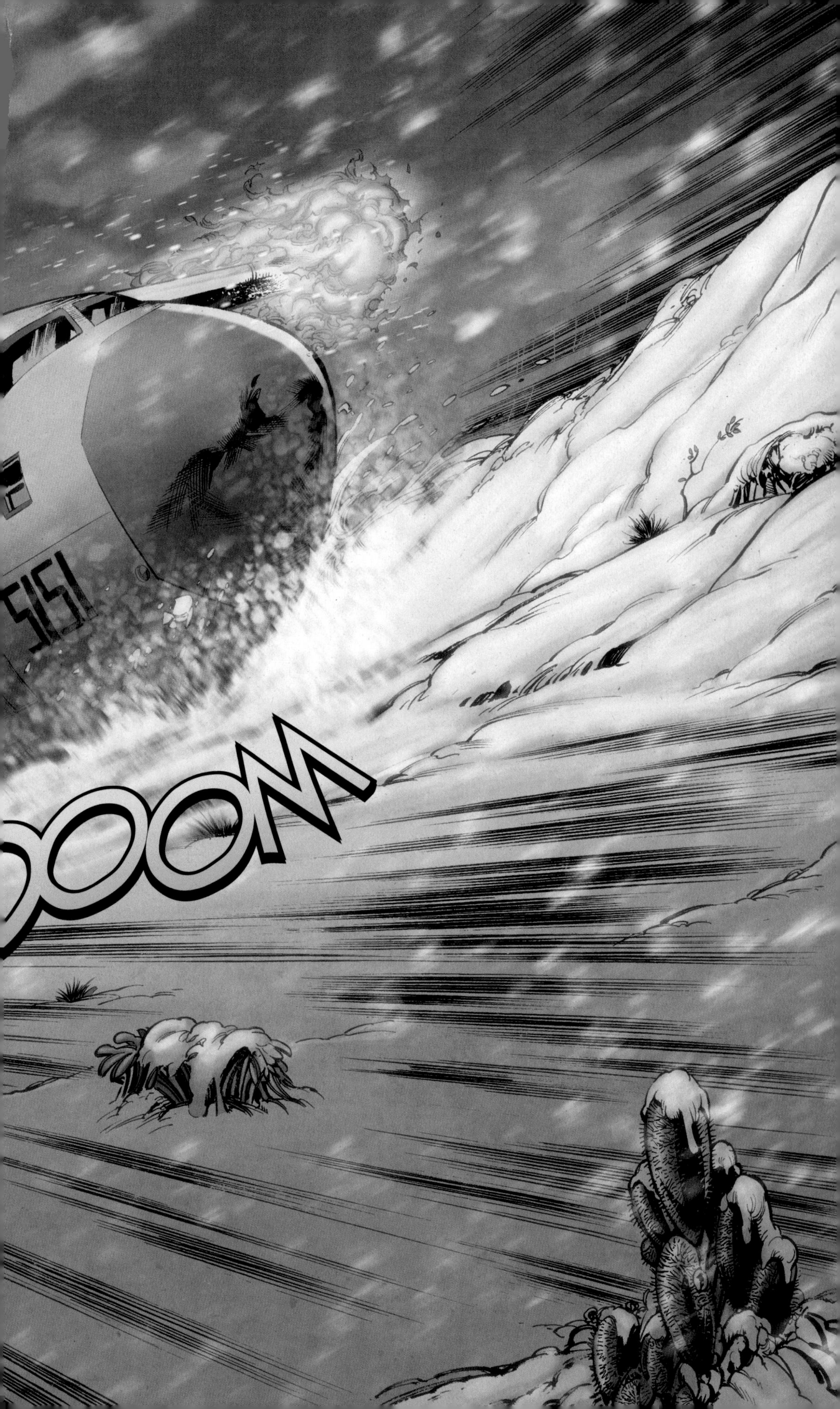
OOM

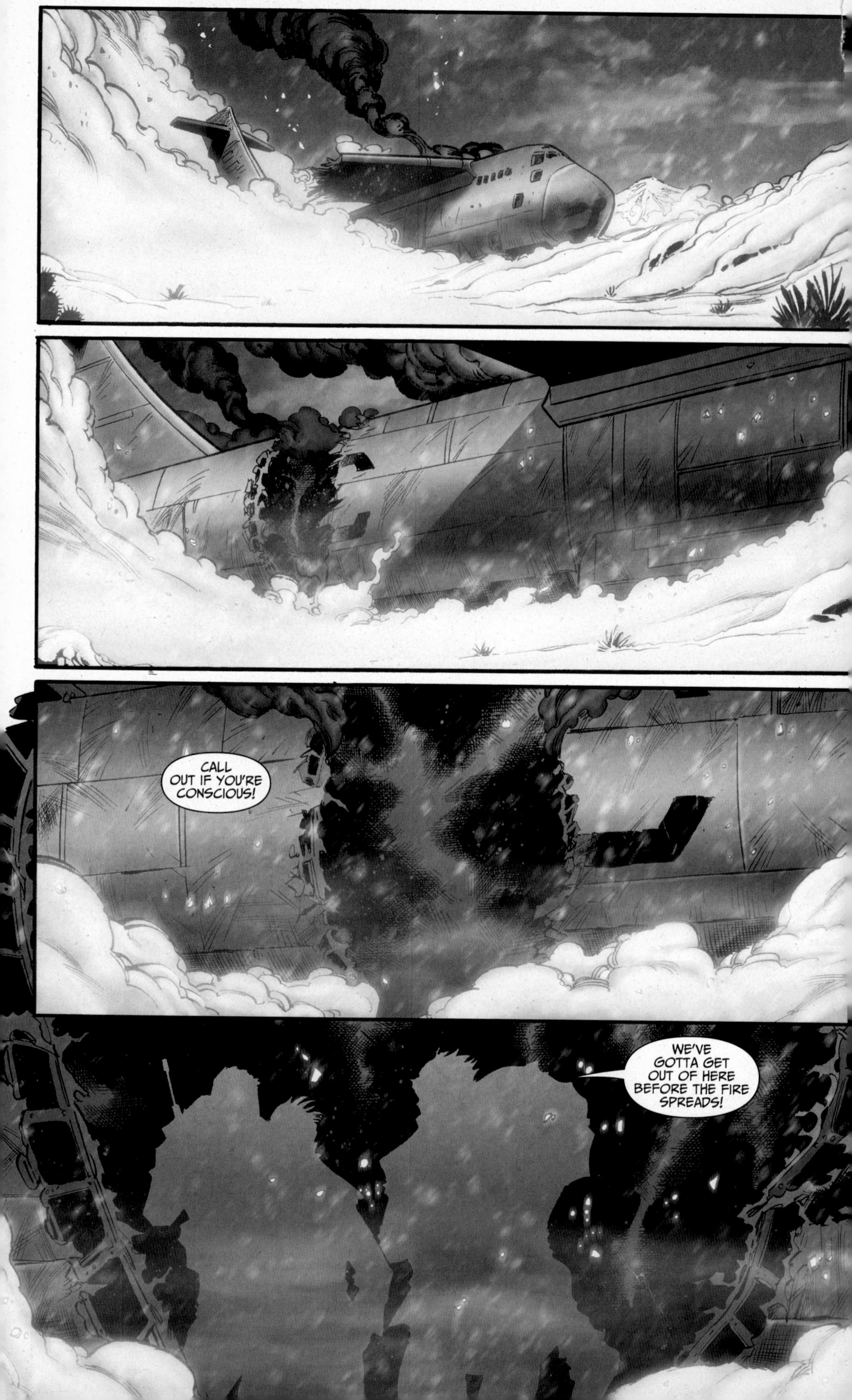
CALL OUT IF YOU'RE CONSCIOUS!
WE'VE GOTTA GET OUT OF HERE BEFORE THE FIRE SPREADS!

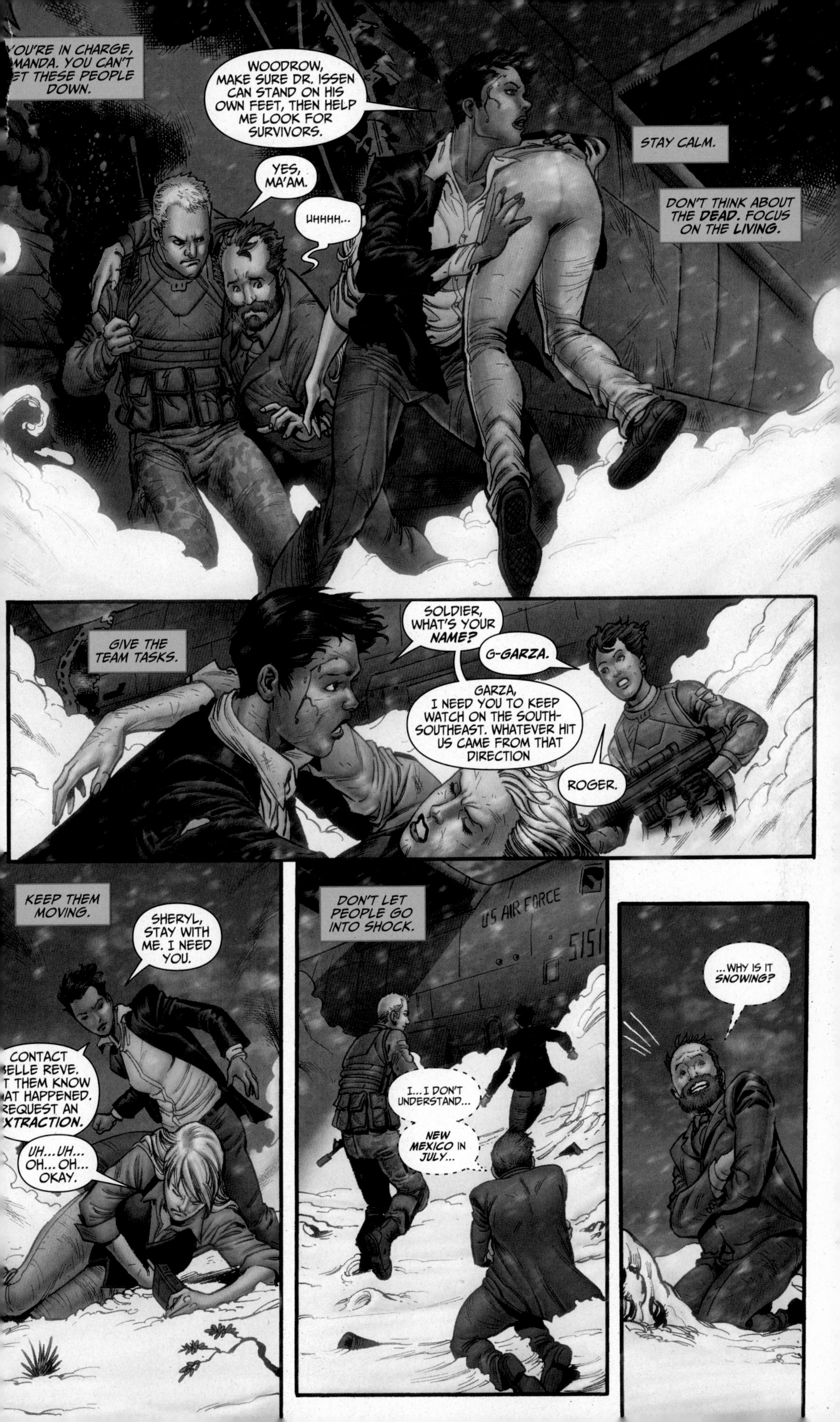

YOU'RE IN CHARGE, AMANDA. YOU CAN'T LET THESE PEOPLE DOWN.
WOODROW, MAKE SURE DR. ISSEN CAN STAND ON HIS OWN FEET, THEN HELP ME LOOK FOR SURVIVORS.
YES, MA'AM.
UHHHH...
STAY CALM.
DON'T THINK ABOUT THE DEAD. FOCUS ON THE LIVING.
GIVE THE TEAM TASKS.
SOLDIER, WHAT'S YOUR NAME?
G-GARZA.
GARZA, I NEED YOU TO KEEP WATCH ON THE SOUTH-SOUTHEAST. WHATEVER HIT US CAME FROM THAT DIRECTION
ROGER.
KEEP THEM MOVING.
SHERYL, STAY WITH ME. I NEED YOU.
CONTACT BELLE REVE. LET THEM KNOW WHAT HAPPENED. REQUEST AN EXTRACTION.
UH...UH... OH...OH... OKAY.
DON'T LET PEOPLE GO INTO SHOCK.
US AIR FORCE
5151
I...I DON'T UNDERSTAND...
NEW MEXICO IN JULY...
...WHY IS IT SNOWING?

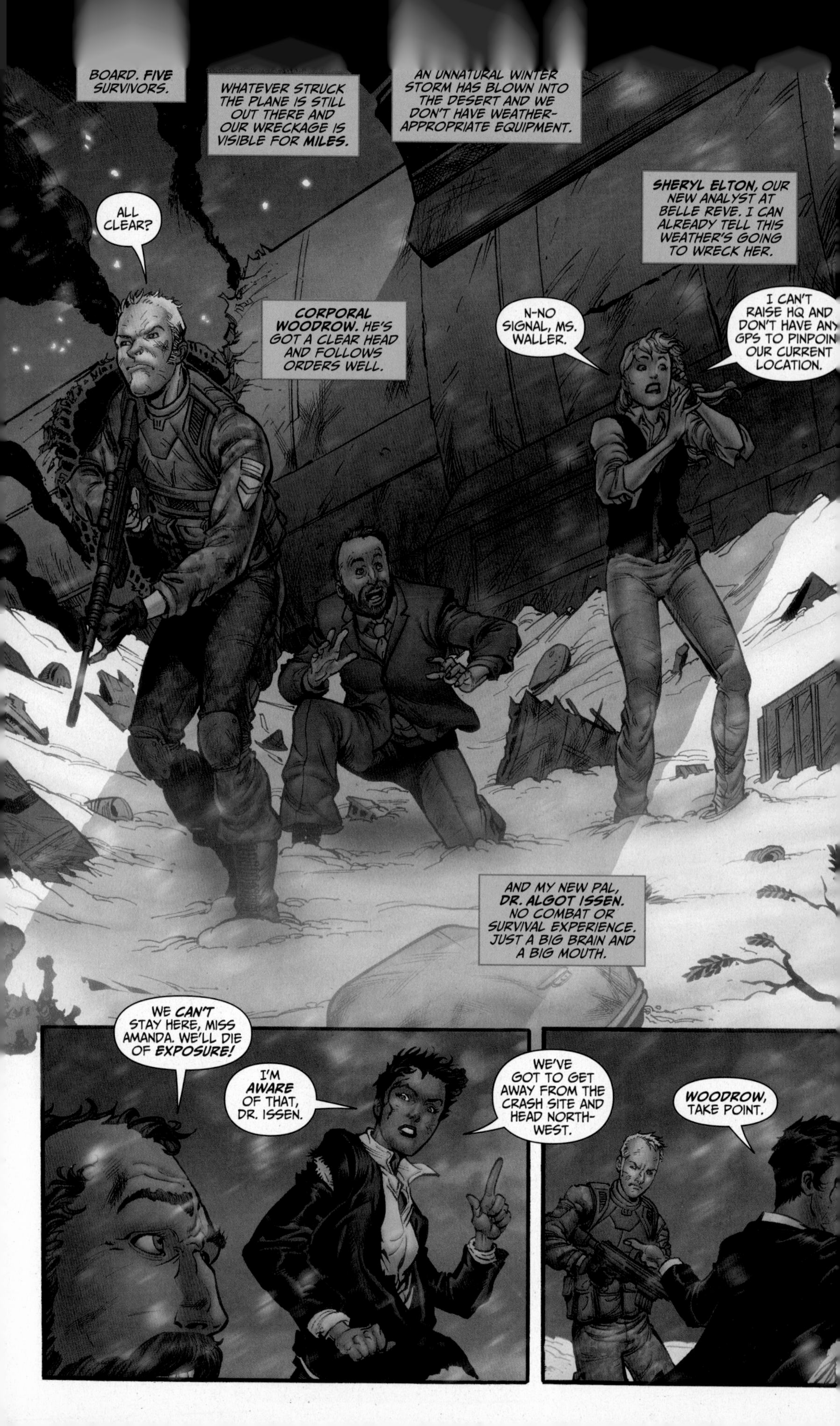
BOARD. FIVE SURVIVORS.
WHATEVER STRUCK THE PLANE IS STILL OUT THERE AND OUR WRECKAGE IS VISIBLE FOR MILES.
AN UNNATURAL WINTER STORM HAS BLOWN INTO THE DESERT AND WE DON'T HAVE WEATHER-APPROPRIATE EQUIPMENT.
ALL CLEAR?
CORPORAL WOODROW. HE'S GOT A CLEAR HEAD AND FOLLOWS ORDERS WELL.
SHERYL ELTON, OUR NEW ANALYST AT BELLE REVE. I CAN ALREADY TELL THIS WEATHER'S GOING TO WRECK HER.
N-NO SIGNAL, MS. WALLER.
I CAN'T RAISE HQ AND DON'T HAVE ANY GPS TO PINPOINT OUR CURRENT LOCATION.
AND MY NEW PAL, DR. ALGOT ISSEN. NO COMBAT OR SURVIVAL EXPERIENCE. JUST A BIG BRAIN AND A BIG MOUTH.
WE CAN'T STAY HERE, MISS AMANDA. WE'LL DIE OF EXPOSURE!
I'M AWARE OF THAT, DR. ISSEN.
WE'VE GOT TO GET AWAY FROM THE CRASH SITE AND HEAD NORTH-WEST.
WOODROW, TAKE POINT.

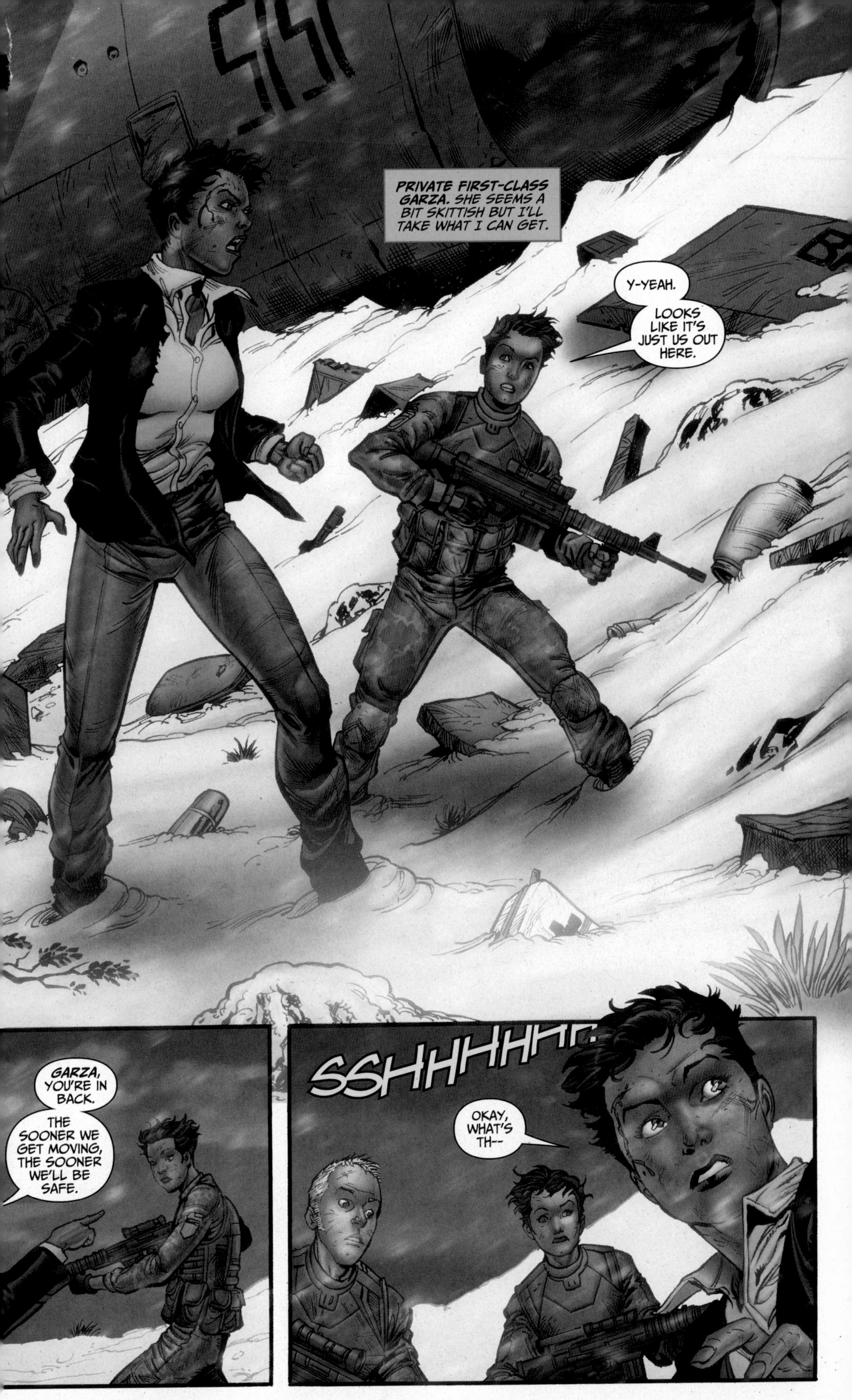
PRIVATE FIRST-CLASS GARZA. SHE SEEMS A BIT SKITTISH BUT I'LL TAKE WHAT I CAN GET.
Y-YEAH.
LOOKS LIKE IT'S JUST US OUT HERE.
GARZA, YOU'RE IN BACK.
THE SOONER WE GET MOVING, THE SOONER WE'LL BE SAFE.
SSHHHHHH
OKAY, WHAT'S TH--

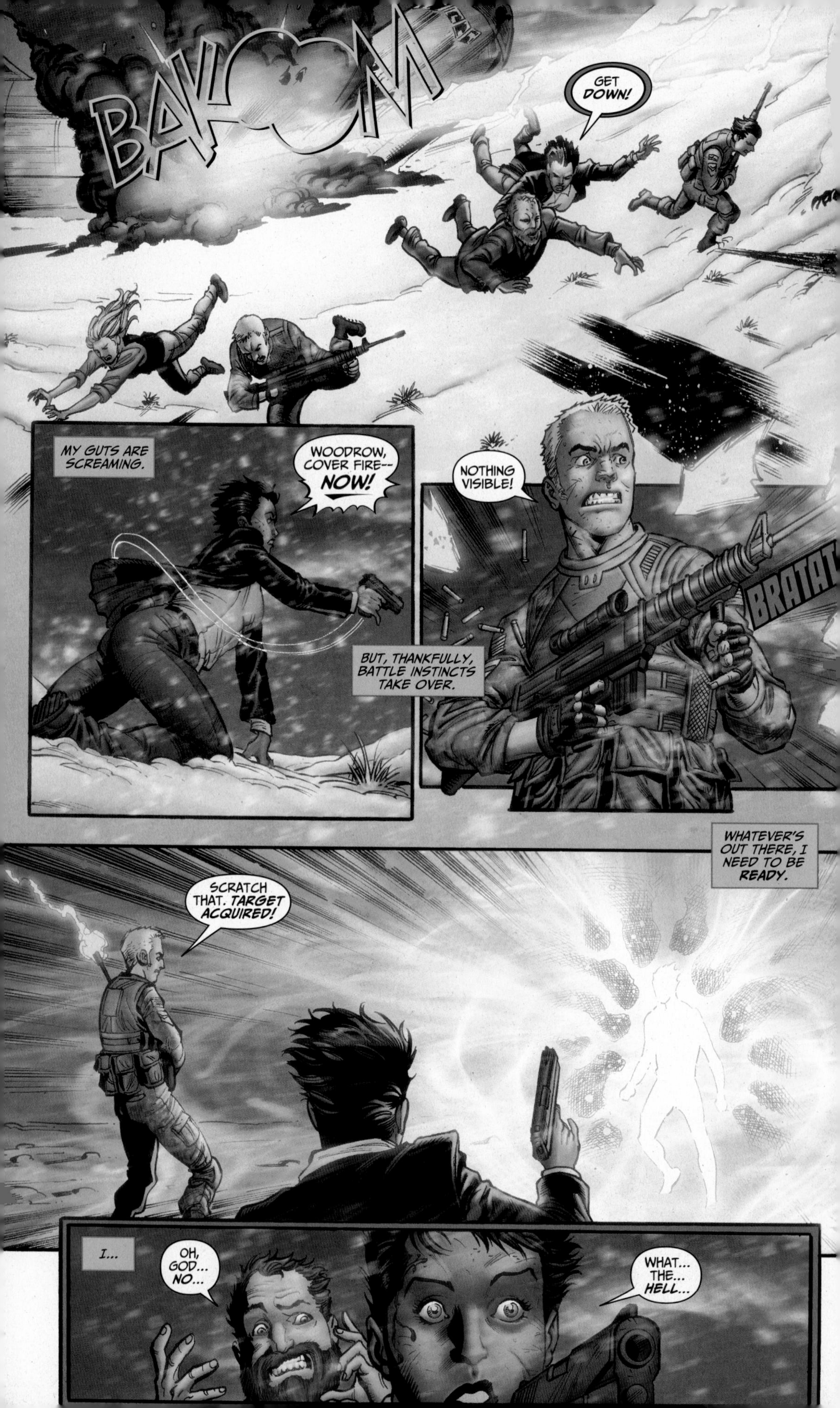
BAKOOM
GET DOWN!
MY GUTS ARE SCREAMING.
WOODROW, COVER FIRE-- NOW!
NOTHING VISIBLE!
BRATAT
BUT, THANKFULLY, BATTLE INSTINCTS TAKE OVER.
WHATEVER'S OUT THERE, I NEED TO BE READY.
SCRATCH THAT. TARGET ACQUIRED!
I...
OH, GOD... NO...
WHAT... THE... HELL...

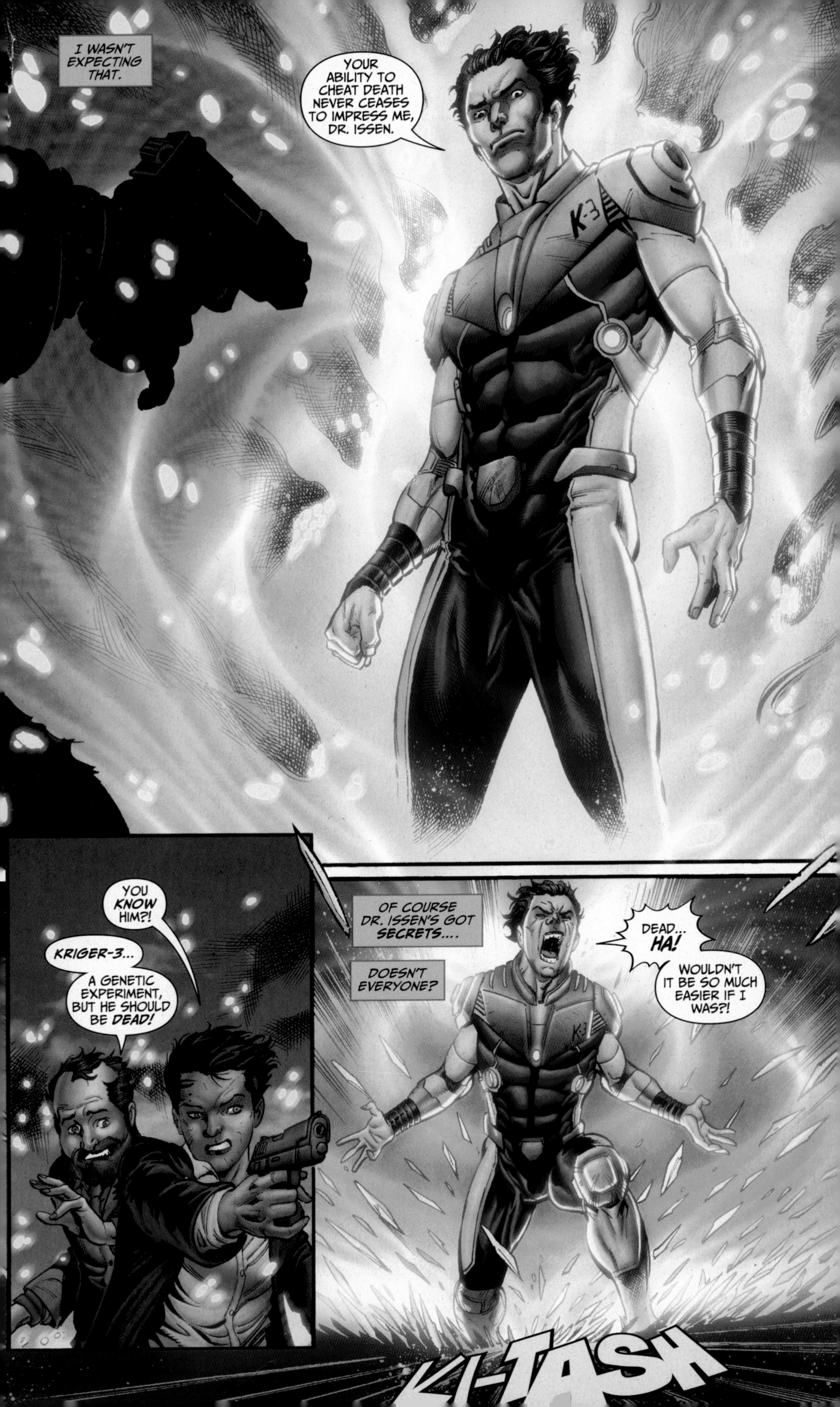
I WASN'T EXPECTING THAT.
YOUR ABILITY TO CHEAT DEATH NEVER CEASES TO IMPRESS ME, DR. ISSEN.
YOU KNOW HIM?!
KRIGER-3...
A GENETIC EXPERIMENT, BUT HE SHOULD BE DEAD!
OF COURSE DR. ISSEN'S GOT SECRETS....
DOESN'T EVERYONE?
DEAD... HA!
WOULDN'T IT BE SO MUCH EASIER IF I WAS?!
KI-TASH

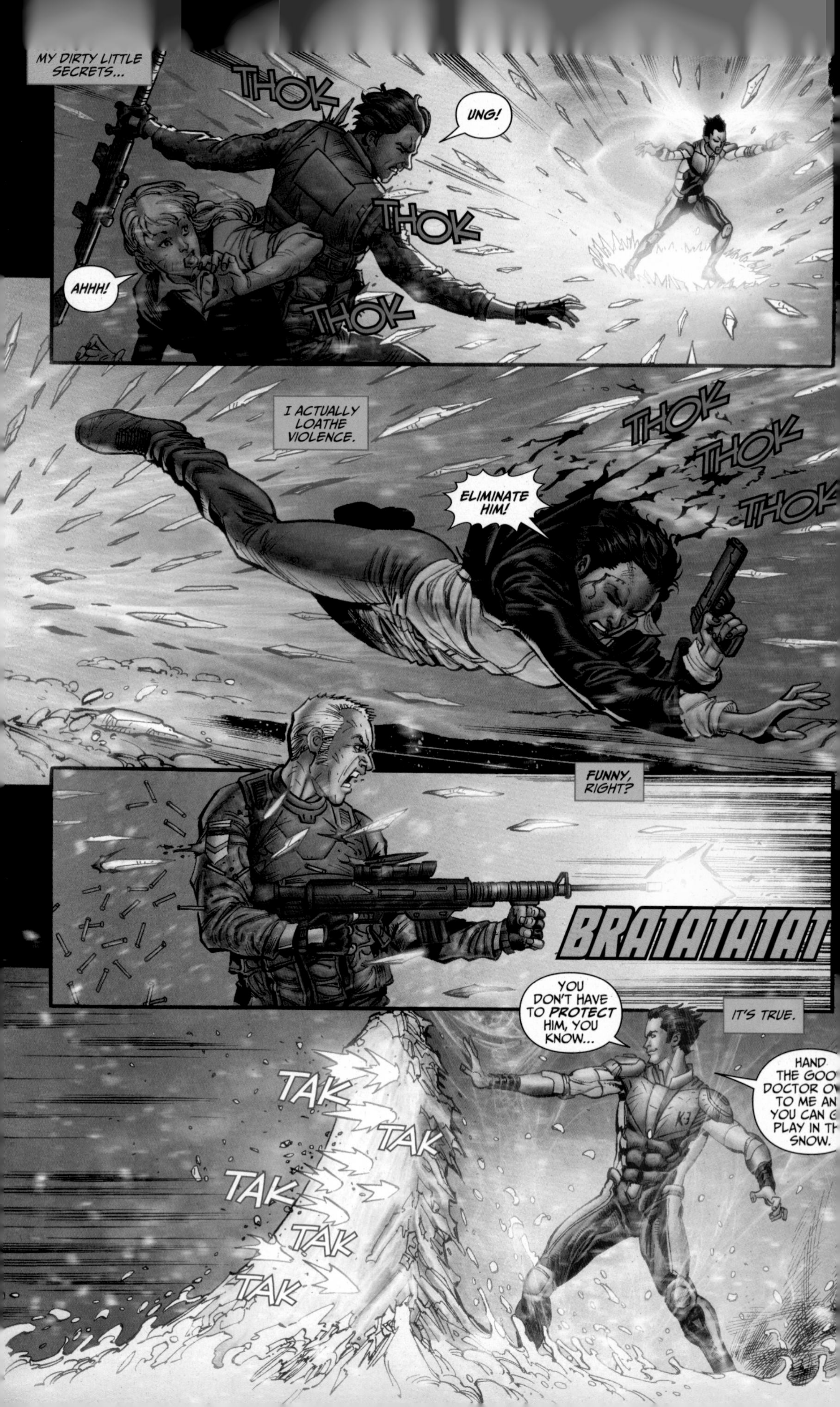

MY DIRTY LITTLE SECRETS...
THOK
UNG!
THOK
AHHH!
THOK
I ACTUALLY LOATHE VIOLENCE.
THOK
THOK
THOK
ELIMINATE HIM!
FUNNY, RIGHT?
BRATATATAT
YOU DON'T HAVE TO *PROTECT* HIM, YOU KNOW...
IT'S TRUE.
TAK
TAK
TAK
TAK
TAK

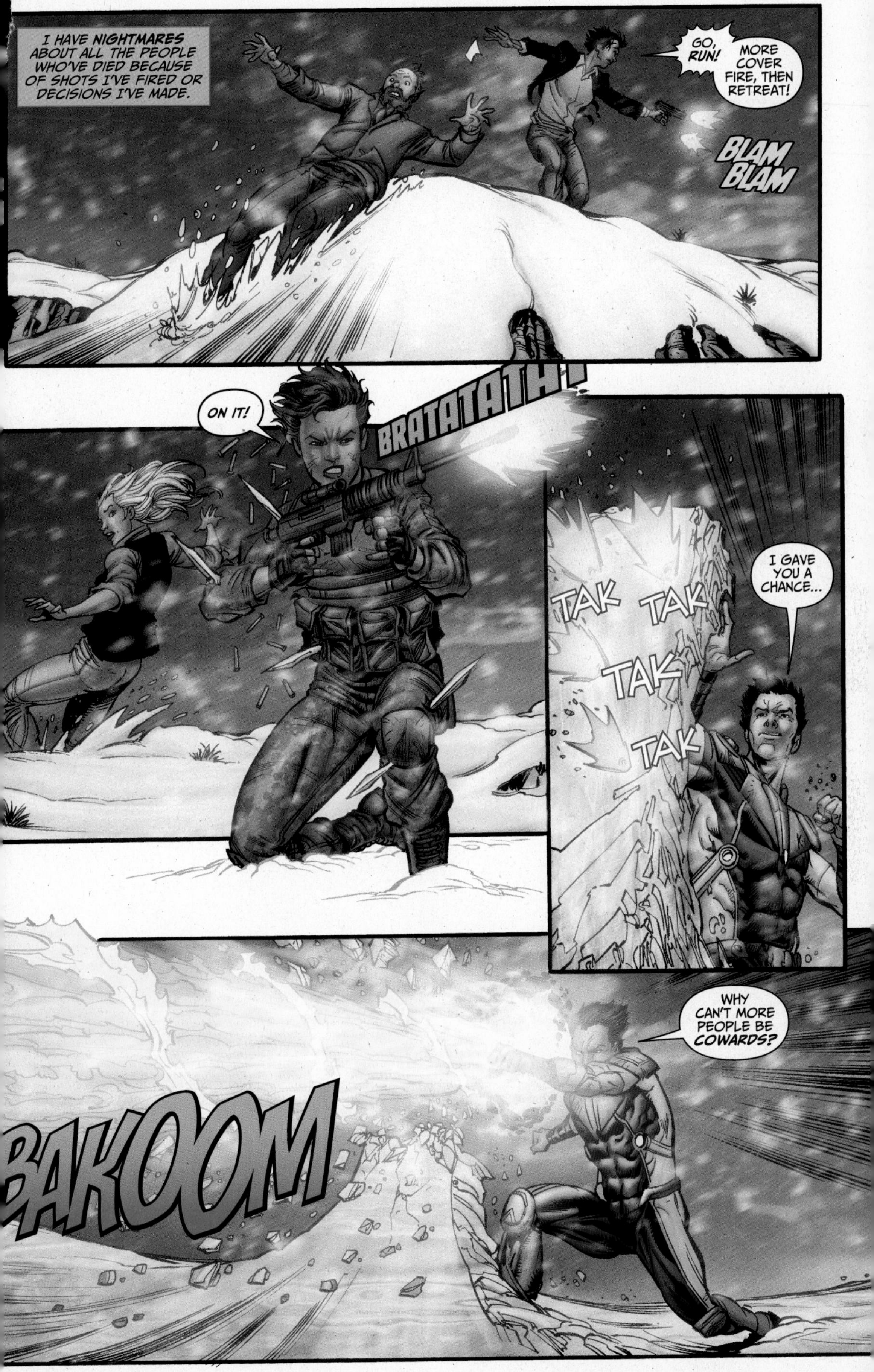
I HAVE NIGHTMARES ABOUT ALL THE PEOPLE WHO'VE DIED BECAUSE OF SHOTS I'VE FIRED OR DECISIONS I'VE MADE.
GO, RUN!
MORE COVER FIRE, THEN RETREAT!
BLAM BLAM
ON IT!
BRATATATATT
TAK TAK TAK TAK
I GAVE YOU A CHANCE...
WHY CAN'T MORE PEOPLE BE COWARDS?
BAKOOM

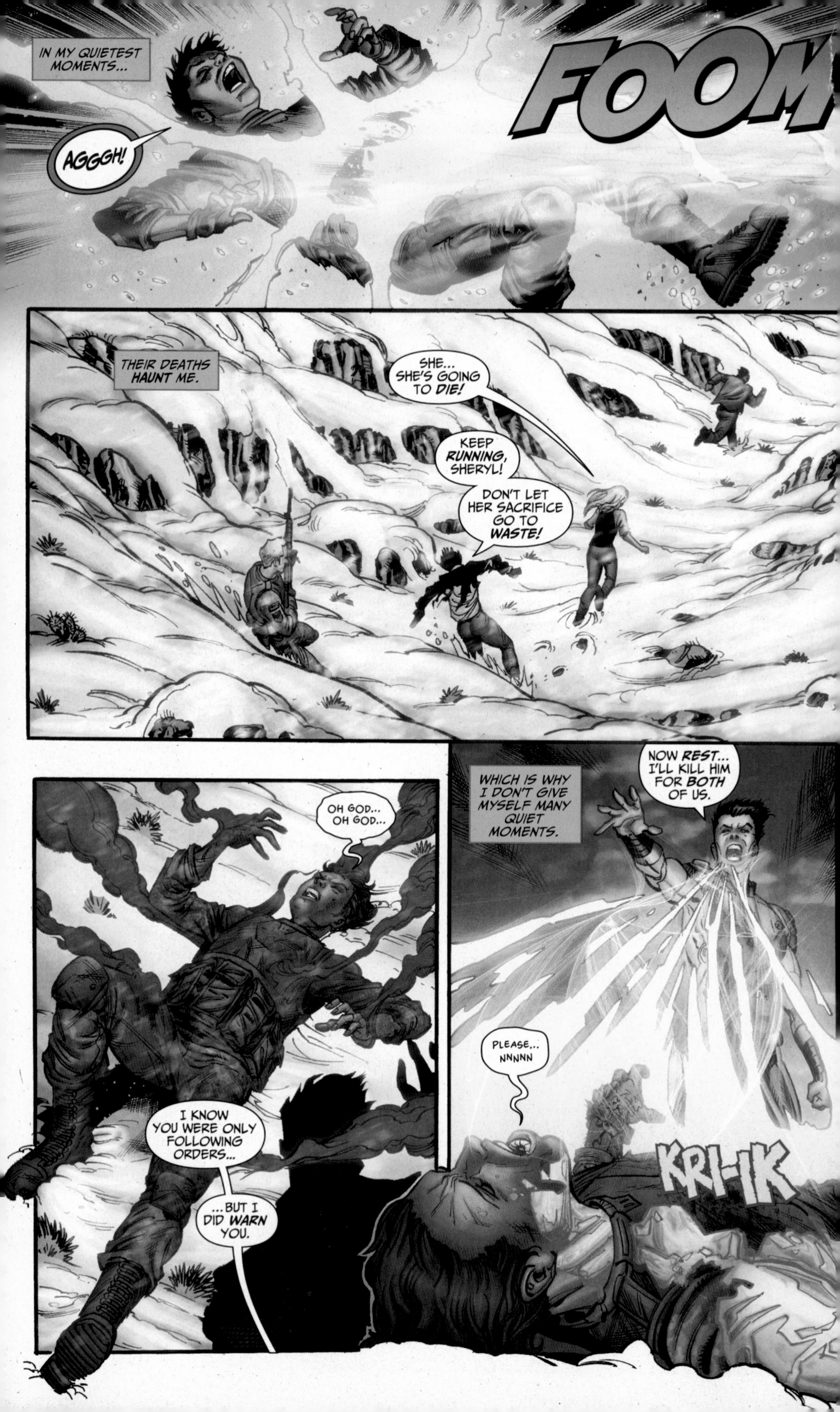
IN MY QUIETEST MOMENTS...
AGGGH!
FOOM
THEIR DEATHS HAUNT ME.
SHE... SHE'S GOING TO DIE!
KEEP RUNNING, SHERYL!
DON'T LET HER SACRIFICE GO TO WASTE!
OH GOD... OH GOD...
I KNOW YOU WERE ONLY FOLLOWING ORDERS...
...BUT I DID WARN YOU.
WHICH IS WHY I DON'T GIVE MYSELF MANY QUIET MOMENTS.
NOW REST... I'LL KILL HIM FOR BOTH OF US.
PLEASE... NNNNN
KRI-IK

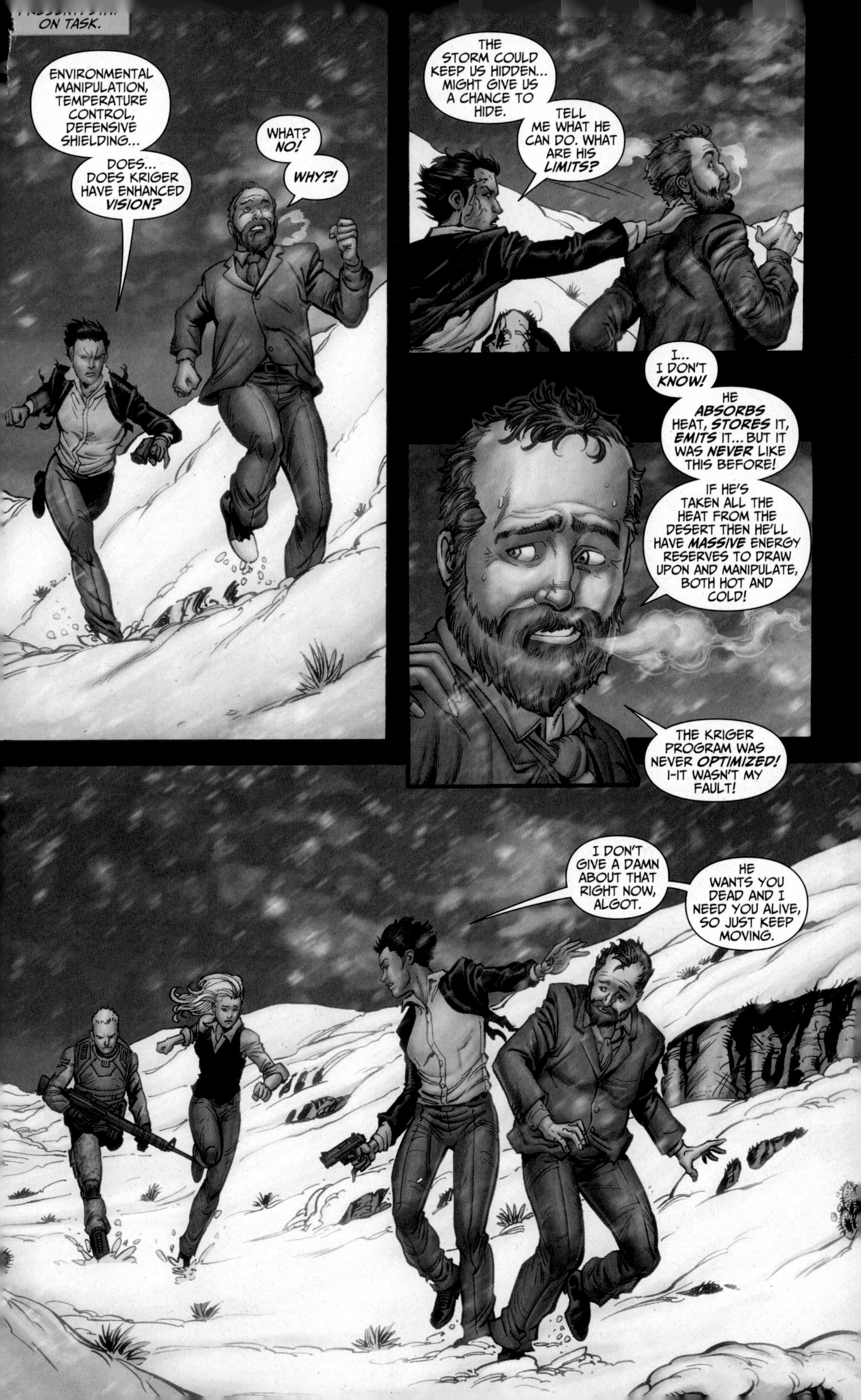
ON TASK.
ENVIRONMENTAL MANIPULATION, TEMPERATURE CONTROL, DEFENSIVE SHIELDING...
DOES... DOES KRIGER HAVE ENHANCED *VISION?*
WHAT? *NO!*
WHY?!
THE STORM COULD KEEP US HIDDEN... MIGHT GIVE US A CHANCE TO HIDE.
TELL ME WHAT HE CAN DO. WHAT ARE HIS *LIMITS?*
I... I DON'T *KNOW!*
HE **ABSORBS** HEAT, **STORES** IT, **EMITS** IT... BUT IT WAS **NEVER** LIKE THIS BEFORE!
IF HE'S TAKEN ALL THE HEAT FROM THE DESERT THEN HE'LL HAVE **MASSIVE** ENERGY RESERVES TO DRAW UPON AND MANIPULATE, BOTH HOT AND COLD!
THE KRIGER PROGRAM WAS NEVER *OPTIMIZED!* I-IT WASN'T MY FAULT!
I DON'T GIVE A DAMN ABOUT THAT RIGHT NOW, ALGOT.
HE WANTS YOU DEAD AND I NEED YOU ALIVE, SO JUST KEEP MOVING.

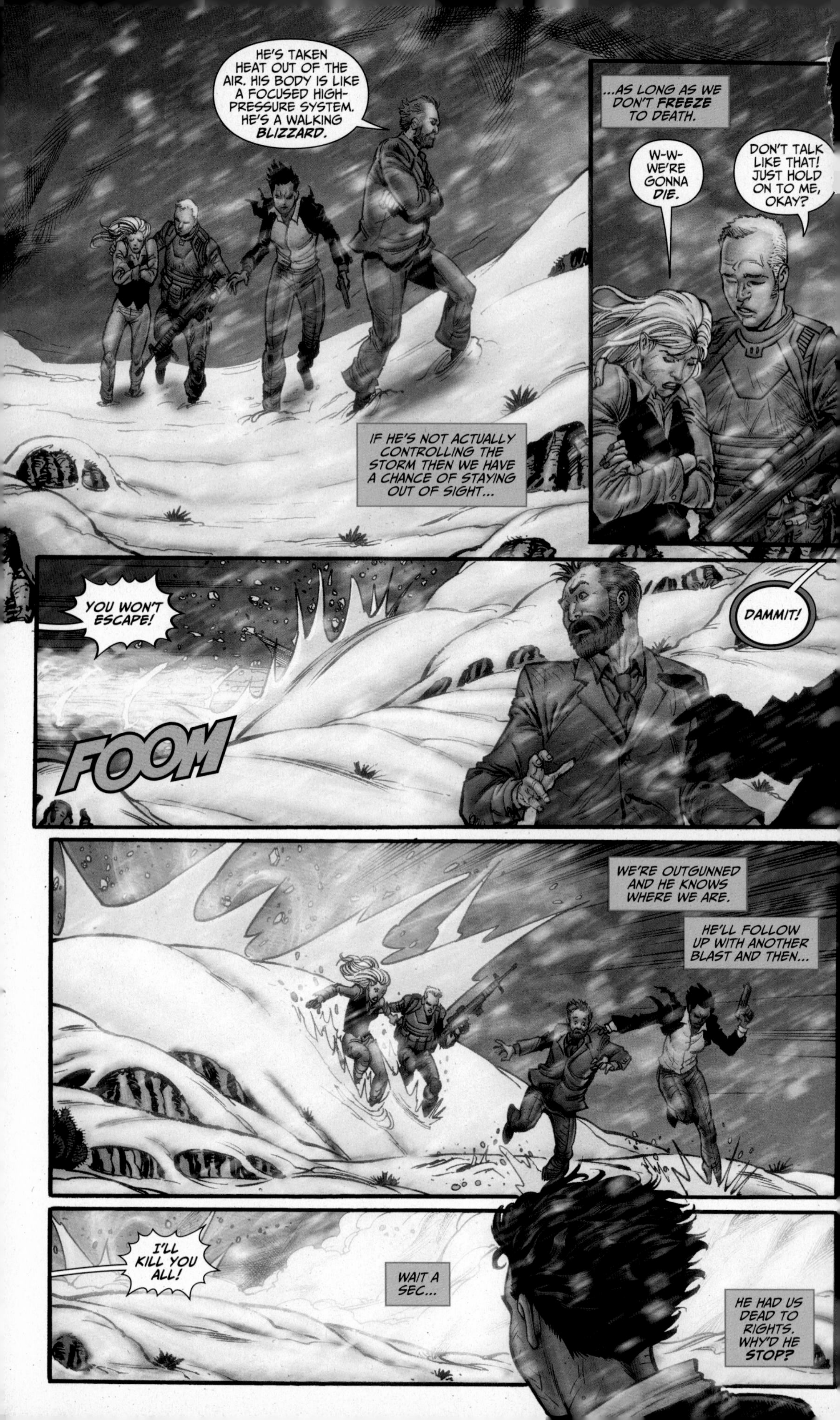

HE'S TAKEN HEAT OUT OF THE AIR. HIS BODY IS LIKE A FOCUSED HIGH-PRESSURE SYSTEM. HE'S A WALKING BLIZZARD.
IF HE'S NOT ACTUALLY CONTROLLING THE STORM THEN WE HAVE A CHANCE OF STAYING OUT OF SIGHT...
...AS LONG AS WE DON'T FREEZE TO DEATH.
W-W-WE'RE GONNA DIE.
DON'T TALK LIKE THAT! JUST HOLD ON TO ME, OKAY?
YOU WON'T ESCAPE!
FOOM
DAMMIT!
WE'RE OUTGUNNED AND HE KNOWS WHERE WE ARE.
HE'LL FOLLOW UP WITH ANOTHER BLAST AND THEN...
I'LL KILL YOU ALL!
WAIT A SEC...
HE HAD US DEAD TO RIGHTS. WHY'D HE STOP?

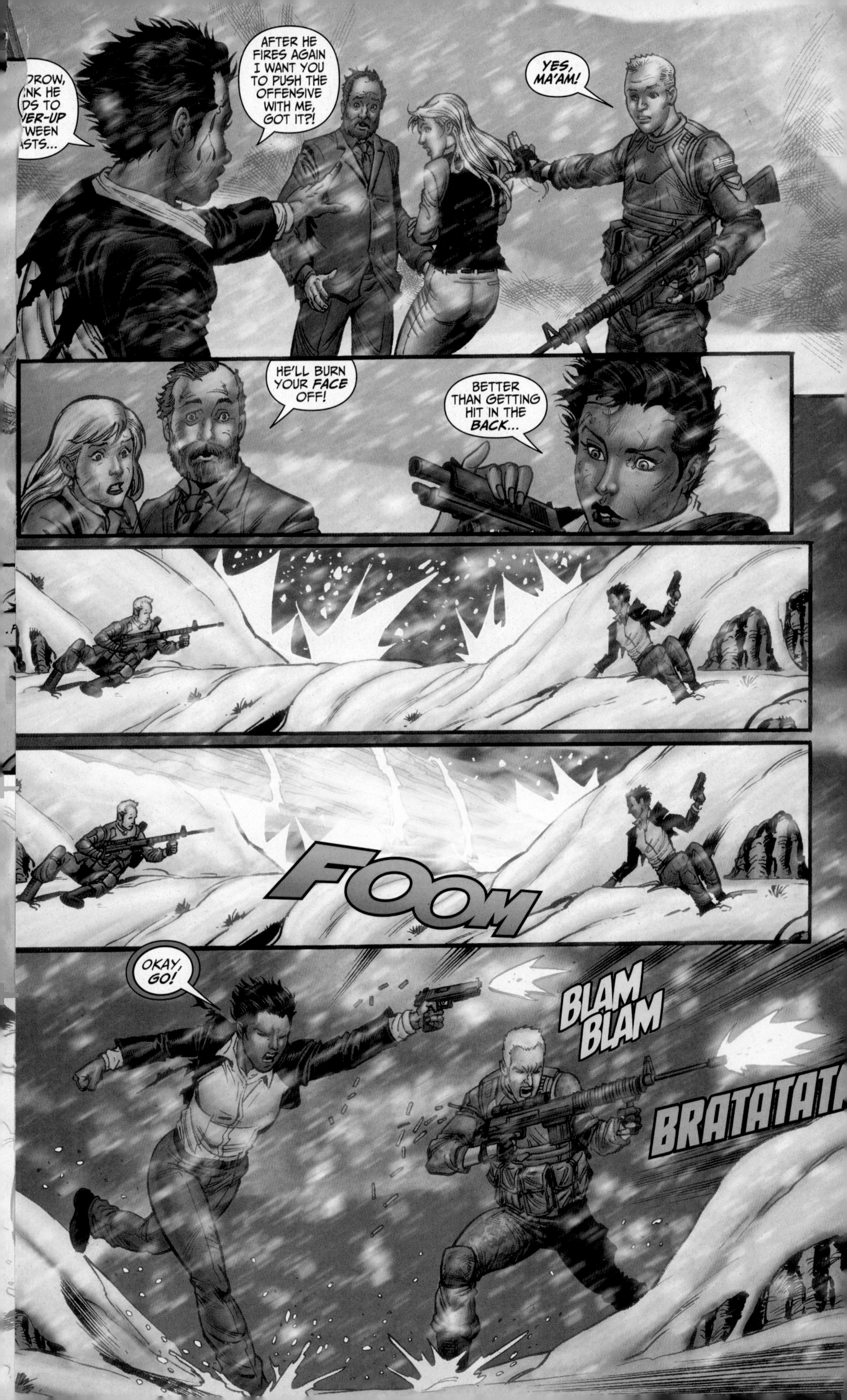

DROW,
NK HE
DS TO
VER-UP
TWEEN
ASTS...
AFTER HE FIRES AGAIN I WANT YOU TO PUSH THE OFFENSIVE WITH ME, GOT IT?!
YES, MA'AM!
HE'LL BURN YOUR FACE OFF!
BETTER THAN GETTING HIT IN THE BACK...
FOOM
OKAY, GO!
BLAM BLAM
BRATATATA

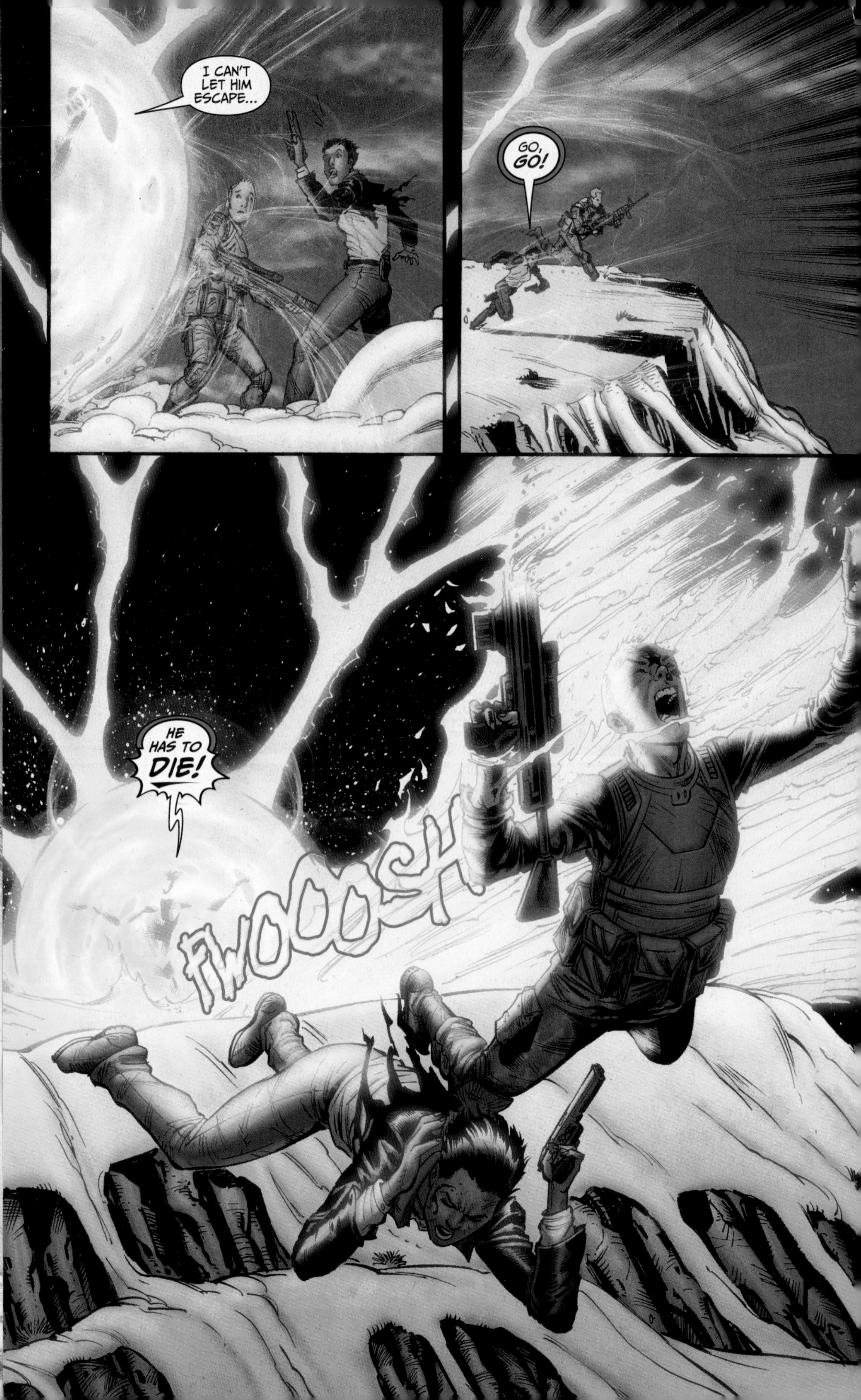
I CAN'T LET HIM ESCAPE...
GO, GO!
HE HAS TO DIE!
FWOOOSH

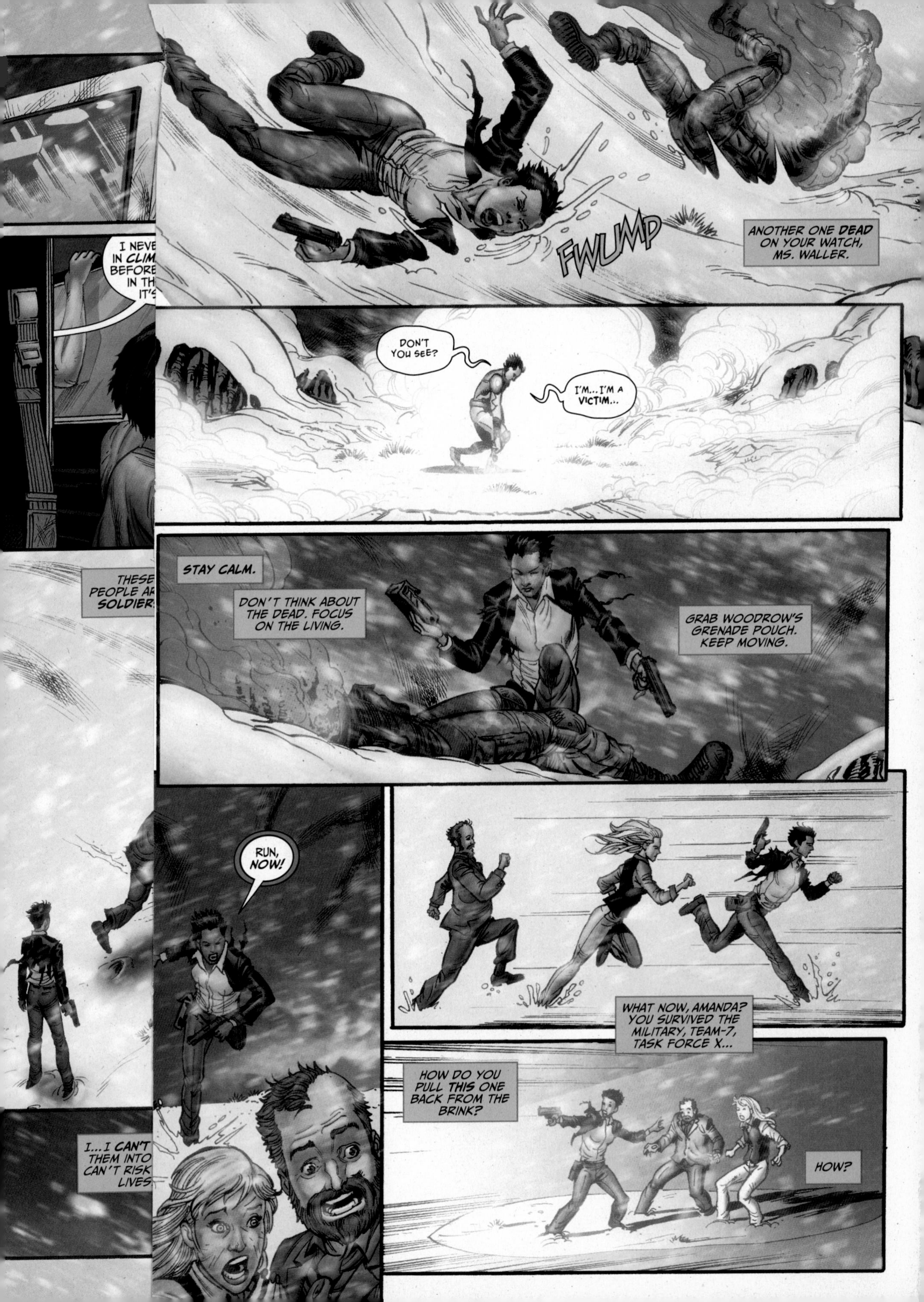
FWUMP
ANOTHER ONE DEAD ON YOUR WATCH, MS. WALLER.
DON'T YOU SEE?
I'M... I'M A VICTIM...
STAY CALM.
DON'T THINK ABOUT THE DEAD. FOCUS ON THE LIVING.
GRAB WOODROW'S GRENADE POUCH. KEEP MOVING.
RUN, NOW!
WHAT NOW, AMANDA? YOU SURVIVED THE MILITARY, TEAM-7, TASK FORCE X...
HOW DO YOU PULL THIS ONE BACK FROM THE BRINK?
HOW?

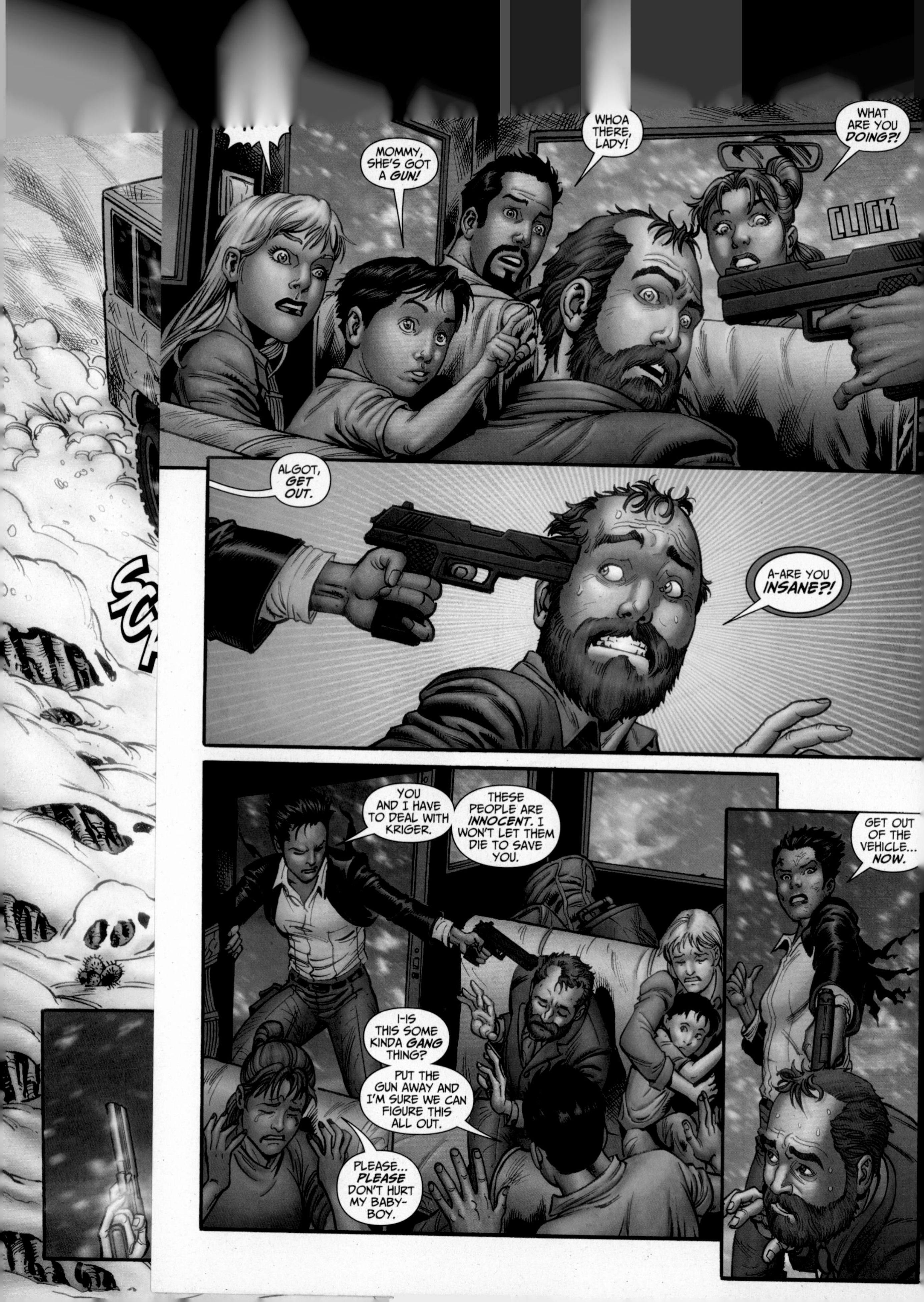
MOMMY, SHE'S GOT A GUN!
WHOA THERE, LADY!
WHAT ARE YOU DOING?!
CLICK
ALGOT, GET OUT.
A-ARE YOU INSANE?!
YOU AND I HAVE TO DEAL WITH KRIGER.
THESE PEOPLE ARE INNOCENT. I WON'T LET THEM DIE TO SAVE YOU.
I-IS THIS SOME KINDA GANG THING?
PUT THE GUN AWAY AND I'M SURE WE CAN FIGURE THIS ALL OUT.
PLEASE... PLEASE DON'T HURT MY BABY-BOY.
GET OUT OF THE VEHICLE... NOW.

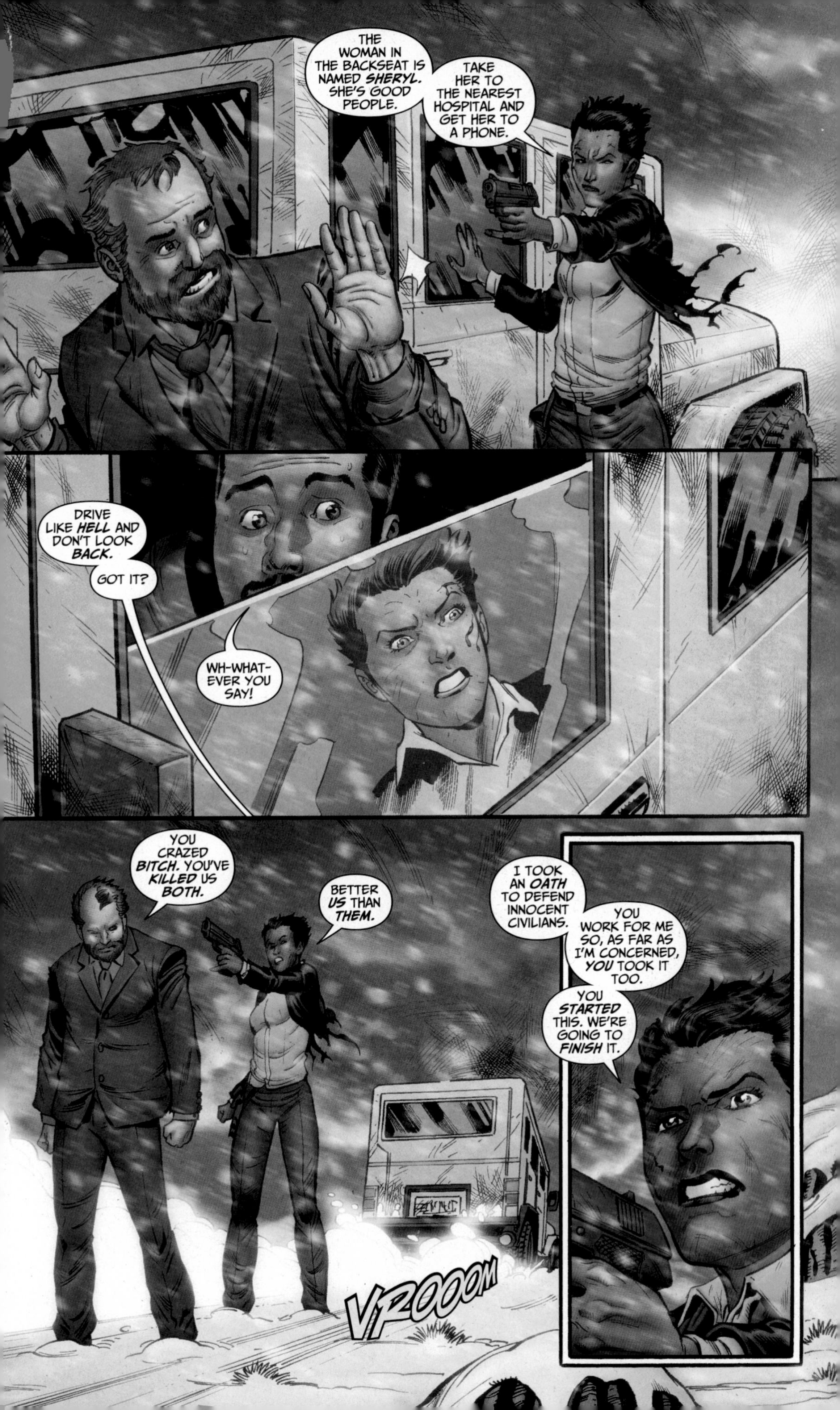
THE WOMAN IN THE BACKSEAT IS NAMED SHERYL. SHE'S GOOD PEOPLE.
TAKE HER TO THE NEAREST HOSPITAL AND GET HER TO A PHONE.
DRIVE LIKE HELL AND DON'T LOOK BACK.
GOT IT?
WH-WHAT-EVER YOU SAY!
YOU CRAZED BITCH. YOU'VE KILLED US BOTH.
BETTER US THAN THEM.
I TOOK AN OATH TO DEFEND INNOCENT CIVILIANS.
YOU WORK FOR ME SO, AS FAR AS I'M CONCERNED, YOU TOOK IT TOO.
YOU STARTED THIS. WE'RE GOING TO FINISH IT.
VROOOM

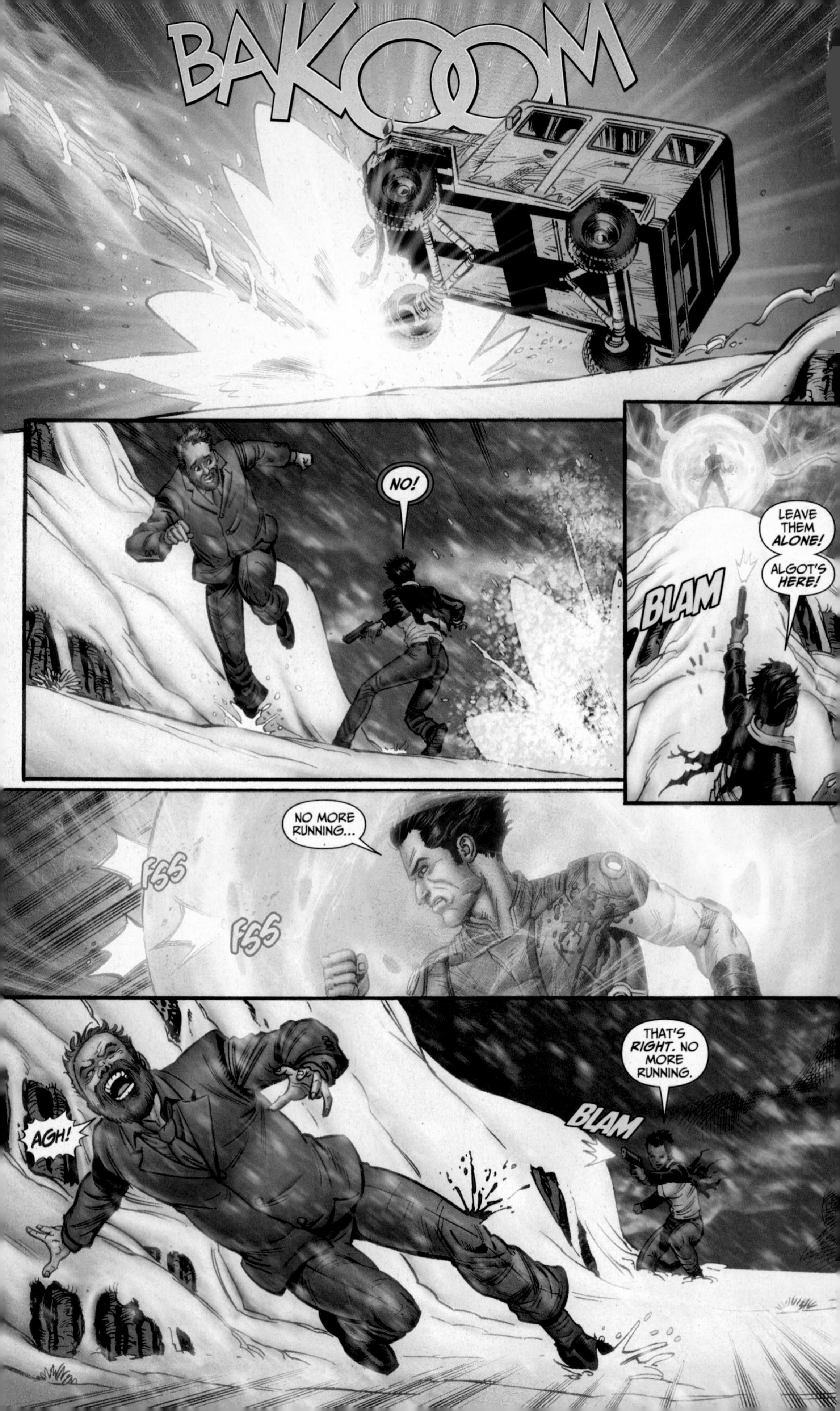
BAKOOM
NO!
LEAVE THEM ALONE!
ALGOT'S HERE!
BLAM
NO MORE RUNNING...
FSS
FSS
AGH!
BLAM
THAT'S RIGHT. NO MORE RUNNING.

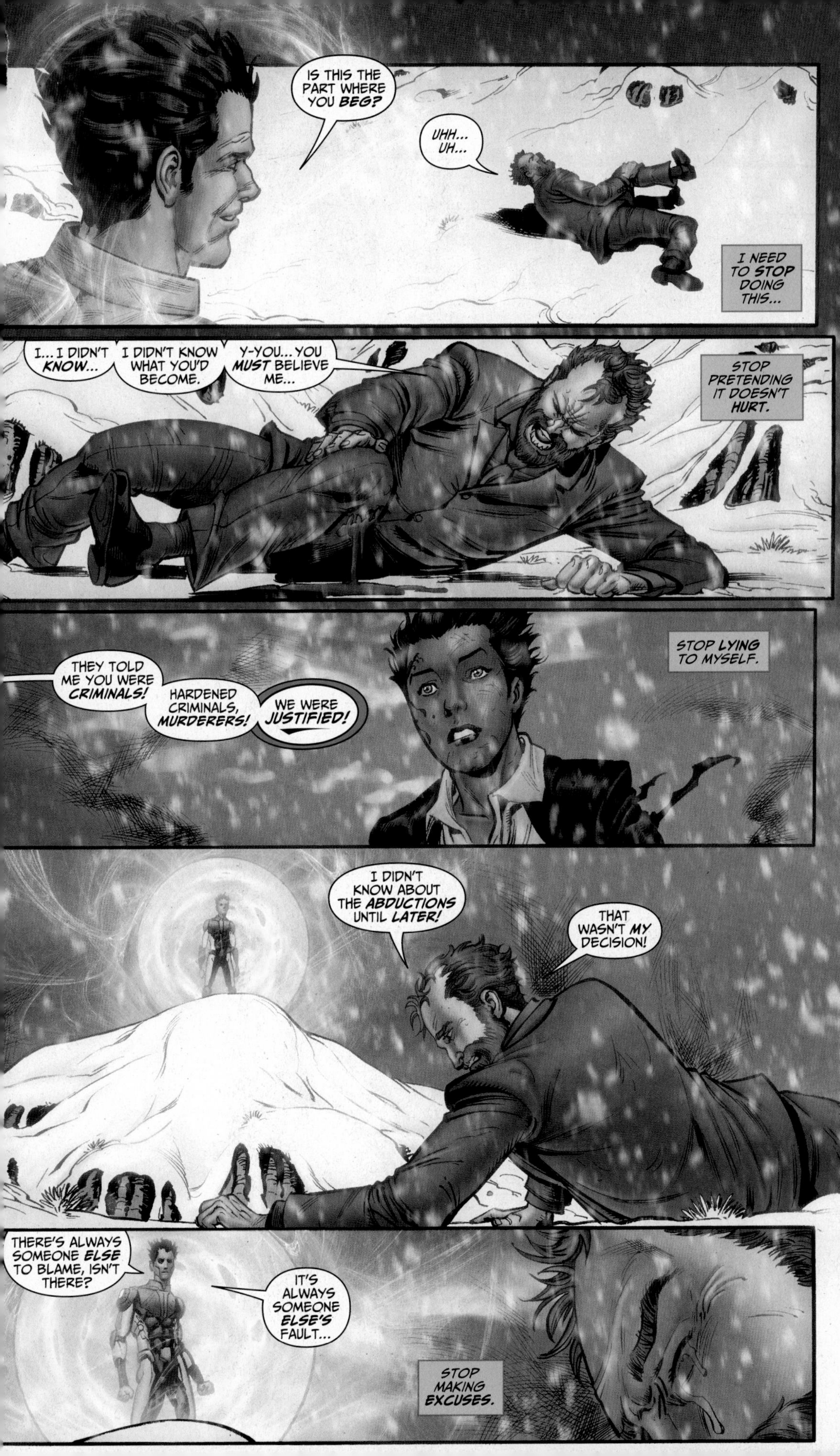
IS THIS THE PART WHERE YOU BEG?
UHH... UH...
I NEED TO STOP DOING THIS...
I... I DIDN'T KNOW...
I DIDN'T KNOW WHAT YOU'D BECOME.
Y-YOU... YOU MUST BELIEVE ME...
STOP PRETENDING IT DOESN'T HURT.
THEY TOLD ME YOU WERE CRIMINALS!
HARDENED CRIMINALS, MURDERERS!
WE WERE JUSTIFIED!
STOP LYING TO MYSELF.
I DIDN'T KNOW ABOUT THE ABDUCTIONS UNTIL LATER!
THAT WASN'T MY DECISION!
THERE'S ALWAYS SOMEONE ELSE TO BLAME, ISN'T THERE?
IT'S ALWAYS SOMEONE ELSE'S FAULT...
STOP MAKING EXCUSES.

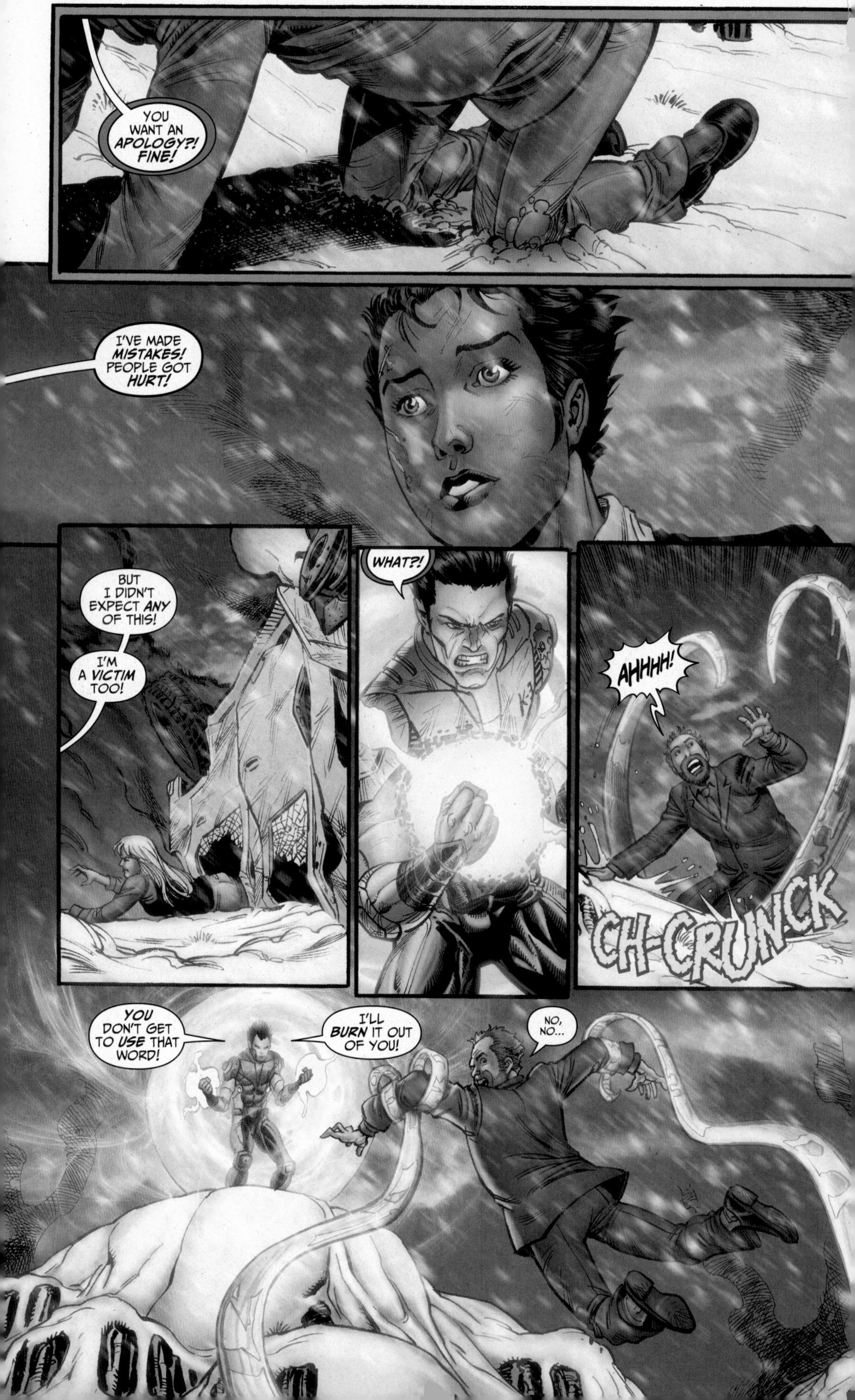
YOU WANT AN APOLOGY?! FINE!
I'VE MADE MISTAKES! PEOPLE GOT HURT!
BUT I DIDN'T EXPECT ANY OF THIS!
I'M A VICTIM TOO!
WHAT?!
AHHHH!
CH-CRUNCK
YOU DON'T GET TO USE THAT WORD!
I'LL BURN IT OUT OF YOU!
NO, NO...

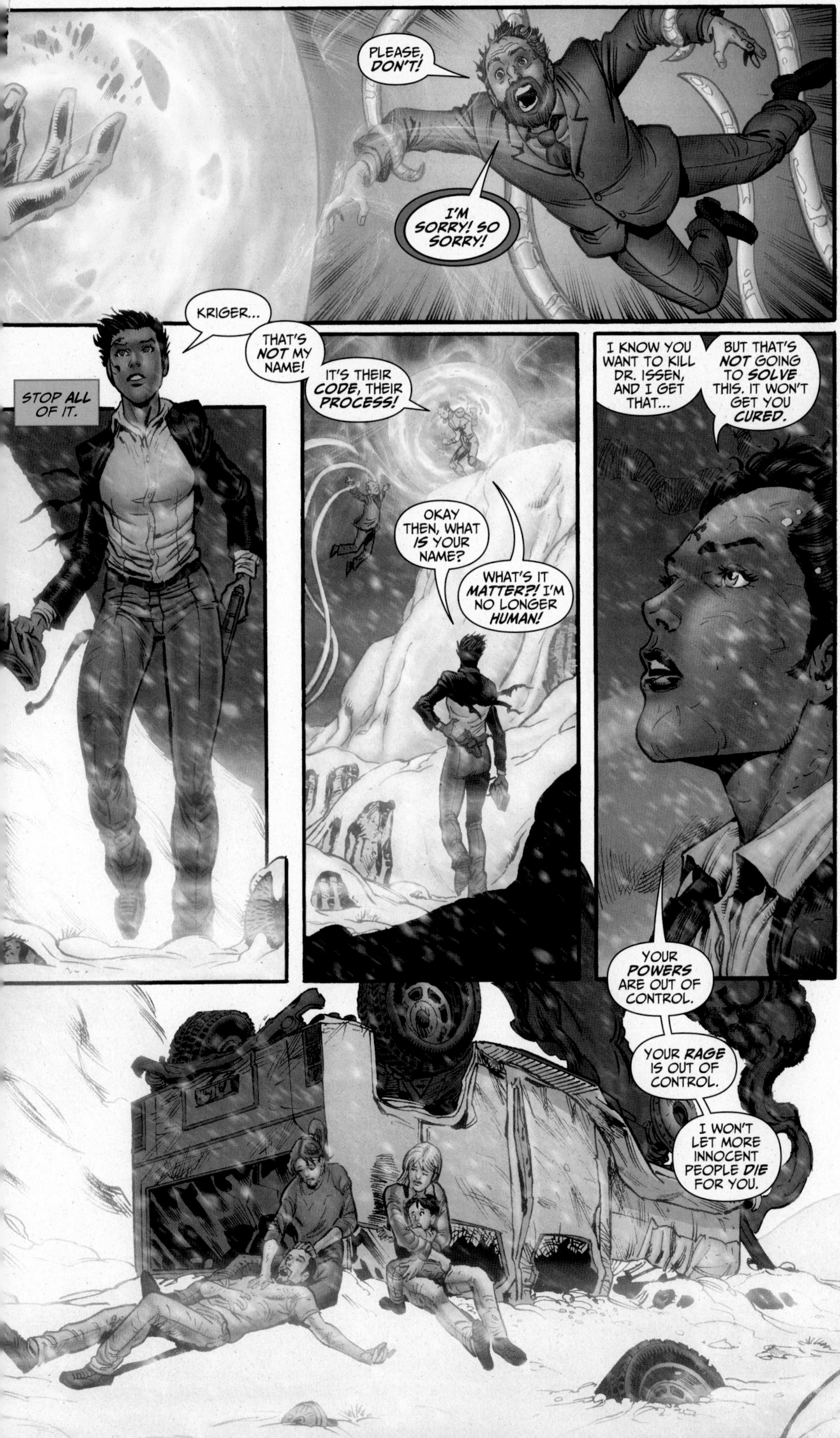
PLEASE, DON'T!
I'M SORRY! SO SORRY!
KRIGER...
THAT'S NOT MY NAME!
IT'S THEIR CODE, THEIR PROCESS!
STOP ALL OF IT.
OKAY THEN, WHAT IS YOUR NAME?
WHAT'S IT MATTER?! I'M NO LONGER HUMAN!
I KNOW YOU WANT TO KILL DR. ISSEN, AND I GET THAT...
BUT THAT'S NOT GOING TO SOLVE THIS. IT WON'T GET YOU CURED.
YOUR POWERS ARE OUT OF CONTROL.
YOUR RAGE IS OUT OF CONTROL.
I WON'T LET MORE INNOCENT PEOPLE DIE FOR YOU.

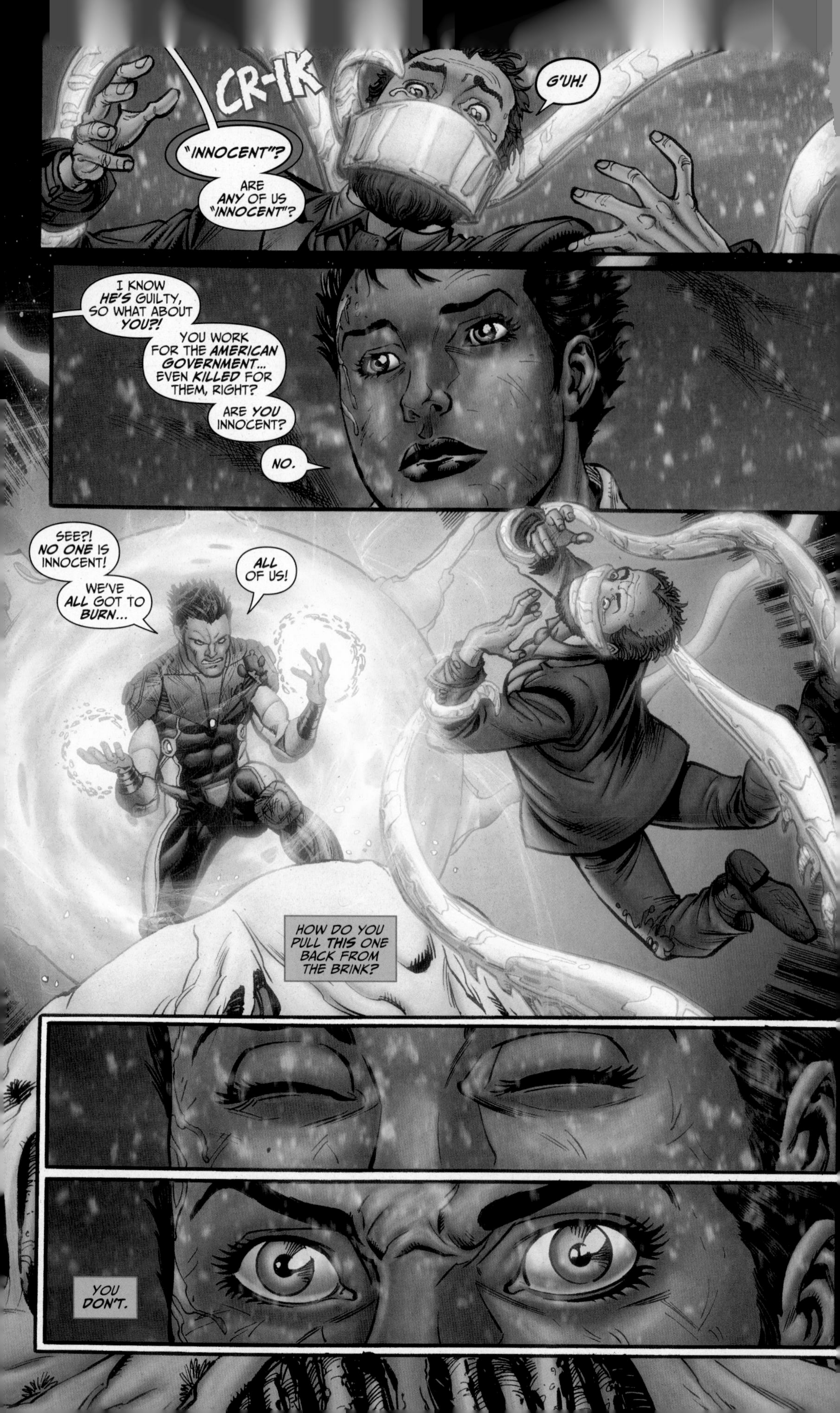
CR-IK
"INNOCENT"?
ARE ANY OF US "INNOCENT"?
G'UH!
I KNOW HE'S GUILTY, SO WHAT ABOUT YOU?!
YOU WORK FOR THE AMERICAN GOVERNMENT... EVEN KILLED FOR THEM, RIGHT?
ARE YOU INNOCENT?
NO.
SEE?! NO ONE IS INNOCENT!
WE'VE ALL GOT TO BURN...
ALL OF US!
HOW DO YOU PULL THIS ONE BACK FROM THE BRINK?
YOU DON'T.

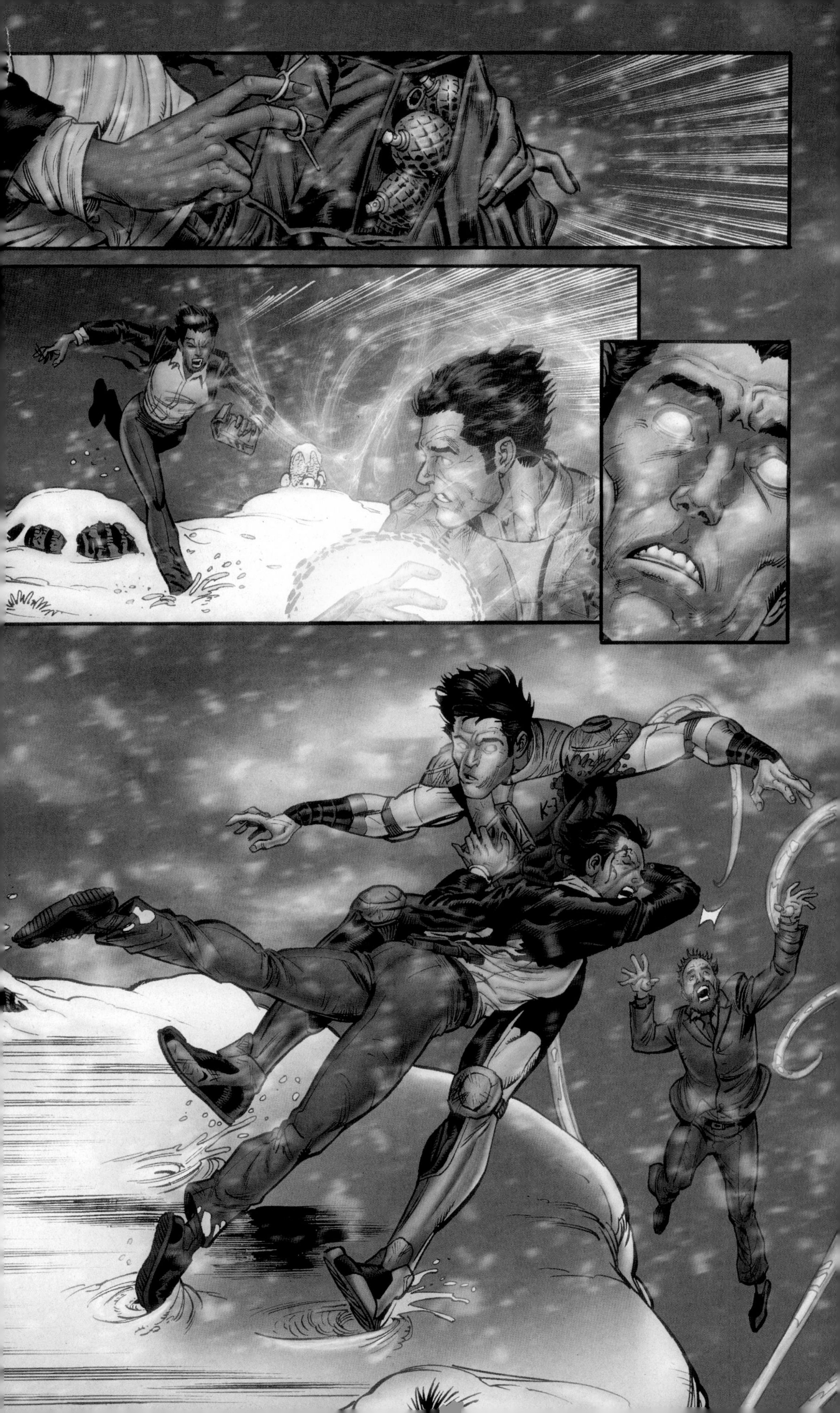

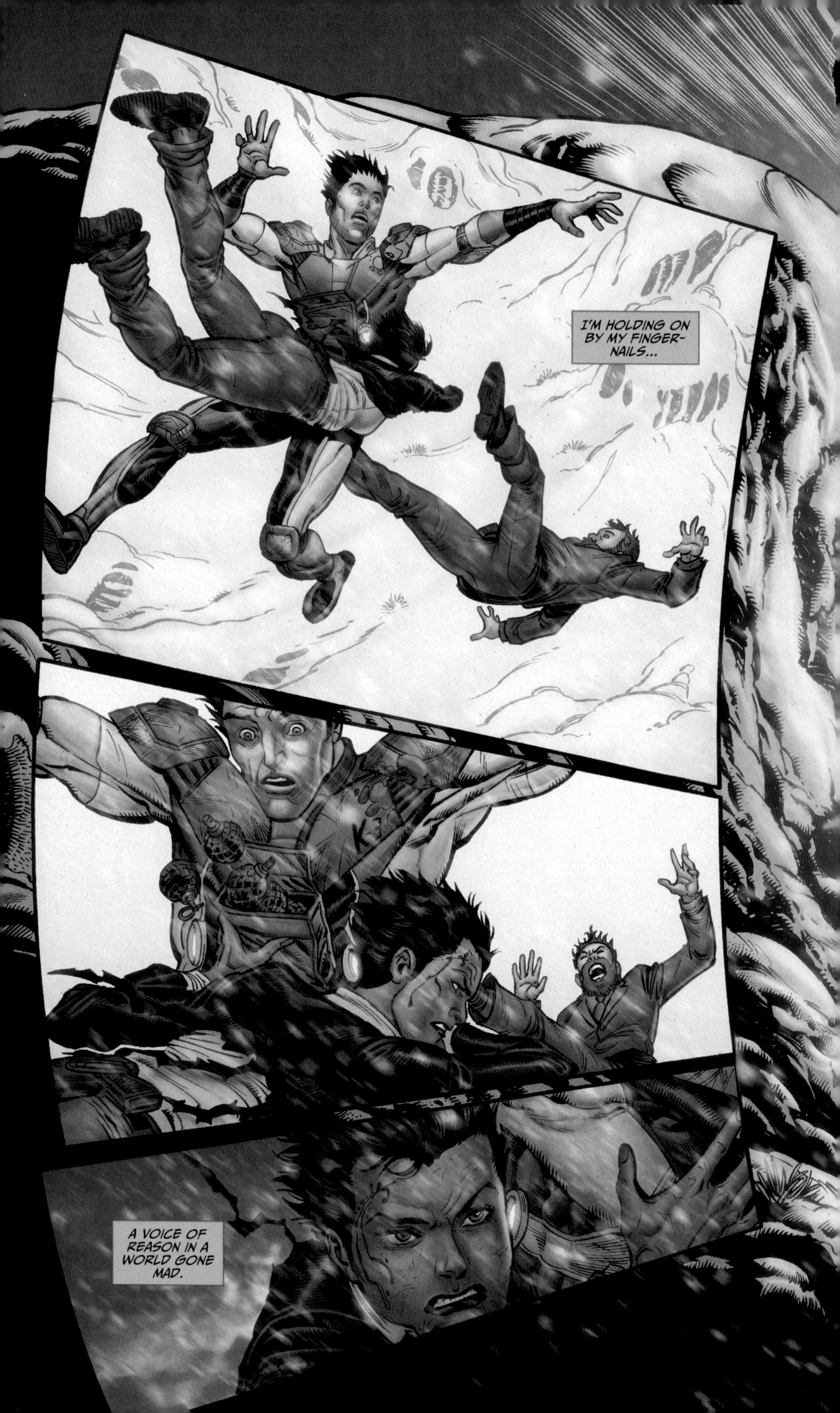
I'M HOLDING ON BY MY FINGER-NAILS...
A VOICE OF REASON IN A WORLD GONE MAD.

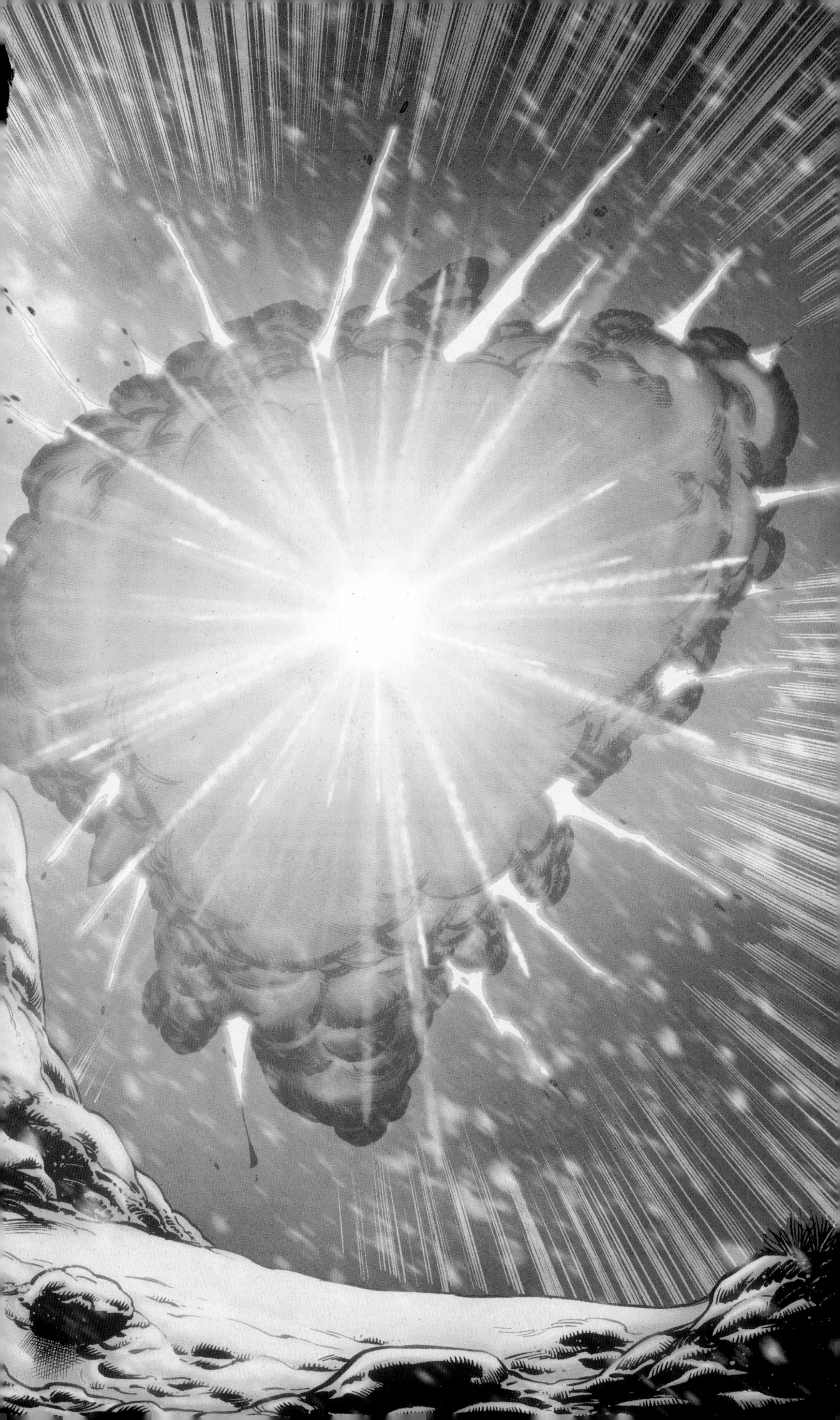

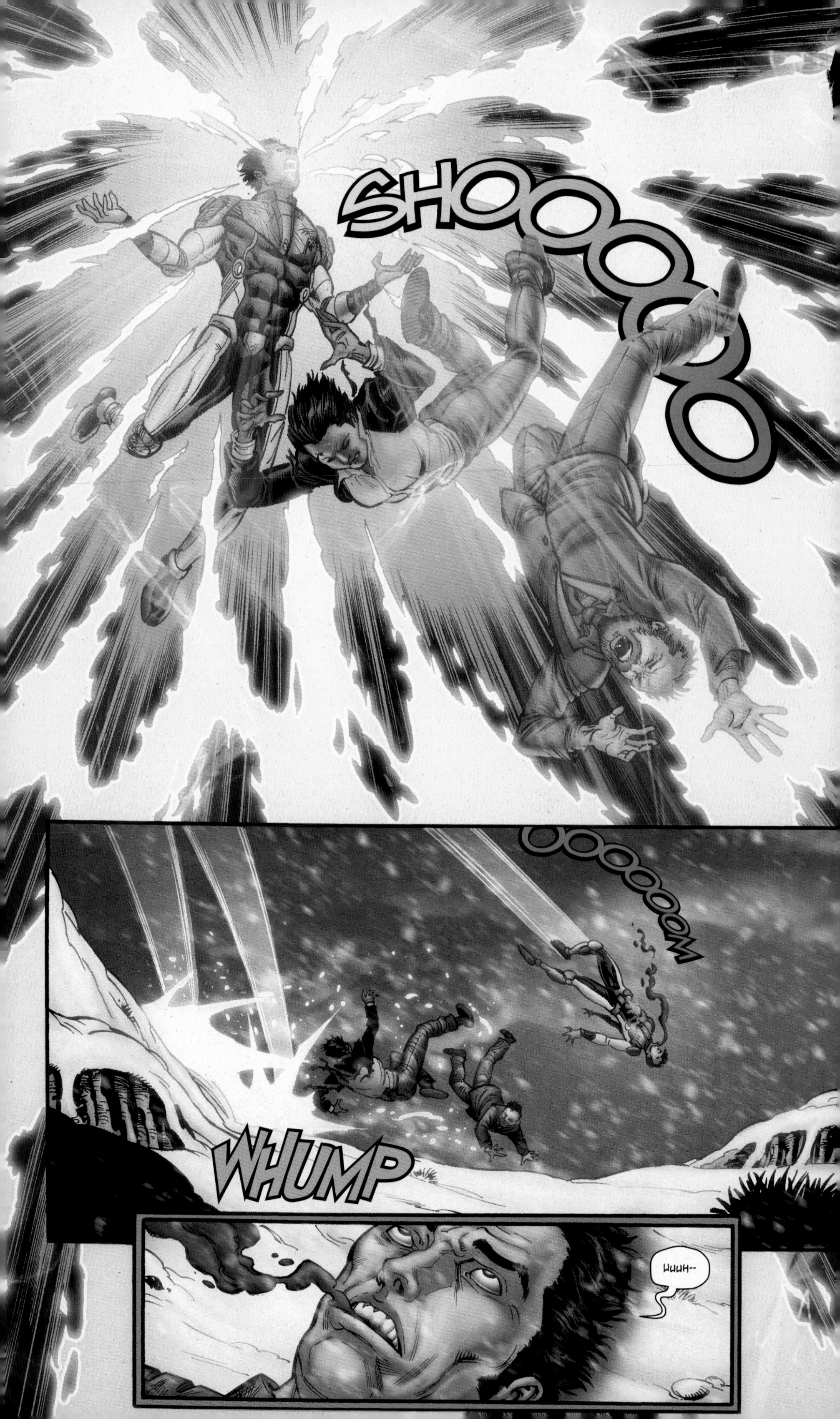

SHOOOOOO
OOOOOOM
WHUMP
HUUH--

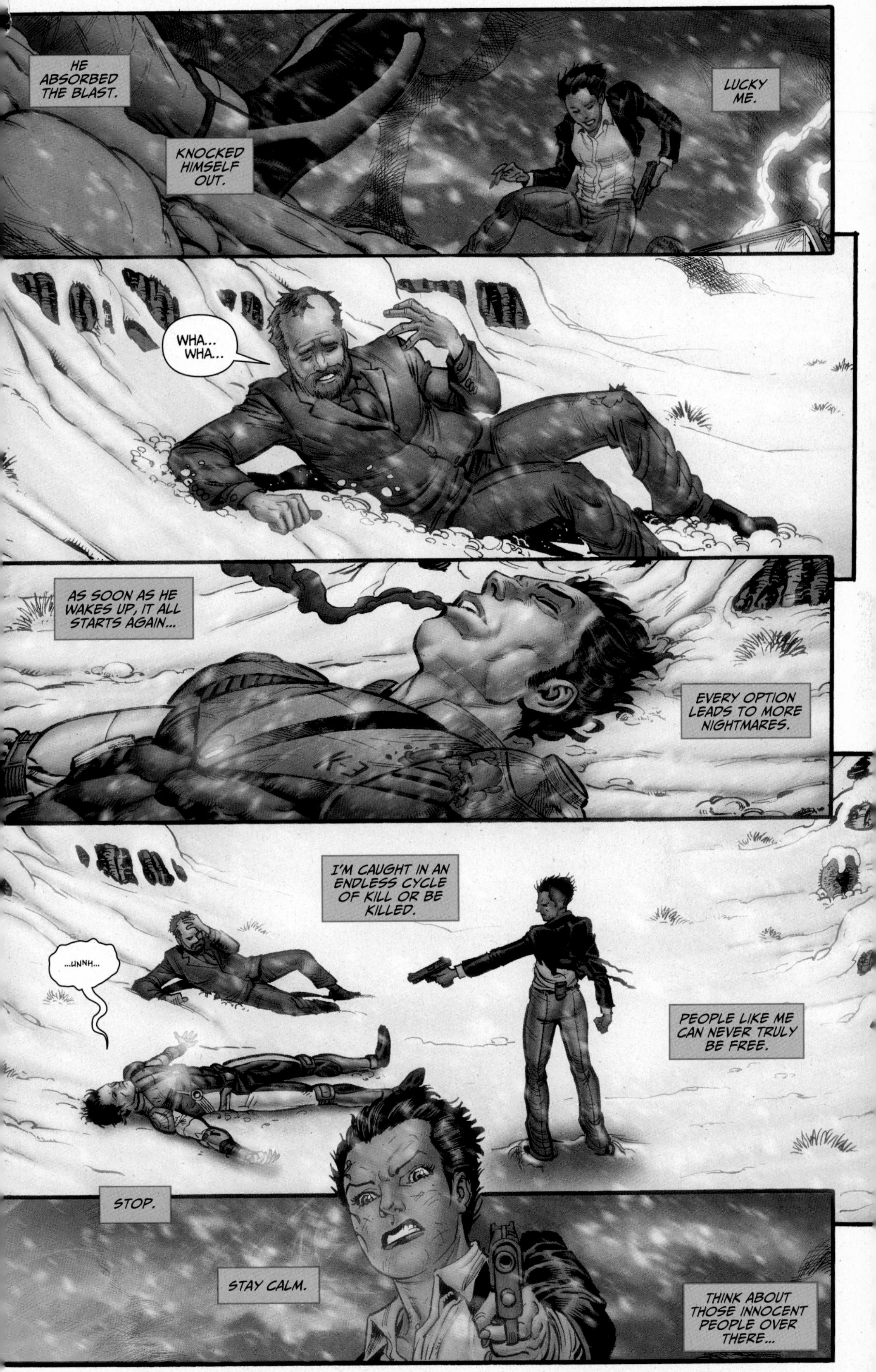
HE ABSORBED THE BLAST.
KNOCKED HIMSELF OUT.
LUCKY ME.
WHA... WHA...
AS SOON AS HE WAKES UP, IT ALL STARTS AGAIN...
EVERY OPTION LEADS TO MORE NIGHTMARES.
I'M CAUGHT IN AN ENDLESS CYCLE OF KILL OR BE KILLED.
...UNNH...
PEOPLE LIKE ME CAN NEVER TRULY BE FREE.
STOP.
STAY CALM.
THINK ABOUT THOSE INNOCENT PEOPLE OVER THERE...

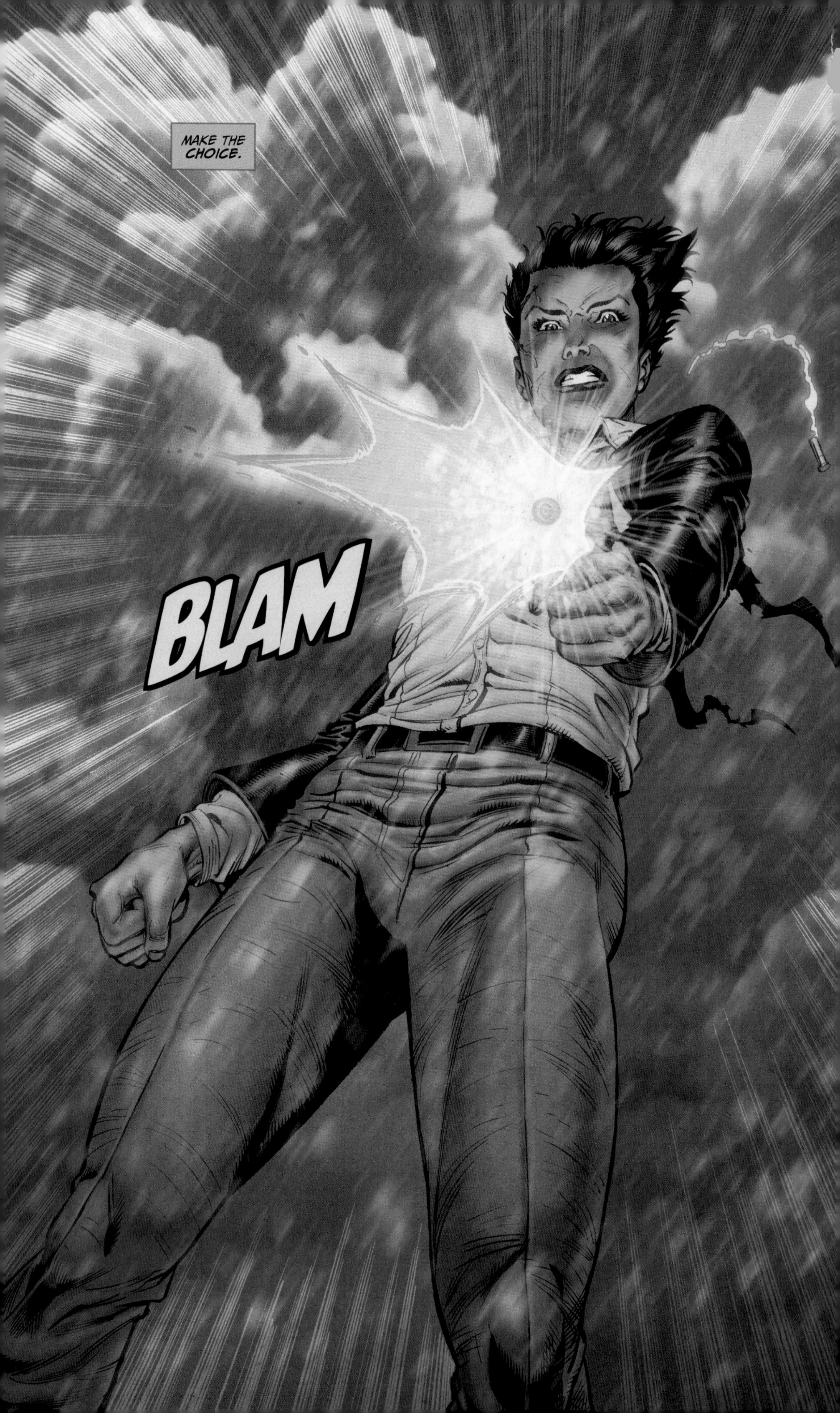
MAKE THE CHOICE.
BLAM

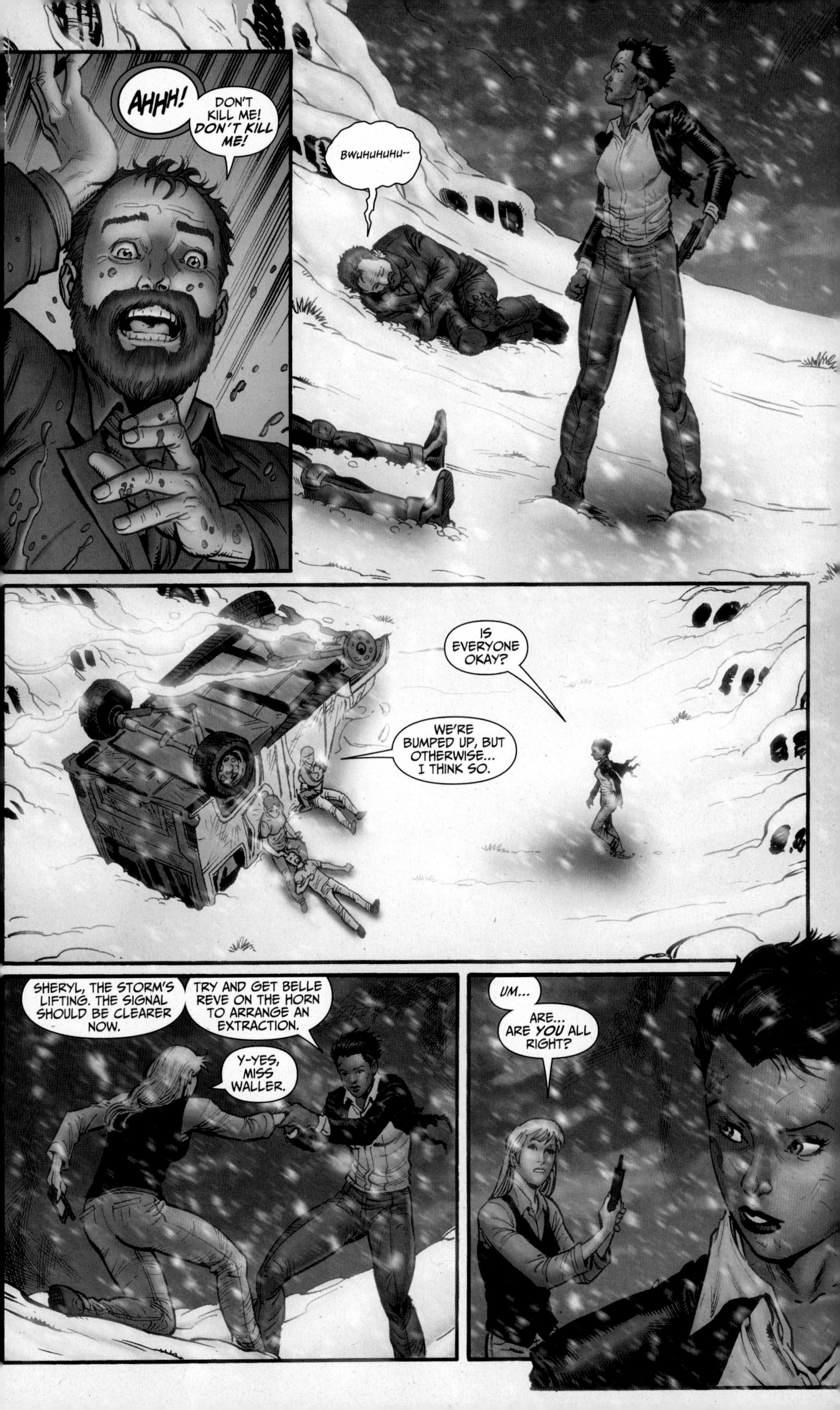
AHHH!
DON'T KILL ME! DON'T KILL ME!
BWUHUHUHU--
IS EVERYONE OKAY?
WE'RE BUMPED UP, BUT OTHERWISE... I THINK SO.
SHERYL, THE STORM'S LIFTING. THE SIGNAL SHOULD BE CLEARER NOW.
TRY AND GET BELLE REVE ON THE HORN TO ARRANGE AN EXTRACTION.
Y-YES, MISS WALLER.
UM...
ARE... ARE YOU ALL RIGHT?

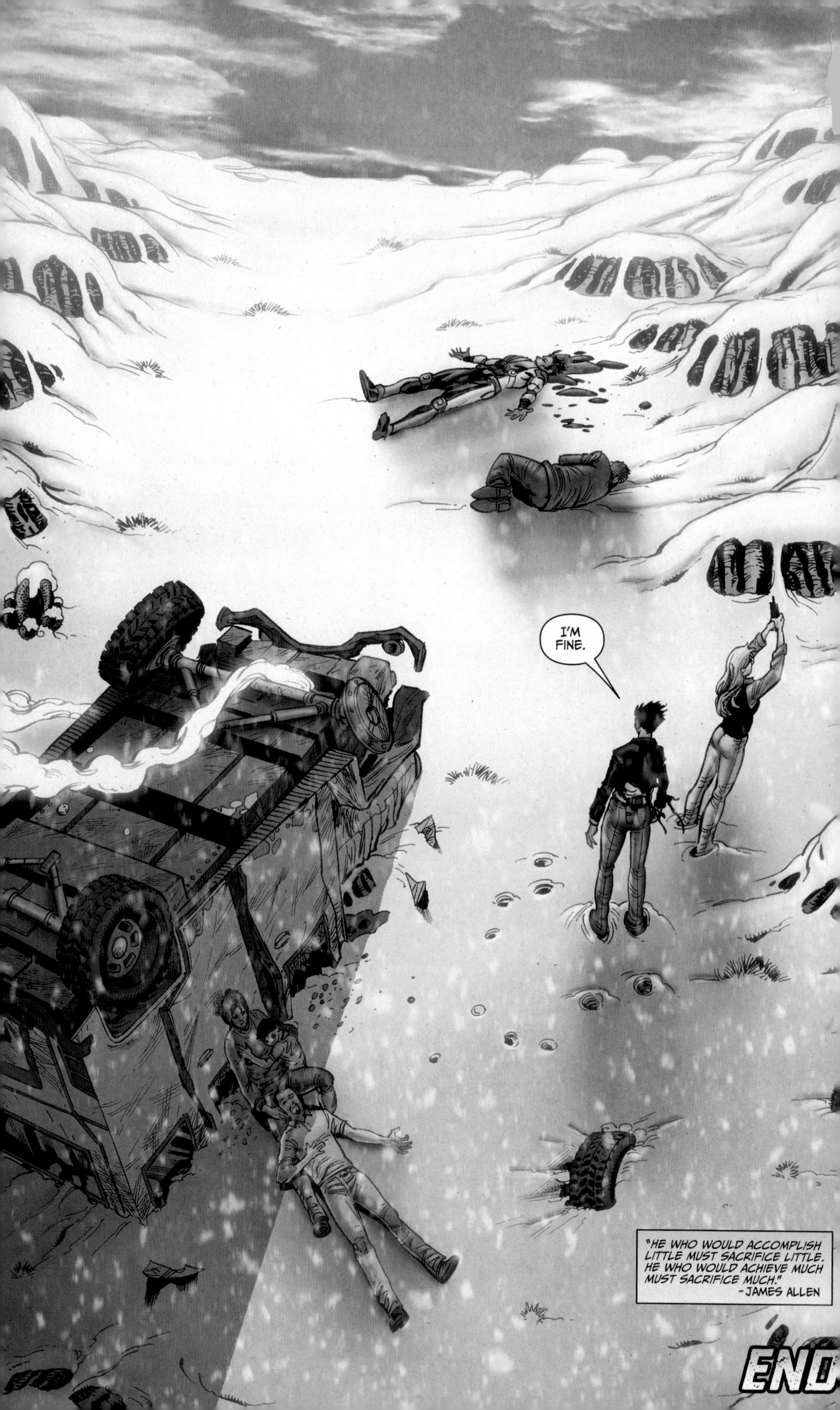
I'M FINE.
"HE WHO WOULD ACCOMPLISH LITTLE MUST SACRIFICE LITTLE. HE WHO WOULD ACHIEVE MUCH MUST SACRIFICE MUCH." -JAMES ALLEN
END

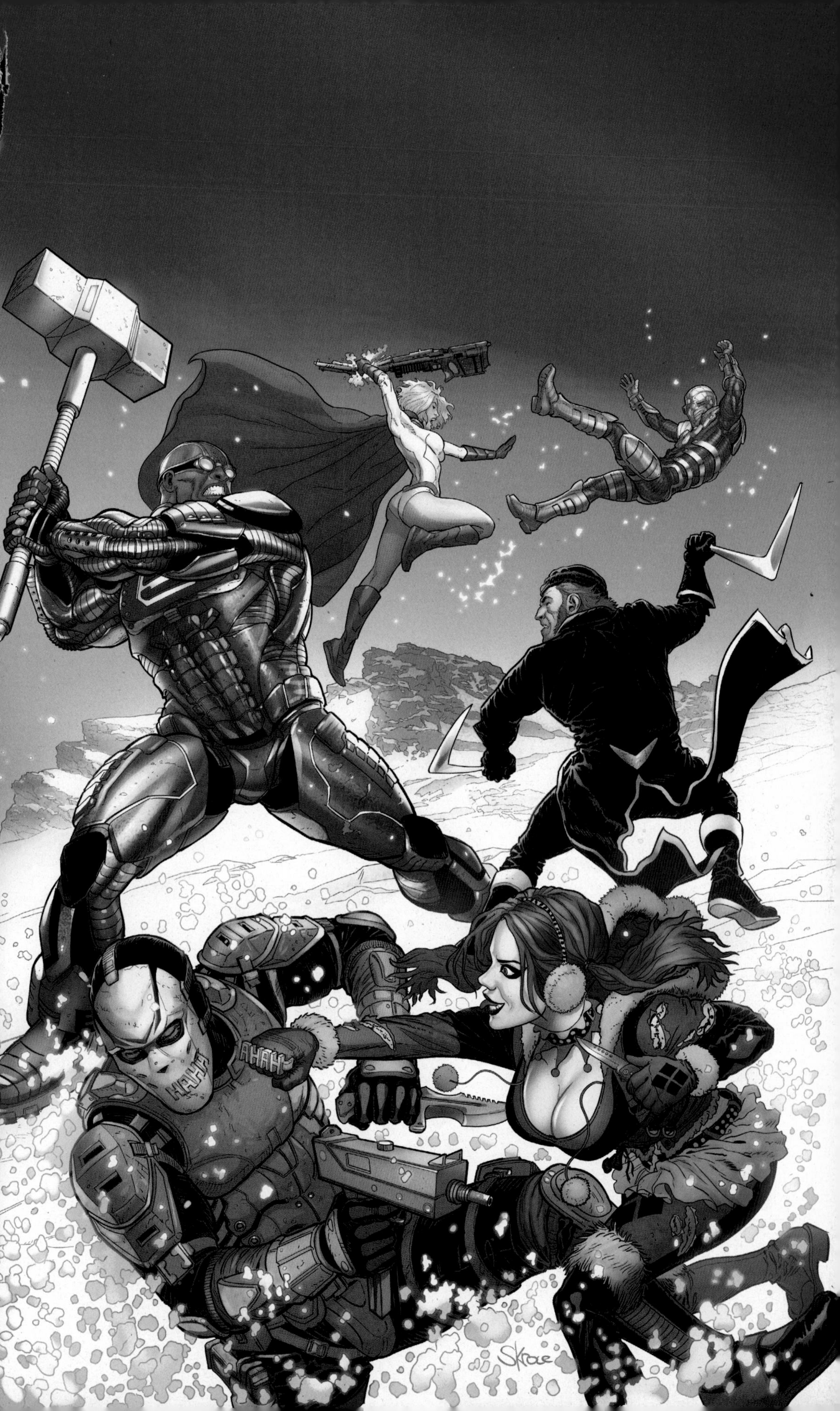
HAHA
AHAH

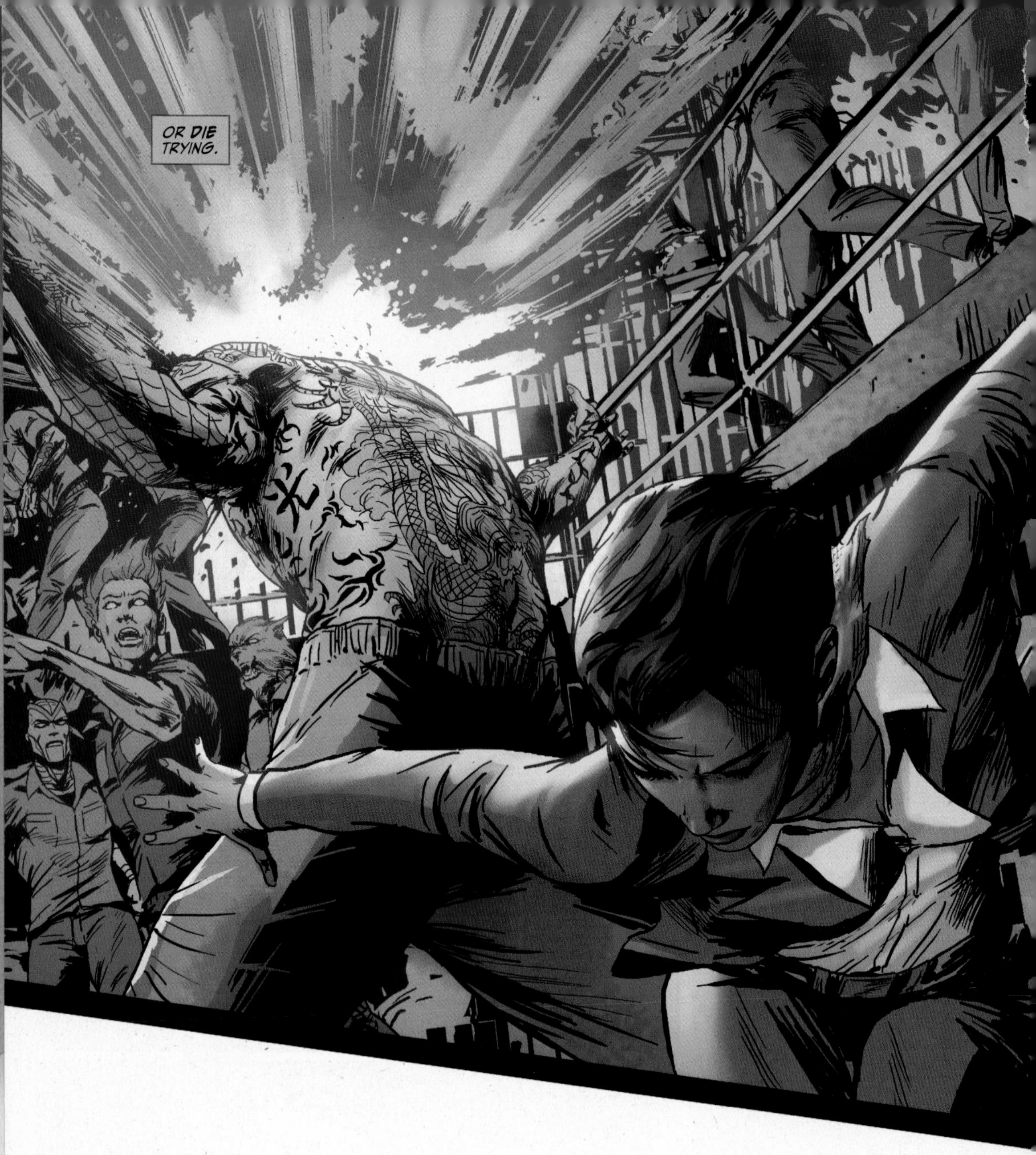
OR DIE TRYING.

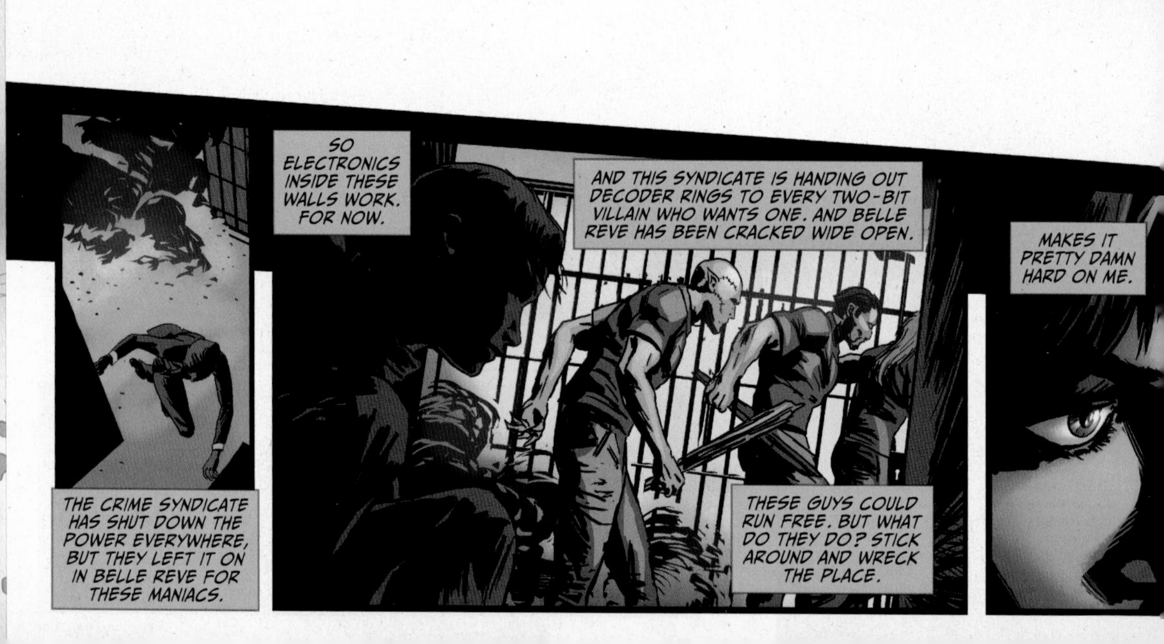
THE CRIME SYNDICATE HAS SHUT DOWN THE POWER EVERYWHERE, BUT THEY LEFT IT ON IN BELLE REVE FOR THESE MANIACS.
SO ELECTRONICS INSIDE THESE WALLS WORK. FOR NOW.
AND THIS SYNDICATE IS HANDING OUT DECODER RINGS TO EVERY TWO-BIT VILLAIN WHO WANTS ONE. AND BELLE REVE HAS BEEN CRACKED WIDE OPEN.
THESE GUYS COULD RUN FREE. BUT WHAT DO THEY DO? STICK AROUND AND WRECK THE PLACE.
MAKES IT PRETTY DAMN HARD ON ME.

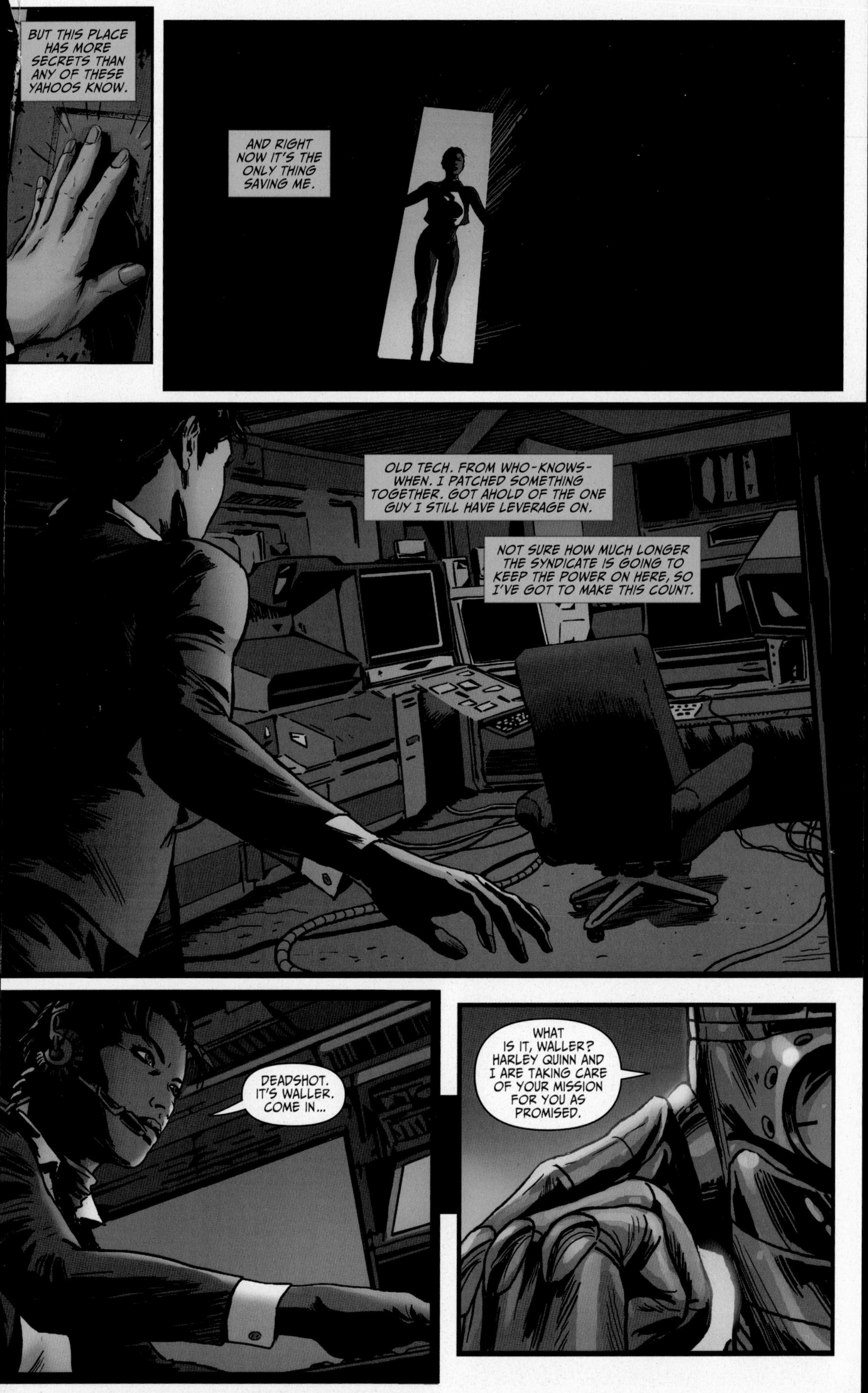
BUT THIS PLACE HAS MORE SECRETS THAN ANY OF THESE YAHOOS KNOW.
AND RIGHT NOW IT'S THE ONLY THING SAVING ME.
OLD TECH. FROM WHO-KNOWS-WHEN. I PATCHED SOMETHING TOGETHER. GOT AHOLD OF THE ONE GUY I STILL HAVE LEVERAGE ON.
NOT SURE HOW MUCH LONGER THE SYNDICATE IS GOING TO KEEP THE POWER ON HERE, SO I'VE GOT TO MAKE THIS COUNT.
DEADSHOT. IT'S WALLER. COME IN...
WHAT IS IT, WALLER? HARLEY QUINN AND I ARE TAKING CARE OF YOUR MISSION FOR YOU AS PROMISED.

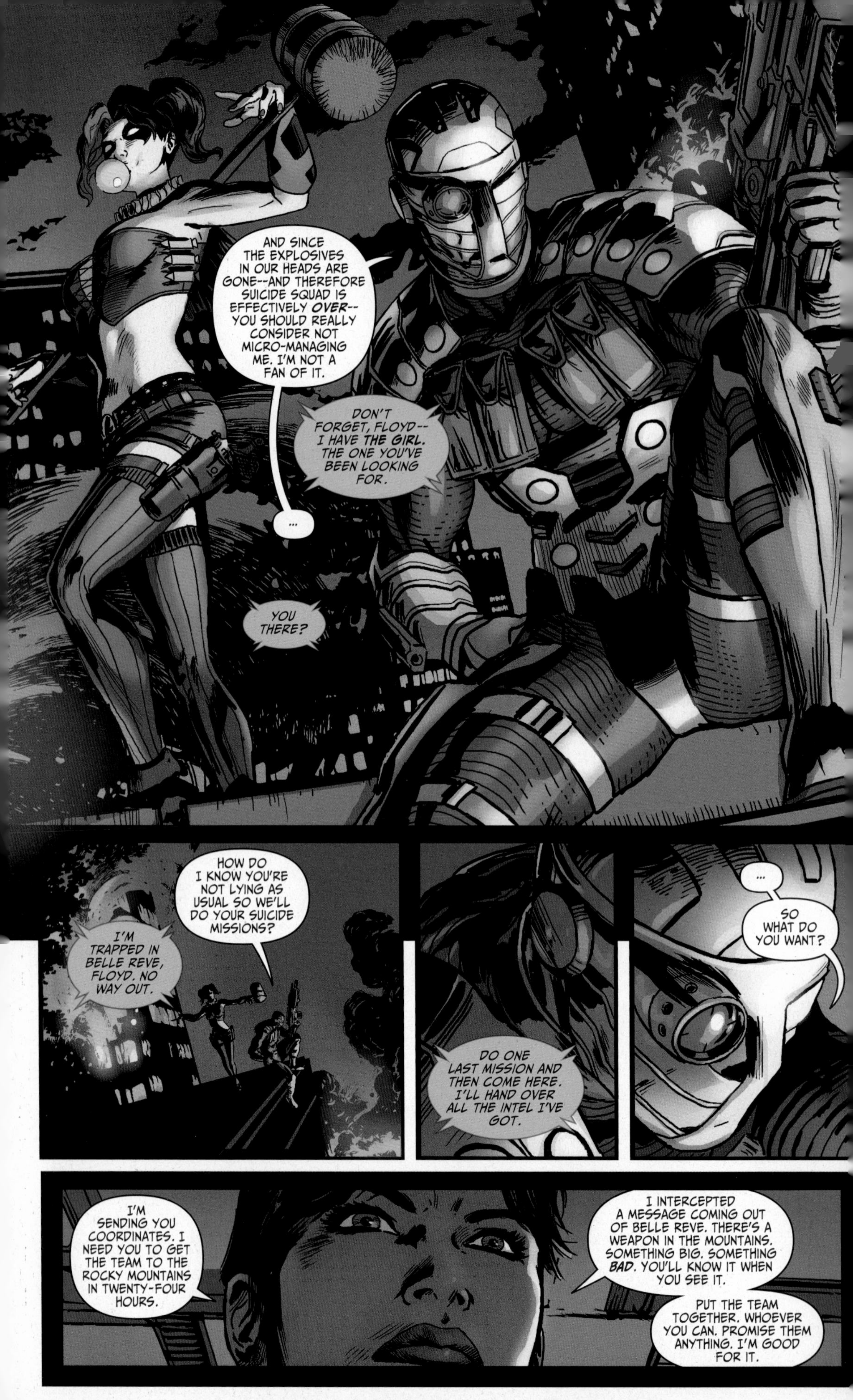
AND SINCE THE EXPLOSIVES IN OUR HEADS ARE GONE--AND THEREFORE SUICIDE SQUAD IS EFFECTIVELY OVER--YOU SHOULD REALLY CONSIDER NOT MICRO-MANAGING ME. I'M NOT A FAN OF IT.
DON'T FORGET, FLOYD--I HAVE THE GIRL. THE ONE YOU'VE BEEN LOOKING FOR.
...
YOU THERE?
HOW DO I KNOW YOU'RE NOT LYING AS USUAL SO WE'LL DO YOUR SUICIDE MISSIONS?
I'M TRAPPED IN BELLE REVE, FLOYD. NO WAY OUT.
DO ONE LAST MISSION AND THEN COME HERE. I'LL HAND OVER ALL THE INTEL I'VE GOT.
...
SO WHAT DO YOU WANT?
I'M SENDING YOU COORDINATES. I NEED YOU TO GET THE TEAM TO THE ROCKY MOUNTAINS IN TWENTY-FOUR HOURS.
I INTERCEPTED A MESSAGE COMING OUT OF BELLE REVE. THERE'S A WEAPON IN THE MOUNTAINS. SOMETHING BIG. SOMETHING BAD. YOU'LL KNOW IT WHEN YOU SEE IT.
PUT THE TEAM TOGETHER. WHOEVER YOU CAN. PROMISE THEM ANYTHING. I'M GOOD FOR IT.

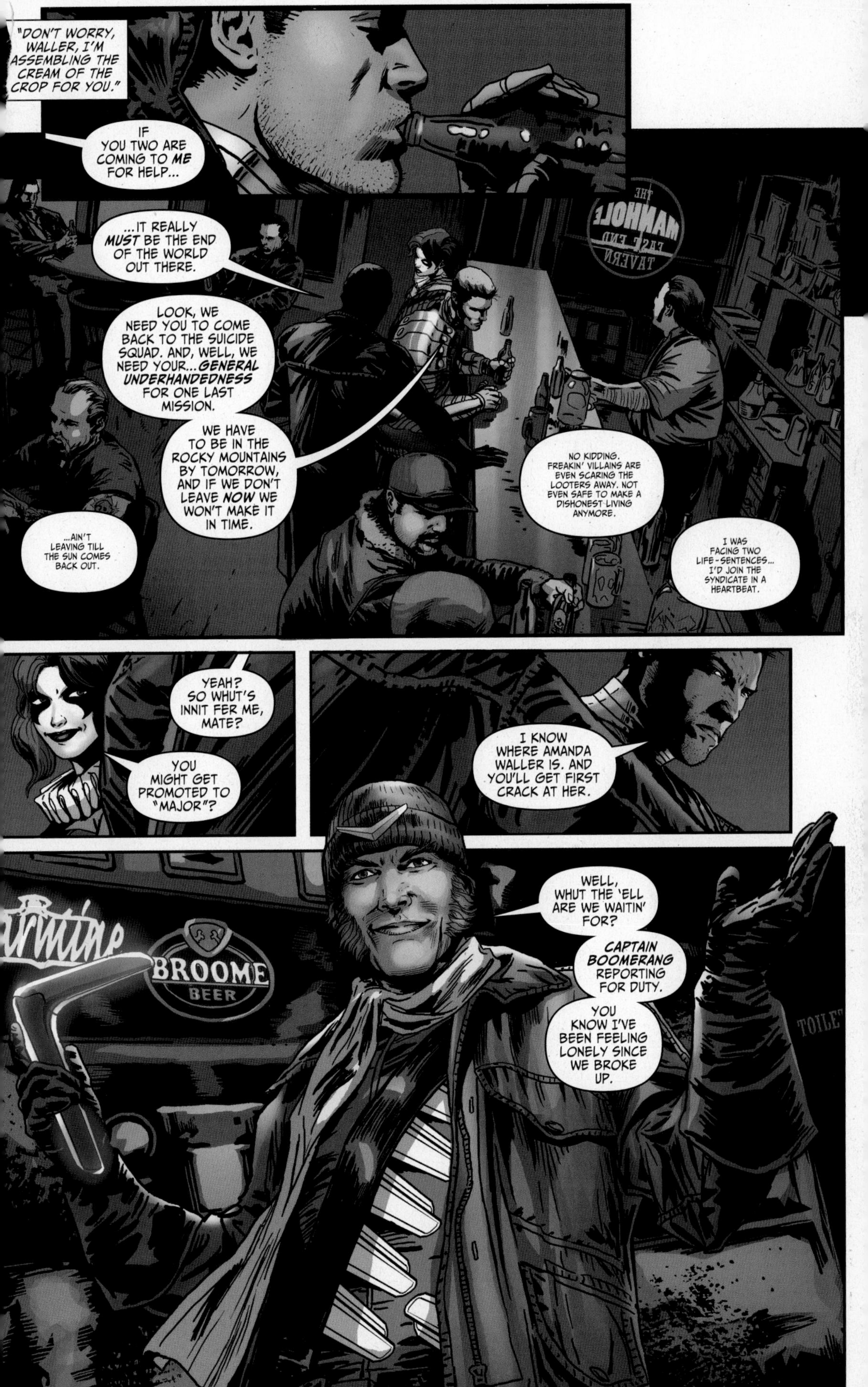

"DON'T WORRY, WALLER, I'M ASSEMBLING THE CREAM OF THE CROP FOR YOU."
IF YOU TWO ARE COMING TO ME FOR HELP...
...IT REALLY MUST BE THE END OF THE WORLD OUT THERE.
THE MANHOLE EAST END TAVERN
LOOK, WE NEED YOU TO COME BACK TO THE SUICIDE SQUAD. AND, WELL, WE NEED YOUR...GENERAL UNDERHANDEDNESS FOR ONE LAST MISSION.
WE HAVE TO BE IN THE ROCKY MOUNTAINS BY TOMORROW, AND IF WE DON'T LEAVE NOW WE WON'T MAKE IT IN TIME.
...AIN'T LEAVING TILL THE SUN COMES BACK OUT.
NO KIDDING. FREAKIN' VILLAINS ARE EVEN SCARING THE LOOTERS AWAY. NOT EVEN SAFE TO MAKE A DISHONEST LIVING ANYMORE.
I WAS FACING TWO LIFE-SENTENCES... I'D JOIN THE SYNDICATE IN A HEARTBEAT.
YEAH? SO WHUT'S INNIT FER ME, MATE?
YOU MIGHT GET PROMOTED TO "MAJOR"?
I KNOW WHERE AMANDA WALLER IS. AND YOU'LL GET FIRST CRACK AT HER.
WELL, WHUT THE 'ELL ARE WE WAITIN' FOR?
CAPTAIN BOOMERANG REPORTING FOR DUTY.
YOU KNOW I'VE BEEN FEELING LONELY SINCE WE BROKE UP.
BROOME BEER

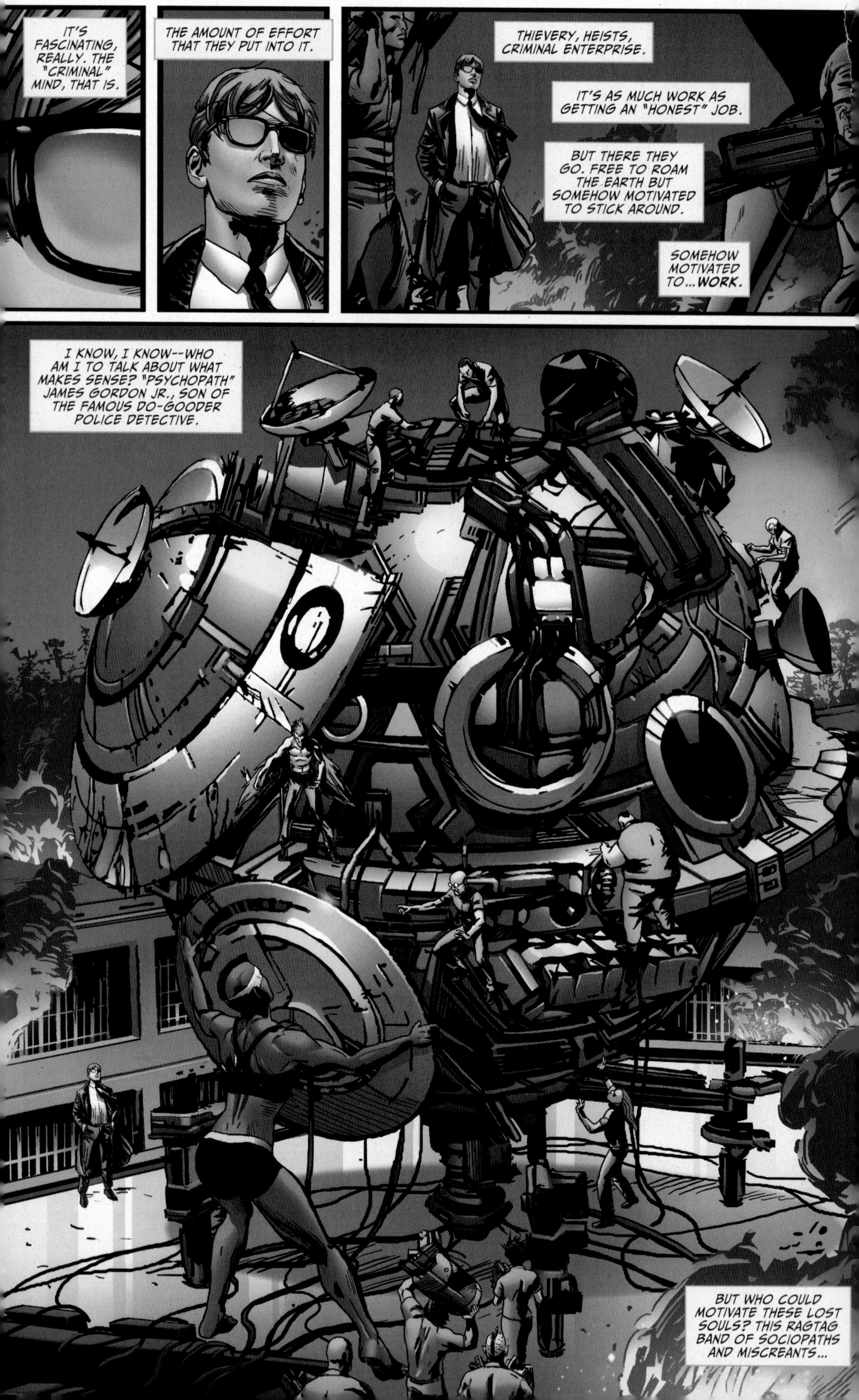
IT'S FASCINATING, REALLY. THE "CRIMINAL" MIND, THAT IS.
THE AMOUNT OF EFFORT THAT THEY PUT INTO IT.
THIEVERY, HEISTS, CRIMINAL ENTERPRISE.
IT'S AS MUCH WORK AS GETTING AN "HONEST" JOB.
BUT THERE THEY GO. FREE TO ROAM THE EARTH BUT SOMEHOW MOTIVATED TO STICK AROUND.
SOMEHOW MOTIVATED TO...WORK.
I KNOW, I KNOW--WHO AM I TO TALK ABOUT WHAT MAKES SENSE? "PSYCHOPATH" JAMES GORDON JR., SON OF THE FAMOUS DO-GOODER POLICE DETECTIVE.
BUT WHO COULD MOTIVATE THESE LOST SOULS? THIS RAGTAG BAND OF SOCIOPATHS AND MISCREANTS...

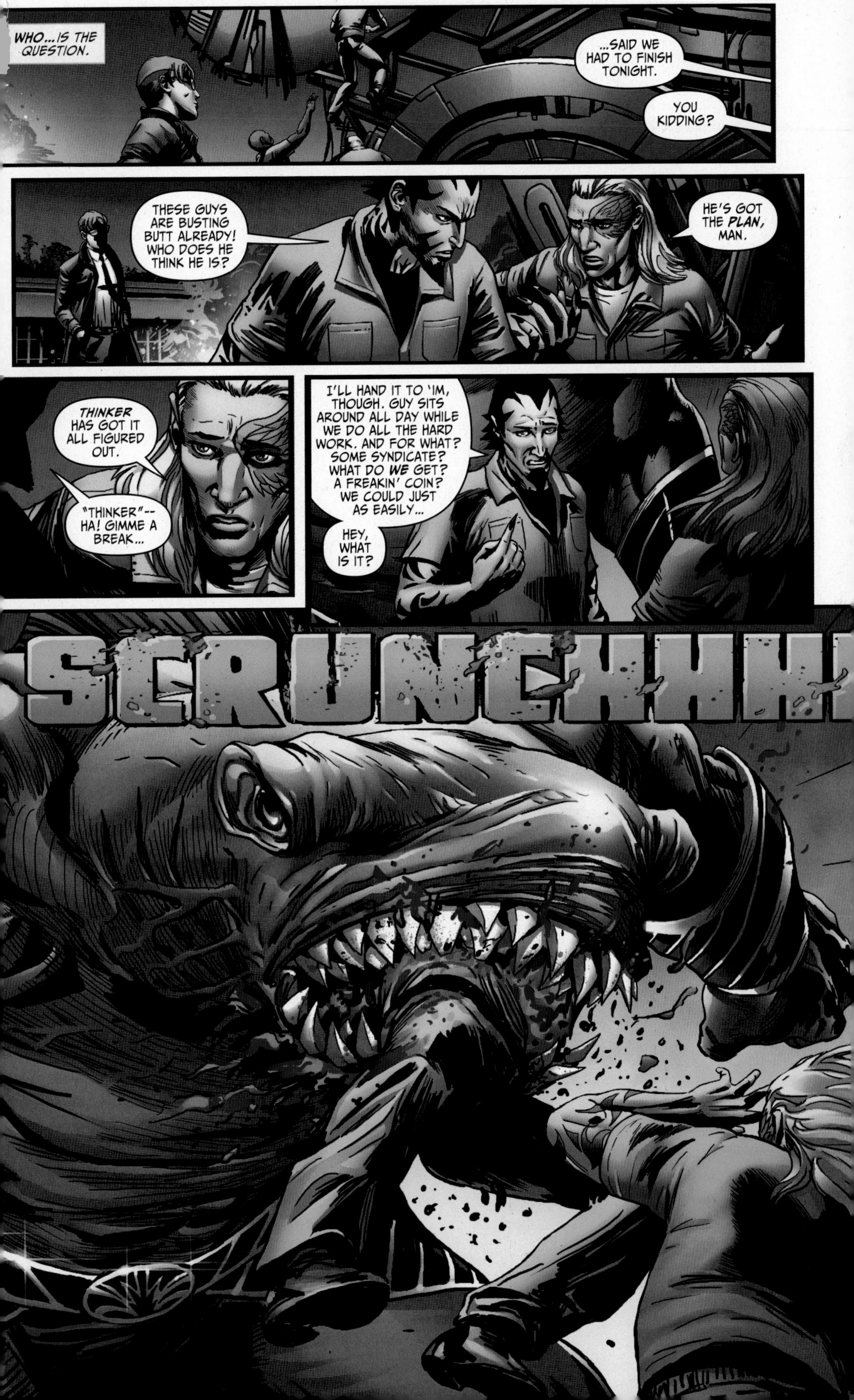
WHO... IS THE QUESTION.
...SAID WE HAD TO FINISH TONIGHT.
YOU KIDDING?
THESE GUYS ARE BUSTING BUTT ALREADY! WHO DOES HE THINK HE IS?
HE'S GOT THE *PLAN*, MAN.
THINKER HAS GOT IT ALL FIGURED OUT.
"THINKER"--HA! GIMME A BREAK...
I'LL HAND IT TO 'IM, THOUGH. GUY SITS AROUND ALL DAY WHILE WE DO ALL THE HARD WORK. AND FOR WHAT? SOME SYNDICATE? WHAT DO *WE* GET? A FREAKIN' COIN? WE COULD JUST AS EASILY...
HEY, WHAT IS IT?
SCRUNCHHH

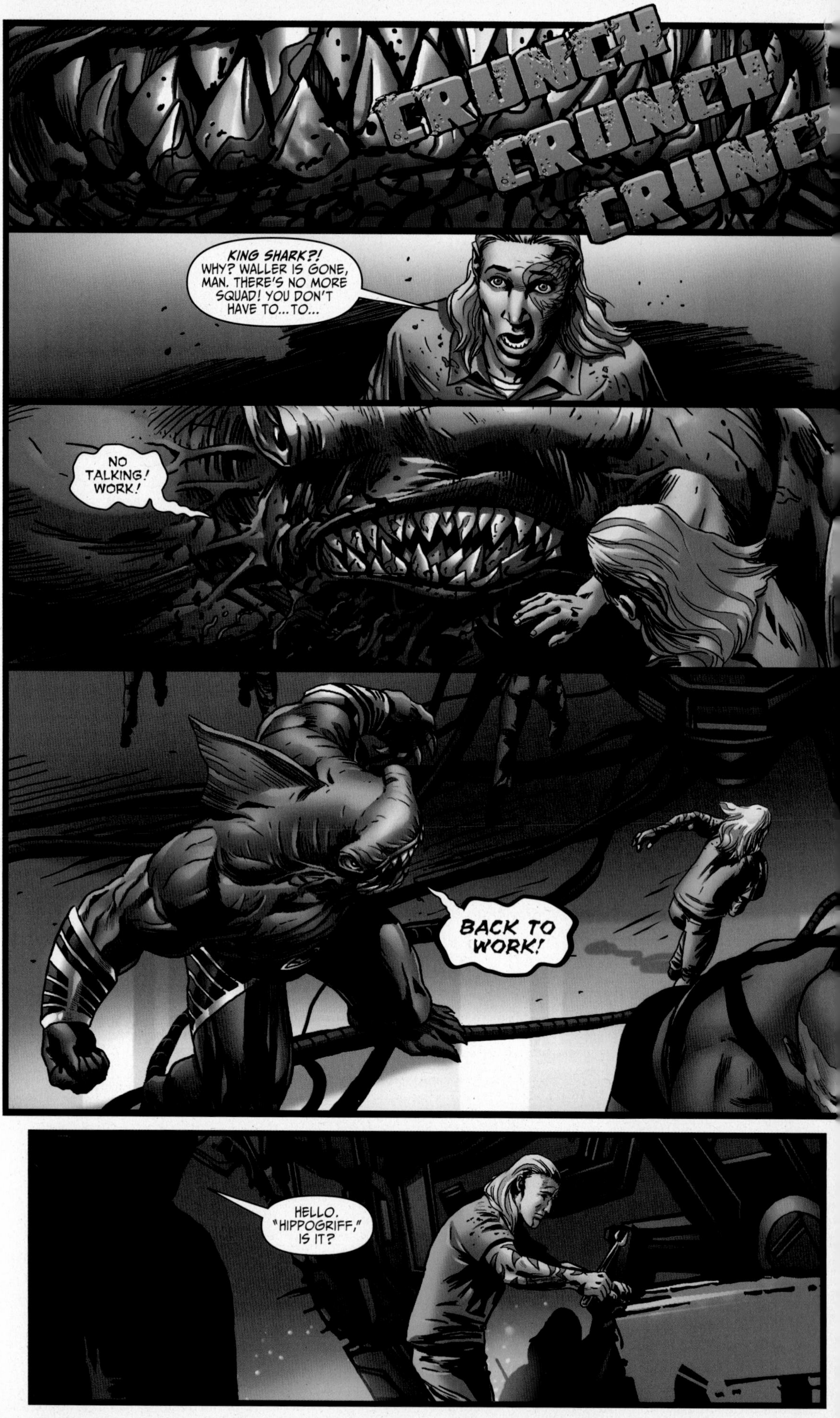

CRUNCH CRUNCH CRUNCH
KING SHARK?! WHY? WALLER IS GONE, MAN. THERE'S NO MORE SQUAD! YOU DON'T HAVE TO...TO...
NO TALKING! WORK!
BACK TO WORK!
HELLO. "HIPPOGRIFF," IS IT?

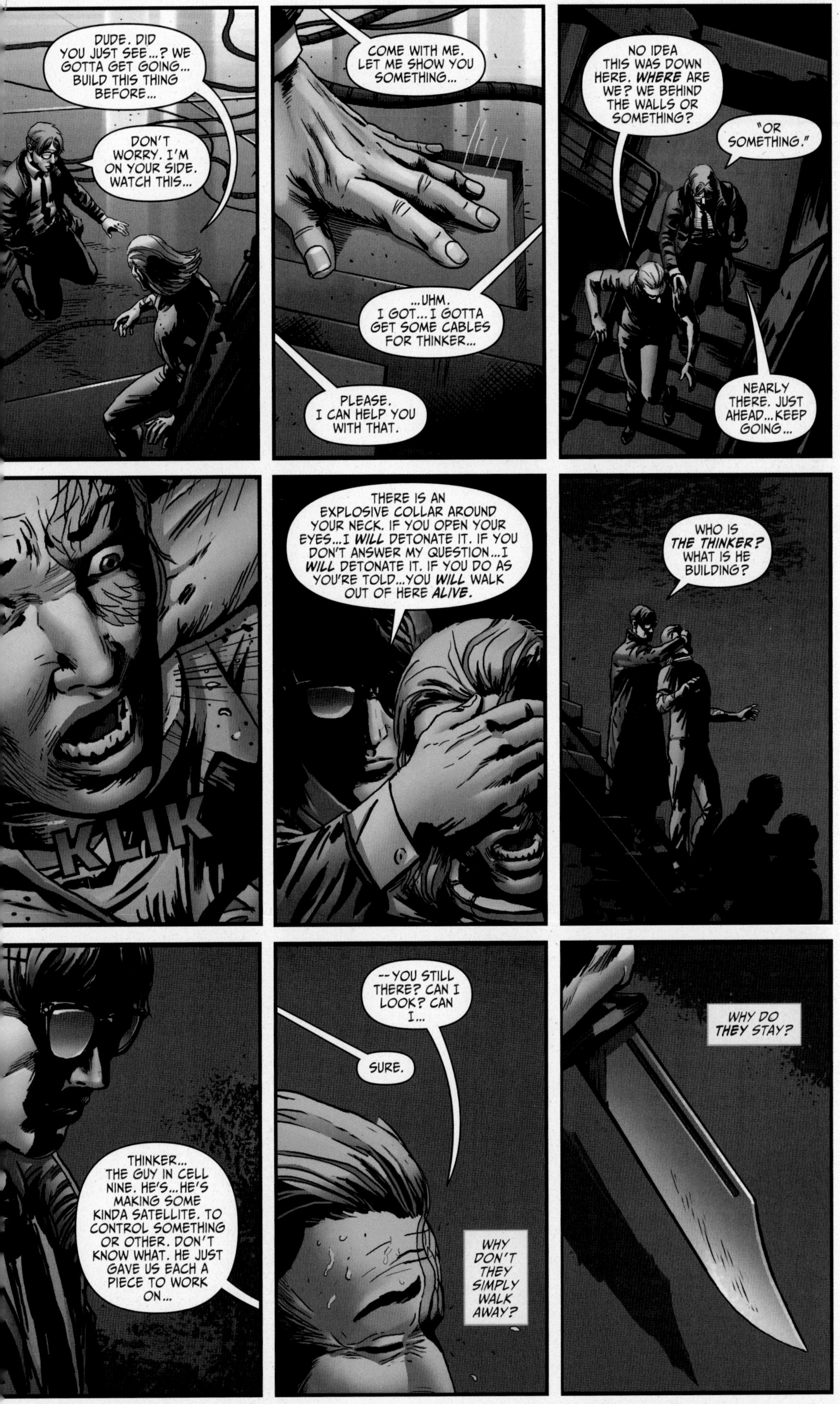
DUDE. DID YOU JUST SEE...? WE GOTTA GET GOING... BUILD THIS THING BEFORE...
DON'T WORRY. I'M ON YOUR SIDE. WATCH THIS...
COME WITH ME. LET ME SHOW YOU SOMETHING...
...UHM. I GOT... I GOTTA GET SOME CABLES FOR THINKER...
PLEASE. I CAN HELP YOU WITH THAT.
NO IDEA THIS WAS DOWN HERE. WHERE ARE WE? WE BEHIND THE WALLS OR SOMETHING?
"OR SOMETHING."
NEARLY THERE. JUST AHEAD...KEEP GOING...
KLIK
THERE IS AN EXPLOSIVE COLLAR AROUND YOUR NECK. IF YOU OPEN YOUR EYES...I WILL DETONATE IT. IF YOU DON'T ANSWER MY QUESTION...I WILL DETONATE IT. IF YOU DO AS YOU'RE TOLD...YOU WILL WALK OUT OF HERE ALIVE.
WHO IS THE THINKER? WHAT IS HE BUILDING?
THINKER... THE GUY IN CELL NINE. HE'S...HE'S MAKING SOME KINDA SATELLITE. TO CONTROL SOMETHING OR OTHER. DON'T KNOW WHAT. HE JUST GAVE US EACH A PIECE TO WORK ON...
--YOU STILL THERE? CAN I LOOK? CAN I...
SURE.
WHY DON'T THEY SIMPLY WALK AWAY?
WHY DO THEY STAY?

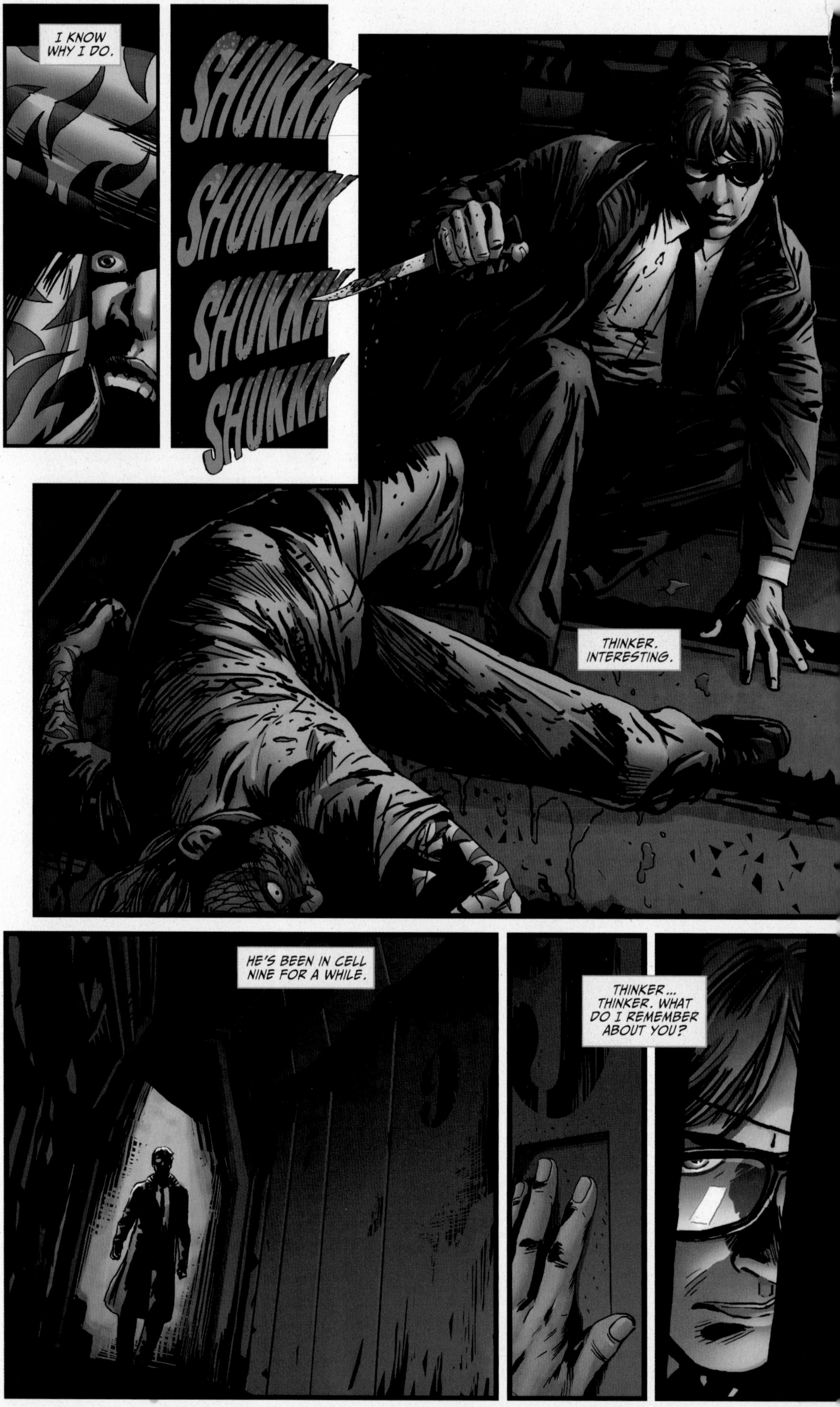
I KNOW WHY I DO.
SHUKKK
SHUKKK
SHUKKK
SHUKKK
THINKER. INTERESTING.
HE'S BEEN IN CELL NINE FOR A WHILE.
THINKER... THINKER. WHAT DO I REMEMBER ABOUT YOU?

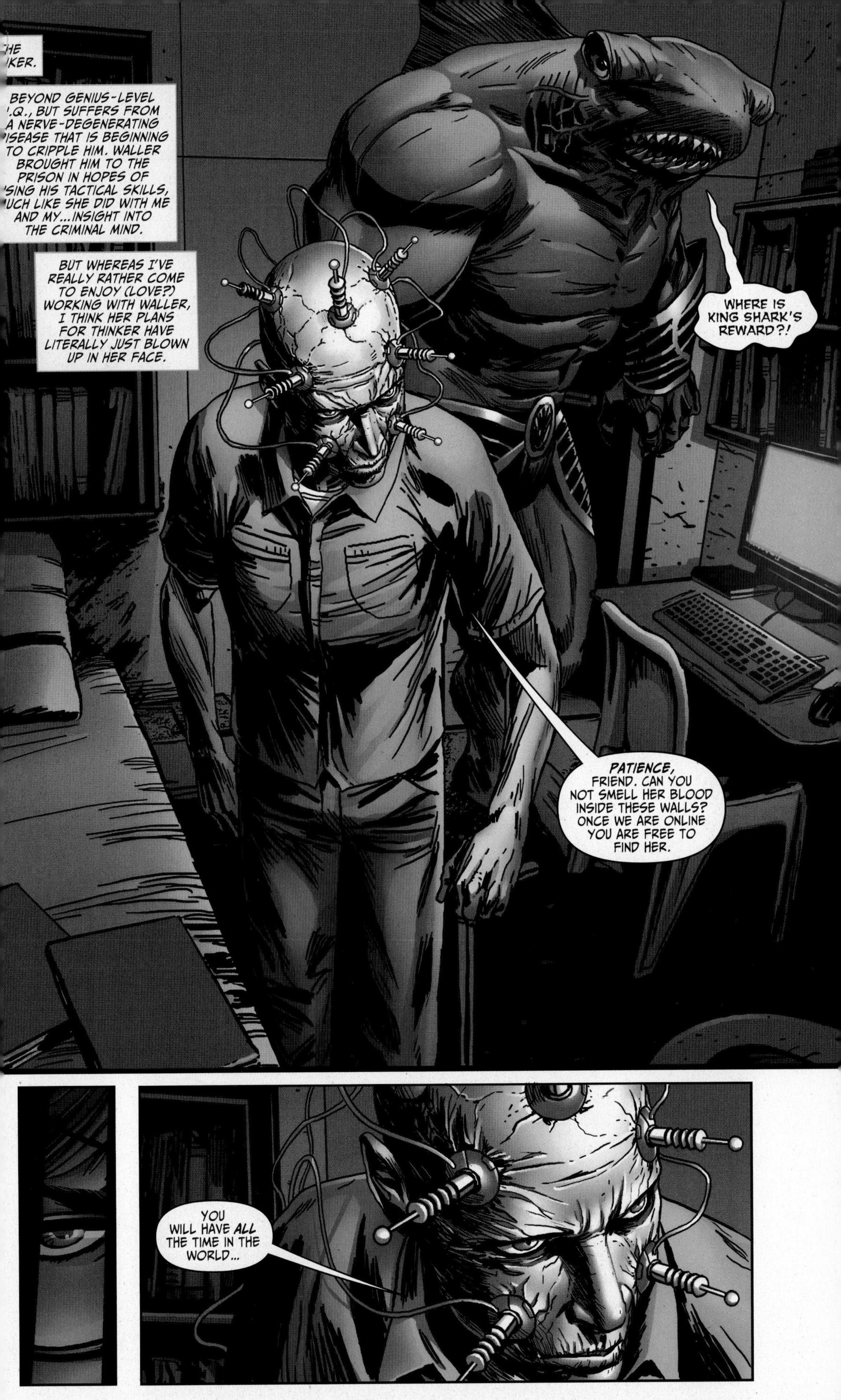

THE ...KER.
BEYOND GENIUS-LEVEL I.Q., BUT SUFFERS FROM A NERVE-DEGENERATING DISEASE THAT IS BEGINNING TO CRIPPLE HIM. WALLER BROUGHT HIM TO THE PRISON IN HOPES OF USING HIS TACTICAL SKILLS, MUCH LIKE SHE DID WITH ME AND MY...INSIGHT INTO THE CRIMINAL MIND.
BUT WHEREAS I'VE REALLY RATHER COME TO ENJOY (LOVE?) WORKING WITH WALLER, I THINK HER PLANS FOR THINKER HAVE LITERALLY JUST BLOWN UP IN HER FACE.
WHERE IS KING SHARK'S REWARD?!
PATIENCE, FRIEND. CAN YOU NOT SMELL HER BLOOD INSIDE THESE WALLS? ONCE WE ARE ONLINE YOU ARE FREE TO FIND HER.
YOU WILL HAVE ALL THE TIME IN THE WORLD...

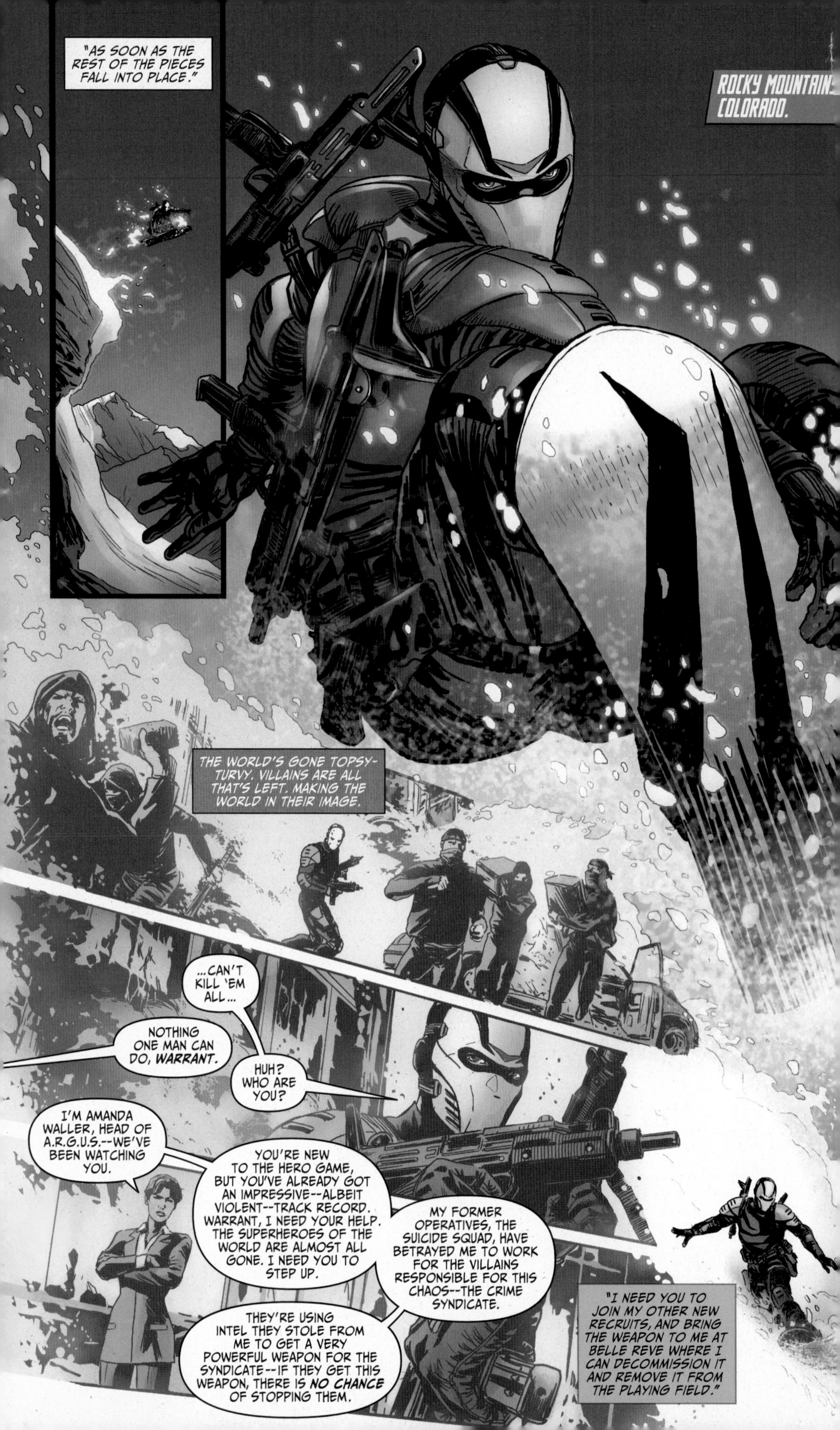
"AS SOON AS THE REST OF THE PIECES FALL INTO PLACE."
ROCKY MOUNTAINS, COLORADO.
THE WORLD'S GONE TOPSY-TURVY. VILLAINS ARE ALL THAT'S LEFT. MAKING THE WORLD IN THEIR IMAGE.
...CAN'T KILL 'EM ALL...
NOTHING ONE MAN CAN DO, WARRANT.
HUH? WHO ARE YOU?
I'M AMANDA WALLER, HEAD OF A.R.G.U.S.--WE'VE BEEN WATCHING YOU.
YOU'RE NEW TO THE HERO GAME, BUT YOU'VE ALREADY GOT AN IMPRESSIVE--ALBEIT VIOLENT--TRACK RECORD. WARRANT, I NEED YOUR HELP. THE SUPERHEROES OF THE WORLD ARE ALMOST ALL GONE. I NEED YOU TO STEP UP.
MY FORMER OPERATIVES, THE SUICIDE SQUAD, HAVE BETRAYED ME TO WORK FOR THE VILLAINS RESPONSIBLE FOR THIS CHAOS--THE CRIME SYNDICATE.
THEY'RE USING INTEL THEY STOLE FROM ME TO GET A VERY POWERFUL WEAPON FOR THE SYNDICATE--IF THEY GET THIS WEAPON, THERE IS NO CHANCE OF STOPPING THEM.
"I NEED YOU TO JOIN MY OTHER NEW RECRUITS, AND BRING THE WEAPON TO ME AT BELLE REVE WHERE I CAN DECOMMISSION IT AND REMOVE IT FROM THE PLAYING FIELD."

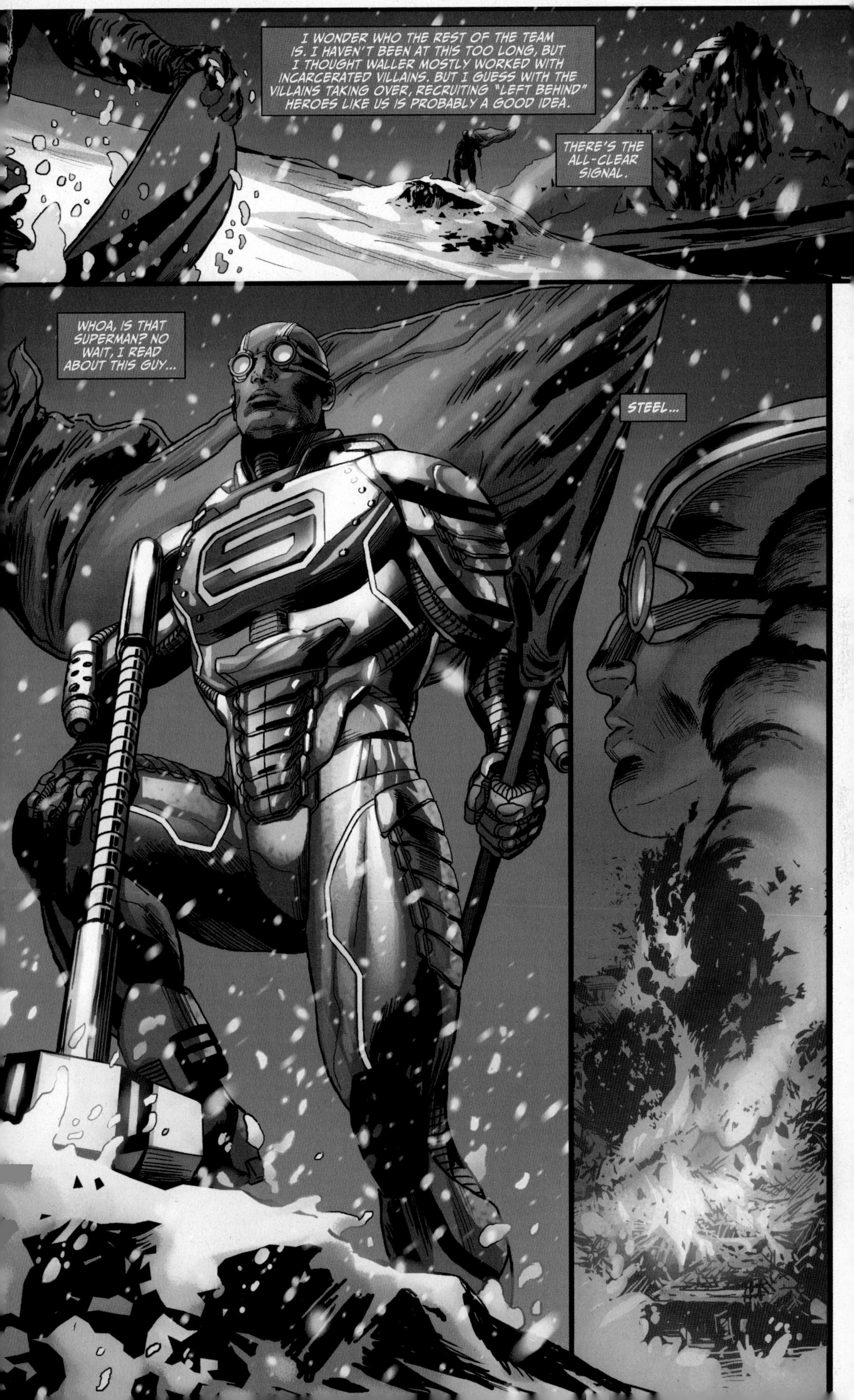
I WONDER WHO THE REST OF THE TEAM IS. I HAVEN'T BEEN AT THIS TOO LONG, BUT I THOUGHT WALLER MOSTLY WORKED WITH INCARCERATED VILLAINS. BUT I GUESS WITH THE VILLAINS TAKING OVER, RECRUITING "LEFT BEHIND" HEROES LIKE US IS PROBABLY A GOOD IDEA.
THERE'S THE ALL-CLEAR SIGNAL.
WHOA, IS THAT SUPERMAN? NO WAIT, I READ ABOUT THIS GUY...
STEEL...

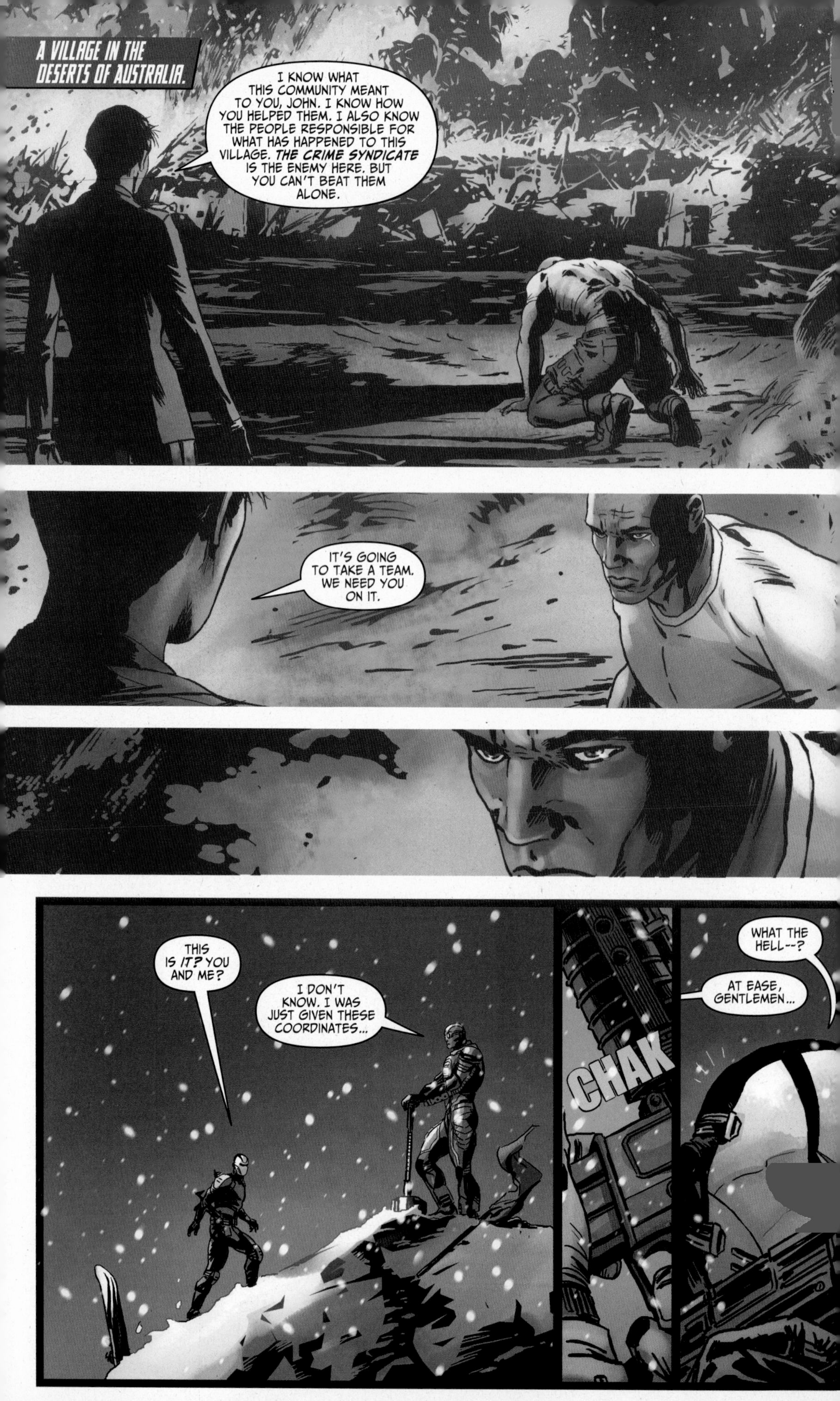

A VILLAGE IN THE DESERTS OF AUSTRALIA.
I KNOW WHAT THIS COMMUNITY MEANT TO YOU, JOHN. I KNOW HOW YOU HELPED THEM. I ALSO KNOW THE PEOPLE RESPONSIBLE FOR WHAT HAS HAPPENED TO THIS VILLAGE. THE CRIME SYNDICATE IS THE ENEMY HERE. BUT YOU CAN'T BEAT THEM ALONE.
IT'S GOING TO TAKE A TEAM. WE NEED YOU ON IT.
THIS IS IT? YOU AND ME?
I DON'T KNOW. I WAS JUST GIVEN THESE COORDINATES...
CHAK
WHAT THE HELL--?
AT EASE, GENTLEMEN...

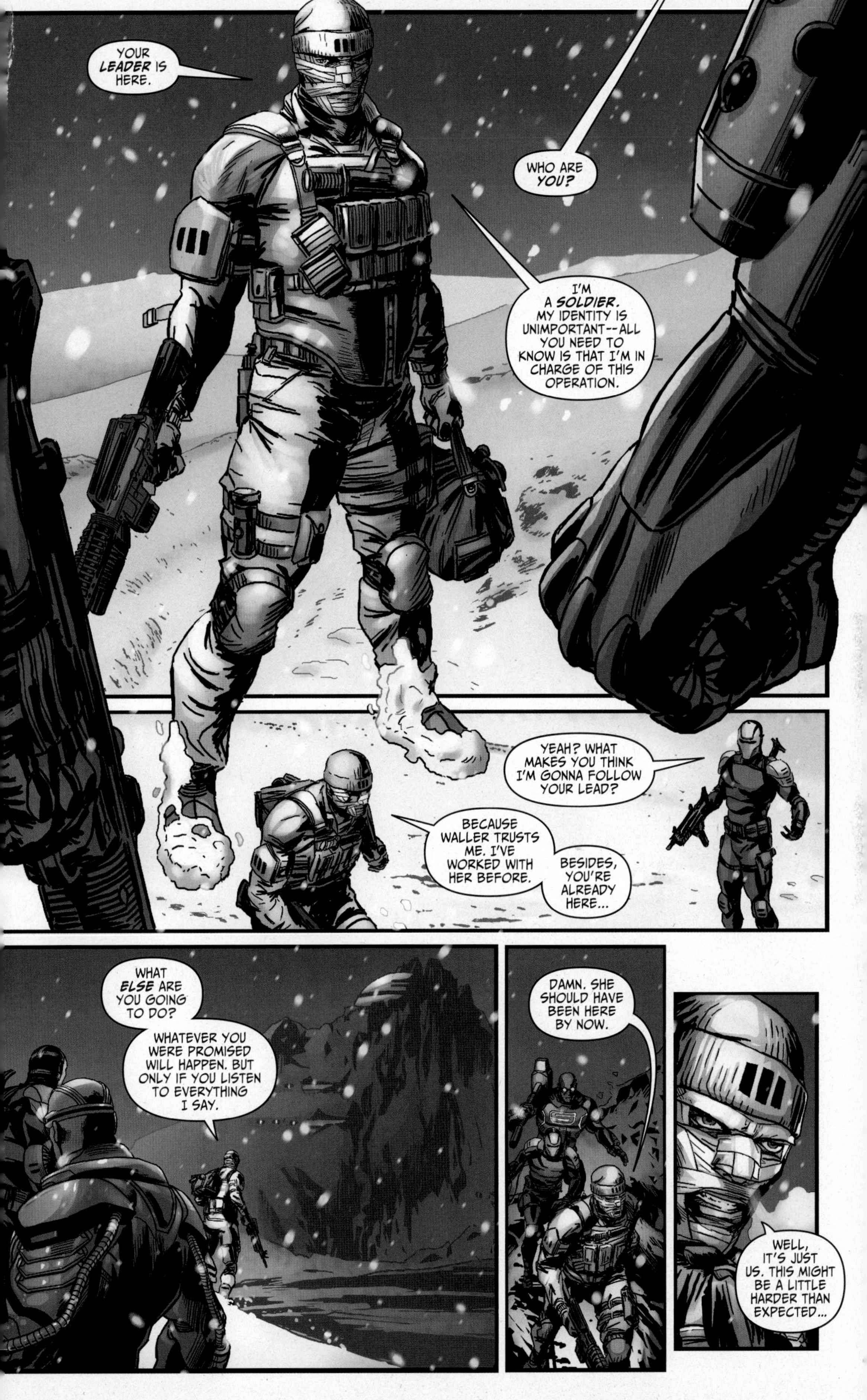
YOUR LEADER IS HERE.
WHO ARE YOU?
I'M A SOLDIER. MY IDENTITY IS UNIMPORTANT--ALL YOU NEED TO KNOW IS THAT I'M IN CHARGE OF THIS OPERATION.
YEAH? WHAT MAKES YOU THINK I'M GONNA FOLLOW YOUR LEAD?
BECAUSE WALLER TRUSTS ME. I'VE WORKED WITH HER BEFORE.
BESIDES, YOU'RE ALREADY HERE...
WHAT ELSE ARE YOU GOING TO DO?
WHATEVER YOU WERE PROMISED WILL HAPPEN. BUT ONLY IF YOU LISTEN TO EVERYTHING I SAY.
DAMN. SHE SHOULD HAVE BEEN HERE BY NOW.
WELL, IT'S JUST US. THIS MIGHT BE A LITTLE HARDER THAN EXPECTED...

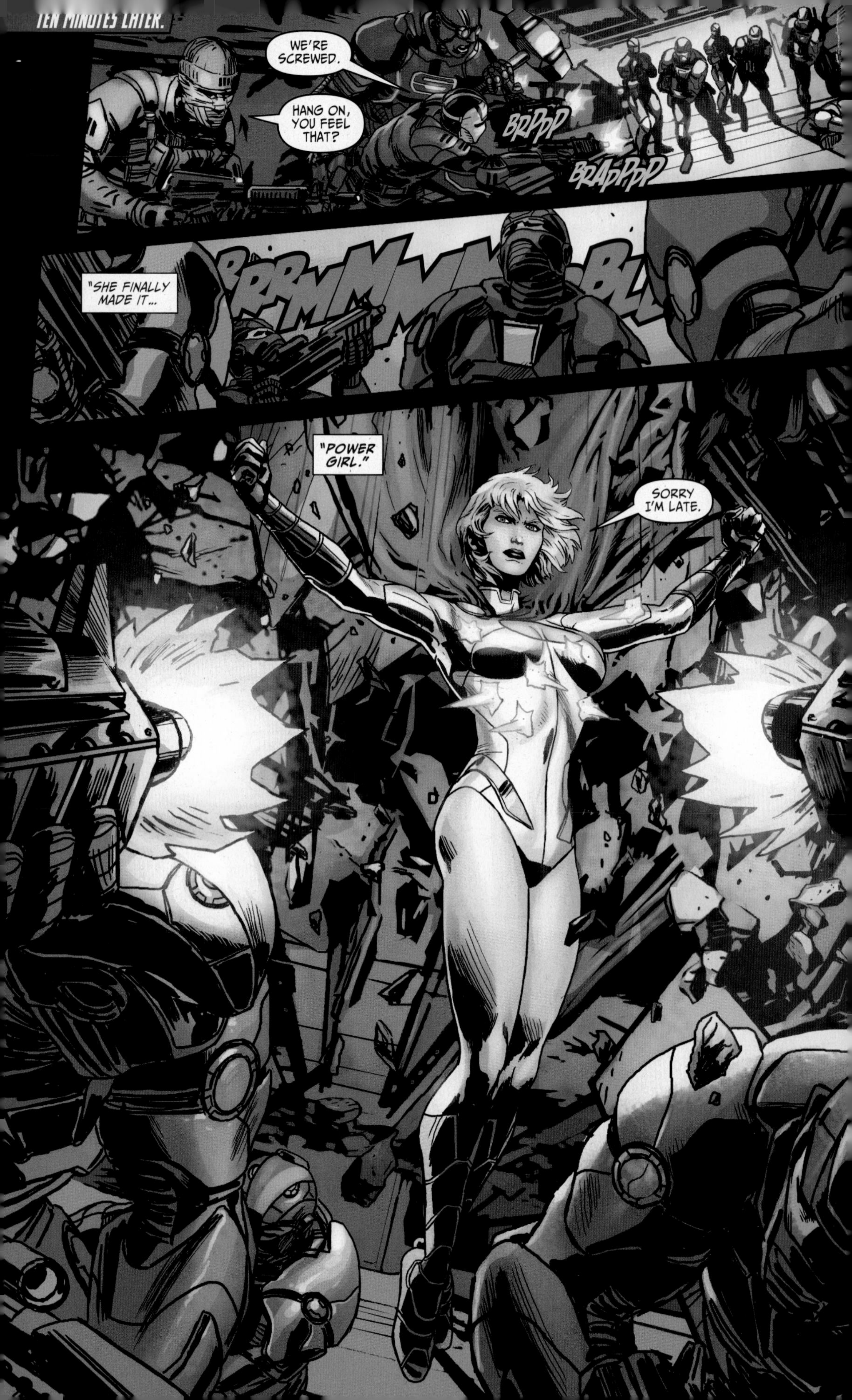
TEN MINUTES LATER.
WE'RE SCREWED.
HANG ON, YOU FEEL THAT?
BRPPP
BRAPPPP
"SHE FINALLY MADE IT...
"POWER GIRL."
SORRY I'M LATE.

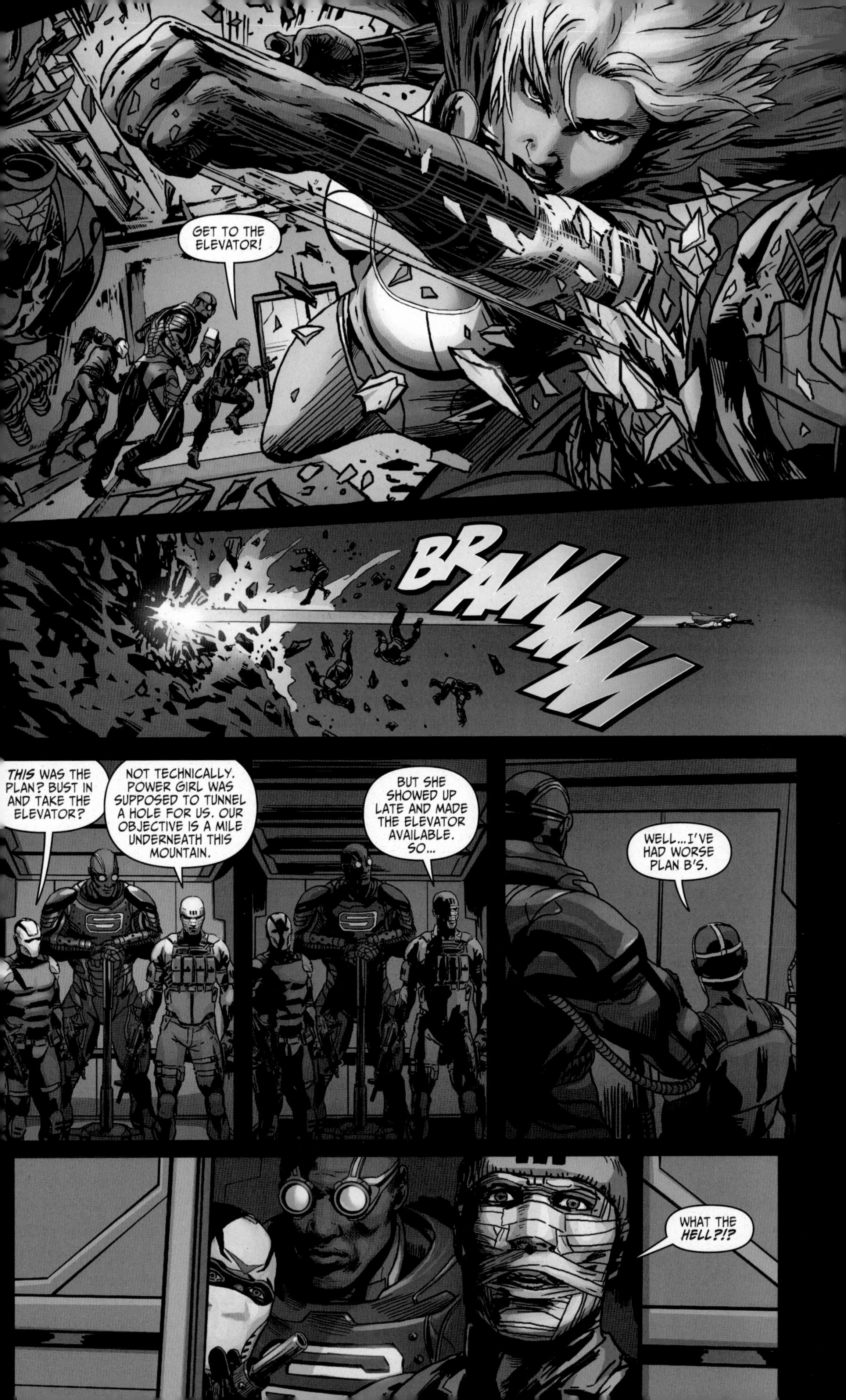
GET TO THE ELEVATOR!
BRAMMM
THIS WAS THE PLAN? BUST IN AND TAKE THE ELEVATOR?
NOT TECHNICALLY. POWER GIRL WAS SUPPOSED TO TUNNEL A HOLE FOR US. OUR OBJECTIVE IS A MILE UNDERNEATH THIS MOUNTAIN.
BUT SHE SHOWED UP LATE AND MADE THE ELEVATOR AVAILABLE. SO...
WELL...I'VE HAD WORSE PLAN B'S.
WHAT THE HELL?!?

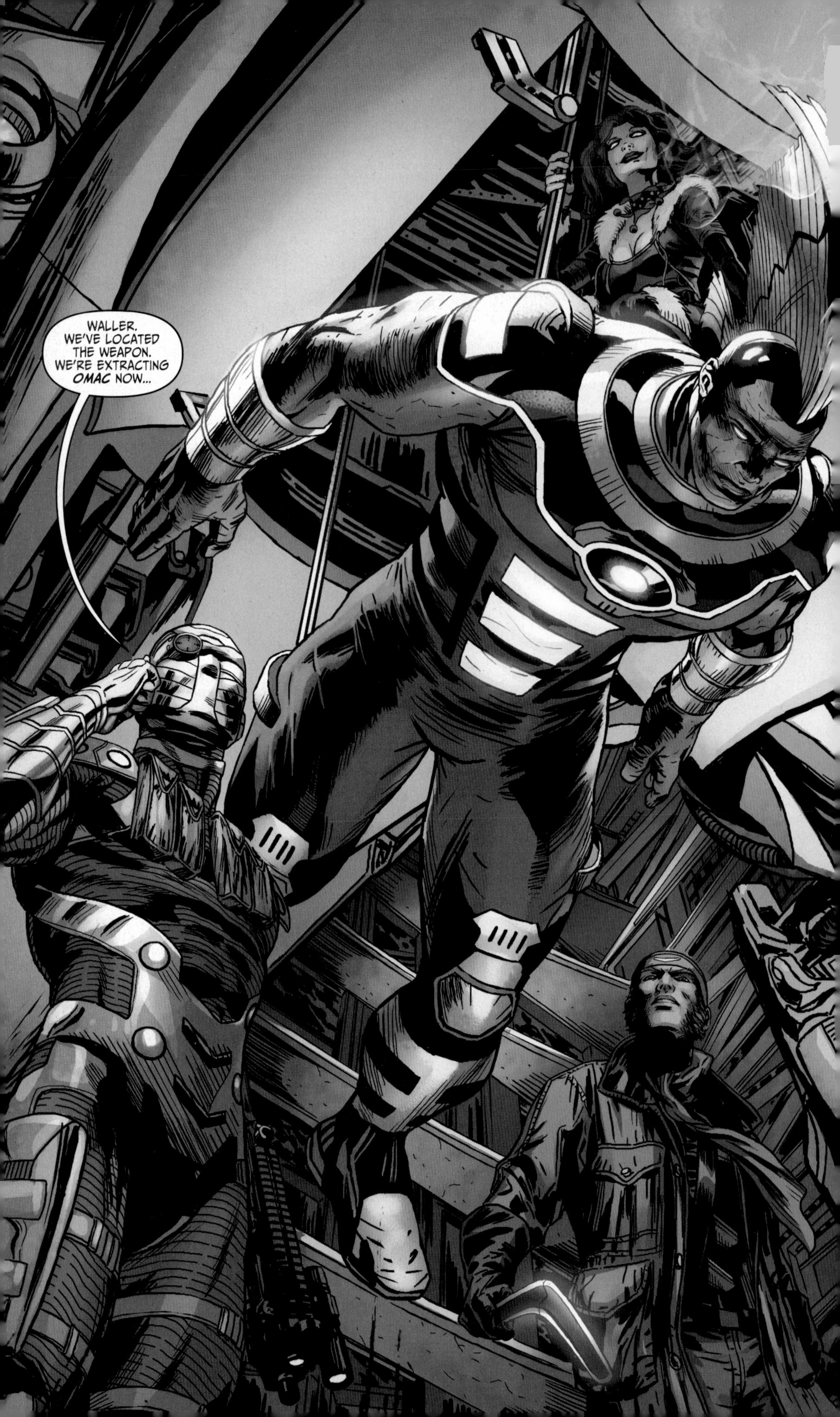

WALLER. WE'VE LOCATED THE WEAPON. WE'RE EXTRACTING **OMAC** NOW...

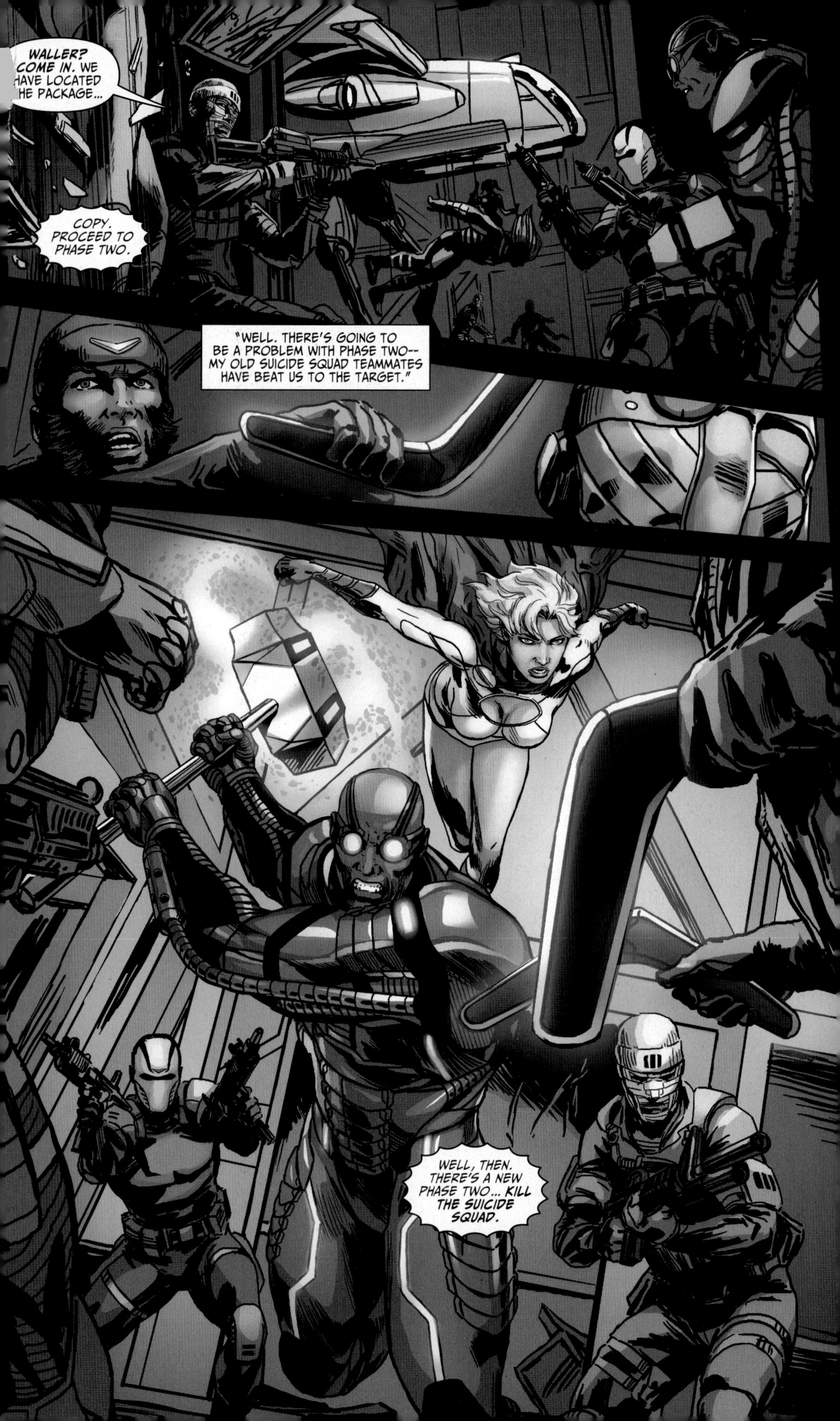
WALLER? COME IN. WE HAVE LOCATED THE PACKAGE...
COPY. PROCEED TO PHASE TWO.
"WELL. THERE'S GOING TO BE A PROBLEM WITH PHASE TWO-- MY OLD SUICIDE SQUAD TEAMMATES HAVE BEAT US TO THE TARGET."
WELL, THEN. THERE'S A NEW PHASE TWO... KILL THE SUICIDE SQUAD.

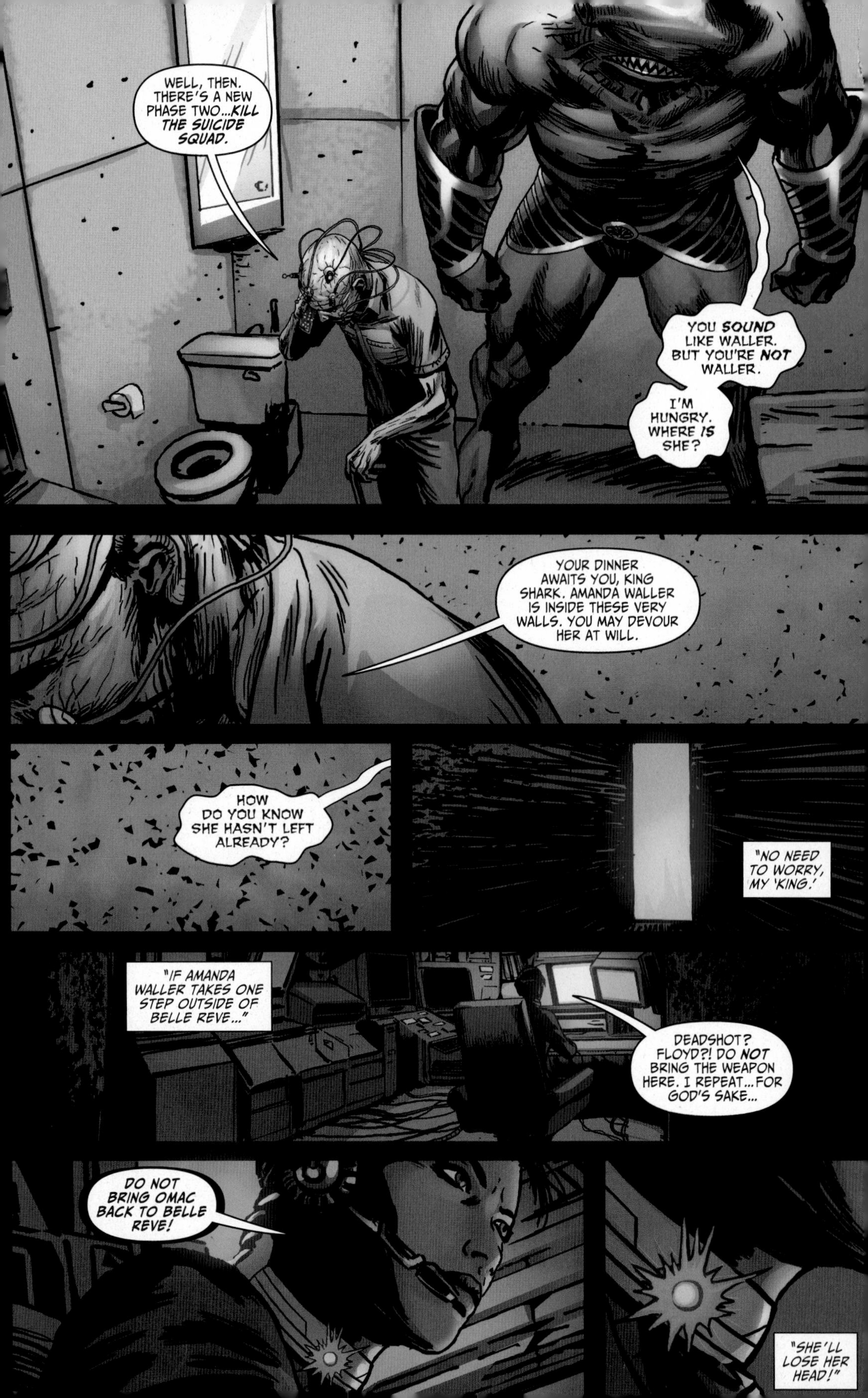
WELL, THEN. THERE'S A NEW PHASE TWO...KILL THE SUICIDE SQUAD.
YOU SOUND LIKE WALLER. BUT YOU'RE NOT WALLER.
I'M HUNGRY. WHERE IS SHE?
YOUR DINNER AWAITS YOU, KING SHARK. AMANDA WALLER IS INSIDE THESE VERY WALLS. YOU MAY DEVOUR HER AT WILL.
HOW DO YOU KNOW SHE HASN'T LEFT ALREADY?
"NO NEED TO WORRY, MY 'KING.'
"IF AMANDA WALLER TAKES ONE STEP OUTSIDE OF BELLE REVE..."
DEADSHOT? FLOYD?! DO NOT BRING THE WEAPON HERE. I REPEAT...FOR GOD'S SAKE...
DO NOT BRING OMAC BACK TO BELLE REVE!
"SHE'LL LOSE HER HEAD!"

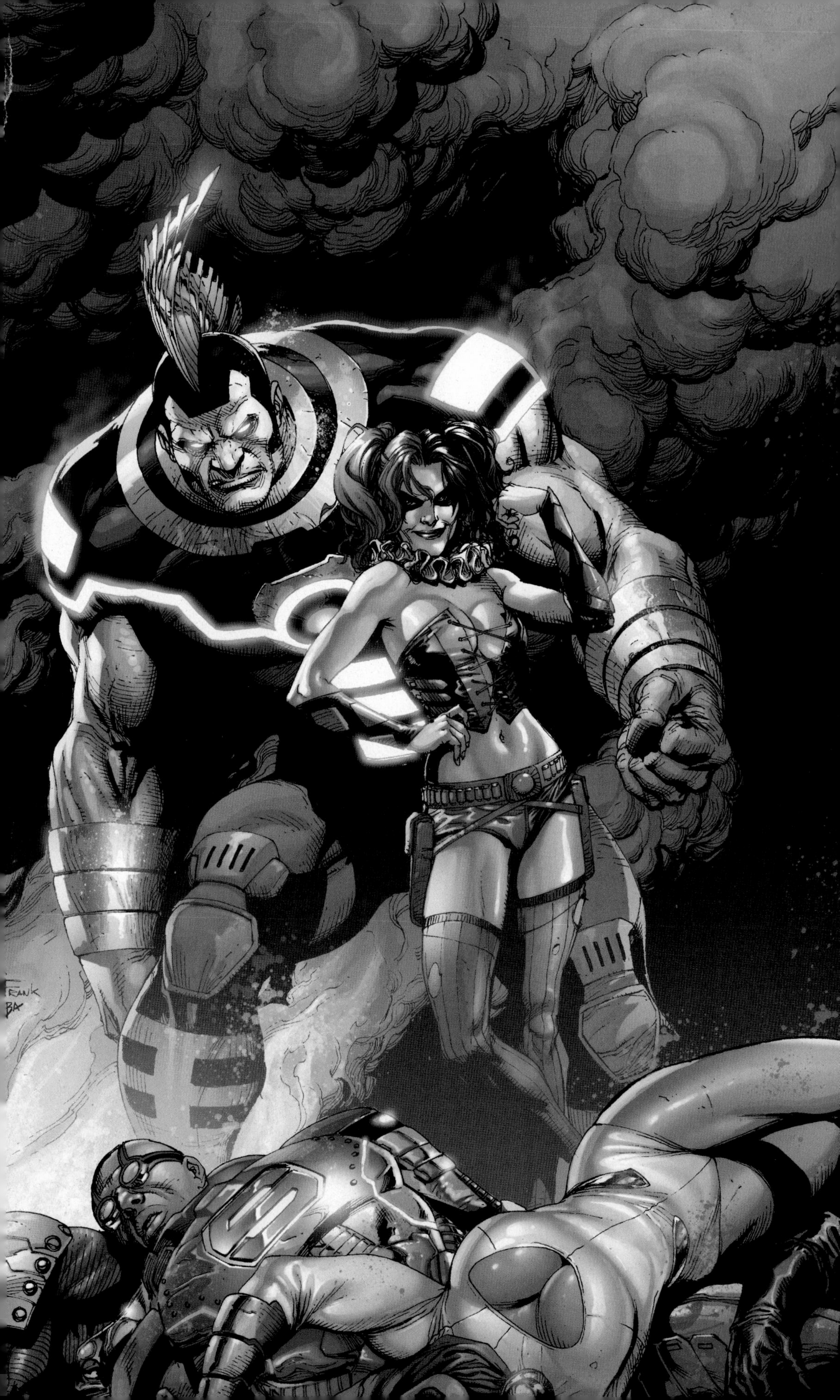

CLEANING OUT THE CLOSET

MATT KINDT writer **PATRICK ZIRCHER** artist **JASON KEITH** colorist **JARED K. FLETCHER** letterer

cover by **GARY FRANK** and **BRAD ANDERSON**

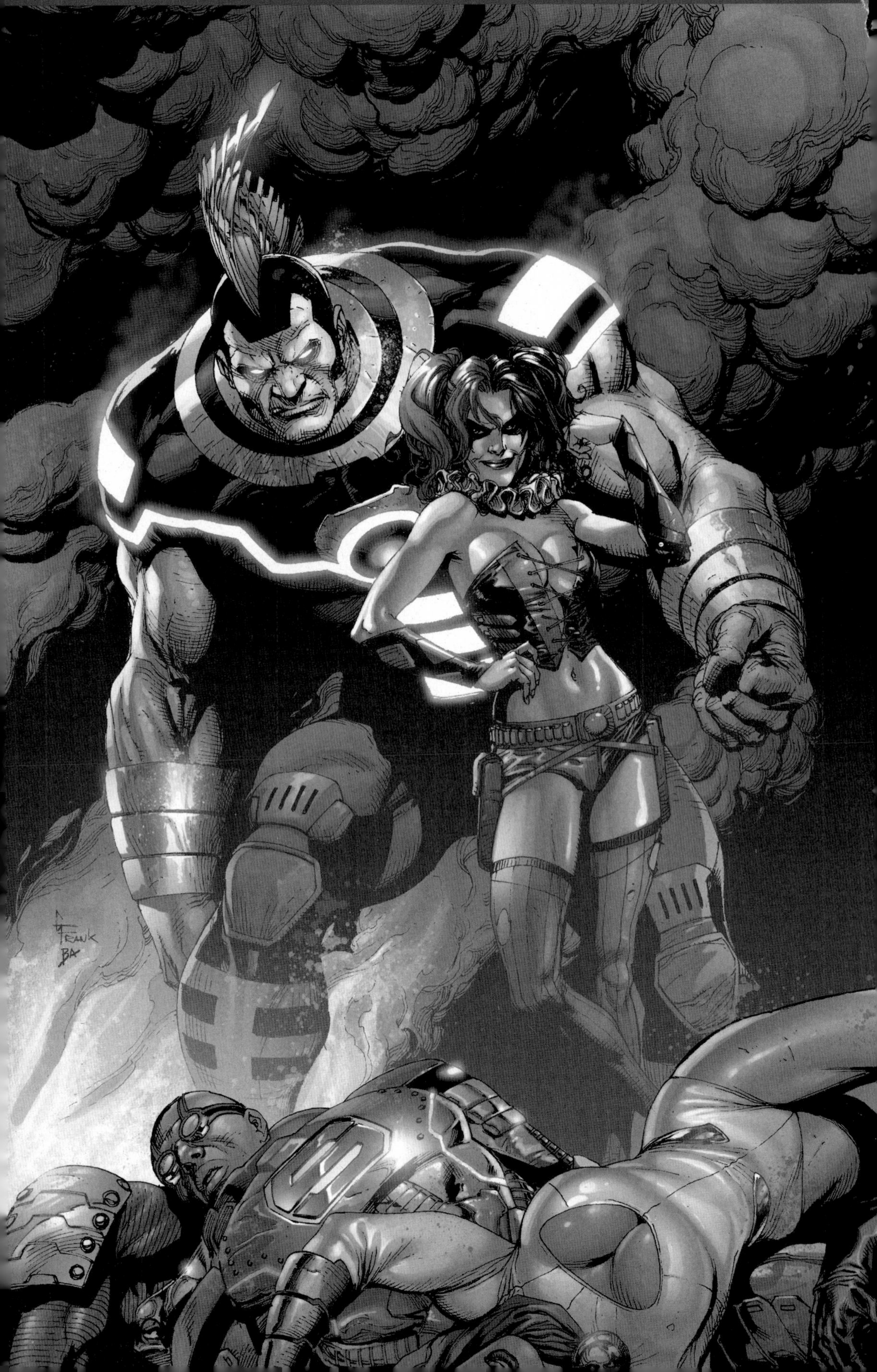

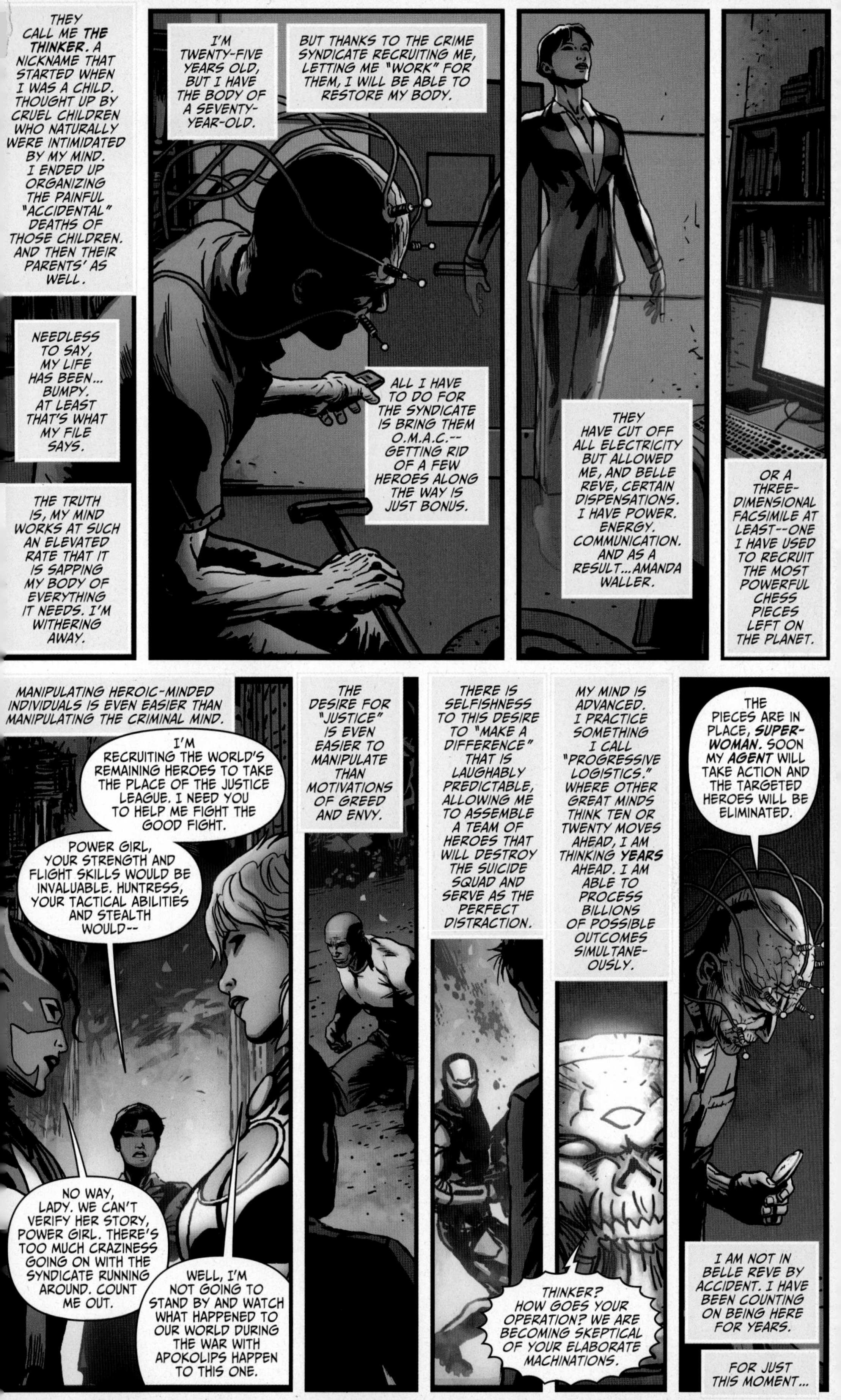
THEY CALL ME THE THINKER. A NICKNAME THAT STARTED WHEN I WAS A CHILD. THOUGHT UP BY CRUEL CHILDREN WHO NATURALLY WERE INTIMIDATED BY MY MIND. I ENDED UP ORGANIZING THE PAINFUL "ACCIDENTAL" DEATHS OF THOSE CHILDREN. AND THEN THEIR PARENTS' AS WELL.
NEEDLESS TO SAY, MY LIFE HAS BEEN... BUMPY. AT LEAST THAT'S WHAT MY FILE SAYS.
THE TRUTH IS, MY MIND WORKS AT SUCH AN ELEVATED RATE THAT IT IS SAPPING MY BODY OF EVERYTHING IT NEEDS. I'M WITHERING AWAY.
I'M TWENTY-FIVE YEARS OLD, BUT I HAVE THE BODY OF A SEVENTY-YEAR-OLD.
BUT THANKS TO THE CRIME SYNDICATE RECRUITING ME, LETTING ME "WORK" FOR THEM, I WILL BE ABLE TO RESTORE MY BODY.
ALL I HAVE TO DO FOR THE SYNDICATE IS BRING THEM O.M.A.C.-- GETTING RID OF A FEW HEROES ALONG THE WAY IS JUST BONUS.
THEY HAVE CUT OFF ALL ELECTRICITY BUT ALLOWED ME, AND BELLE REVE, CERTAIN DISPENSATIONS. I HAVE POWER. ENERGY. COMMUNICATION. AND AS A RESULT...AMANDA WALLER.
OR A THREE-DIMENSIONAL FACSIMILE AT LEAST--ONE I HAVE USED TO RECRUIT THE MOST POWERFUL CHESS PIECES LEFT ON THE PLANET.
MANIPULATING HEROIC-MINDED INDIVIDUALS IS EVEN EASIER THAN MANIPULATING THE CRIMINAL MIND.
I'M RECRUITING THE WORLD'S REMAINING HEROES TO TAKE THE PLACE OF THE JUSTICE LEAGUE. I NEED YOU TO HELP ME FIGHT THE GOOD FIGHT.
POWER GIRL, YOUR STRENGTH AND FLIGHT SKILLS WOULD BE INVALUABLE. HUNTRESS, YOUR TACTICAL ABILITIES AND STEALTH WOULD--
NO WAY, LADY. WE CAN'T VERIFY HER STORY, POWER GIRL. THERE'S TOO MUCH CRAZINESS GOING ON WITH THE SYNDICATE RUNNING AROUND. COUNT ME OUT.
WELL, I'M NOT GOING TO STAND BY AND WATCH WHAT HAPPENED TO OUR WORLD DURING THE WAR WITH APOKOLIPS HAPPEN TO THIS ONE.
THE DESIRE FOR "JUSTICE" IS EVEN EASIER TO MANIPULATE THAN MOTIVATIONS OF GREED AND ENVY.
THERE IS SELFISHNESS TO THIS DESIRE TO "MAKE A DIFFERENCE" THAT IS LAUGHABLY PREDICTABLE, ALLOWING ME TO ASSEMBLE A TEAM OF HEROES THAT WILL DESTROY THE SUICIDE SQUAD AND SERVE AS THE PERFECT DISTRACTION.
MY MIND IS ADVANCED. I PRACTICE SOMETHING I CALL "PROGRESSIVE LOGISTICS." WHERE OTHER GREAT MINDS THINK TEN OR TWENTY MOVES AHEAD, I AM THINKING YEARS AHEAD. I AM ABLE TO PROCESS BILLIONS OF POSSIBLE OUTCOMES SIMULTANEOUSLY.
THINKER? HOW GOES YOUR OPERATION? WE ARE BECOMING SKEPTICAL OF YOUR ELABORATE MACHINATIONS.
THE PIECES ARE IN PLACE, SUPERWOMAN. SOON MY AGENT WILL TAKE ACTION AND THE TARGETED HEROES WILL BE ELIMINATED.
I AM NOT IN BELLE REVE BY ACCIDENT. I HAVE BEEN COUNTING ON BEING HERE FOR YEARS.
FOR JUST THIS MOMENT...

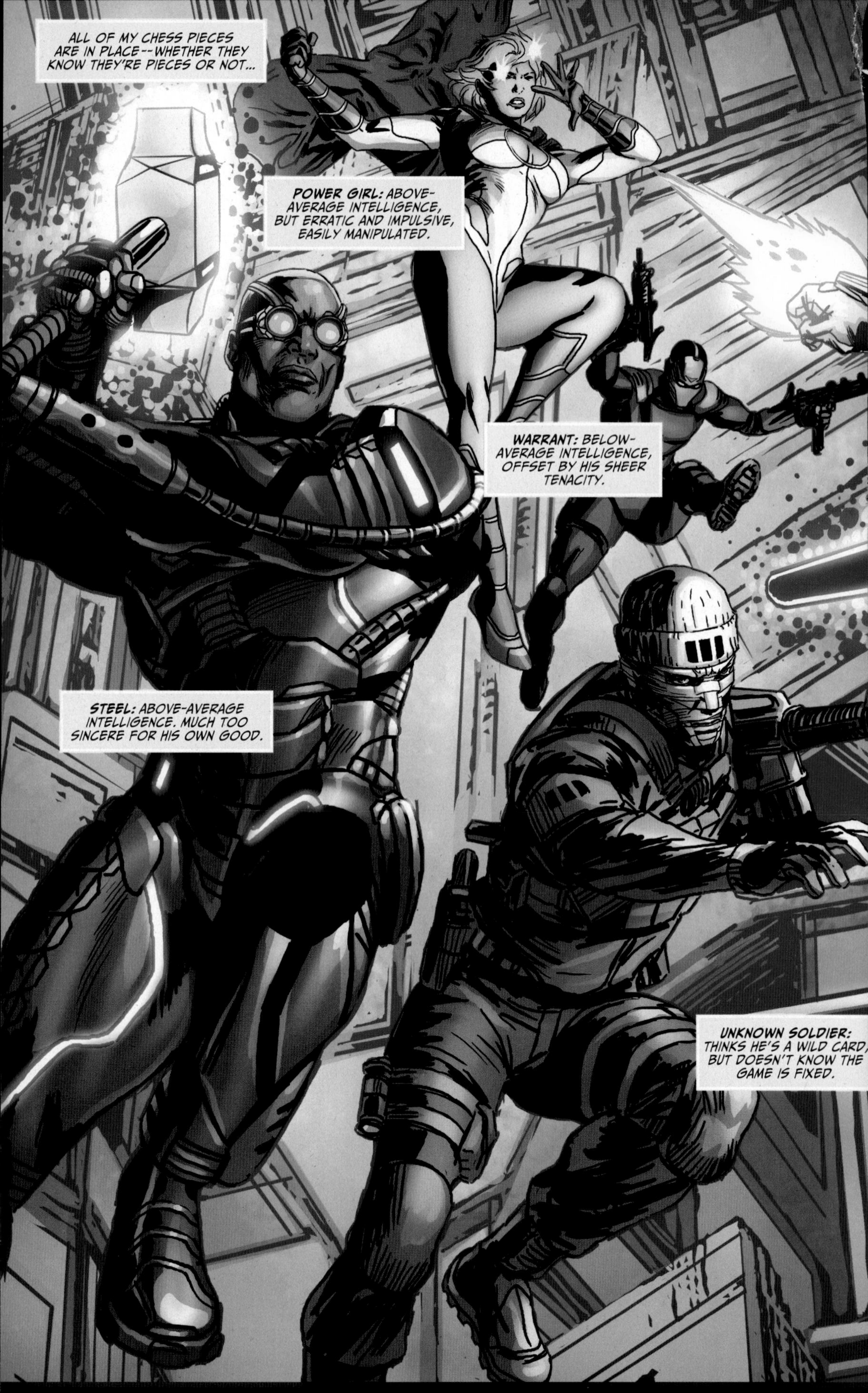
ALL OF MY CHESS PIECES ARE IN PLACE--WHETHER THEY KNOW THEY'RE PIECES OR NOT...
POWER GIRL: ABOVE-AVERAGE INTELLIGENCE, BUT ERRATIC AND IMPULSIVE, EASILY MANIPULATED.
WARRANT: BELOW-AVERAGE INTELLIGENCE, OFFSET BY HIS SHEER TENACITY.
STEEL: ABOVE-AVERAGE INTELLIGENCE. MUCH TOO SINCERE FOR HIS OWN GOOD.
UNKNOWN SOLDIER: THINKS HE'S A WILD CARD, BUT DOESN'T KNOW THE GAME IS FIXED.

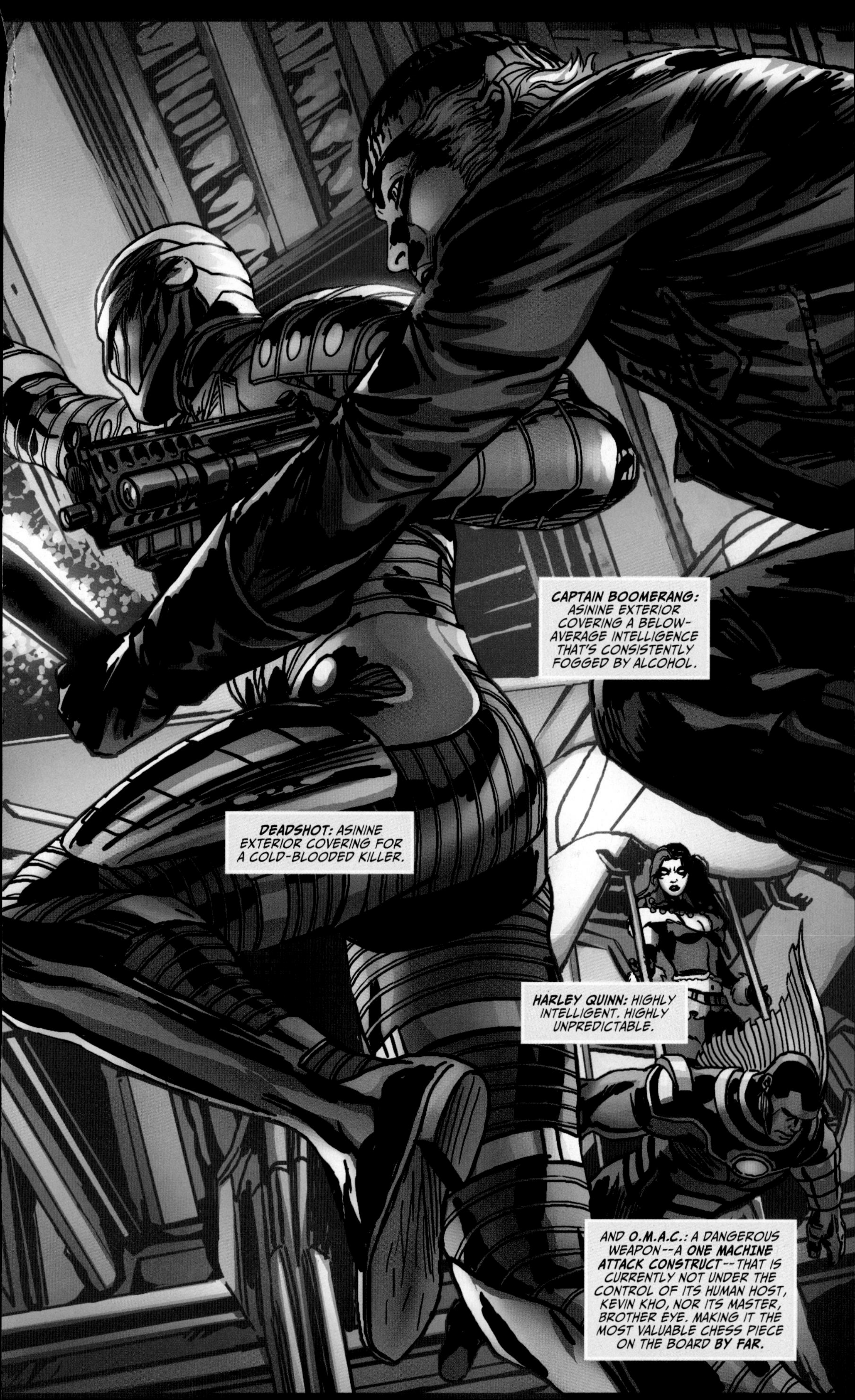
CAPTAIN BOOMERANG: ASININE EXTERIOR COVERING A BELOW-AVERAGE INTELLIGENCE THAT'S CONSISTENTLY FOGGED BY ALCOHOL.
DEADSHOT: ASININE EXTERIOR COVERING FOR A COLD-BLOODED KILLER.
HARLEY QUINN: HIGHLY INTELLIGENT. HIGHLY UNPREDICTABLE.
AND O.M.A.C.: A DANGEROUS WEAPON--A ONE MACHINE ATTACK CONSTRUCT--THAT IS CURRENTLY NOT UNDER THE CONTROL OF ITS HUMAN HOST, KEVIN KHO, NOR ITS MASTER, BROTHER EYE. MAKING IT THE MOST VALUABLE CHESS PIECE ON THE BOARD BY FAR.

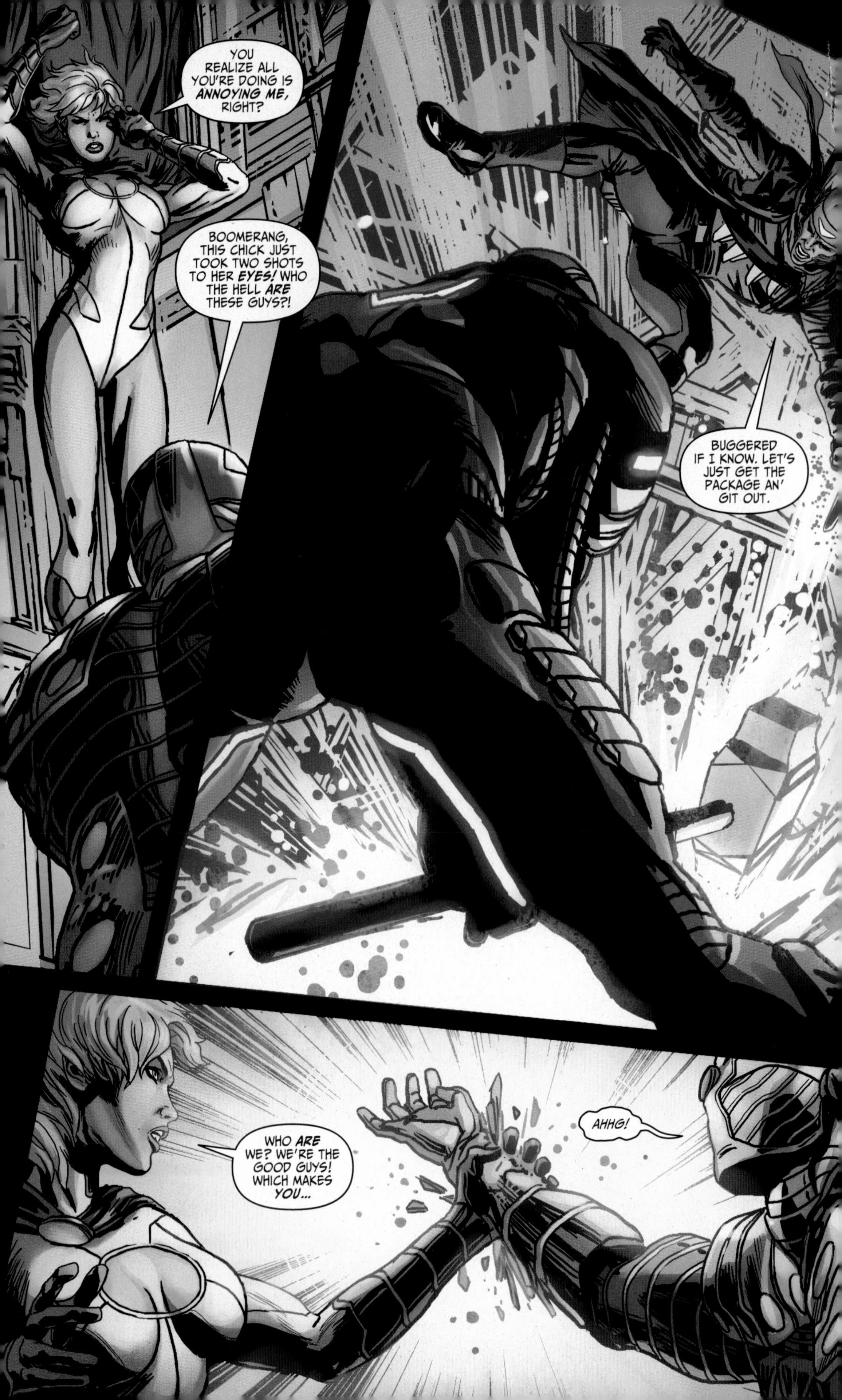
YOU REALIZE ALL YOU'RE DOING IS ANNOYING ME, RIGHT?
BOOMERANG, THIS CHICK JUST TOOK TWO SHOTS TO HER EYES! WHO THE HELL ARE THESE GUYS?!
BUGGERED IF I KNOW. LET'S JUST GET THE PACKAGE AN' GIT OUT.
WHO ARE WE? WE'RE THE GOOD GUYS! WHICH MAKES YOU...
AHHG!

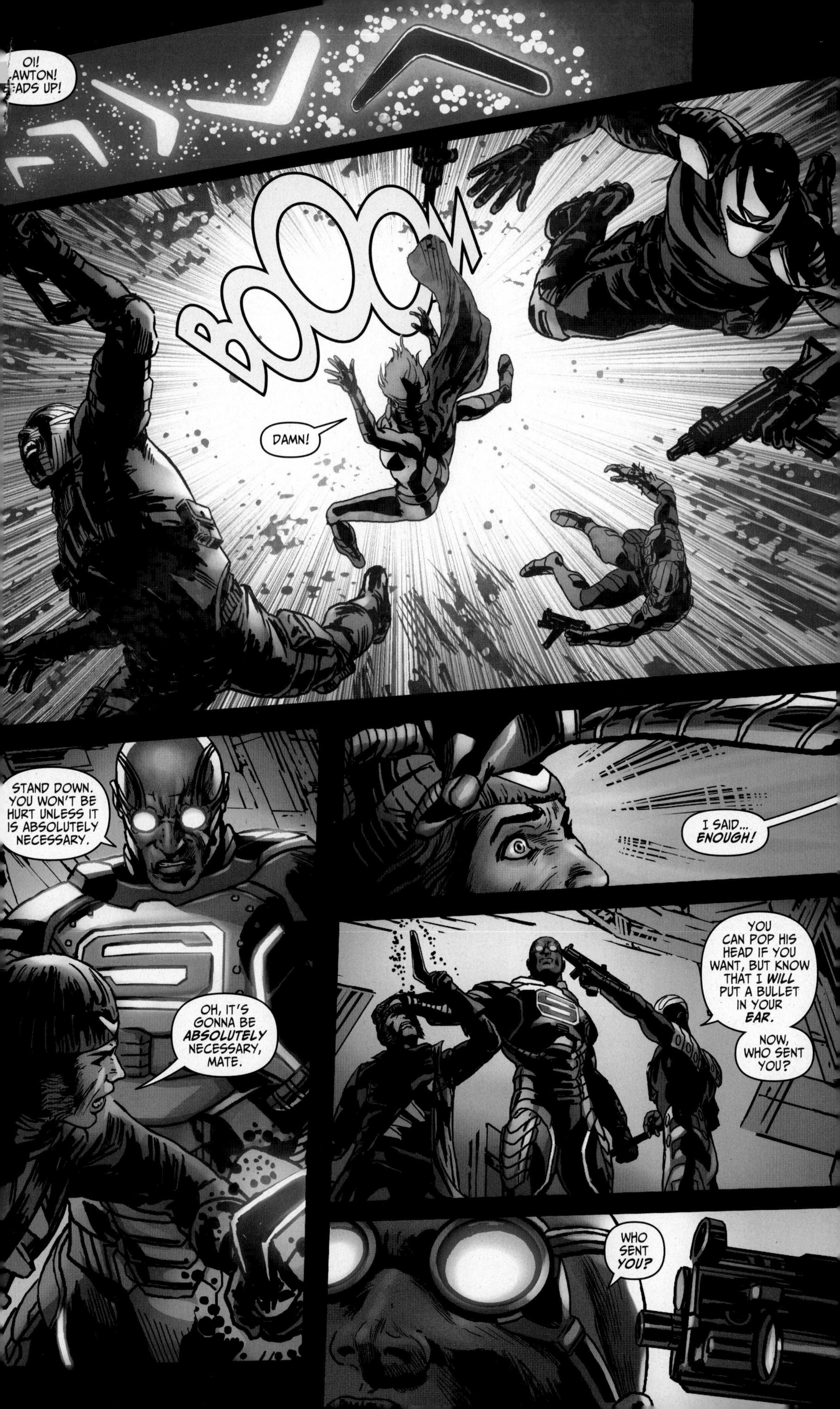
OI! AWTON! EADS UP!
BOOOOM
DAMN!
STAND DOWN. YOU WON'T BE HURT UNLESS IT IS ABSOLUTELY NECESSARY.
OH, IT'S GONNA BE ABSOLUTELY NECESSARY, MATE.
I SAID... ENOUGH!
YOU CAN POP HIS HEAD IF YOU WANT, BUT KNOW THAT I WILL PUT A BULLET IN YOUR EAR.
NOW, WHO SENT YOU?
WHO SENT YOU?

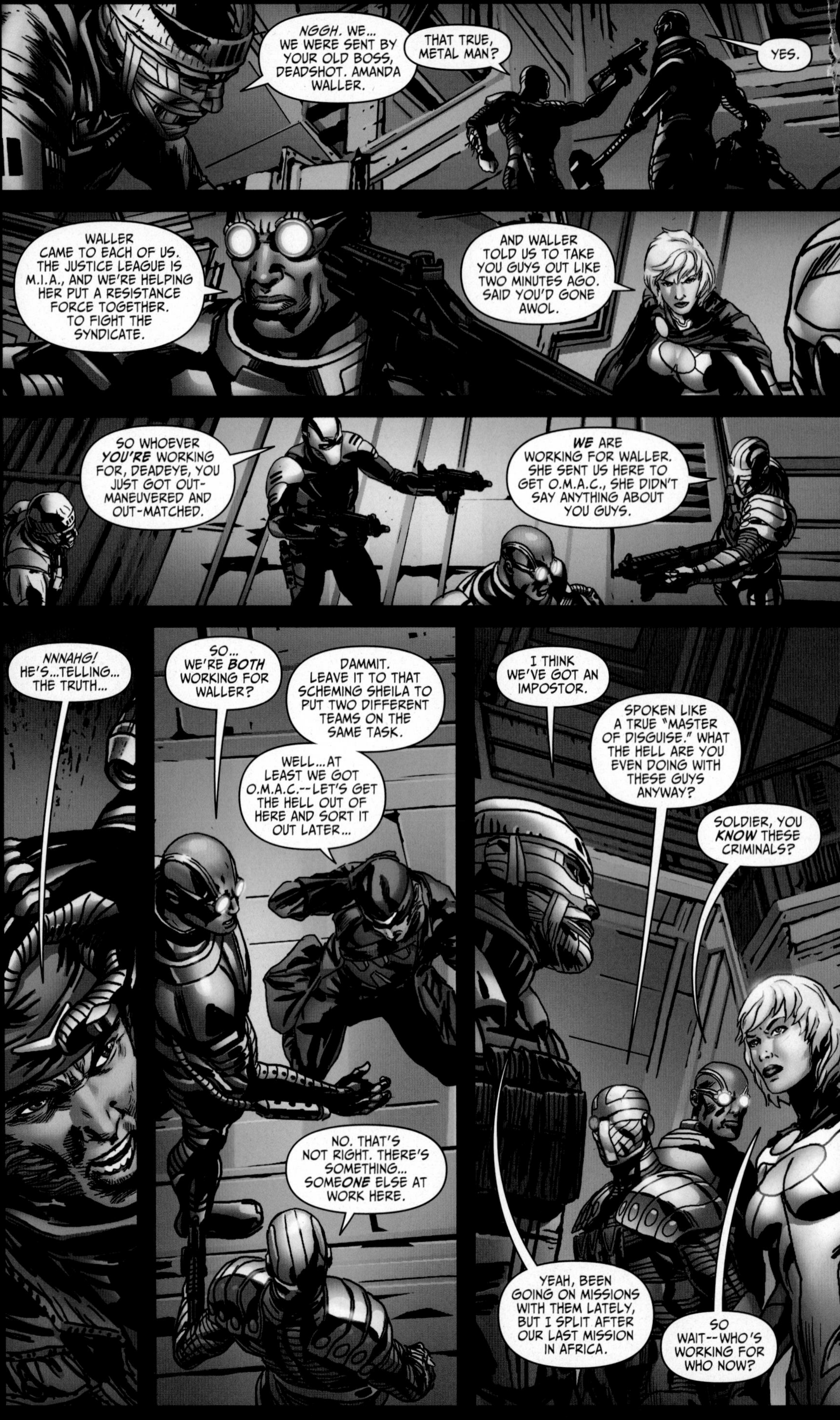
NGGH. WE... WE WERE SENT BY YOUR OLD BOSS, DEADSHOT. AMANDA WALLER.
THAT TRUE, METAL MAN?
YES.
WALLER CAME TO EACH OF US. THE JUSTICE LEAGUE IS M.I.A., AND WE'RE HELPING HER PUT A RESISTANCE FORCE TOGETHER. TO FIGHT THE SYNDICATE.
AND WALLER TOLD US TO TAKE YOU GUYS OUT LIKE TWO MINUTES AGO. SAID YOU'D GONE AWOL.
SO WHOEVER YOU'RE WORKING FOR, DEADEYE, YOU JUST GOT OUT-MANEUVERED AND OUT-MATCHED.
WE ARE WORKING FOR WALLER. SHE SENT US HERE TO GET O.M.A.C., SHE DIDN'T SAY ANYTHING ABOUT YOU GUYS.
NNNAHG! HE'S...TELLING... THE TRUTH...
SO... WE'RE BOTH WORKING FOR WALLER?
DAMMIT. LEAVE IT TO THAT SCHEMING SHEILA TO PUT TWO DIFFERENT TEAMS ON THE SAME TASK.
WELL...AT LEAST WE GOT O.M.A.C.--LET'S GET THE HELL OUT OF HERE AND SORT IT OUT LATER...
NO. THAT'S NOT RIGHT. THERE'S SOMETHING... SOMEONE ELSE AT WORK HERE.
I THINK WE'VE GOT AN IMPOSTOR.
SPOKEN LIKE A TRUE "MASTER OF DISGUISE." WHAT THE HELL ARE YOU EVEN DOING WITH THESE GUYS ANYWAY?
SOLDIER, YOU KNOW THESE CRIMINALS?
YEAH, BEEN GOING ON MISSIONS WITH THEM LATELY, BUT I SPLIT AFTER OUR LAST MISSION IN AFRICA.
SO WAIT--WHO'S WORKING FOR WHO NOW?

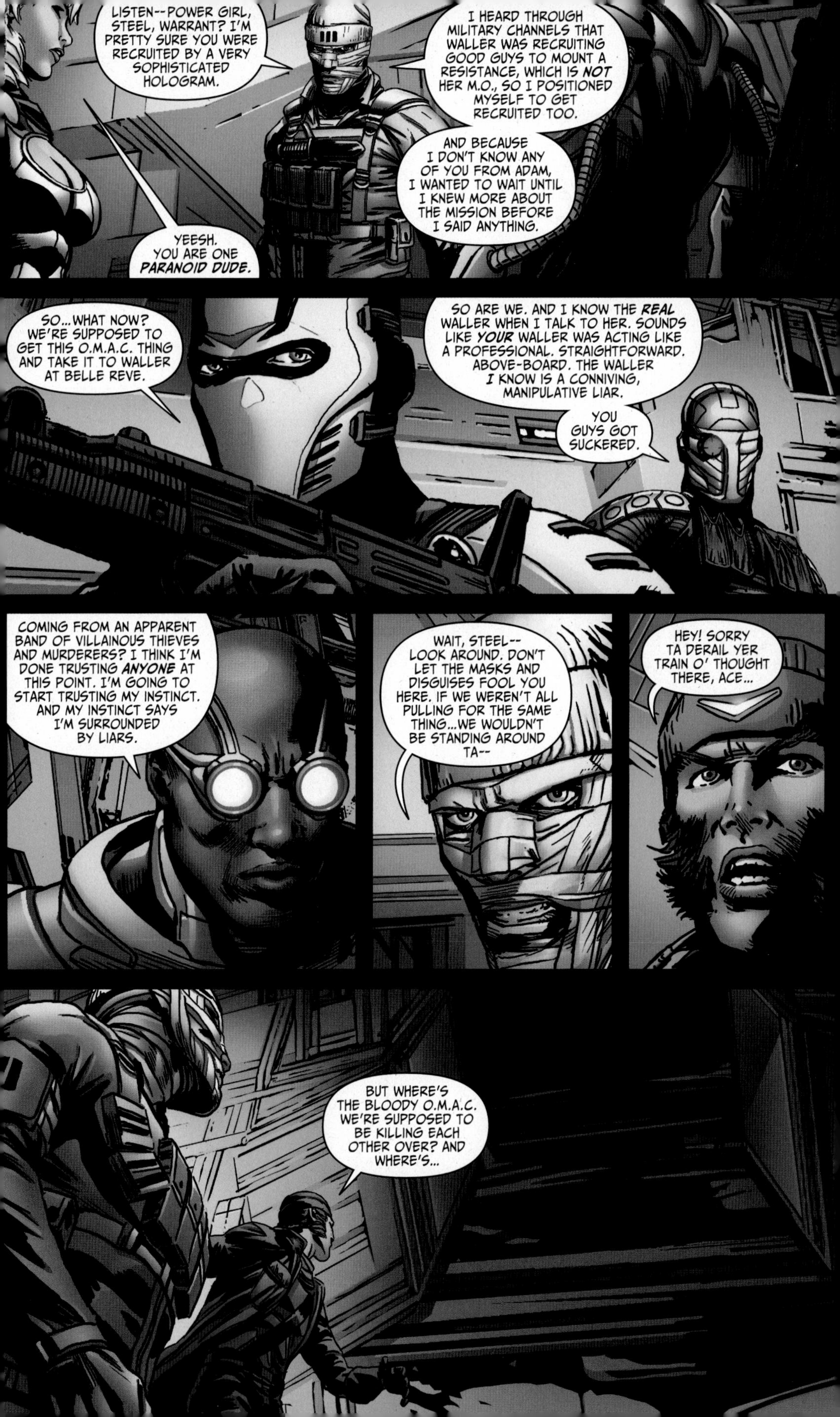
LISTEN--POWER GIRL, STEEL, WARRANT? I'M PRETTY SURE YOU WERE RECRUITED BY A VERY SOPHISTICATED HOLOGRAM.
I HEARD THROUGH MILITARY CHANNELS THAT WALLER WAS RECRUITING GOOD GUYS TO MOUNT A RESISTANCE, WHICH IS NOT HER M.O., SO I POSITIONED MYSELF TO GET RECRUITED TOO.
AND BECAUSE I DON'T KNOW ANY OF YOU FROM ADAM, I WANTED TO WAIT UNTIL I KNEW MORE ABOUT THE MISSION BEFORE I SAID ANYTHING.
YEESH. YOU ARE ONE PARANOID DUDE.
SO...WHAT NOW? WE'RE SUPPOSED TO GET THIS O.M.A.C. THING AND TAKE IT TO WALLER AT BELLE REVE.
SO ARE WE. AND I KNOW THE REAL WALLER WHEN I TALK TO HER. SOUNDS LIKE YOUR WALLER WAS ACTING LIKE A PROFESSIONAL. STRAIGHTFORWARD. ABOVE-BOARD. THE WALLER I KNOW IS A CONNIVING, MANIPULATIVE LIAR.
YOU GUYS GOT SUCKERED.
COMING FROM AN APPARENT BAND OF VILLAINOUS THIEVES AND MURDERERS? I THINK I'M DONE TRUSTING ANYONE AT THIS POINT. I'M GOING TO START TRUSTING MY INSTINCT. AND MY INSTINCT SAYS I'M SURROUNDED BY LIARS.
WAIT, STEEL-- LOOK AROUND. DON'T LET THE MASKS AND DISGUISES FOOL YOU HERE. IF WE WEREN'T ALL PULLING FOR THE SAME THING...WE WOULDN'T BE STANDING AROUND TA--
HEY! SORRY TA DERAIL YER TRAIN O' THOUGHT THERE, ACE...
BUT WHERE'S THE BLOODY O.M.A.C. WE'RE SUPPOSED TO BE KILLING EACH OTHER OVER? AND WHERE'S...

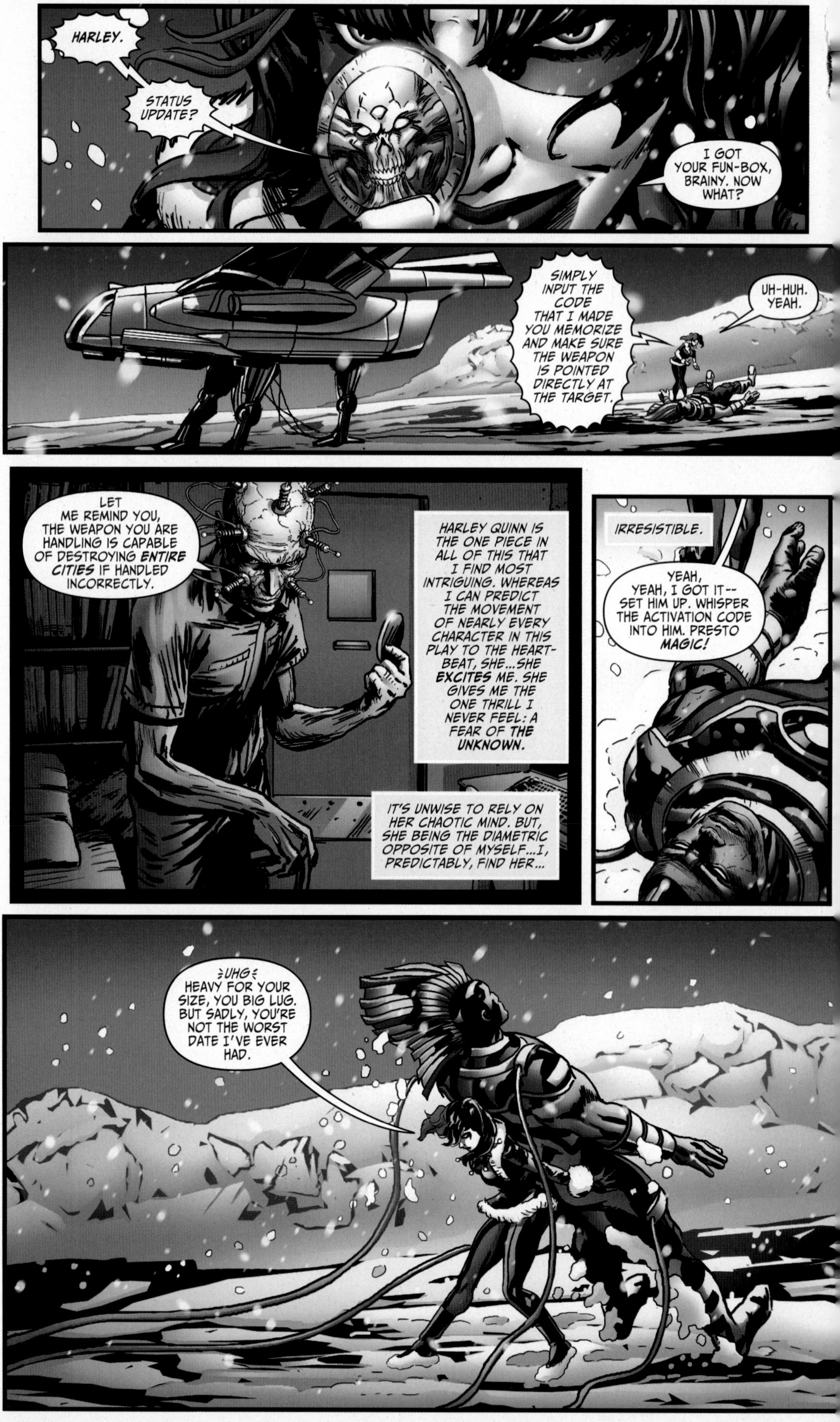
HARLEY.
STATUS UPDATE?
I GOT YOUR FUN-BOX, BRAINY. NOW WHAT?
SIMPLY INPUT THE CODE THAT I MADE YOU MEMORIZE AND MAKE SURE THE WEAPON IS POINTED DIRECTLY AT THE TARGET.
UH-HUH. YEAH.
LET ME REMIND YOU, THE WEAPON YOU ARE HANDLING IS CAPABLE OF DESTROYING ENTIRE CITIES IF HANDLED INCORRECTLY.
HARLEY QUINN IS THE ONE PIECE IN ALL OF THIS THAT I FIND MOST INTRIGUING. WHEREAS I CAN PREDICT THE MOVEMENT OF NEARLY EVERY CHARACTER IN THIS PLAY TO THE HEART-BEAT, SHE...SHE EXCITES ME. SHE GIVES ME THE ONE THRILL I NEVER FEEL: A FEAR OF THE UNKNOWN.
IT'S UNWISE TO RELY ON HER CHAOTIC MIND. BUT, SHE BEING THE DIAMETRIC OPPOSITE OF MYSELF...I, PREDICTABLY, FIND HER...
IRRESISTIBLE.
YEAH, YEAH, I GOT IT-- SET HIM UP. WHISPER THE ACTIVATION CODE INTO HIM. PRESTO MAGIC!
UHG
HEAVY FOR YOUR SIZE, YOU BIG LUG. BUT SADLY, YOU'RE NOT THE WORST DATE I'VE EVER HAD.

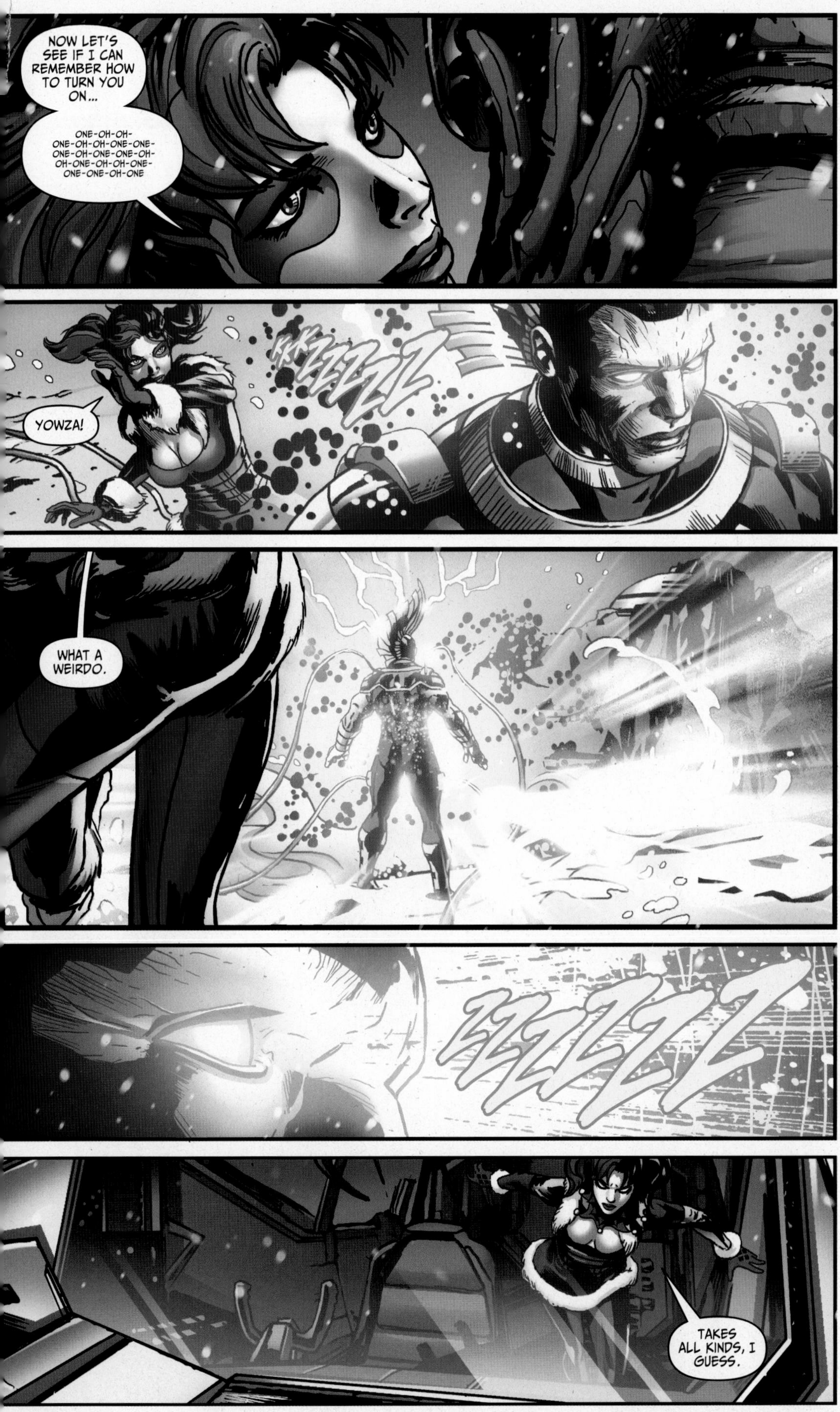
NOW LET'S SEE IF I CAN REMEMBER HOW TO TURN YOU ON...
ONE-OH-OH-ONE-OH-OH-ONE-ONE-ONE-OH-ONE-ONE-ONE-OH-OH-ONE-OH-OH-ONE-ONE-ONE-OH-ONE
KKZZZZZ
YOWZA!
WHAT A WEIRDO.
ZZZZZZZ
TAKES ALL KINDS, I GUESS.

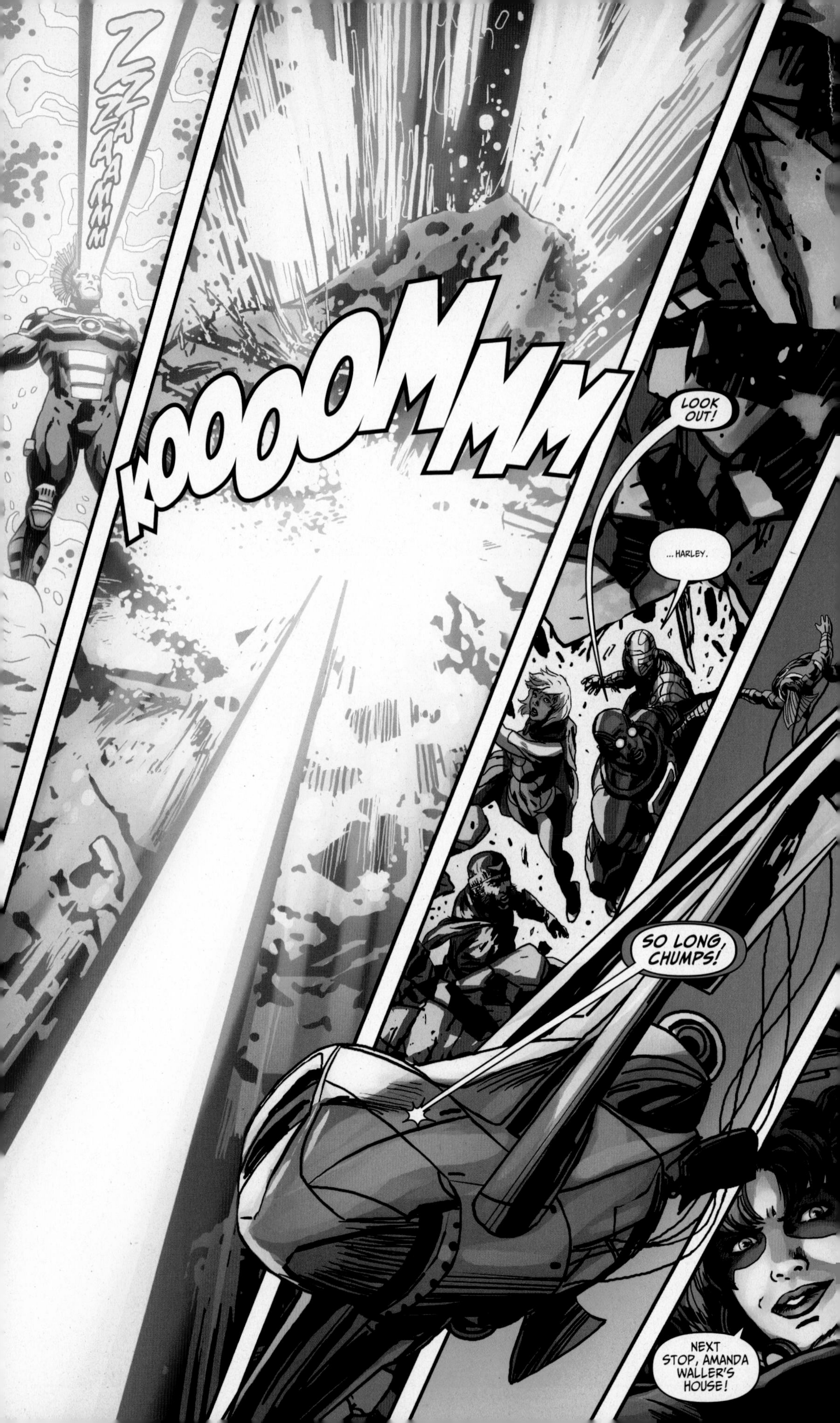
ZZZAAAMMM
KOOOOMMMM
LOOK OUT!
...HARLEY.
SO LONG, CHUMPS!
NEXT STOP, AMANDA WALLER'S HOUSE!

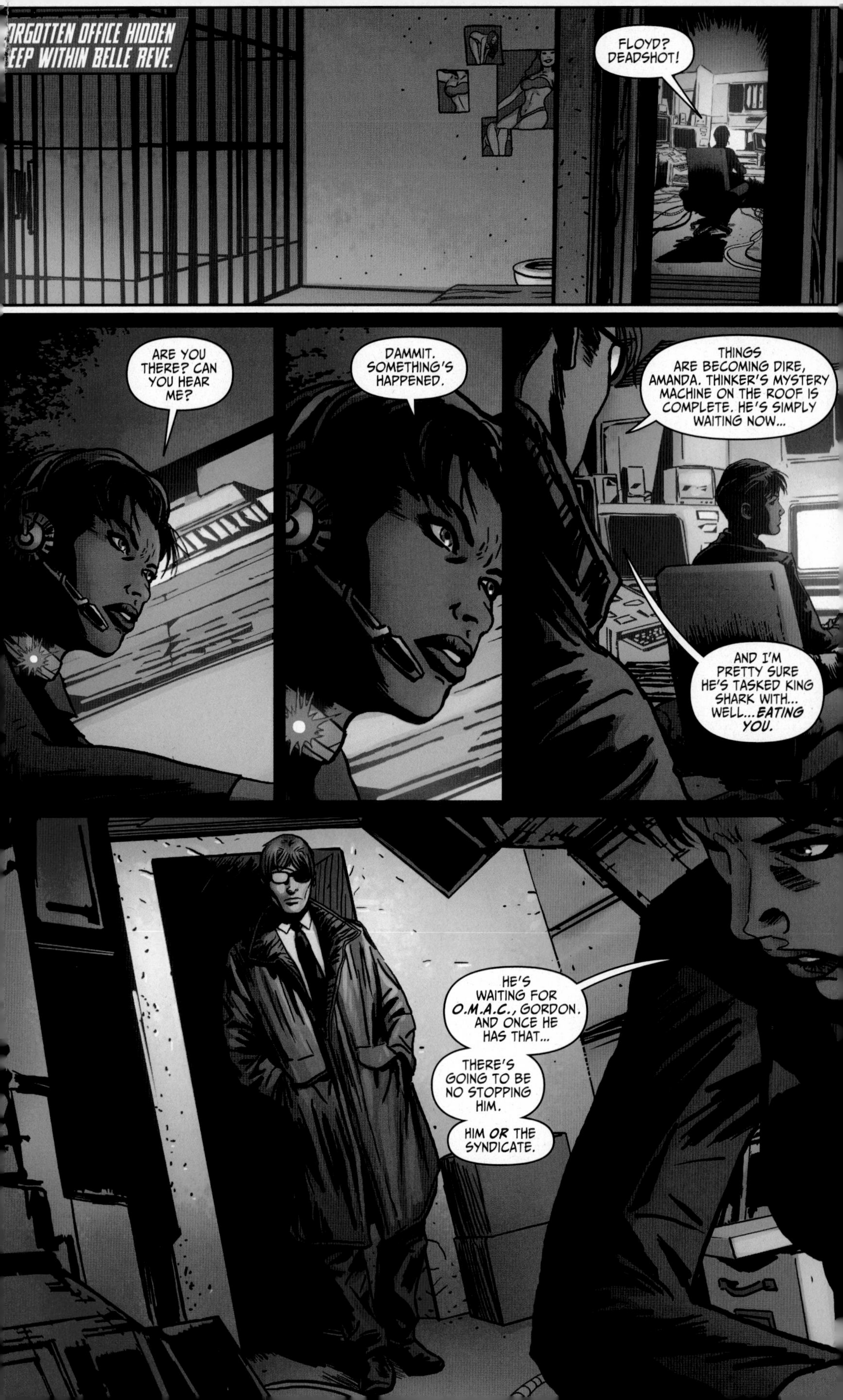
ORGOTTEN OFFICE HIDDEN
EEP WITHIN BELLE REVE.
FLOYD? DEADSHOT!
ARE YOU THERE? CAN YOU HEAR ME?
DAMMIT. SOMETHING'S HAPPENED.
THINGS ARE BECOMING DIRE, AMANDA. THINKER'S MYSTERY MACHINE ON THE ROOF IS COMPLETE. HE'S SIMPLY WAITING NOW...
AND I'M PRETTY SURE HE'S TASKED KING SHARK WITH... WELL...EATING YOU.
HE'S WAITING FOR O.M.A.C., GORDON. AND ONCE HE HAS THAT...
THERE'S GOING TO BE NO STOPPING HIM.
HIM OR THE SYNDICATE.

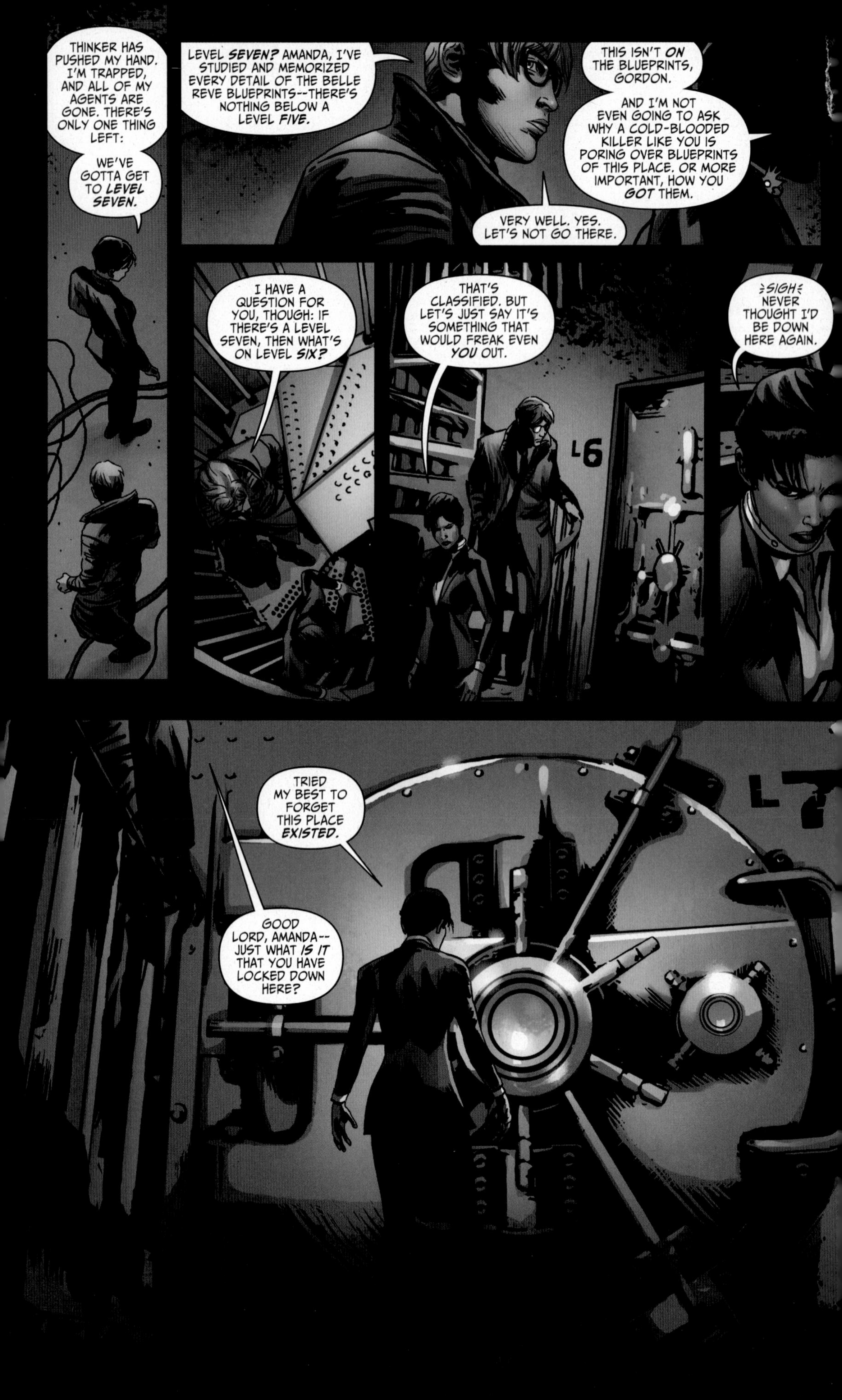
THINKER HAS PUSHED MY HAND. I'M TRAPPED, AND ALL OF MY AGENTS ARE GONE. THERE'S ONLY ONE THING LEFT:
WE'VE GOTTA GET TO LEVEL SEVEN.
LEVEL SEVEN? AMANDA, I'VE STUDIED AND MEMORIZED EVERY DETAIL OF THE BELLE REVE BLUEPRINTS--THERE'S NOTHING BELOW A LEVEL FIVE.
THIS ISN'T ON THE BLUEPRINTS, GORDON.
AND I'M NOT EVEN GOING TO ASK WHY A COLD-BLOODED KILLER LIKE YOU IS PORING OVER BLUEPRINTS OF THIS PLACE. OR MORE IMPORTANT, HOW YOU GOT THEM.
VERY WELL. YES. LET'S NOT GO THERE.
I HAVE A QUESTION FOR YOU, THOUGH: IF THERE'S A LEVEL SEVEN, THEN WHAT'S ON LEVEL SIX?
THAT'S CLASSIFIED. BUT LET'S JUST SAY IT'S SOMETHING THAT WOULD FREAK EVEN YOU OUT.
L6
SIGH NEVER THOUGHT I'D BE DOWN HERE AGAIN.
L7
TRIED MY BEST TO FORGET THIS PLACE EXISTED.
GOOD LORD, AMANDA--JUST WHAT IS IT THAT YOU HAVE LOCKED DOWN HERE?

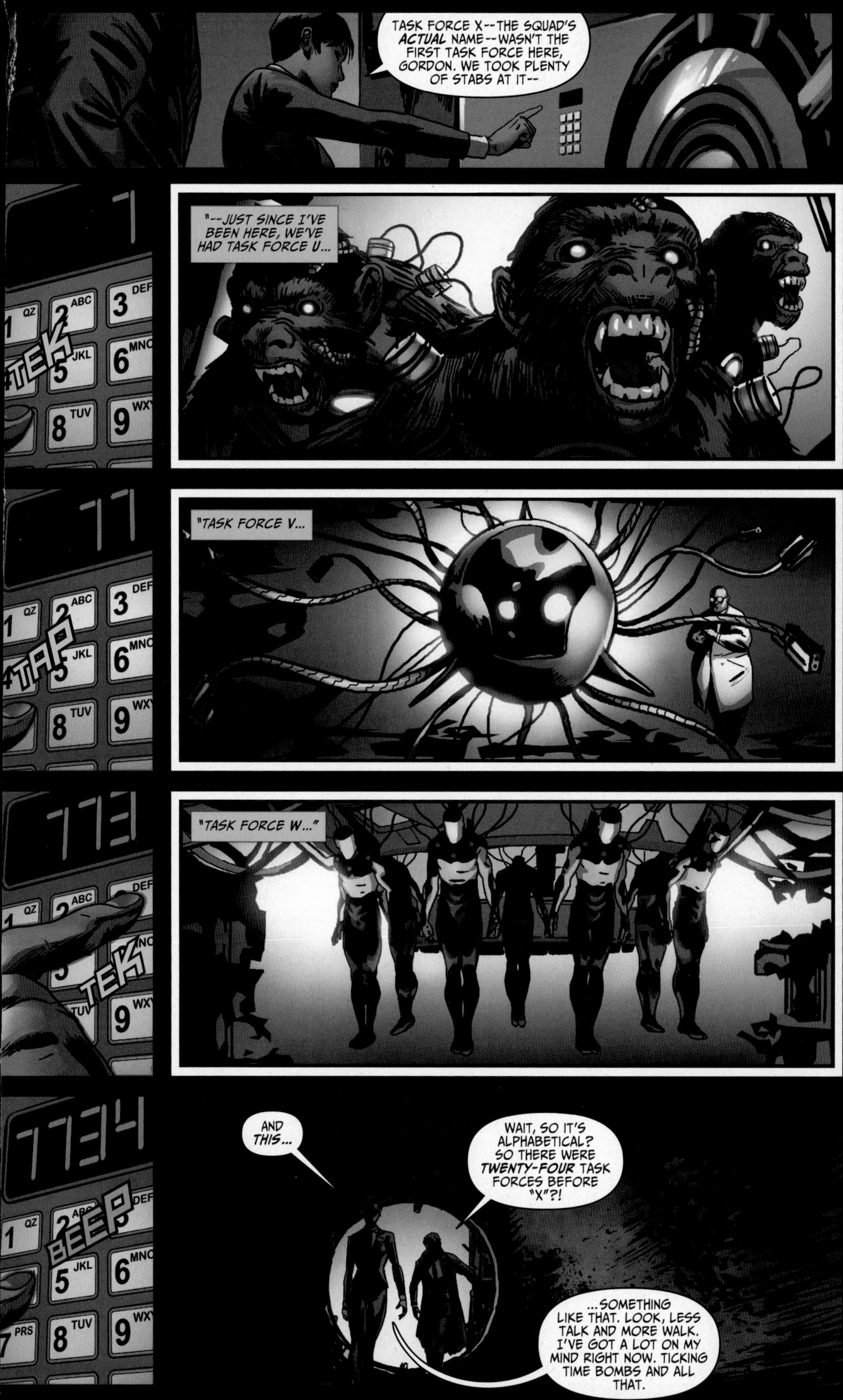
TASK FORCE X--THE SQUAD'S ACTUAL NAME--WASN'T THE FIRST TASK FORCE HERE, GORDON. WE TOOK PLENTY OF STABS AT IT--
"--JUST SINCE I'VE BEEN HERE, WE'VE HAD TASK FORCE U...
TEK
"TASK FORCE V...
TAP
"TASK FORCE W..."
TEK
BEEP
AND THIS...
WAIT, SO IT'S ALPHABETICAL? SO THERE WERE TWENTY-FOUR TASK FORCES BEFORE "X"?!
...SOMETHING LIKE THAT. LOOK, LESS TALK AND MORE WALK. I'VE GOT A LOT ON MY MIND RIGHT NOW. TICKING TIME BOMBS AND ALL THAT.

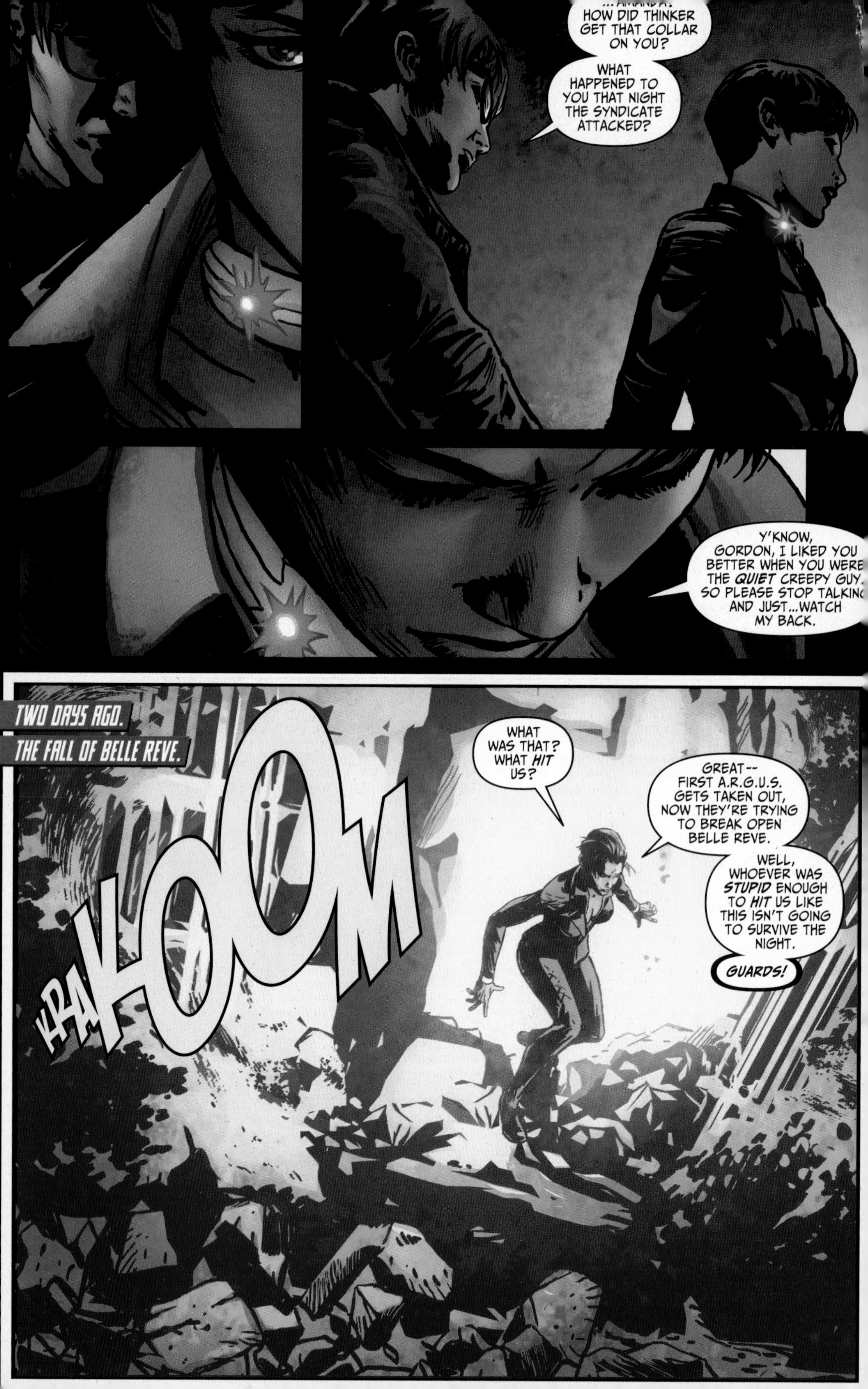
HOW DID THINKER GET THAT COLLAR ON YOU?
WHAT HAPPENED TO YOU THAT NIGHT THE SYNDICATE ATTACKED?
Y'KNOW, GORDON, I LIKED YOU BETTER WHEN YOU WERE THE QUIET CREEPY GUY. SO PLEASE STOP TALKIN AND JUST...WATCH MY BACK.
TWO DAYS AGO.
THE FALL OF BELLE REVE.
KRAKOOM
WHAT WAS THAT? WHAT HIT US?
GREAT-- FIRST A.R.G.U.S. GETS TAKEN OUT, NOW THEY'RE TRYING TO BREAK OPEN BELLE REVE.
WELL, WHOEVER WAS STUPID ENOUGH TO HIT US LIKE THIS ISN'T GOING TO SURVIVE THE NIGHT.
GUARDS!

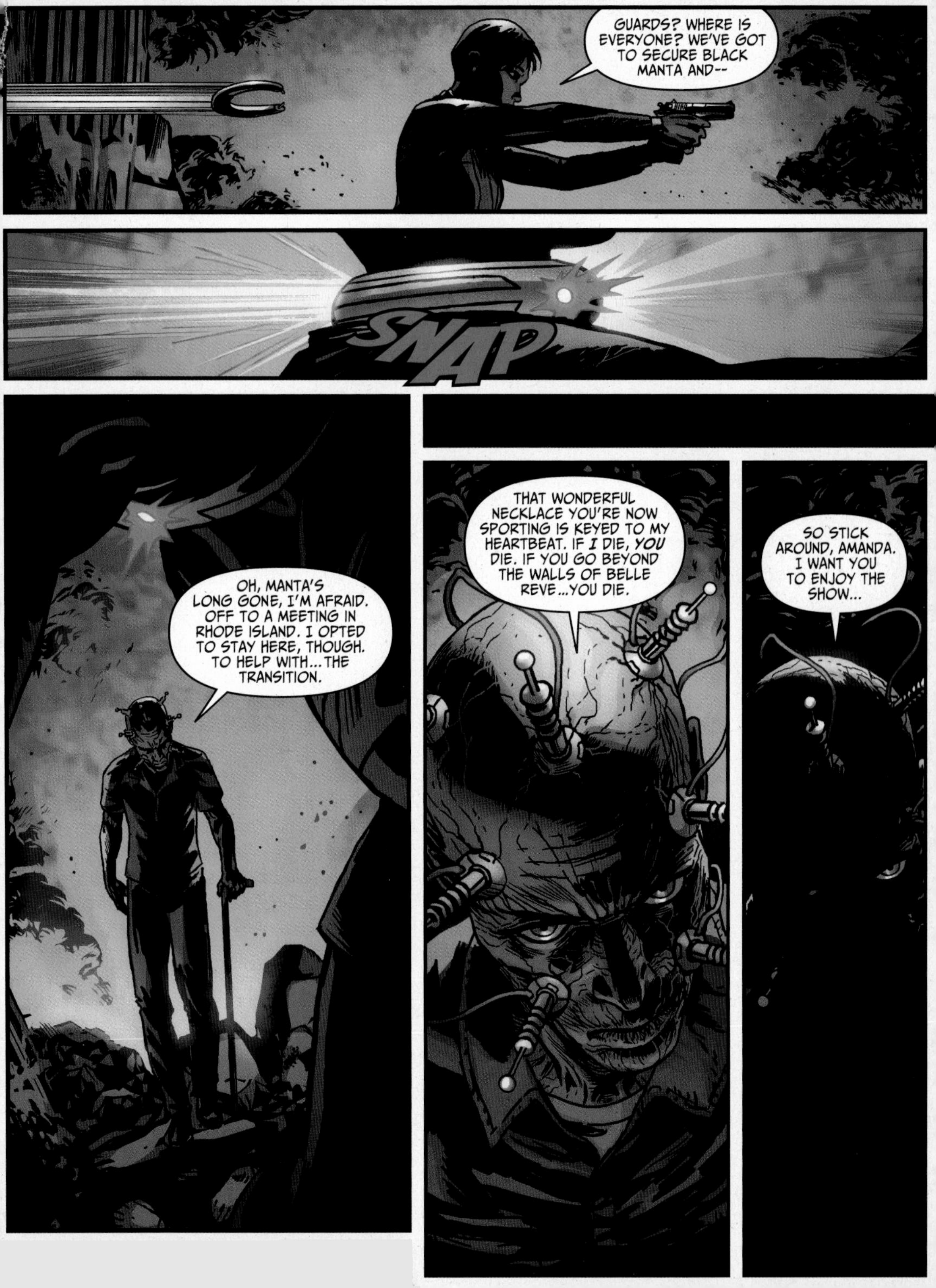
GUARDS? WHERE IS EVERYONE? WE'VE GOT TO SECURE BLACK MANTA AND--
SNAP
OH, MANTA'S LONG GONE, I'M AFRAID. OFF TO A MEETING IN RHODE ISLAND. I OPTED TO STAY HERE, THOUGH. TO HELP WITH... THE TRANSITION.
THAT WONDERFUL NECKLACE YOU'RE NOW SPORTING IS KEYED TO MY HEARTBEAT. IF I DIE, YOU DIE. IF YOU GO BEYOND THE WALLS OF BELLE REVE... YOU DIE.
SO STICK AROUND, AMANDA. I WANT YOU TO ENJOY THE SHOW...

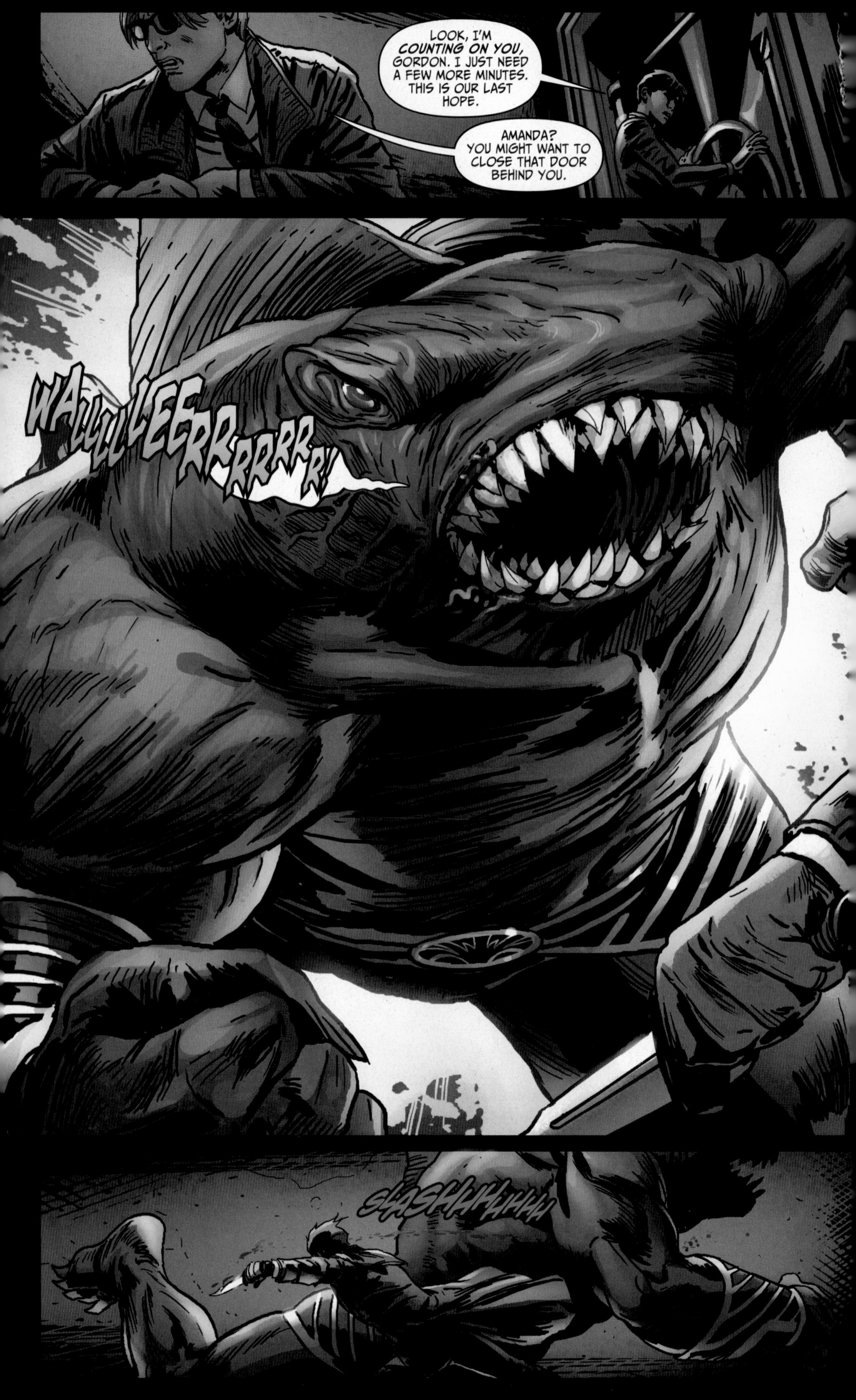
LOOK, I'M *COUNTING ON YOU,* GORDON. I JUST NEED A FEW MORE MINUTES. THIS IS OUR LAST HOPE.
AMANDA? YOU MIGHT WANT TO CLOSE THAT DOOR BEHIND YOU.
WALLLLEERRRRRRRR!
SLASHHHHHHH

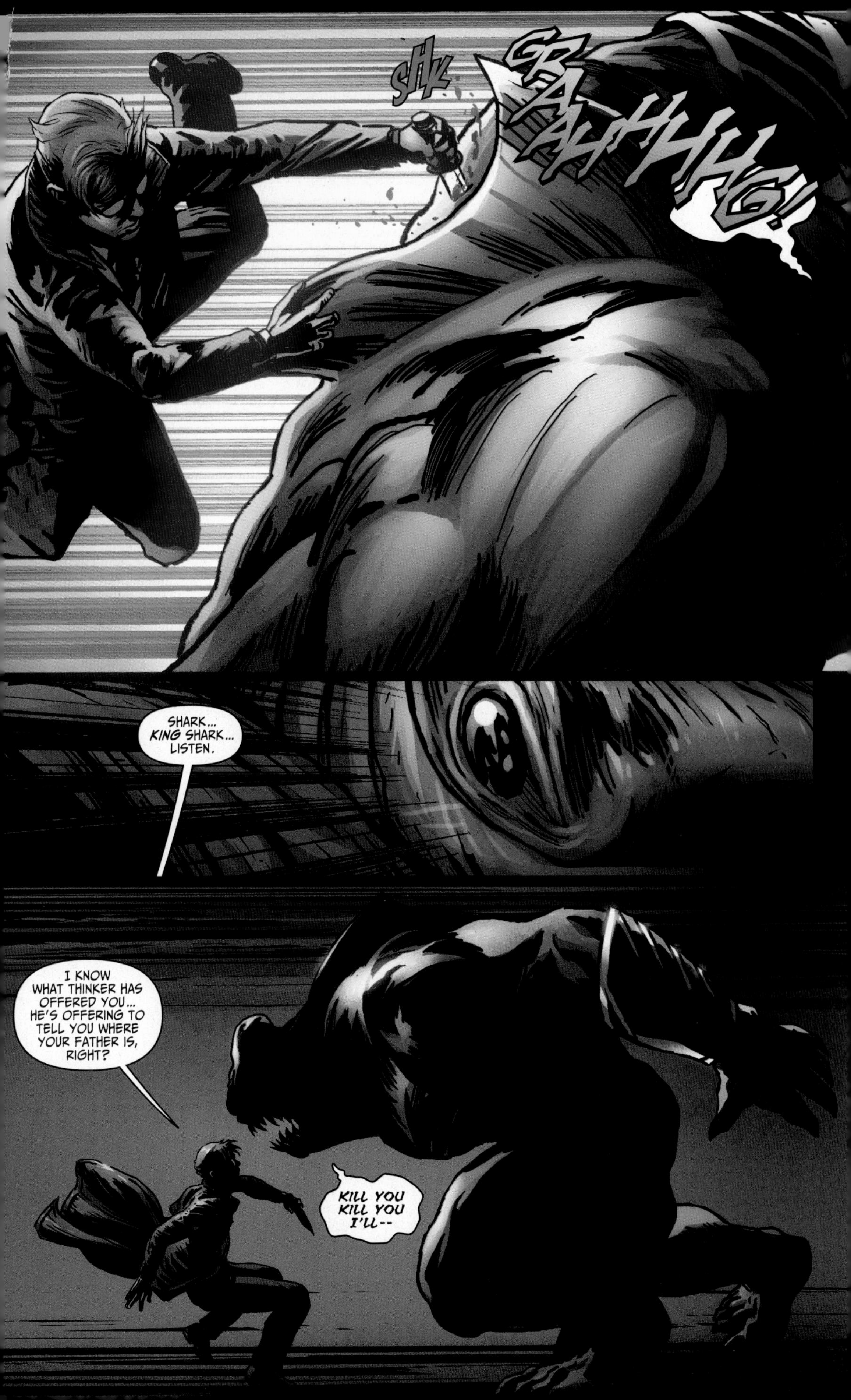
SHK
GRAAHHHHG!!
SHARK... KING SHARK... LISTEN.
I KNOW WHAT THINKER HAS OFFERED YOU... HE'S OFFERING TO TELL YOU WHERE YOUR FATHER IS, RIGHT?
KILL YOU KILL YOU I'LL--

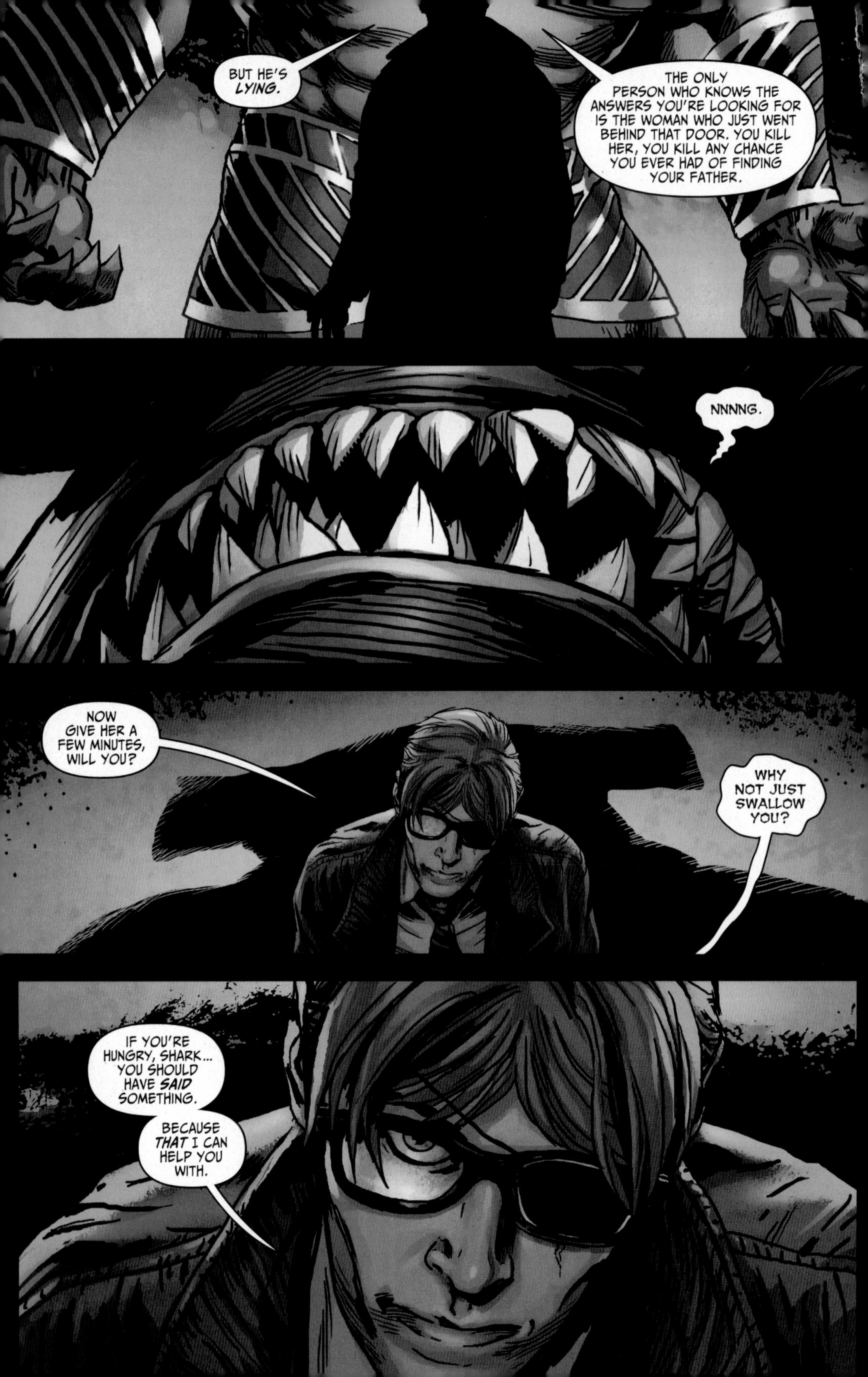
BUT HE'S *LYING.*
THE ONLY PERSON WHO KNOWS THE ANSWERS YOU'RE LOOKING FOR IS THE WOMAN WHO JUST WENT BEHIND THAT DOOR. YOU KILL HER, YOU KILL ANY CHANCE YOU EVER HAD OF FINDING YOUR FATHER.
NNNNG.
NOW GIVE HER A FEW MINUTES, WILL YOU?
WHY NOT JUST SWALLOW YOU?
IF YOU'RE HUNGRY, SHARK... YOU SHOULD HAVE *SAID* SOMETHING.
BECAUSE *THAT* I CAN HELP YOU WITH.

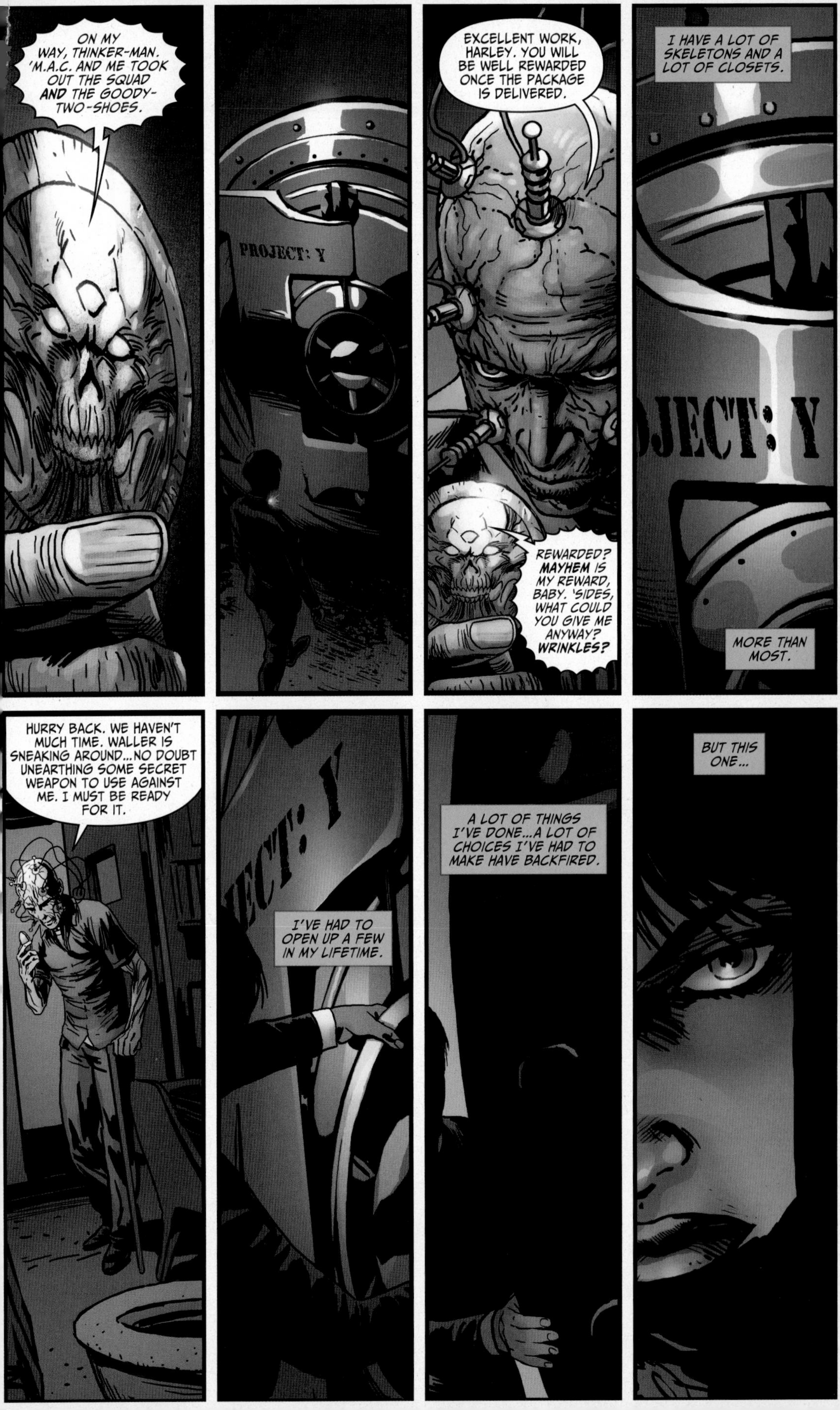
ON MY WAY, THINKER-MAN. 'M.A.C. AND ME TOOK OUT THE SQUAD AND THE GOODY-TWO-SHOES.
PROJECT: Y
EXCELLENT WORK, HARLEY. YOU WILL BE WELL REWARDED ONCE THE PACKAGE IS DELIVERED.
REWARDED? MAYHEM IS MY REWARD, BABY. 'SIDES, WHAT COULD YOU GIVE ME ANYWAY? WRINKLES?
I HAVE A LOT OF SKELETONS AND A LOT OF CLOSETS.
OJECT: Y
MORE THAN MOST.
HURRY BACK. WE HAVEN'T MUCH TIME. WALLER IS SNEAKING AROUND...NO DOUBT UNEARTHING SOME SECRET WEAPON TO USE AGAINST ME. I MUST BE READY FOR IT.
I'VE HAD TO OPEN UP A FEW IN MY LIFETIME.
A LOT OF THINGS I'VE DONE...A LOT OF CHOICES I'VE HAD TO MAKE HAVE BACKFIRED.
BUT THIS ONE...

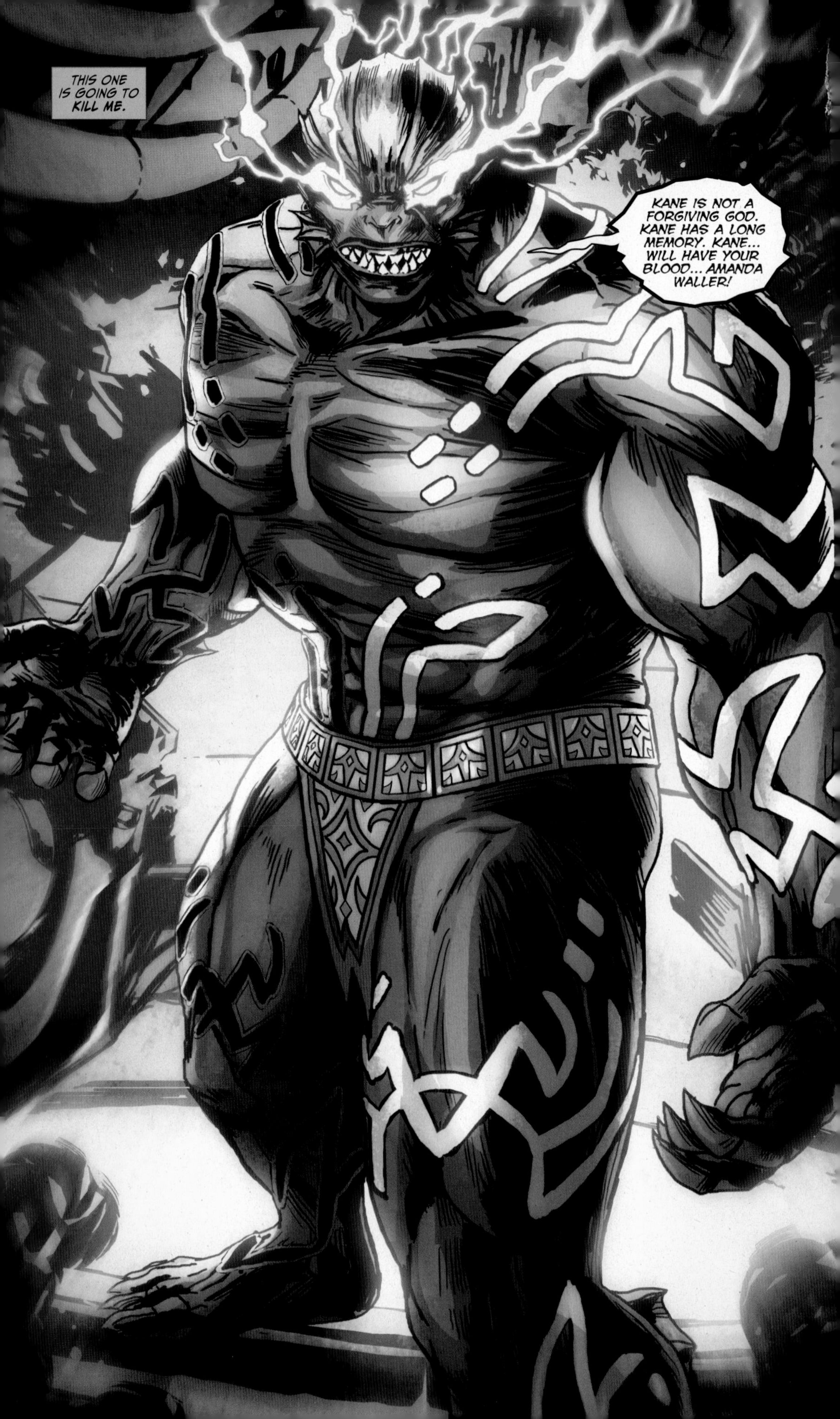
THIS ONE IS GOING TO KILL ME.
KANE IS NOT A FORGIVING GOD. KANE HAS A LONG MEMORY. KANE... WILL HAVE YOUR BLOOD... AMANDA WALLER!

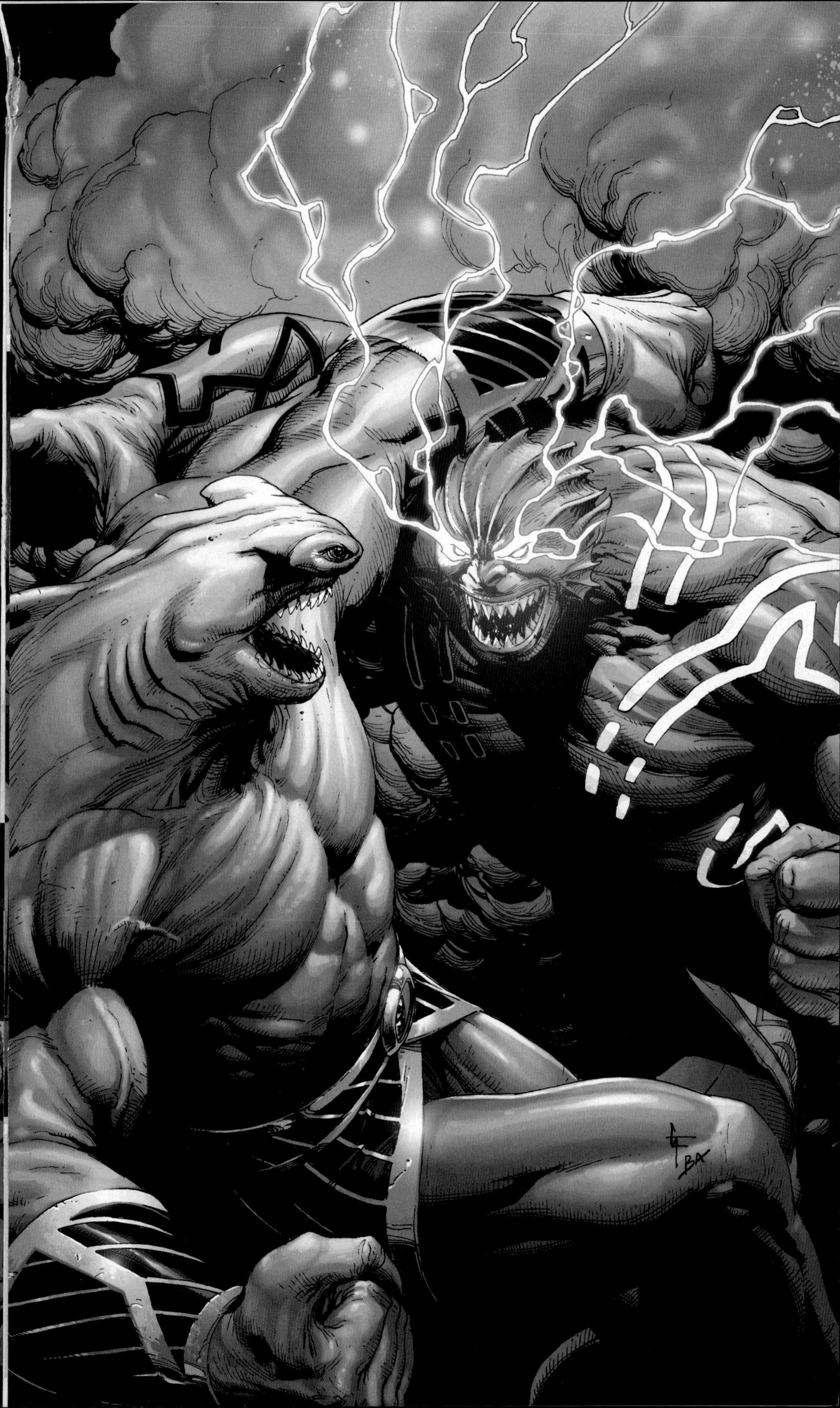

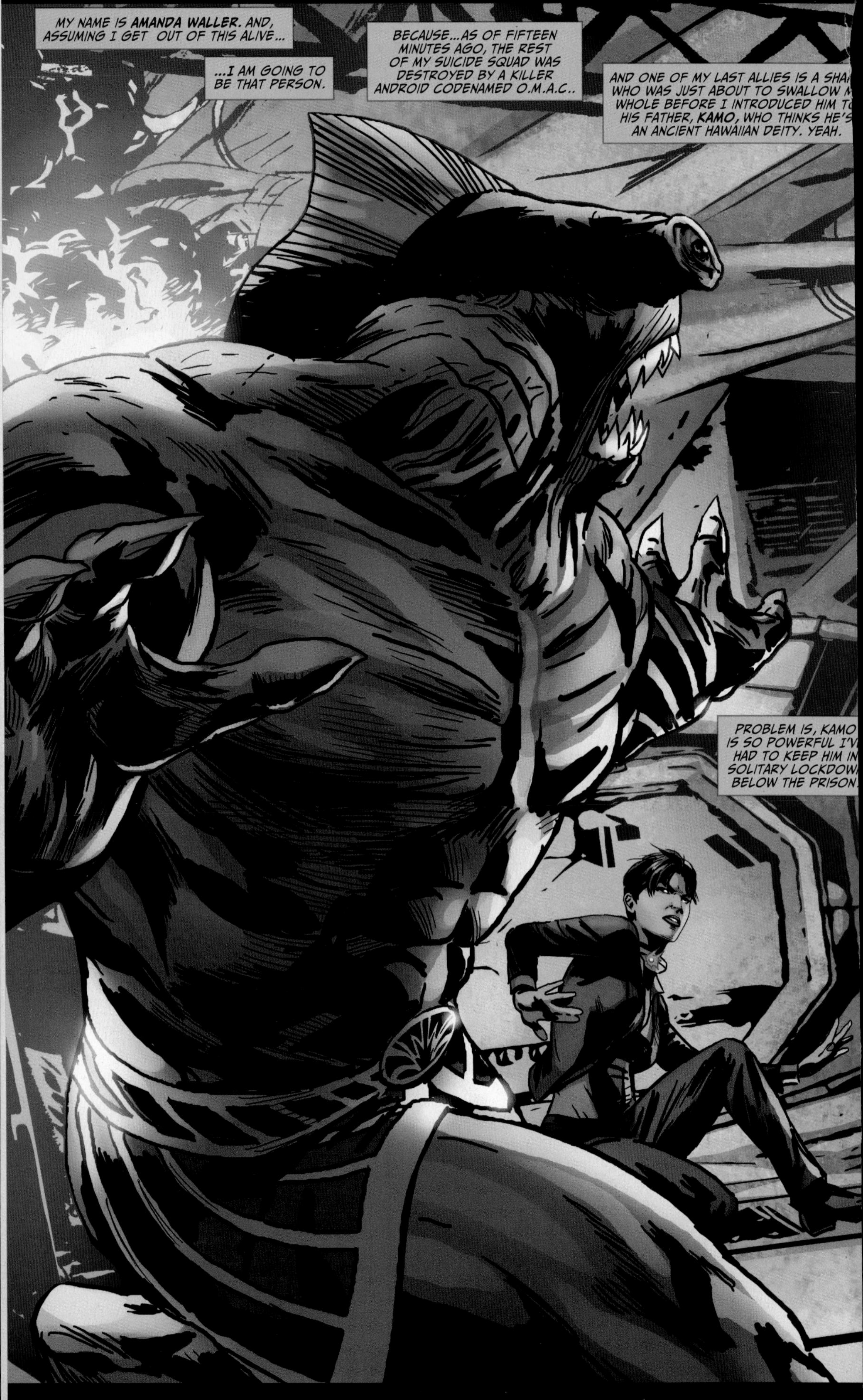
MY NAME IS AMANDA WALLER. AND, ASSUMING I GET OUT OF THIS ALIVE...
...I AM GOING TO BE THAT PERSON.
BECAUSE...AS OF FIFTEEN MINUTES AGO, THE REST OF MY SUICIDE SQUAD WAS DESTROYED BY A KILLER ANDROID CODENAMED O.M.A.C..
AND ONE OF MY LAST ALLIES IS A SHA WHO WAS JUST ABOUT TO SWALLOW M WHOLE BEFORE I INTRODUCED HIM TO HIS FATHER, KAMO, WHO THINKS HE'S AN ANCIENT HAWAIIAN DEITY. YEAH.
PROBLEM IS, KAMO IS SO POWERFUL I'V HAD TO KEEP HIM IN SOLITARY LOCKDOW BELOW THE PRISON

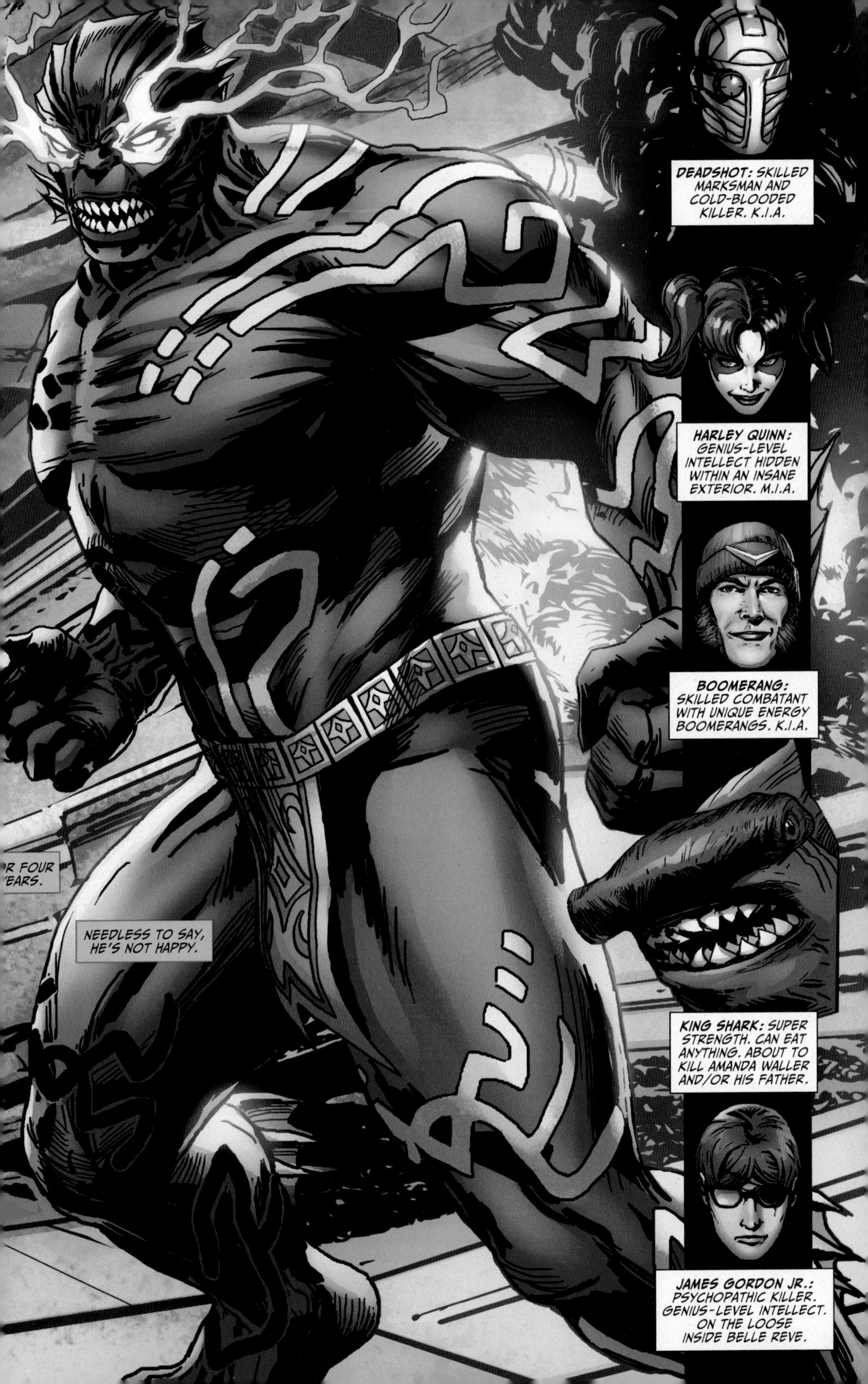

DEADSHOT: SKILLED MARKSMAN AND COLD-BLOODED KILLER. K.I.A.
HARLEY QUINN: GENIUS-LEVEL INTELLECT HIDDEN WITHIN AN INSANE EXTERIOR. M.I.A.
BOOMERANG: SKILLED COMBATANT WITH UNIQUE ENERGY BOOMERANGS. K.I.A.
NEEDLESS TO SAY, HE'S NOT HAPPY.
KING SHARK: SUPER STRENGTH. CAN EAT ANYTHING. ABOUT TO KILL AMANDA WALLER AND/OR HIS FATHER.
JAMES GORDON JR.: PSYCHOPATHIC KILLER. GENIUS-LEVEL INTELLECT. ON THE LOOSE INSIDE BELLE REVE.

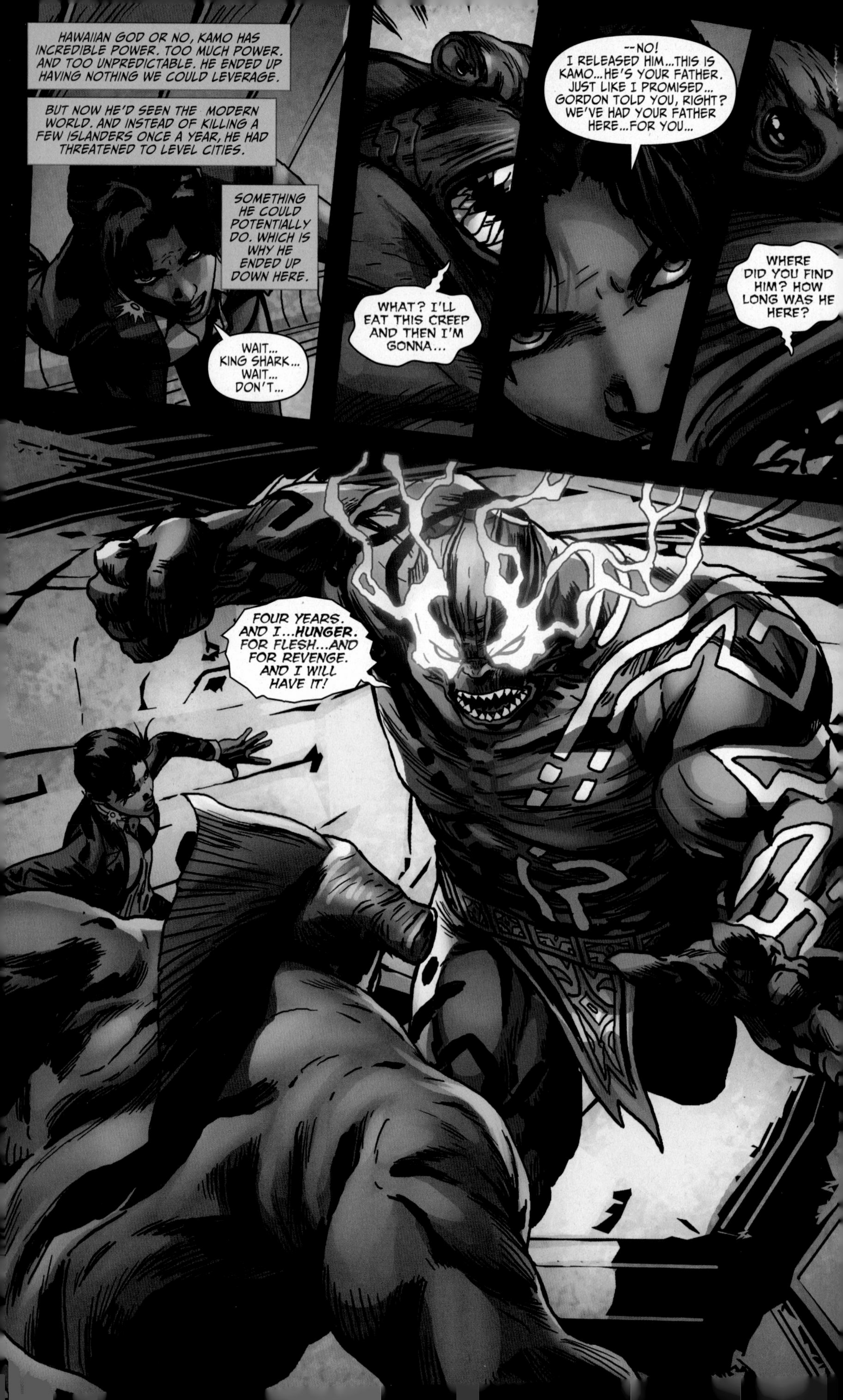
HAWAIIAN GOD OR NO, KAMO HAS INCREDIBLE POWER. TOO MUCH POWER. AND TOO UNPREDICTABLE. HE ENDED UP HAVING NOTHING WE COULD LEVERAGE.
BUT NOW HE'D SEEN THE MODERN WORLD. AND INSTEAD OF KILLING A FEW ISLANDERS ONCE A YEAR, HE HAD THREATENED TO LEVEL CITIES.
SOMETHING HE COULD POTENTIALLY DO. WHICH IS WHY HE ENDED UP DOWN HERE.
WAIT... KING SHARK... WAIT... DON'T...
WHAT? I'LL EAT THIS CREEP AND THEN I'M GONNA...
--NO! I RELEASED HIM...THIS IS KAMO...HE'S YOUR FATHER. JUST LIKE I PROMISED... GORDON TOLD YOU, RIGHT? WE'VE HAD YOUR FATHER HERE...FOR YOU...
WHERE DID YOU FIND HIM? HOW LONG WAS HE HERE?
FOUR YEARS. AND I...HUNGER. FOR FLESH...AND FOR REVENGE. AND I WILL HAVE IT!

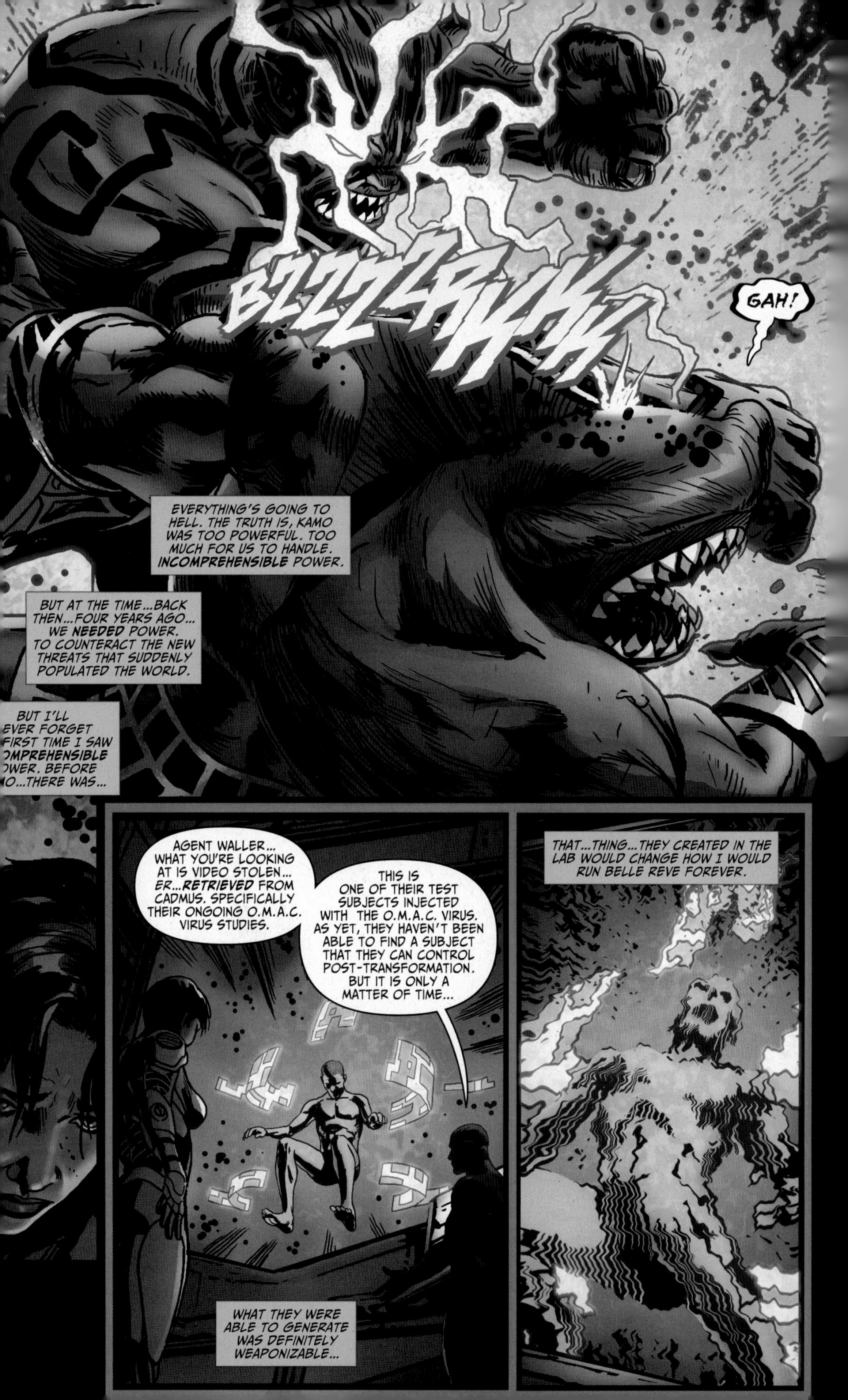
GAH!
EVERYTHING'S GOING TO HELL. THE TRUTH IS, KAMO WAS TOO POWERFUL. TOO MUCH FOR US TO HANDLE. **INCOMPREHENSIBLE** POWER.
BUT AT THE TIME...BACK THEN...FOUR YEARS AGO... WE **NEEDED** POWER. TO COUNTERACT THE NEW THREATS THAT SUDDENLY POPULATED THE WORLD.
BUT I'LL EVER FORGET FIRST TIME I SAW **OMPREHENSIBLE** OWER. BEFORE O...THERE WAS...
AGENT WALLER... WHAT YOU'RE LOOKING AT IS VIDEO STOLEN... ER...**RETRIEVED** FROM CADMUS. SPECIFICALLY THEIR ONGOING O.M.A.C. VIRUS STUDIES.
THIS IS ONE OF THEIR TEST SUBJECTS INJECTED WITH THE O.M.A.C. VIRUS. AS YET, THEY HAVEN'T BEEN ABLE TO FIND A SUBJECT THAT THEY CAN CONTROL POST-TRANSFORMATION. BUT IT IS ONLY A MATTER OF TIME...
WHAT THEY WERE ABLE TO GENERATE WAS DEFINITELY WEAPONIZABLE...
THAT...THING...THEY CREATED IN THE LAB WOULD CHANGE HOW I WOULD RUN BELLE REVE FOREVER.

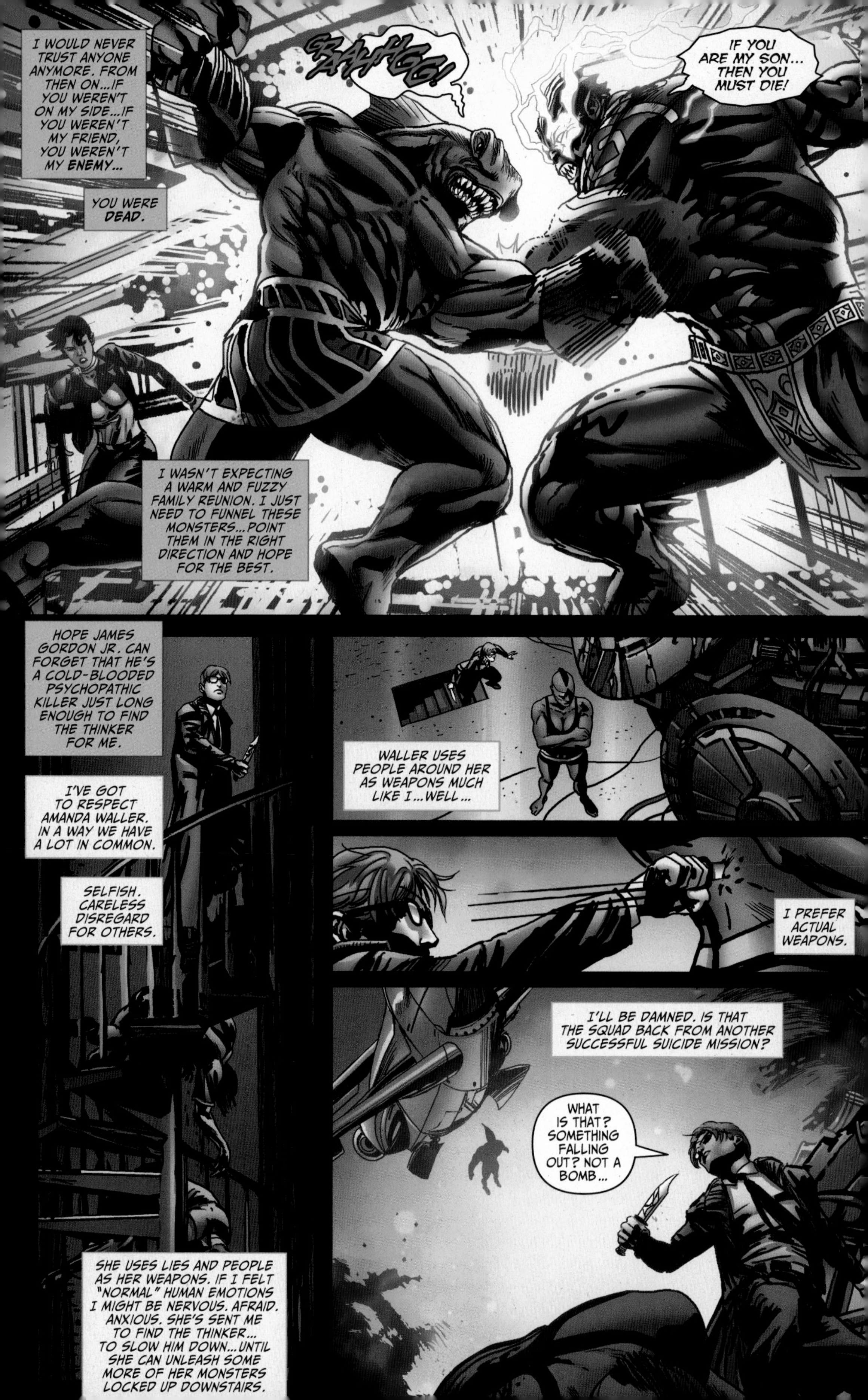

I WOULD NEVER TRUST ANYONE ANYMORE. FROM THEN ON...IF YOU WEREN'T ON MY SIDE...IF YOU WEREN'T MY FRIEND, YOU WEREN'T MY **ENEMY**...
GRAAHGG!
IF YOU ARE MY SON... THEN YOU MUST DIE!
YOU WERE **DEAD**.
I WASN'T EXPECTING A WARM AND FUZZY FAMILY REUNION. I JUST NEED TO FUNNEL THESE MONSTERS...POINT THEM IN THE RIGHT DIRECTION AND HOPE FOR THE BEST.
HOPE JAMES GORDON JR. CAN FORGET THAT HE'S A COLD-BLOODED PSYCHOPATHIC KILLER JUST LONG ENOUGH TO FIND THE THINKER FOR ME.
I'VE GOT TO RESPECT AMANDA WALLER. IN A WAY WE HAVE A LOT IN COMMON.
SELFISH. CARELESS DISREGARD FOR OTHERS.
SHE USES LIES AND PEOPLE AS HER WEAPONS. IF I FELT "NORMAL" HUMAN EMOTIONS I MIGHT BE NERVOUS. AFRAID. ANXIOUS. SHE'S SENT ME TO FIND THE THINKER... TO SLOW HIM DOWN...UNTIL SHE CAN UNLEASH SOME MORE OF HER MONSTERS LOCKED UP DOWNSTAIRS.
WALLER USES PEOPLE AROUND HER AS WEAPONS MUCH LIKE I...WELL...
I PREFER ACTUAL WEAPONS.
I'LL BE DAMNED. IS THAT THE SQUAD BACK FROM ANOTHER SUCCESSFUL SUICIDE MISSION?
WHAT IS THAT? SOMETHING FALLING OUT? NOT A BOMB...

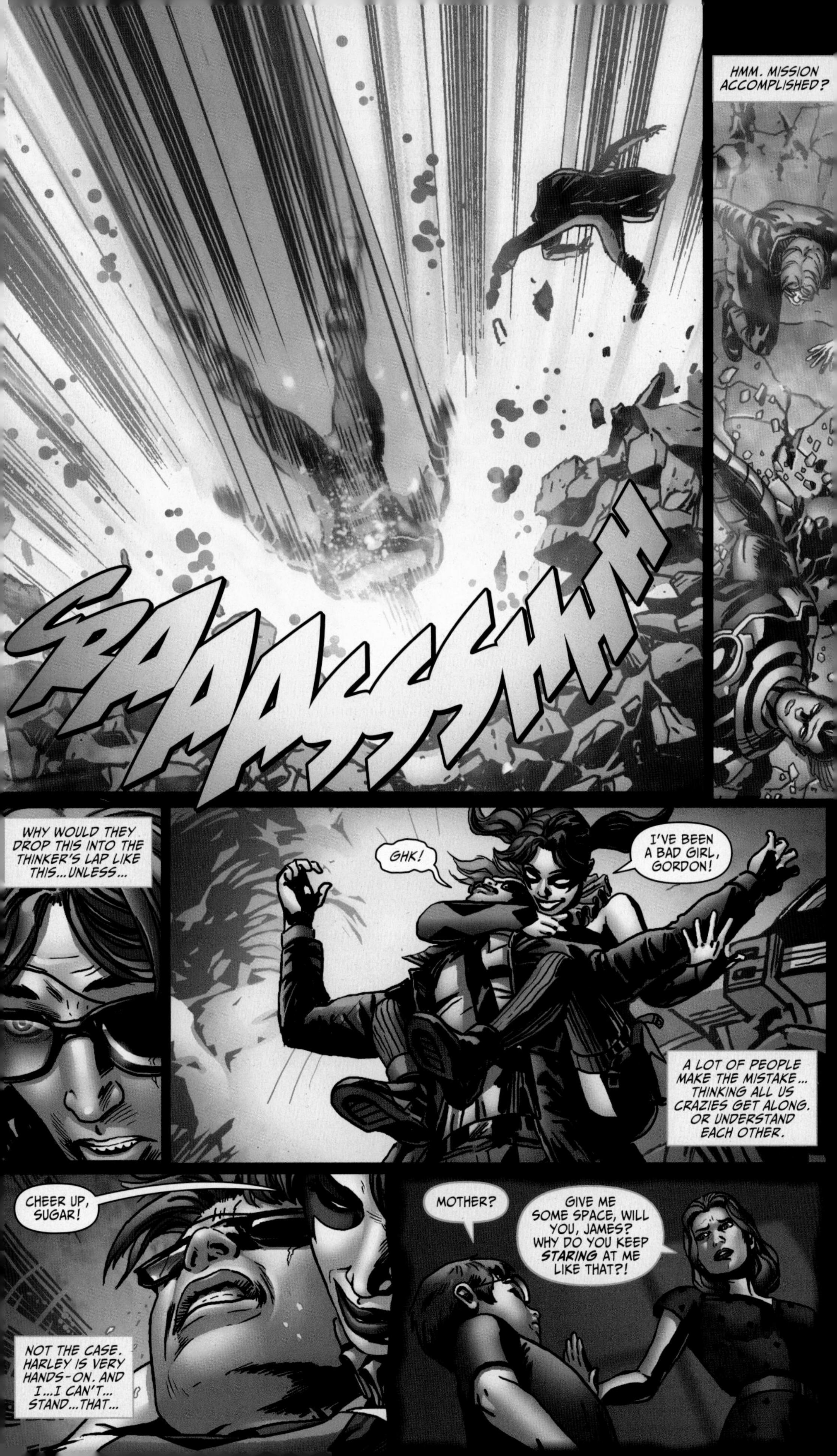

CRAAASSHH
HMM. MISSION ACCOMPLISHED?
WHY WOULD THEY DROP THIS INTO THE THINKER'S LAP LIKE THIS...UNLESS...
GHK!
I'VE BEEN A BAD GIRL, GORDON!
A LOT OF PEOPLE MAKE THE MISTAKE... THINKING ALL US CRAZIES GET ALONG. OR UNDERSTAND EACH OTHER.
CHEER UP, SUGAR!
NOT THE CASE. HARLEY IS VERY HANDS-ON. AND I...I CAN'T... STAND...THAT...
MOTHER?
GIVE ME SOME SPACE, WILL YOU, JAMES? WHY DO YOU KEEP STARING AT ME LIKE THAT?!

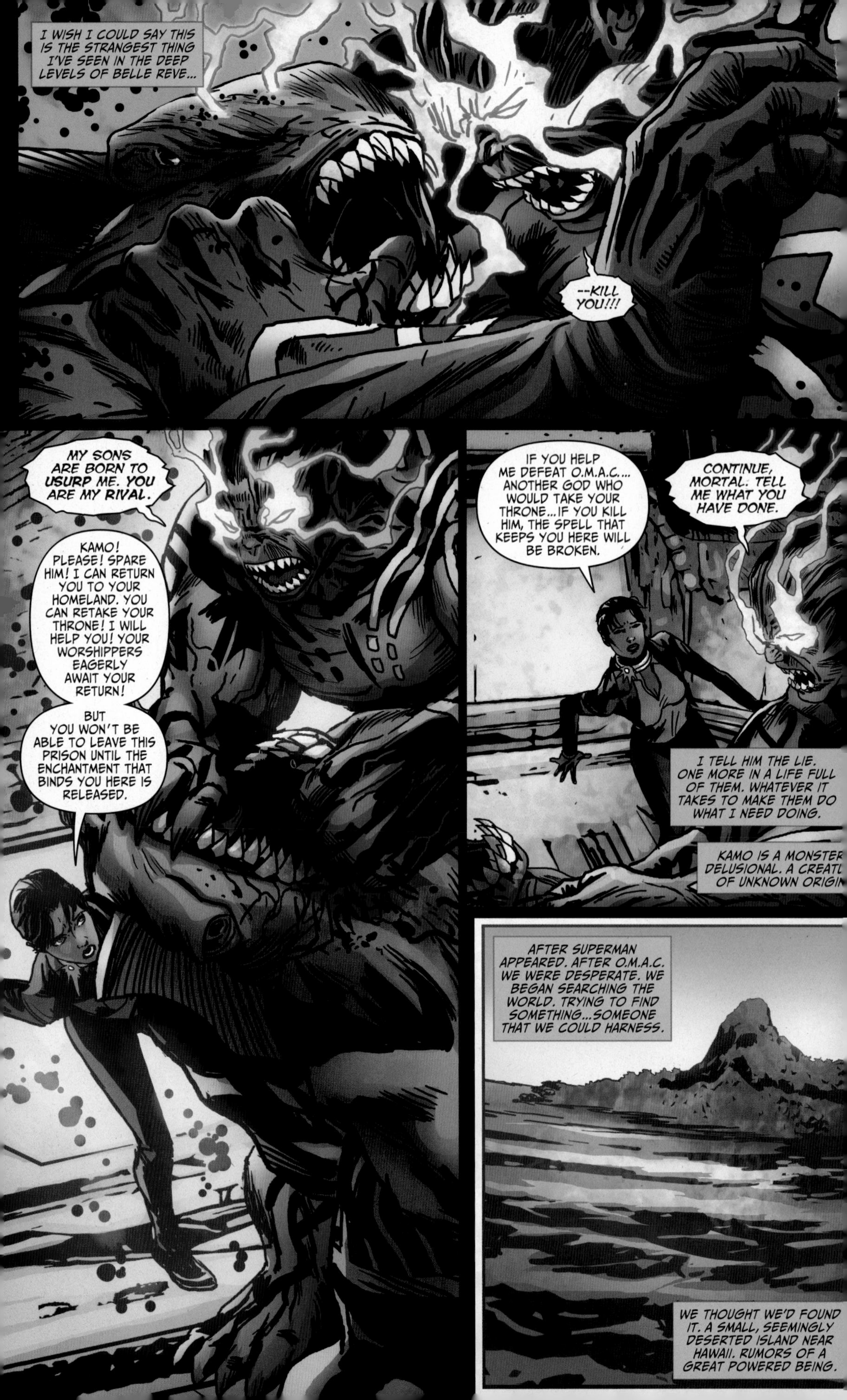
I WISH I COULD SAY THIS IS THE STRANGEST THING I'VE SEEN IN THE DEEP LEVELS OF BELLE REVE...
--KILL YOU!!!
MY SONS ARE BORN TO USURP ME. YOU ARE MY RIVAL.
KAMO! PLEASE! SPARE HIM! I CAN RETURN YOU TO YOUR HOMELAND. YOU CAN RETAKE YOUR THRONE! I WILL HELP YOU! YOUR WORSHIPPERS EAGERLY AWAIT YOUR RETURN!
BUT YOU WON'T BE ABLE TO LEAVE THIS PRISON UNTIL THE ENCHANTMENT THAT BINDS YOU HERE IS RELEASED.
IF YOU HELP ME DEFEAT O.M.A.C.... ANOTHER GOD WHO WOULD TAKE YOUR THRONE...IF YOU KILL HIM, THE SPELL THAT KEEPS YOU HERE WILL BE BROKEN.
CONTINUE, MORTAL. TELL ME WHAT YOU HAVE DONE.
I TELL HIM THE LIE. ONE MORE IN A LIFE FULL OF THEM. WHATEVER IT TAKES TO MAKE THEM DO WHAT I NEED DOING.
KAMO IS A MONSTER DELUSIONAL. A CREATU OF UNKNOWN ORIGIN
AFTER SUPERMAN APPEARED. AFTER O.M.A.C. WE WERE DESPERATE. WE BEGAN SEARCHING THE WORLD. TRYING TO FIND SOMETHING...SOMEONE THAT WE COULD HARNESS.
WE THOUGHT WE'D FOUND IT. A SMALL, SEEMINGLY DESERTED ISLAND NEAR HAWAII. RUMORS OF A GREAT POWERED BEING.

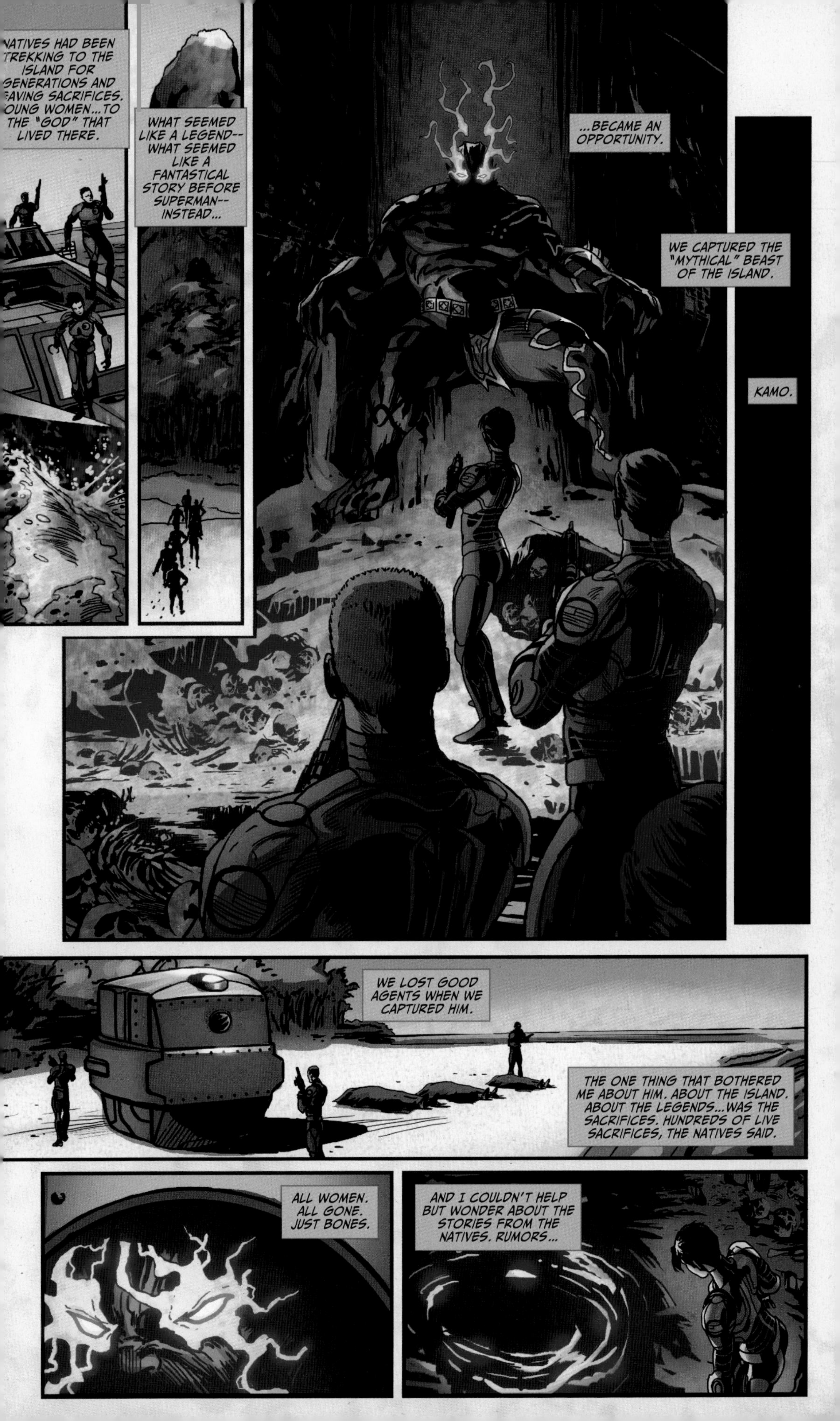
NATIVES HAD BEEN TREKKING TO THE ISLAND FOR GENERATIONS AND LEAVING SACRIFICES. YOUNG WOMEN...TO THE "GOD" THAT LIVED THERE.
WHAT SEEMED LIKE A LEGEND--WHAT SEEMED LIKE A FANTASTICAL STORY BEFORE SUPERMAN--INSTEAD...
...BECAME AN OPPORTUNITY.
WE CAPTURED THE "MYTHICAL" BEAST OF THE ISLAND.
KAMO.
WE LOST GOOD AGENTS WHEN WE CAPTURED HIM.
THE ONE THING THAT BOTHERED ME ABOUT HIM. ABOUT THE ISLAND. ABOUT THE LEGENDS...WAS THE SACRIFICES. HUNDREDS OF LIVE SACRIFICES, THE NATIVES SAID.
ALL WOMEN. ALL GONE. JUST BONES.
AND I COULDN'T HELP BUT WONDER ABOUT THE STORIES FROM THE NATIVES. RUMORS...

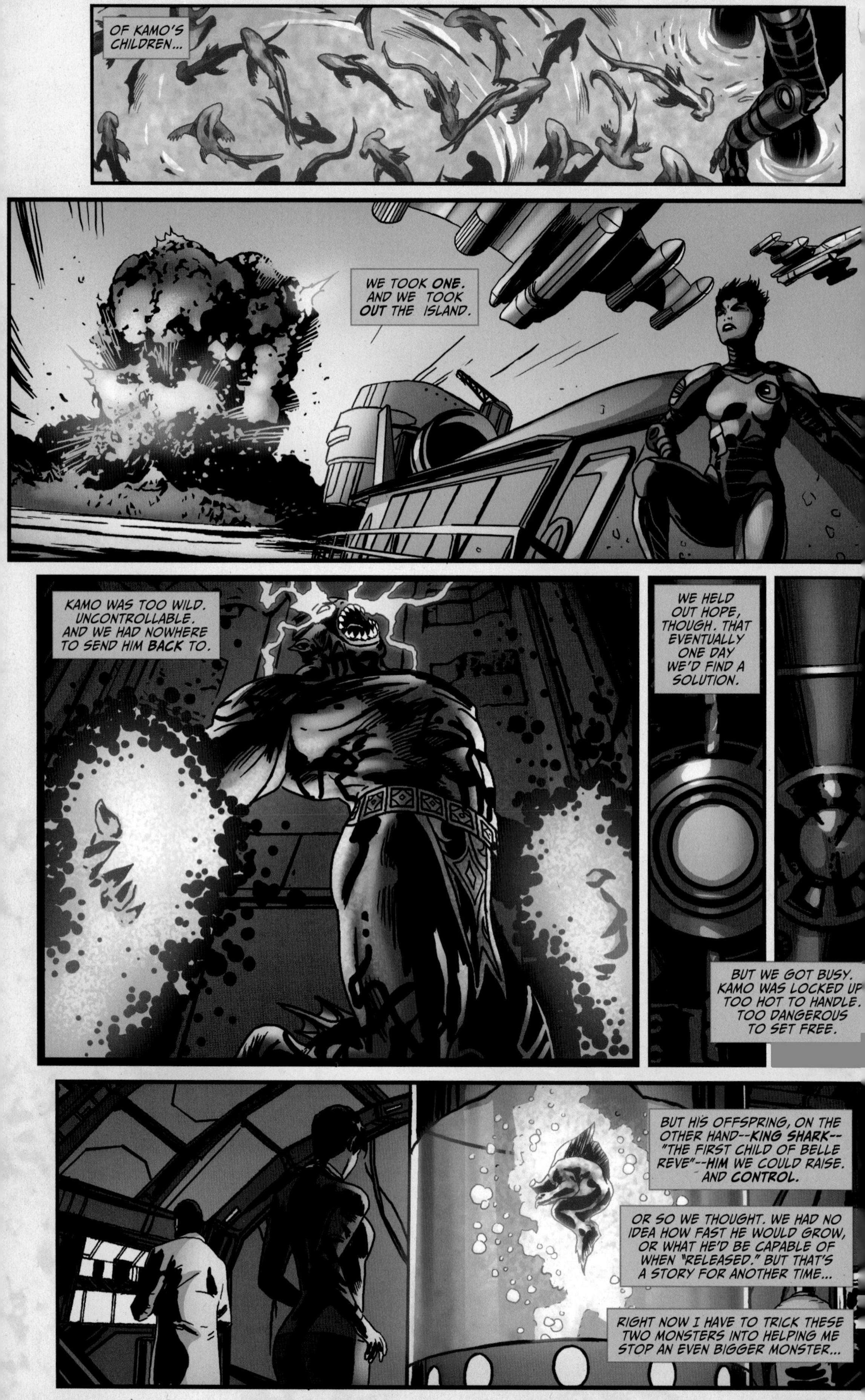

OF KAMO'S CHILDREN...
WE TOOK ONE. AND WE TOOK OUT THE ISLAND.
KAMO WAS TOO WILD. UNCONTROLLABLE. AND WE HAD NOWHERE TO SEND HIM BACK TO.
WE HELD OUT HOPE, THOUGH. THAT EVENTUALLY ONE DAY WE'D FIND A SOLUTION.
BUT WE GOT BUSY. KAMO WAS LOCKED UP TOO HOT TO HANDLE. TOO DANGEROUS TO SET FREE.
BUT HIS OFFSPRING, ON THE OTHER HAND--KING SHARK--"THE FIRST CHILD OF BELLE REVE"--HIM WE COULD RAISE. AND CONTROL.
OR SO WE THOUGHT. WE HAD NO IDEA HOW FAST HE WOULD GROW, OR WHAT HE'D BE CAPABLE OF WHEN "RELEASED." BUT THAT'S A STORY FOR ANOTHER TIME...
RIGHT NOW I HAVE TO TRICK THESE TWO MONSTERS INTO HELPING ME STOP AN EVEN BIGGER MONSTER...

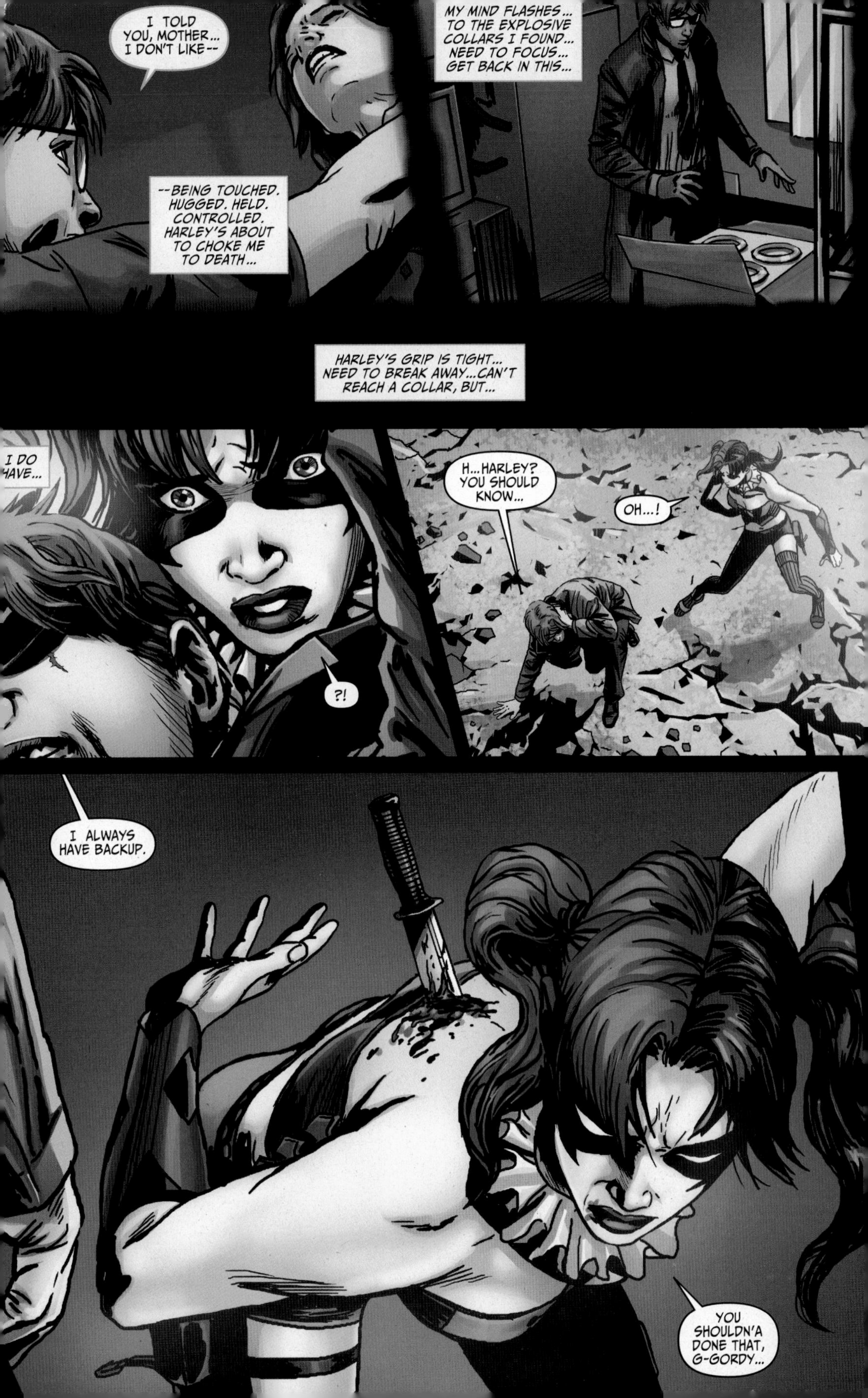
I TOLD YOU, MOTHER... I DON'T LIKE--
--BEING TOUCHED. HUGGED. HELD. CONTROLLED. HARLEY'S ABOUT TO CHOKE ME TO DEATH...
MY MIND FLASHES... TO THE EXPLOSIVE COLLARS I FOUND... NEED TO FOCUS... GET BACK IN THIS...
HARLEY'S GRIP IS TIGHT... NEED TO BREAK AWAY...CAN'T REACH A COLLAR, BUT...
I DO HAVE...
?!
H...HARLEY? YOU SHOULD KNOW...
OH...!
I ALWAYS HAVE BACKUP.
YOU SHOULDN'A DONE THAT, G-GORDY...

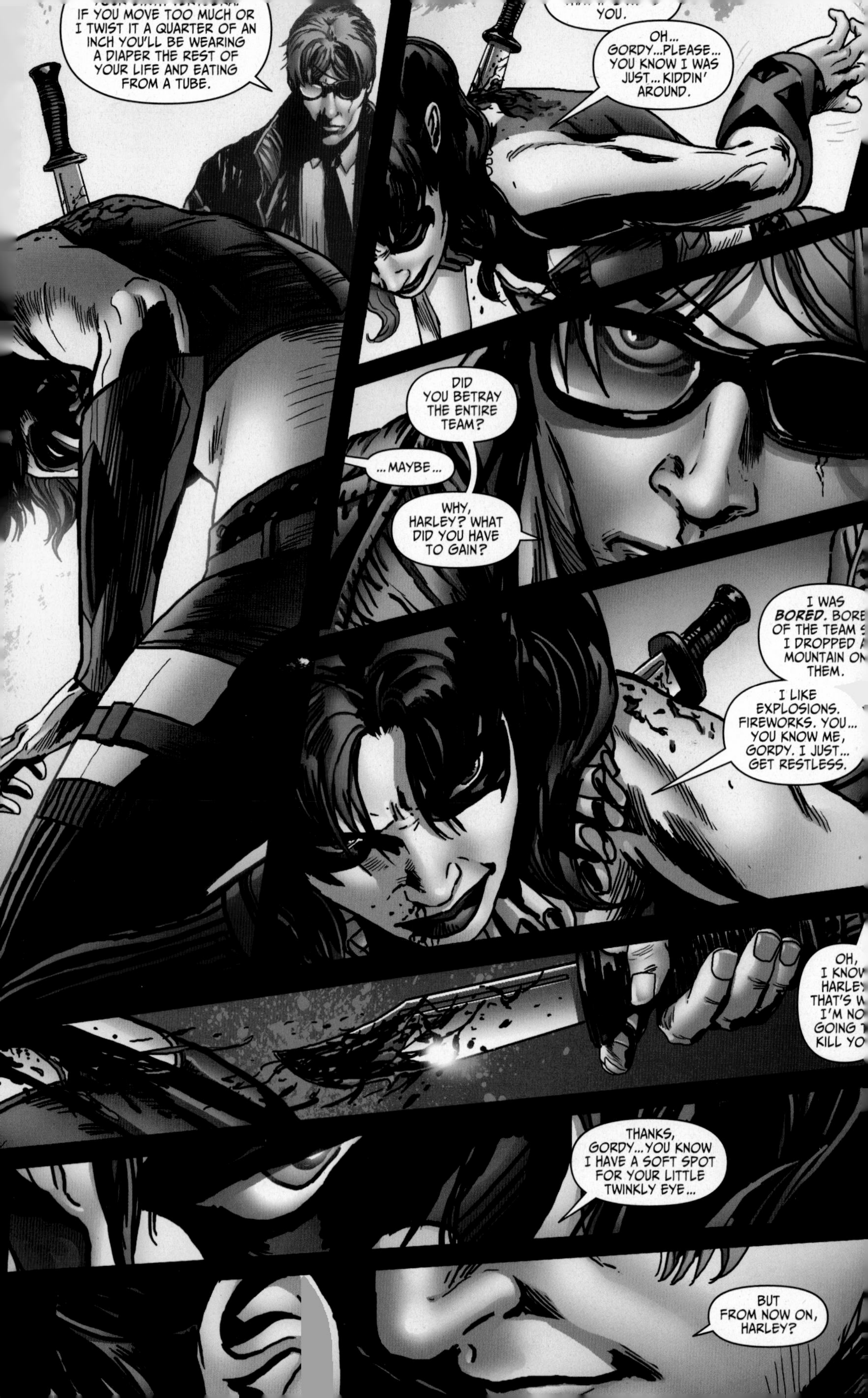
IF YOU MOVE TOO MUCH OR I TWIST IT A QUARTER OF AN INCH YOU'LL BE WEARING A DIAPER THE REST OF YOUR LIFE AND EATING FROM A TUBE.
YOU.
OH... GORDY...PLEASE... YOU KNOW I WAS JUST... KIDDIN' AROUND.
DID YOU BETRAY THE ENTIRE TEAM?
...MAYBE...
WHY, HARLEY? WHAT DID YOU HAVE TO GAIN?
I WAS *BORED*. BORE OF THE TEAM S I DROPPED A MOUNTAIN ON THEM.
I LIKE EXPLOSIONS. FIREWORKS. YOU... YOU KNOW ME, GORDY. I JUST... GET RESTLESS.
OH, I KNOW HARLEY THAT'S I'M NO GOING KILL YO
THANKS, GORDY...YOU KNOW I HAVE A SOFT SPOT FOR YOUR LITTLE TWINKLY EYE...
BUT FROM NOW ON, HARLEY?

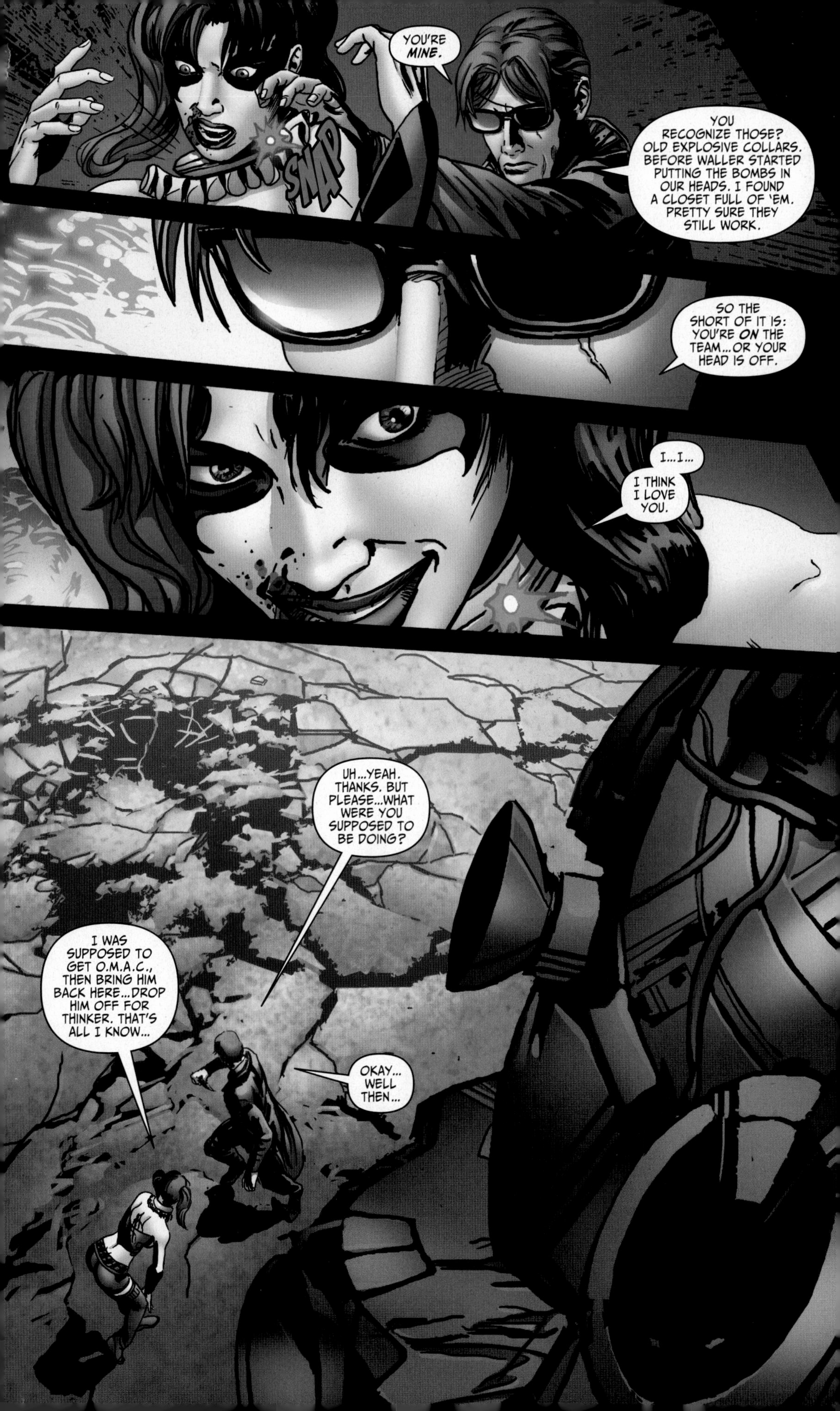

SNAP
YOU'RE MINE.
YOU RECOGNIZE THOSE? OLD EXPLOSIVE COLLARS. BEFORE WALLER STARTED PUTTING THE BOMBS IN OUR HEADS. I FOUND A CLOSET FULL OF 'EM. PRETTY SURE THEY STILL WORK.
SO THE SHORT OF IT IS: YOU'RE ON THE TEAM...OR YOUR HEAD IS OFF.
I...I...
I THINK I LOVE YOU.
UH...YEAH. THANKS. BUT PLEASE...WHAT WERE YOU SUPPOSED TO BE DOING?
I WAS SUPPOSED TO GET O.M.A.C., THEN BRING HIM BACK HERE...DROP HIM OFF FOR THINKER. THAT'S ALL I KNOW...
OKAY... WELL THEN...

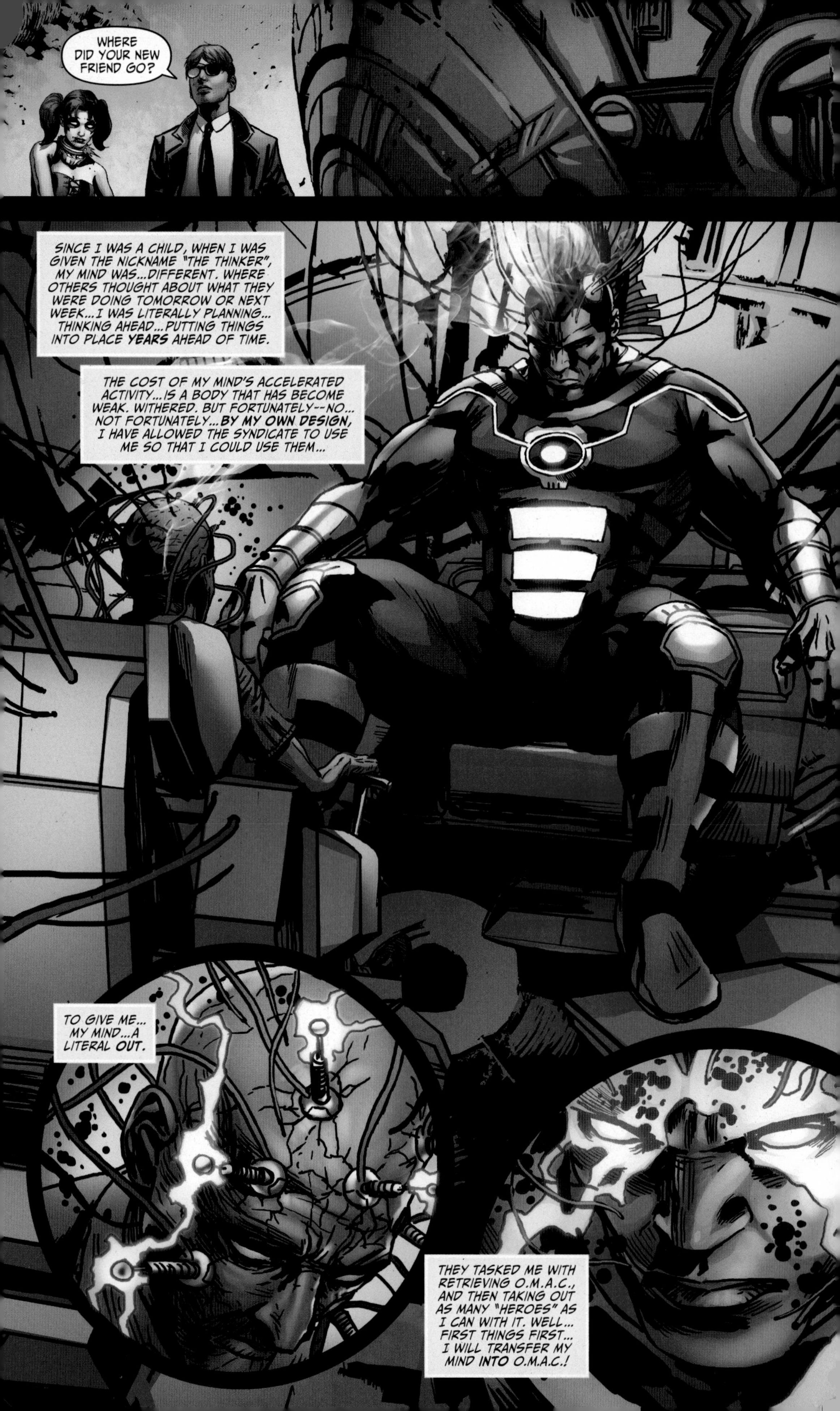
WHERE DID YOUR NEW FRIEND GO?
SINCE I WAS A CHILD, WHEN I WAS GIVEN THE NICKNAME "THE THINKER", MY MIND WAS...DIFFERENT. WHERE OTHERS THOUGHT ABOUT WHAT THEY WERE DOING TOMORROW OR NEXT WEEK...I WAS LITERALLY PLANNING... THINKING AHEAD...PUTTING THINGS INTO PLACE **YEARS** AHEAD OF TIME.
THE COST OF MY MIND'S ACCELERATED ACTIVITY...IS A BODY THAT HAS BECOME WEAK. WITHERED. BUT FORTUNATELY--NO... NOT FORTUNATELY...**BY MY OWN DESIGN**, I HAVE ALLOWED THE SYNDICATE TO USE ME SO THAT I COULD USE THEM...
TO GIVE ME... MY MIND...A LITERAL **OUT**.
THEY TASKED ME WITH RETRIEVING O.M.A.C., AND THEN TAKING OUT AS MANY "HEROES" AS I CAN WITH IT. WELL... FIRST THINGS FIRST... I WILL TRANSFER MY MIND **INTO** O.M.A.C.!

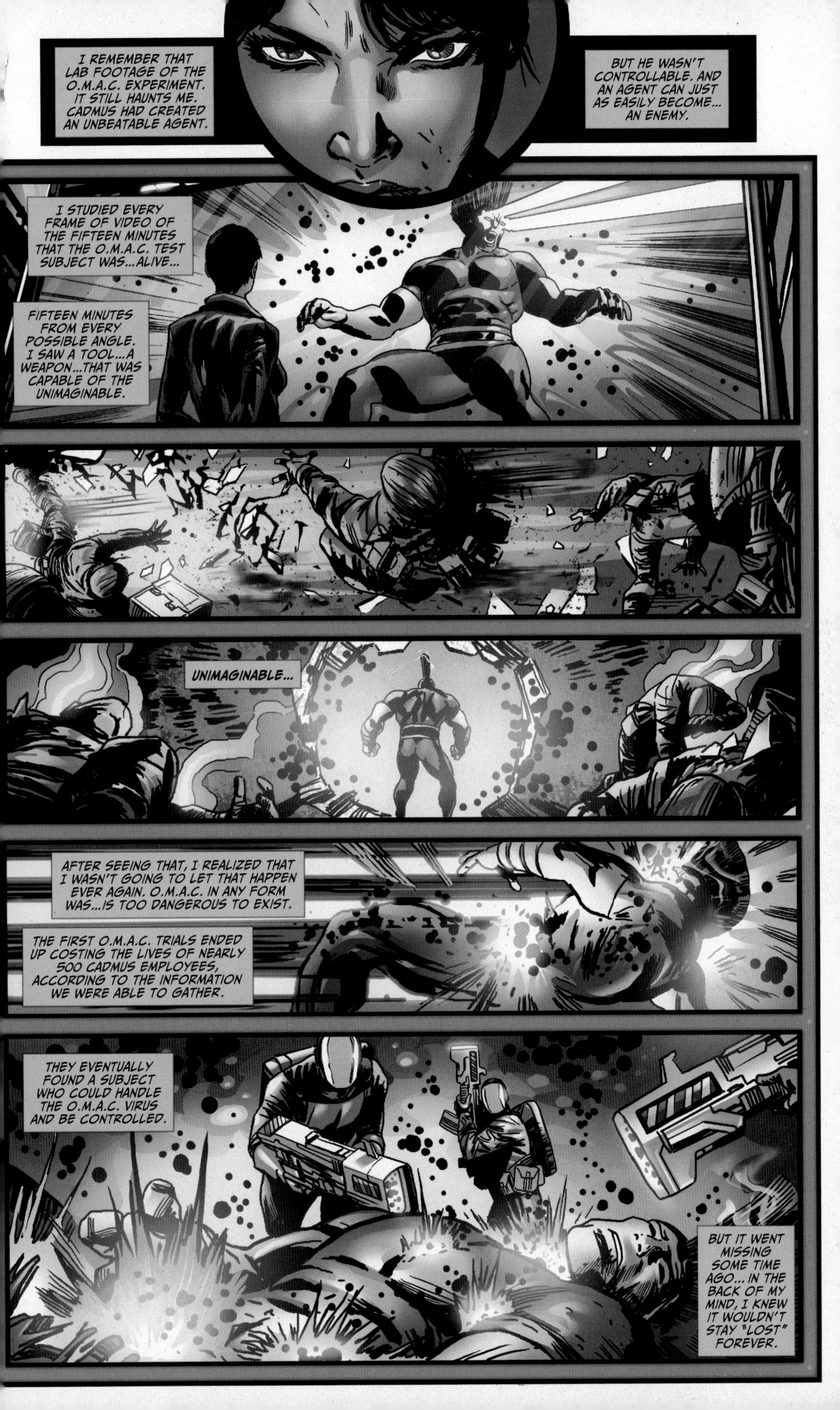
I REMEMBER THAT LAB FOOTAGE OF THE O.M.A.C. EXPERIMENT. IT STILL HAUNTS ME. CADMUS HAD CREATED AN UNBEATABLE AGENT.
BUT HE WASN'T CONTROLLABLE. AND AN AGENT CAN JUST AS EASILY BECOME... AN ENEMY.
I STUDIED EVERY FRAME OF VIDEO OF THE FIFTEEN MINUTES THAT THE O.M.A.C. TEST SUBJECT WAS...ALIVE...
FIFTEEN MINUTES FROM EVERY POSSIBLE ANGLE. I SAW A TOOL...A WEAPON...THAT WAS CAPABLE OF THE UNIMAGINABLE.
UNIMAGINABLE...
AFTER SEEING THAT, I REALIZED THAT I WASN'T GOING TO LET THAT HAPPEN EVER AGAIN. O.M.A.C. IN ANY FORM WAS...IS TOO DANGEROUS TO EXIST.
THE FIRST O.M.A.C. TRIALS ENDED UP COSTING THE LIVES OF NEARLY 500 CADMUS EMPLOYEES, ACCORDING TO THE INFORMATION WE WERE ABLE TO GATHER.
THEY EVENTUALLY FOUND A SUBJECT WHO COULD HANDLE THE O.M.A.C. VIRUS AND BE CONTROLLED.
BUT IT WENT MISSING SOME TIME AGO... IN THE BACK OF MY MIND, I KNEW IT WOULDN'T STAY "LOST" FOREVER.

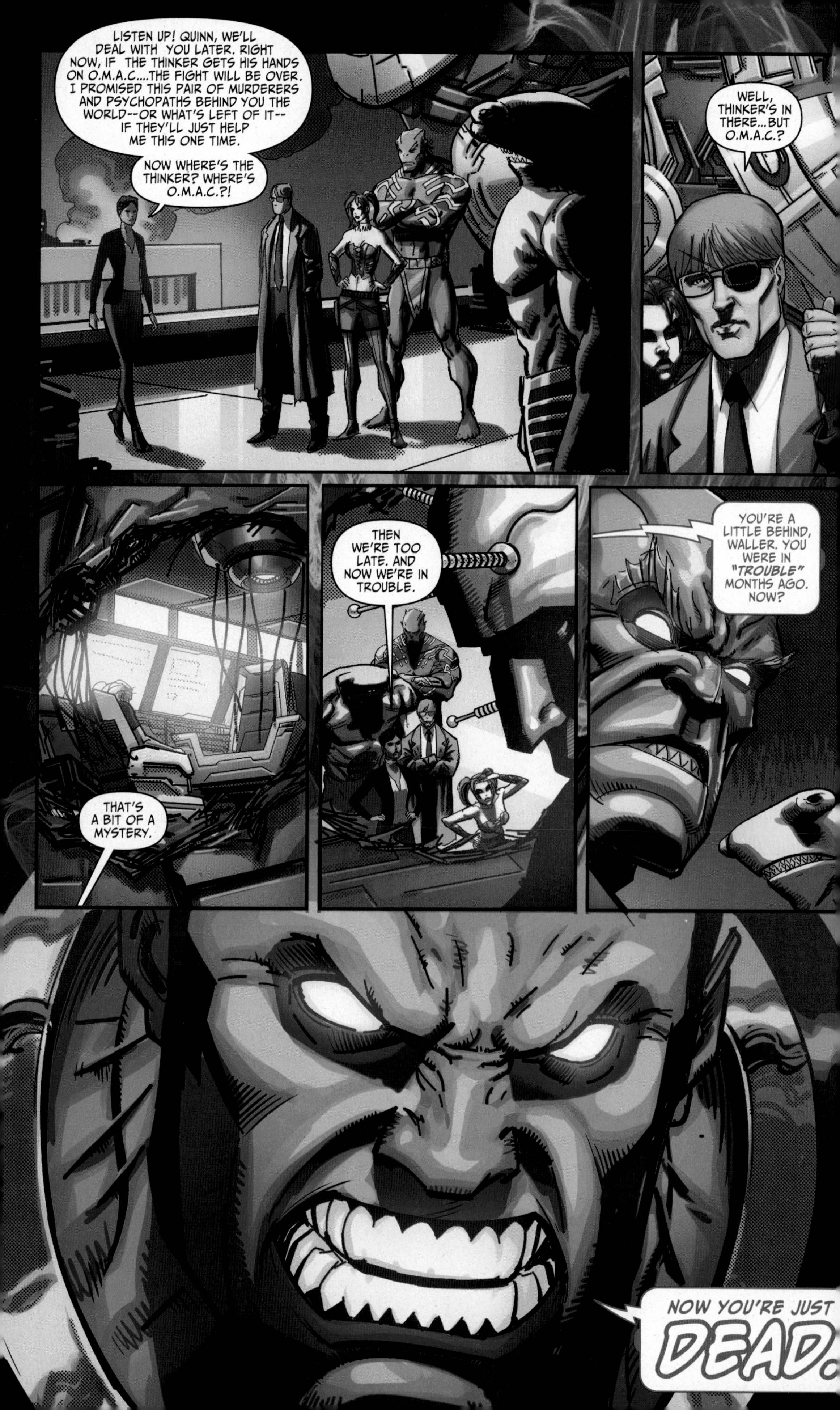
LISTEN UP! QUINN, WE'LL DEAL WITH YOU LATER. RIGHT NOW, IF THE THINKER GETS HIS HANDS ON O.M.A.C....THE FIGHT WILL BE OVER. I PROMISED THIS PAIR OF MURDERERS AND PSYCHOPATHS BEHIND YOU THE WORLD--OR WHAT'S LEFT OF IT--IF THEY'LL JUST HELP ME THIS ONE TIME.
NOW WHERE'S THE THINKER? WHERE'S O.M.A.C.?!
WELL, THINKER'S IN THERE...BUT O.M.A.C.?
THAT'S A BIT OF A MYSTERY.
THEN WE'RE TOO LATE. AND NOW WE'RE IN TROUBLE.
YOU'RE A LITTLE BEHIND, WALLER. YOU WERE IN "TROUBLE" MONTHS AGO. NOW?
NOW YOU'RE JUST
DEAD.

BRASHHHH

...AND HE'S RIGHT. EVERYONE ELSE AROUND ME HASN'T BEEN IN MY LEAGUE. BUT THE THINKER-- HE'S THE FIRST OF THESE "VILLAINS" WHO HAS ACTUALLY BEEN MY MATCH. AND NOW O.M.A.C....I SWORE I WOULD DIE BEFORE I LET SOMETHING THAT POWERFUL FALL INTO THE WRONG HANDS...

AND I'M AFRAID I WAS RIGHT...

I'M GOING TO DIE...

AND O.M.A.C....

...IS GOING TO KILL US ALL.

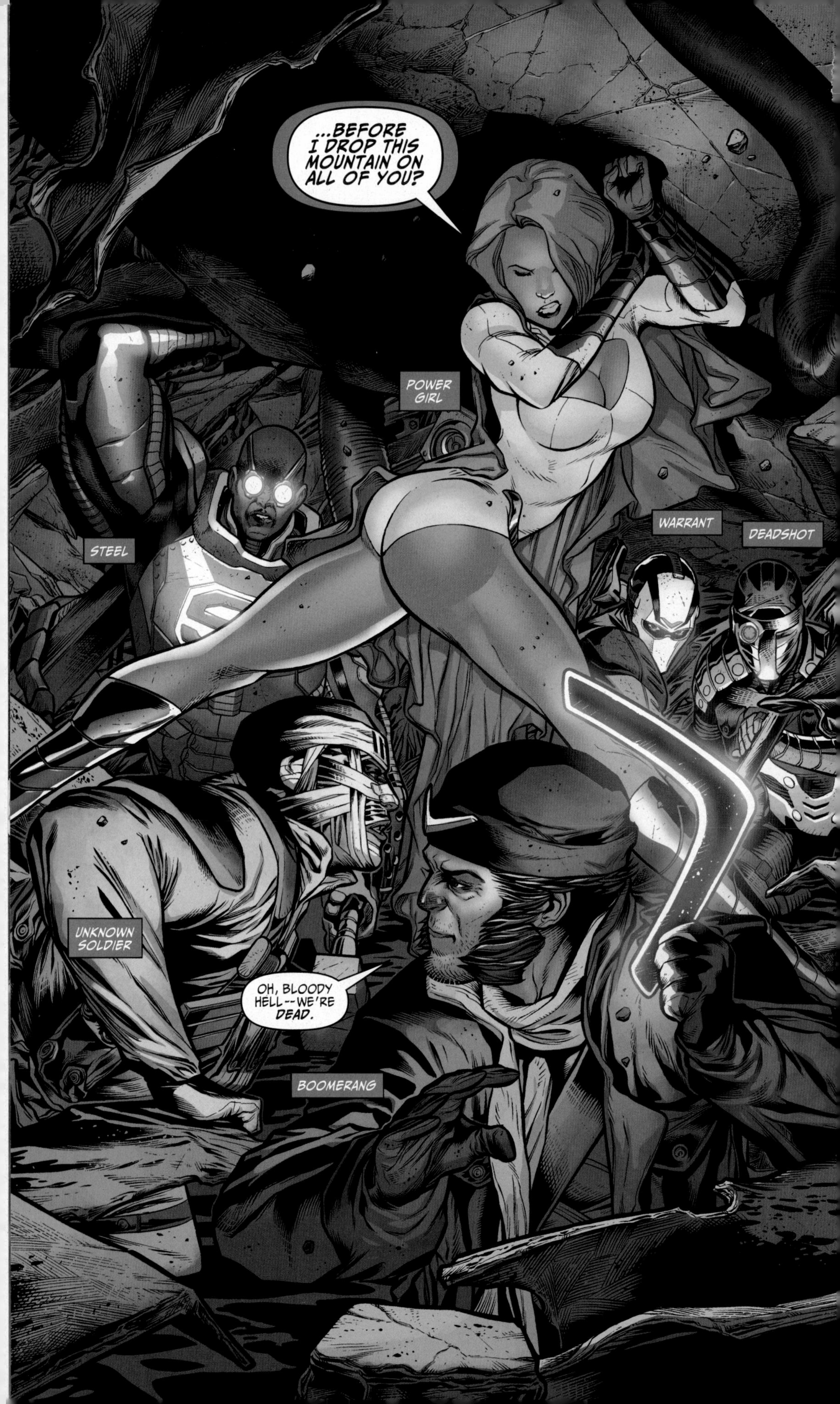
...BEFORE I DROP THIS MOUNTAIN ON ALL OF YOU?
POWER GIRL
STEEL
WARRANT
DEADSHOT
UNKNOWN SOLDIER
OH, BLOODY HELL--WE'RE DEAD.
BOOMERANG

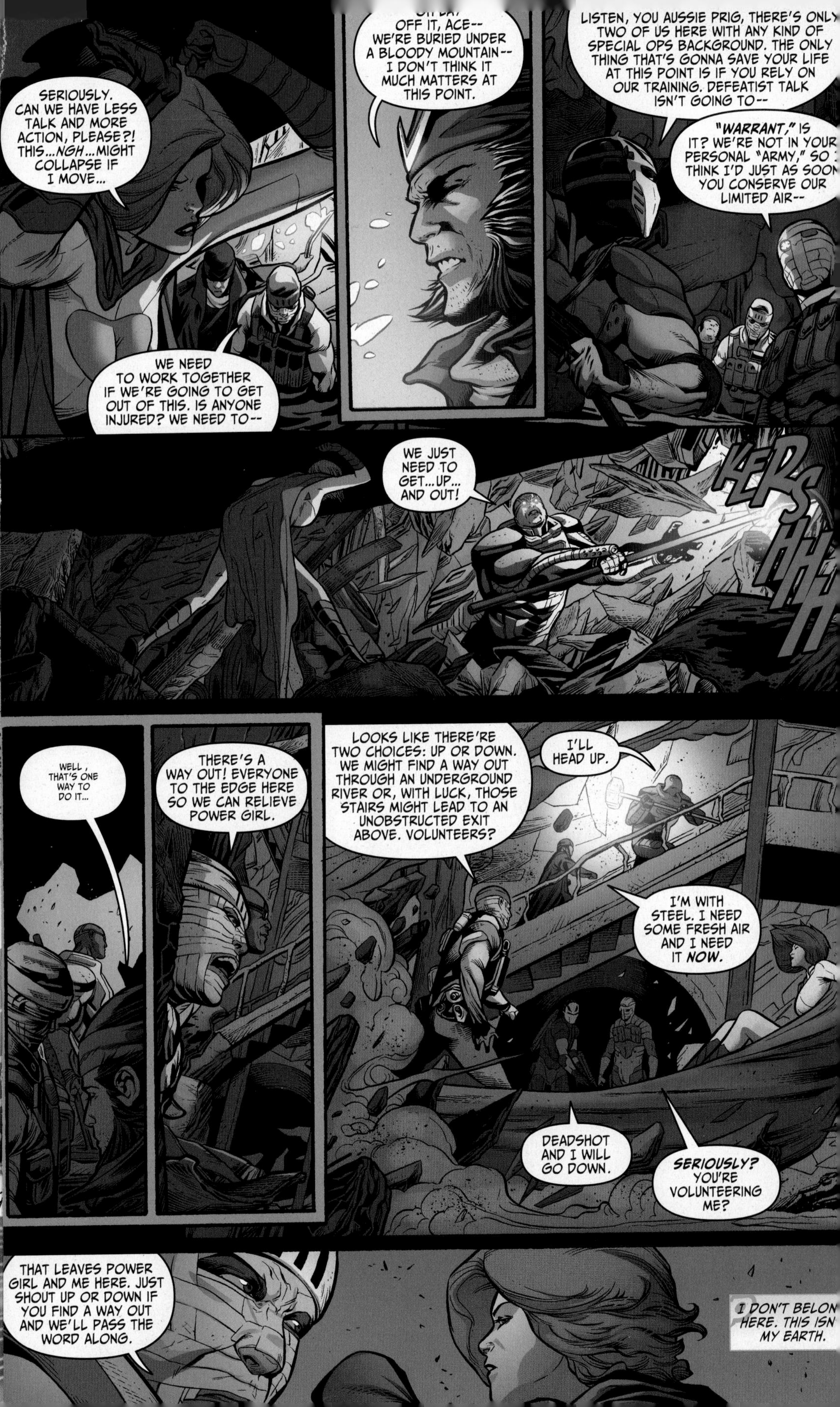
SERIOUSLY. CAN WE HAVE LESS TALK AND MORE ACTION, PLEASE?! THIS...NGH...MIGHT COLLAPSE IF I MOVE...
WE NEED TO WORK TOGETHER IF WE'RE GOING TO GET OUT OF THIS. IS ANYONE INJURED? WE NEED TO--
OFF IT, ACE-- WE'RE BURIED UNDER A BLOODY MOUNTAIN-- I DON'T THINK IT MUCH MATTERS AT THIS POINT.
LISTEN, YOU AUSSIE PRIG, THERE'S ONLY TWO OF US HERE WITH ANY KIND OF SPECIAL OPS BACKGROUND. THE ONLY THING THAT'S GONNA SAVE YOUR LIFE AT THIS POINT IS IF YOU RELY ON OUR TRAINING. DEFEATIST TALK ISN'T GOING TO--
"WARRANT," IS IT? WE'RE NOT IN YOUR PERSONAL "ARMY," SO I THINK I'D JUST AS SOON YOU CONSERVE OUR LIMITED AIR--
WE JUST NEED TO GET...UP... AND OUT!
KERSHHHH
WELL, THAT'S ONE WAY TO DO IT...
THERE'S A WAY OUT! EVERYONE TO THE EDGE HERE SO WE CAN RELIEVE POWER GIRL.
LOOKS LIKE THERE'RE TWO CHOICES: UP OR DOWN. WE MIGHT FIND A WAY OUT THROUGH AN UNDERGROUND RIVER OR, WITH LUCK, THOSE STAIRS MIGHT LEAD TO AN UNOBSTRUCTED EXIT ABOVE. VOLUNTEERS?
I'LL HEAD UP.
I'M WITH STEEL. I NEED SOME FRESH AIR AND I NEED IT NOW.
DEADSHOT AND I WILL GO DOWN.
SERIOUSLY? YOU'RE VOLUNTEERING ME?
THAT LEAVES POWER GIRL AND ME HERE. JUST SHOUT UP OR DOWN IF YOU FIND A WAY OUT AND WE'LL PASS THE WORD ALONG.
I DON'T BELON HERE. THIS ISN MY EARTH.

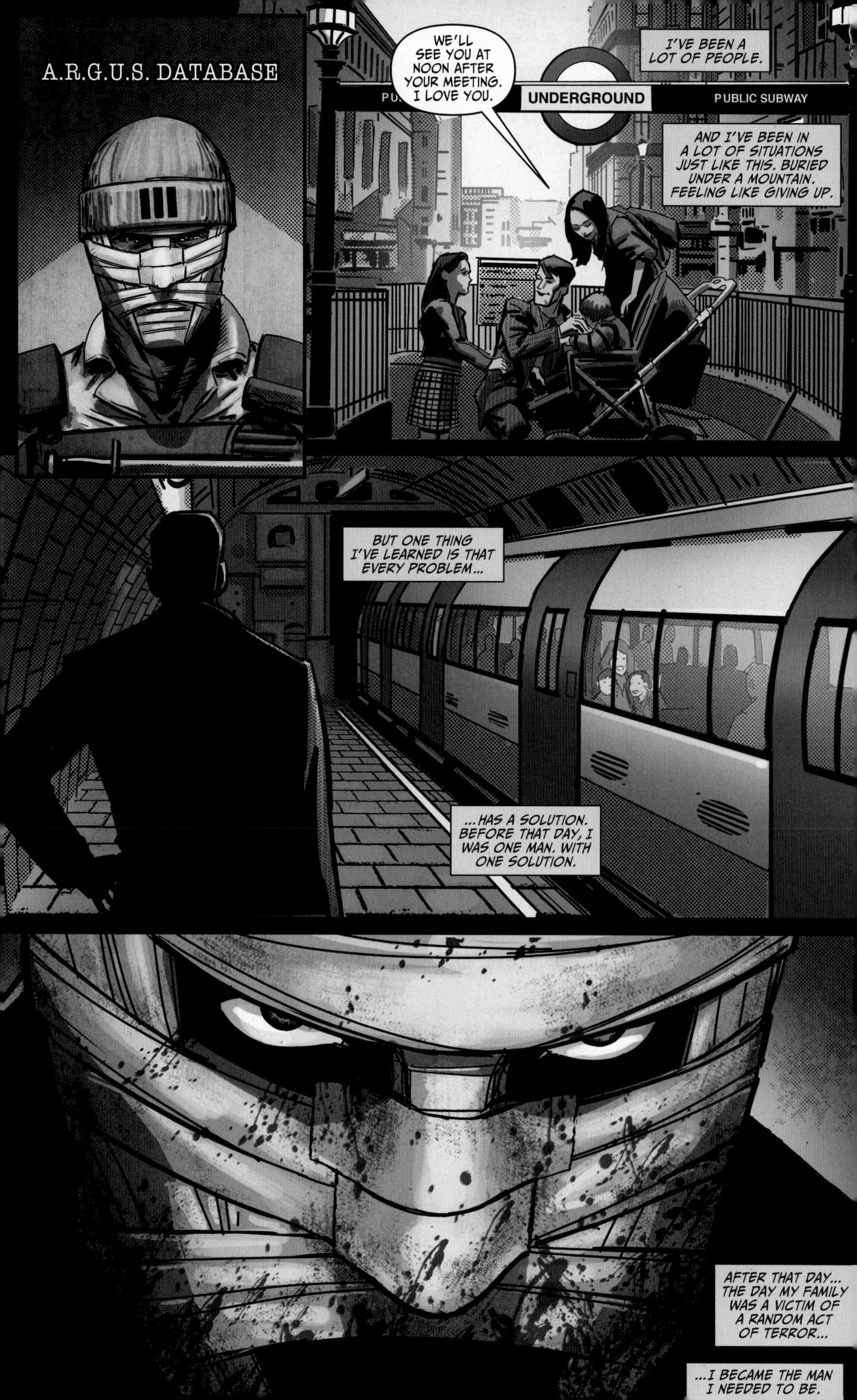
A.R.G.U.S. DATABASE
WE'LL SEE YOU AT NOON AFTER YOUR MEETING. I LOVE YOU.
UNDERGROUND
PUBLIC SUBWAY
I'VE BEEN A LOT OF PEOPLE.
AND I'VE BEEN IN A LOT OF SITUATIONS JUST LIKE THIS. BURIED UNDER A MOUNTAIN. FEELING LIKE GIVING UP.
BUT ONE THING I'VE LEARNED IS THAT EVERY PROBLEM...
...HAS A SOLUTION. BEFORE THAT DAY, I WAS ONE MAN. WITH ONE SOLUTION.
AFTER THAT DAY... THE DAY MY FAMILY WAS A VICTIM OF A RANDOM ACT OF TERROR...
...I BECAME THE MAN I NEEDED TO BE.

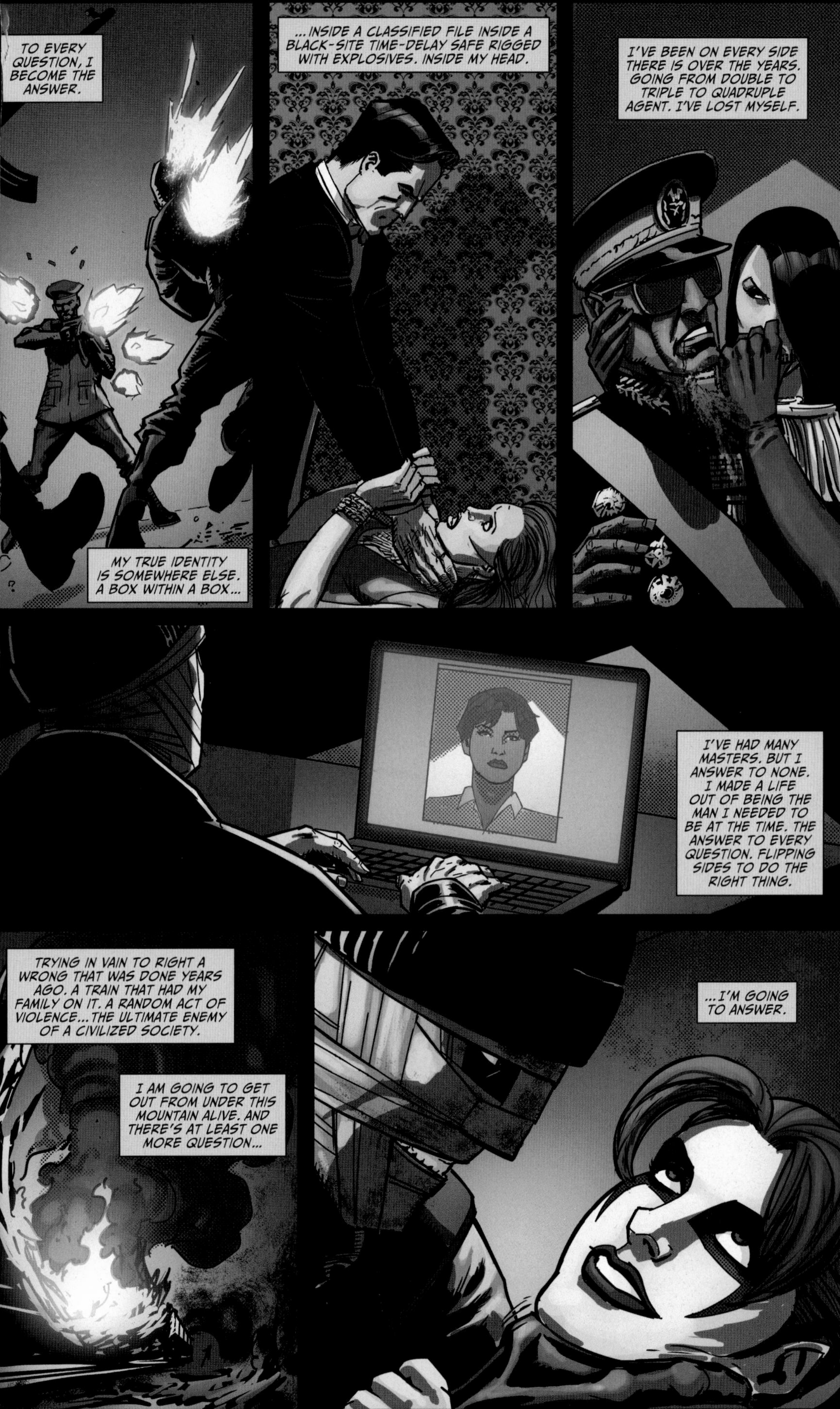
TO EVERY QUESTION, I BECOME THE ANSWER.
MY TRUE IDENTITY IS SOMEWHERE ELSE. A BOX WITHIN A BOX...
...INSIDE A CLASSIFIED FILE INSIDE A BLACK-SITE TIME-DELAY SAFE RIGGED WITH EXPLOSIVES. INSIDE MY HEAD.
I'VE BEEN ON EVERY SIDE THERE IS OVER THE YEARS. GOING FROM DOUBLE TO TRIPLE TO QUADRUPLE AGENT. I'VE LOST MYSELF.
I'VE HAD MANY MASTERS. BUT I ANSWER TO NONE. I MADE A LIFE OUT OF BEING THE MAN I NEEDED TO BE AT THE TIME. THE ANSWER TO EVERY QUESTION. FLIPPING SIDES TO DO THE RIGHT THING.
TRYING IN VAIN TO RIGHT A WRONG THAT WAS DONE YEARS AGO. A TRAIN THAT HAD MY FAMILY ON IT. A RANDOM ACT OF VIOLENCE...THE ULTIMATE ENEMY OF A CIVILIZED SOCIETY.
I AM GOING TO GET OUT FROM UNDER THIS MOUNTAIN ALIVE. AND THERE'S AT LEAST ONE MORE QUESTION...
...I'M GOING TO ANSWER.

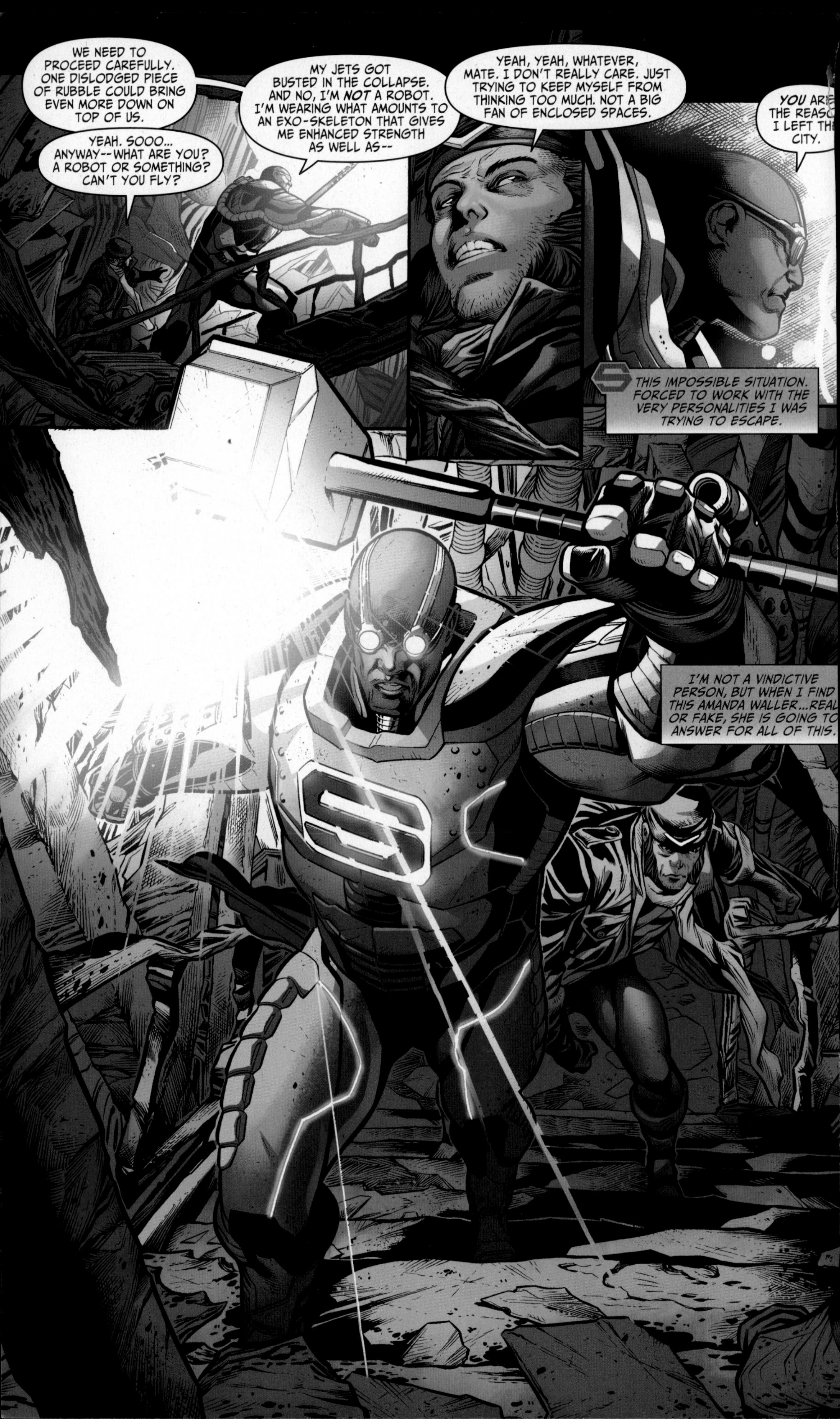
WE NEED TO PROCEED CAREFULLY. ONE DISLODGED PIECE OF RUBBLE COULD BRING EVEN MORE DOWN ON TOP OF US.
YEAH. SOOO... ANYWAY--WHAT ARE YOU? A ROBOT OR SOMETHING? CAN'T YOU FLY?
MY JETS GOT BUSTED IN THE COLLAPSE. AND NO, I'M *NOT* A ROBOT. I'M WEARING WHAT AMOUNTS TO AN EXO-SKELETON THAT GIVES ME ENHANCED STRENGTH AS WELL AS--
YEAH, YEAH, WHATEVER, MATE. I DON'T REALLY CARE. JUST TRYING TO KEEP MYSELF FROM THINKING TOO MUCH. NOT A BIG FAN OF ENCLOSED SPACES.
YOU ARE THE REASO I LEFT TH CITY.
THIS IMPOSSIBLE SITUATION. FORCED TO WORK WITH THE VERY PERSONALITIES I WAS TRYING TO ESCAPE.
I'M NOT A VINDICTIVE PERSON, BUT WHEN I FIND THIS AMANDA WALLER...REAL OR FAKE, SHE IS GOING TO ANSWER FOR ALL OF THIS.

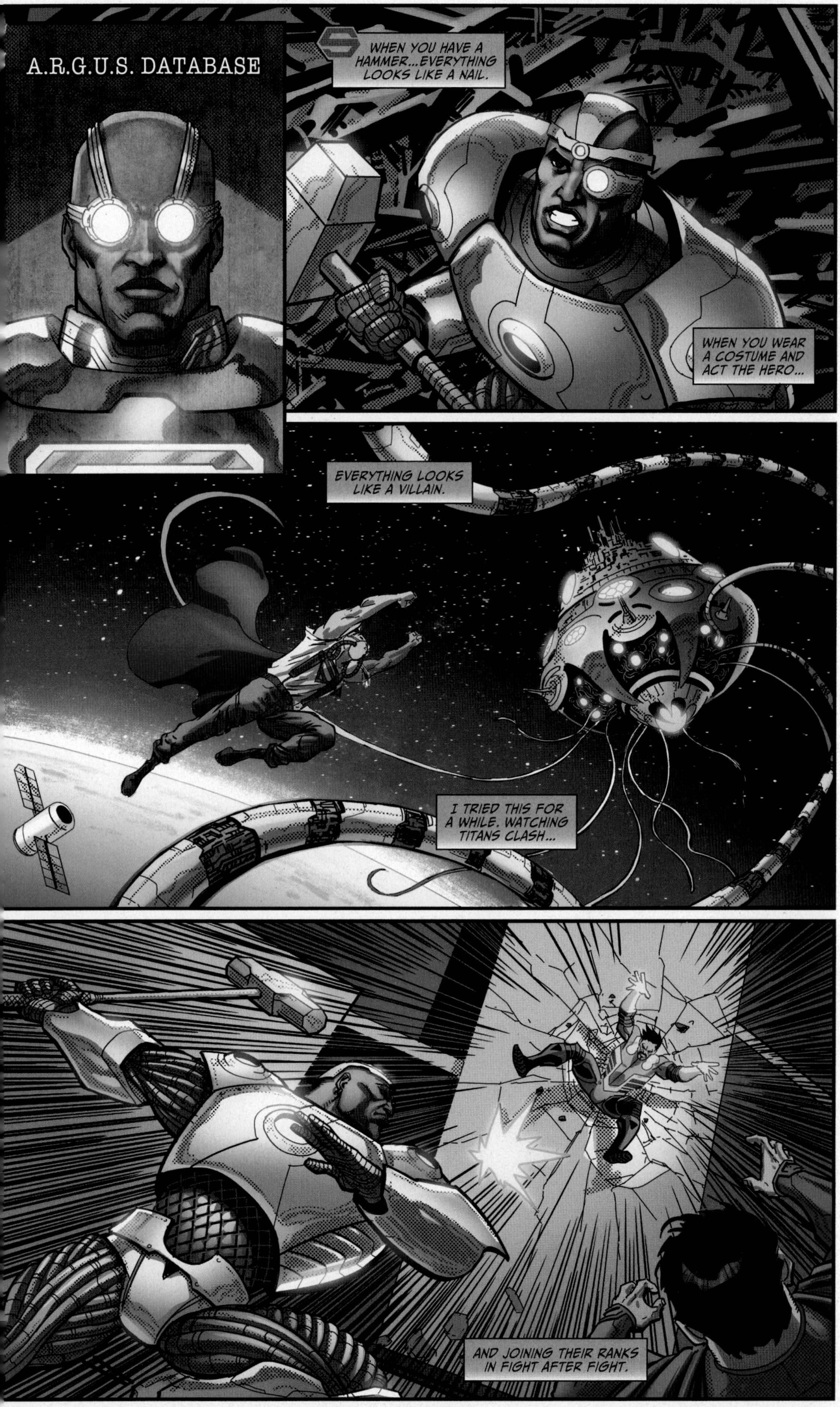
A.R.G.U.S. DATABASE
WHEN YOU HAVE A HAMMER...EVERYTHING LOOKS LIKE A NAIL.
WHEN YOU WEAR A COSTUME AND ACT THE HERO...
EVERYTHING LOOKS LIKE A VILLAIN.
I TRIED THIS FOR A WHILE. WATCHING TITANS CLASH...
AND JOINING THEIR RANKS IN FIGHT AFTER FIGHT.

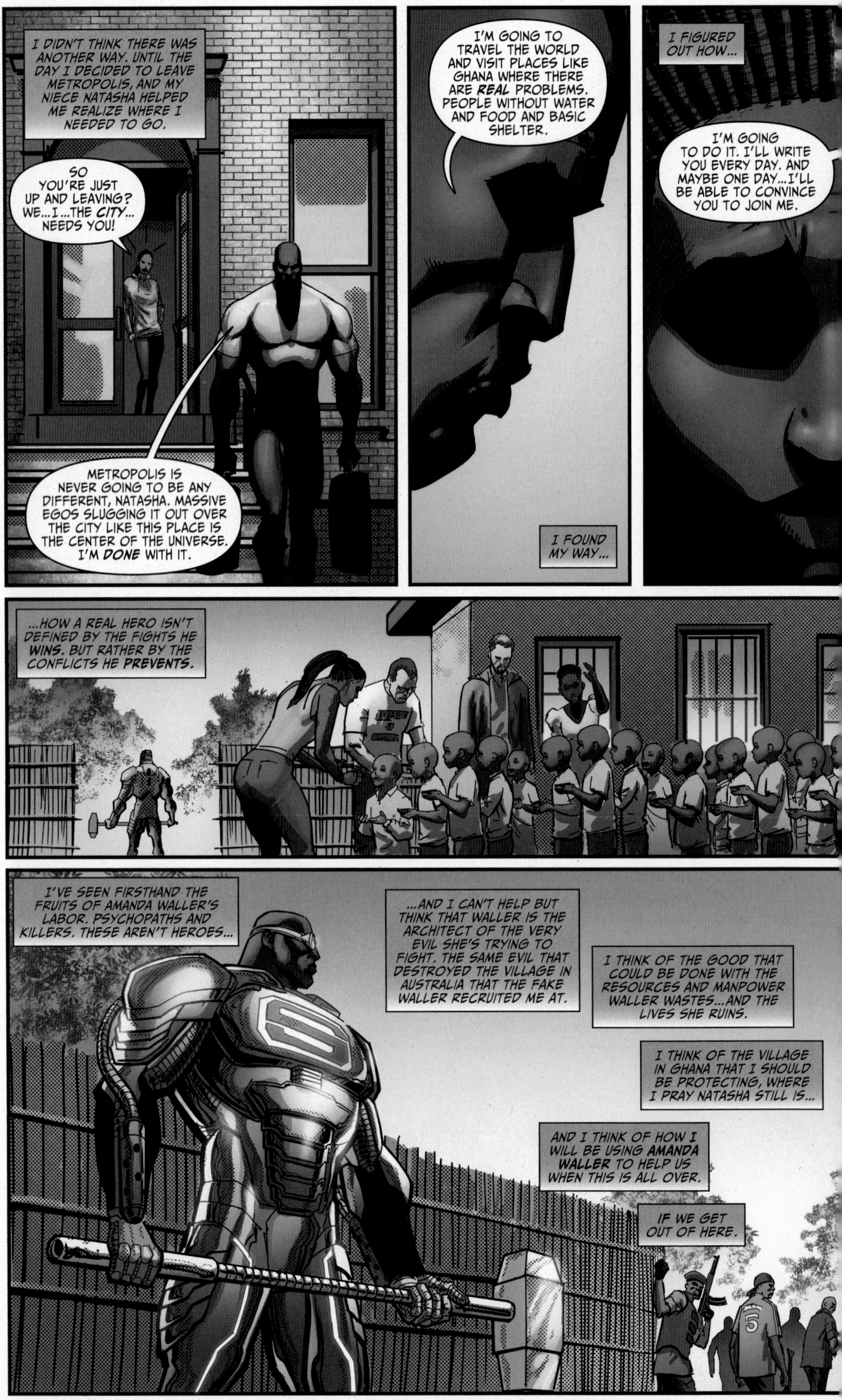
I DIDN'T THINK THERE WAS ANOTHER WAY. UNTIL THE DAY I DECIDED TO LEAVE METROPOLIS, AND MY NIECE NATASHA HELPED ME REALIZE WHERE I NEEDED TO GO.
SO YOU'RE JUST UP AND LEAVING? WE...I...THE CITY... NEEDS YOU!
METROPOLIS IS NEVER GOING TO BE ANY DIFFERENT, NATASHA. MASSIVE EGOS SLUGGING IT OUT OVER THE CITY LIKE THIS PLACE IS THE CENTER OF THE UNIVERSE. I'M DONE WITH IT.
I'M GOING TO TRAVEL THE WORLD AND VISIT PLACES LIKE GHANA WHERE THERE ARE REAL PROBLEMS. PEOPLE WITHOUT WATER AND FOOD AND BASIC SHELTER.
I FOUND MY WAY...
I FIGURED OUT HOW...
I'M GOING TO DO IT. I'LL WRITE YOU EVERY DAY. AND MAYBE ONE DAY...I'LL BE ABLE TO CONVINCE YOU TO JOIN ME.
...HOW A REAL HERO ISN'T DEFINED BY THE FIGHTS HE WINS. BUT RATHER BY THE CONFLICTS HE PREVENTS.
I'VE SEEN FIRSTHAND THE FRUITS OF AMANDA WALLER'S LABOR. PSYCHOPATHS AND KILLERS. THESE AREN'T HEROES...
...AND I CAN'T HELP BUT THINK THAT WALLER IS THE ARCHITECT OF THE VERY EVIL SHE'S TRYING TO FIGHT. THE SAME EVIL THAT DESTROYED THE VILLAGE IN AUSTRALIA THAT THE FAKE WALLER RECRUITED ME AT.
I THINK OF THE GOOD THAT COULD BE DONE WITH THE RESOURCES AND MANPOWER WALLER WASTES...AND THE LIVES SHE RUINS.
I THINK OF THE VILLAGE IN GHANA THAT I SHOULD BE PROTECTING, WHERE I PRAY NATASHA STILL IS...
AND I THINK OF HOW I WILL BE USING AMANDA WALLER TO HELP US WHEN THIS IS ALL OVER.
IF WE GET OUT OF HERE.

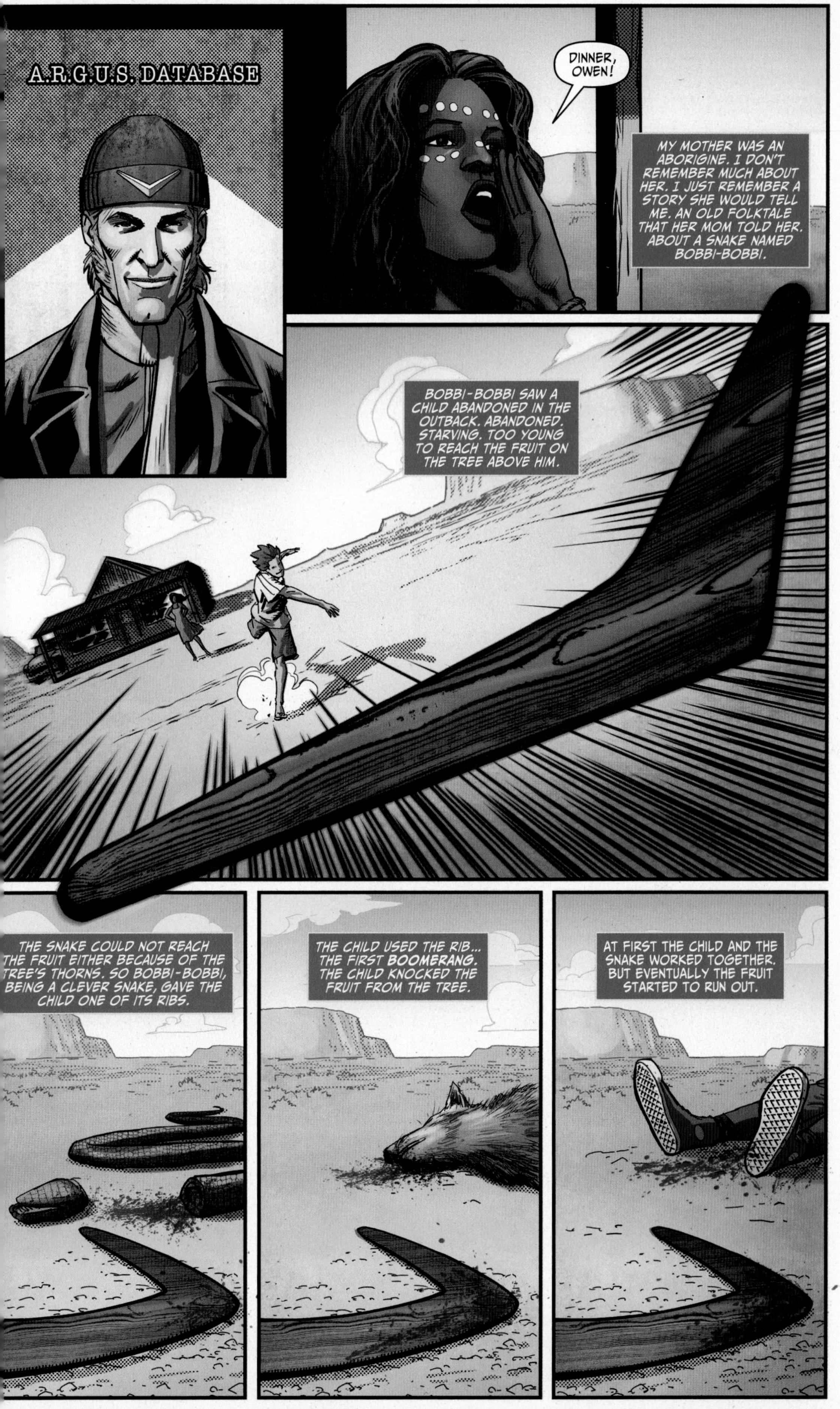
A.R.G.U.S. DATABASE
DINNER, OWEN!
MY MOTHER WAS AN ABORIGINE. I DON'T REMEMBER MUCH ABOUT HER. I JUST REMEMBER A STORY SHE WOULD TELL ME. AN OLD FOLKTALE THAT HER MOM TOLD HER. ABOUT A SNAKE NAMED BOBBI-BOBBI.
BOBBI-BOBBI SAW A CHILD ABANDONED IN THE OUTBACK. ABANDONED. STARVING. TOO YOUNG TO REACH THE FRUIT ON THE TREE ABOVE HIM.
THE SNAKE COULD NOT REACH THE FRUIT EITHER BECAUSE OF THE TREE'S THORNS. SO BOBBI-BOBBI, BEING A CLEVER SNAKE, GAVE THE CHILD ONE OF ITS RIBS.
THE CHILD USED THE RIB... THE FIRST **BOOMERANG.** THE CHILD KNOCKED THE FRUIT FROM THE TREE.
AT FIRST THE CHILD AND THE SNAKE WORKED TOGETHER. BUT EVENTUALLY THE FRUIT STARTED TO RUN OUT.

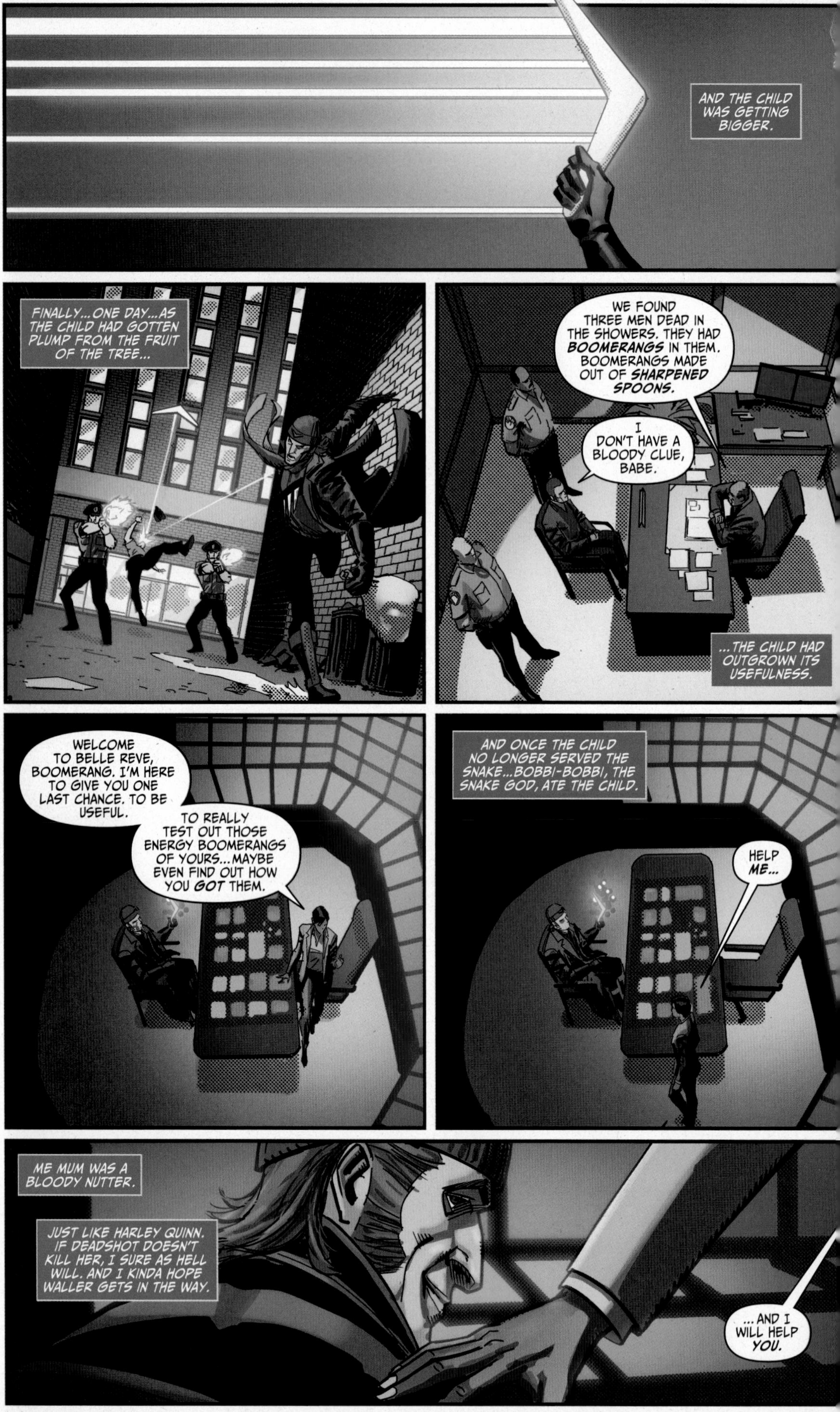
AND THE CHILD WAS GETTING BIGGER.
FINALLY...ONE DAY...AS THE CHILD HAD GOTTEN PLUMP FROM THE FRUIT OF THE TREE...
WE FOUND THREE MEN DEAD IN THE SHOWERS. THEY HAD BOOMERANGS IN THEM. BOOMERANGS MADE OUT OF SHARPENED SPOONS.
I DON'T HAVE A BLOODY CLUE, BABE.
...THE CHILD HAD OUTGROWN ITS USEFULNESS.
WELCOME TO BELLE REVE, BOOMERANG. I'M HERE TO GIVE YOU ONE LAST CHANCE. TO BE USEFUL.
TO REALLY TEST OUT THOSE ENERGY BOOMERANGS OF YOURS...MAYBE EVEN FIND OUT HOW YOU GOT THEM.
AND ONCE THE CHILD NO LONGER SERVED THE SNAKE...BOBBI-BOBBI, THE SNAKE GOD, ATE THE CHILD.
HELP ME...
ME MUM WAS A BLOODY NUTTER.
JUST LIKE HARLEY QUINN. IF DEADSHOT DOESN'T KILL HER, I SURE AS HELL WILL. AND I KINDA HOPE WALLER GETS IN THE WAY.
...AND I WILL HELP YOU.

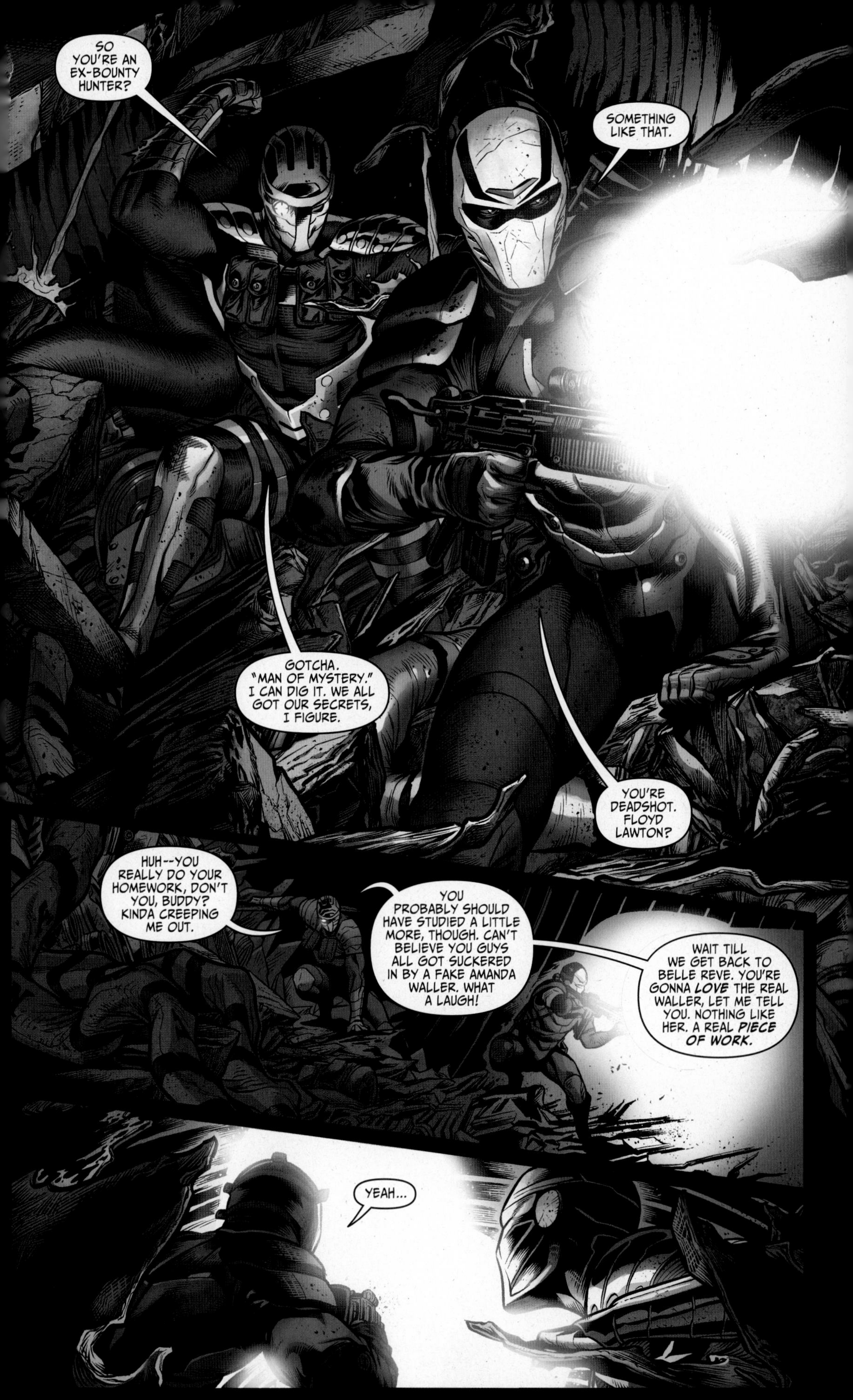
SO YOU'RE AN EX-BOUNTY HUNTER?
SOMETHING LIKE THAT.
GOTCHA. "MAN OF MYSTERY." I CAN DIG IT. WE ALL GOT OUR SECRETS, I FIGURE.
YOU'RE DEADSHOT. FLOYD LAWTON?
HUH--YOU REALLY DO YOUR HOMEWORK, DON'T YOU, BUDDY? KINDA CREEPING ME OUT.
YOU PROBABLY SHOULD HAVE STUDIED A LITTLE MORE, THOUGH. CAN'T BELIEVE YOU GUYS ALL GOT SUCKERED IN BY A FAKE AMANDA WALLER. WHAT A LAUGH!
WAIT TILL WE GET BACK TO BELLE REVE. YOU'RE GONNA *LOVE* THE REAL WALLER, LET ME TELL YOU. NOTHING LIKE HER. A REAL *PIECE OF WORK.*
YEAH...

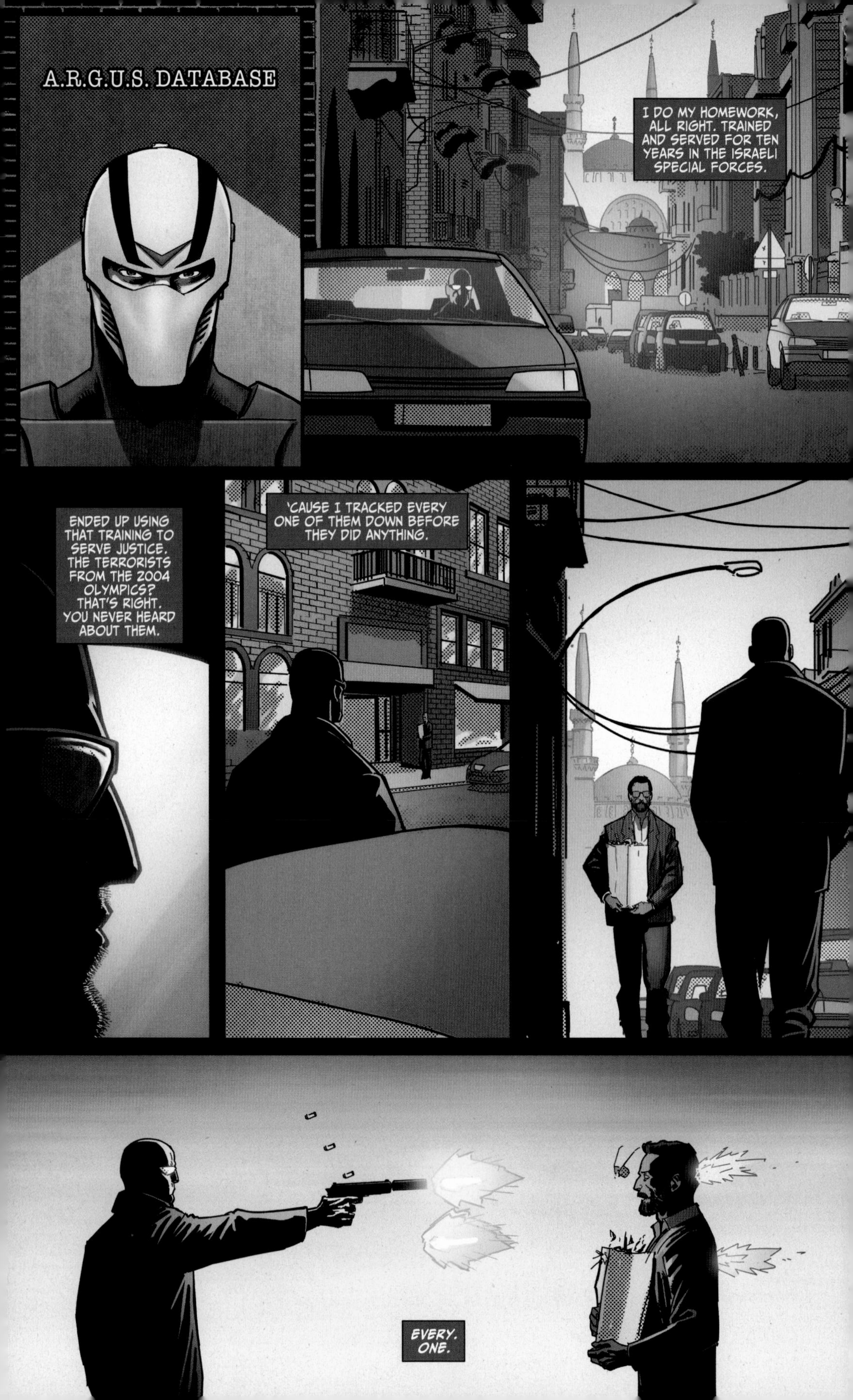
A.R.G.U.S. DATABASE
I DO MY HOMEWORK, ALL RIGHT. TRAINED AND SERVED FOR TEN YEARS IN THE ISRAELI SPECIAL FORCES.
ENDED UP USING THAT TRAINING TO SERVE JUSTICE. THE TERRORISTS FROM THE 2004 OLYMPICS? THAT'S RIGHT. YOU NEVER HEARD ABOUT THEM.
'CAUSE I TRACKED EVERY ONE OF THEM DOWN BEFORE THEY DID ANYTHING.
EVERY. ONE.

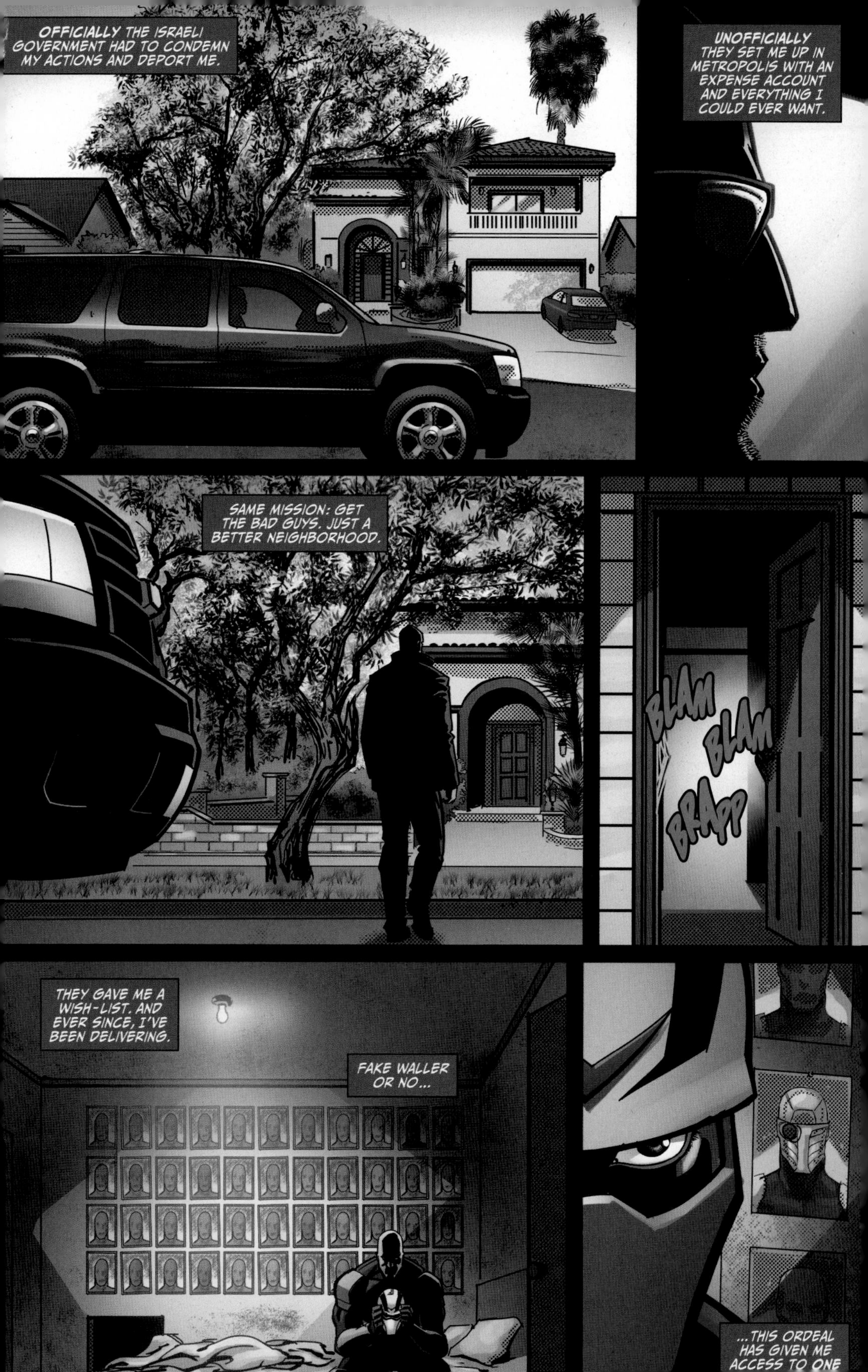
OFFICIALLY THE ISRAELI GOVERNMENT HAD TO CONDEMN MY ACTIONS AND DEPORT ME.
UNOFFICIALLY THEY SET ME UP IN METROPOLIS WITH AN EXPENSE ACCOUNT AND EVERYTHING I COULD EVER WANT.
SAME MISSION: GET THE BAD GUYS. JUST A BETTER NEIGHBORHOOD.
BLAM
BLAM
BRAPP
THEY GAVE ME A WISH-LIST. AND EVER SINCE, I'VE BEEN DELIVERING.
FAKE WALLER OR NO...
...THIS ORDEAL HAS GIVEN ME ACCESS TO ONE

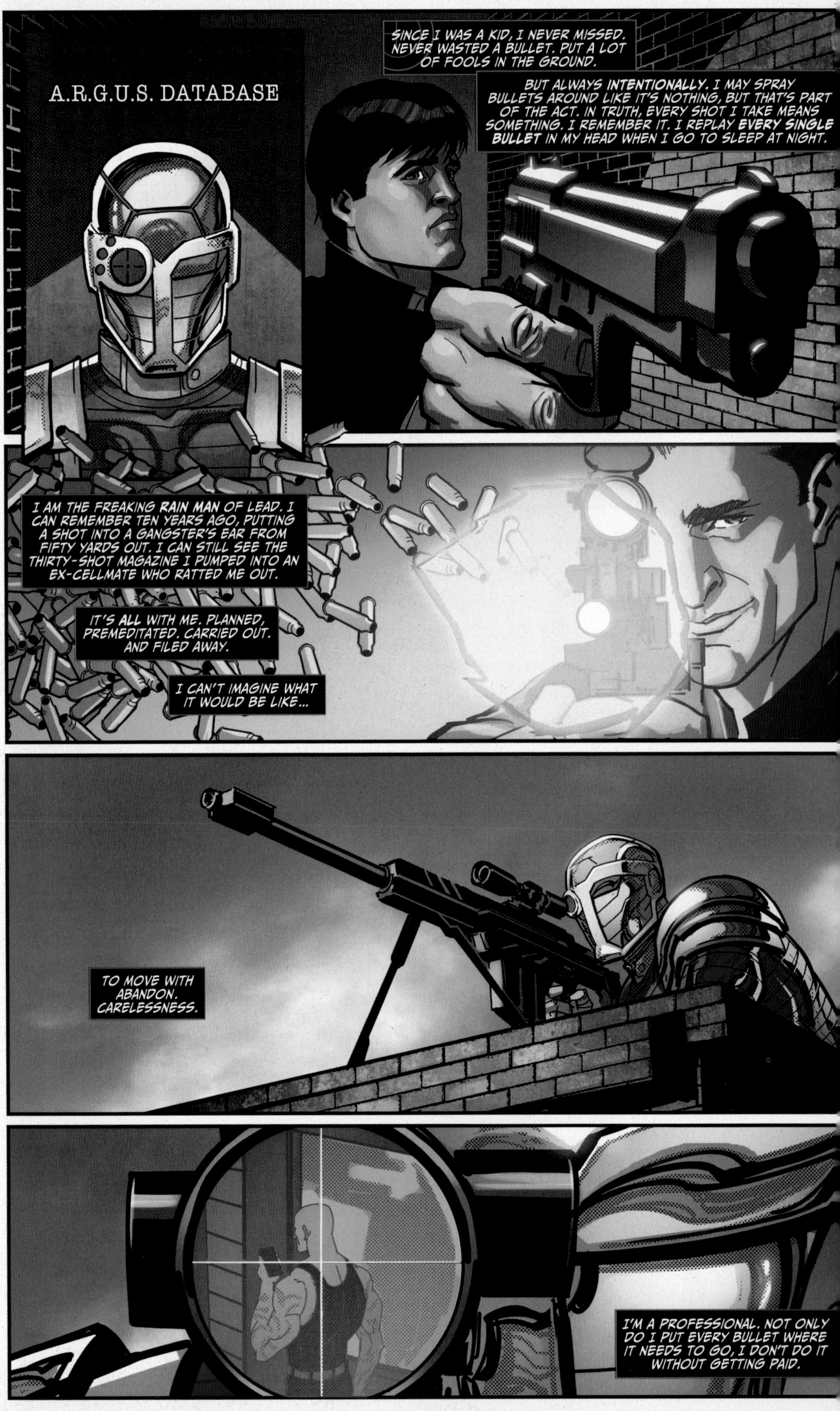
A.R.G.U.S. DATABASE
SINCE I WAS A KID, I NEVER MISSED. NEVER WASTED A BULLET. PUT A LOT OF FOOLS IN THE GROUND.
BUT ALWAYS INTENTIONALLY. I MAY SPRAY BULLETS AROUND LIKE IT'S NOTHING, BUT THAT'S PART OF THE ACT. IN TRUTH, EVERY SHOT I TAKE MEANS SOMETHING. I REMEMBER IT. I REPLAY EVERY SINGLE BULLET IN MY HEAD WHEN I GO TO SLEEP AT NIGHT.
I AM THE FREAKING RAIN MAN OF LEAD. I CAN REMEMBER TEN YEARS AGO, PUTTING A SHOT INTO A GANGSTER'S EAR FROM FIFTY YARDS OUT. I CAN STILL SEE THE THIRTY-SHOT MAGAZINE I PUMPED INTO AN EX-CELLMATE WHO RATTED ME OUT.
IT'S ALL WITH ME. PLANNED, PREMEDITATED. CARRIED OUT. AND FILED AWAY.
I CAN'T IMAGINE WHAT IT WOULD BE LIKE...
TO MOVE WITH ABANDON. CARELESSNESS.
I'M A PROFESSIONAL. NOT ONLY DO I PUT EVERY BULLET WHERE IT NEEDS TO GO, I DON'T DO IT WITHOUT GETTING PAID.

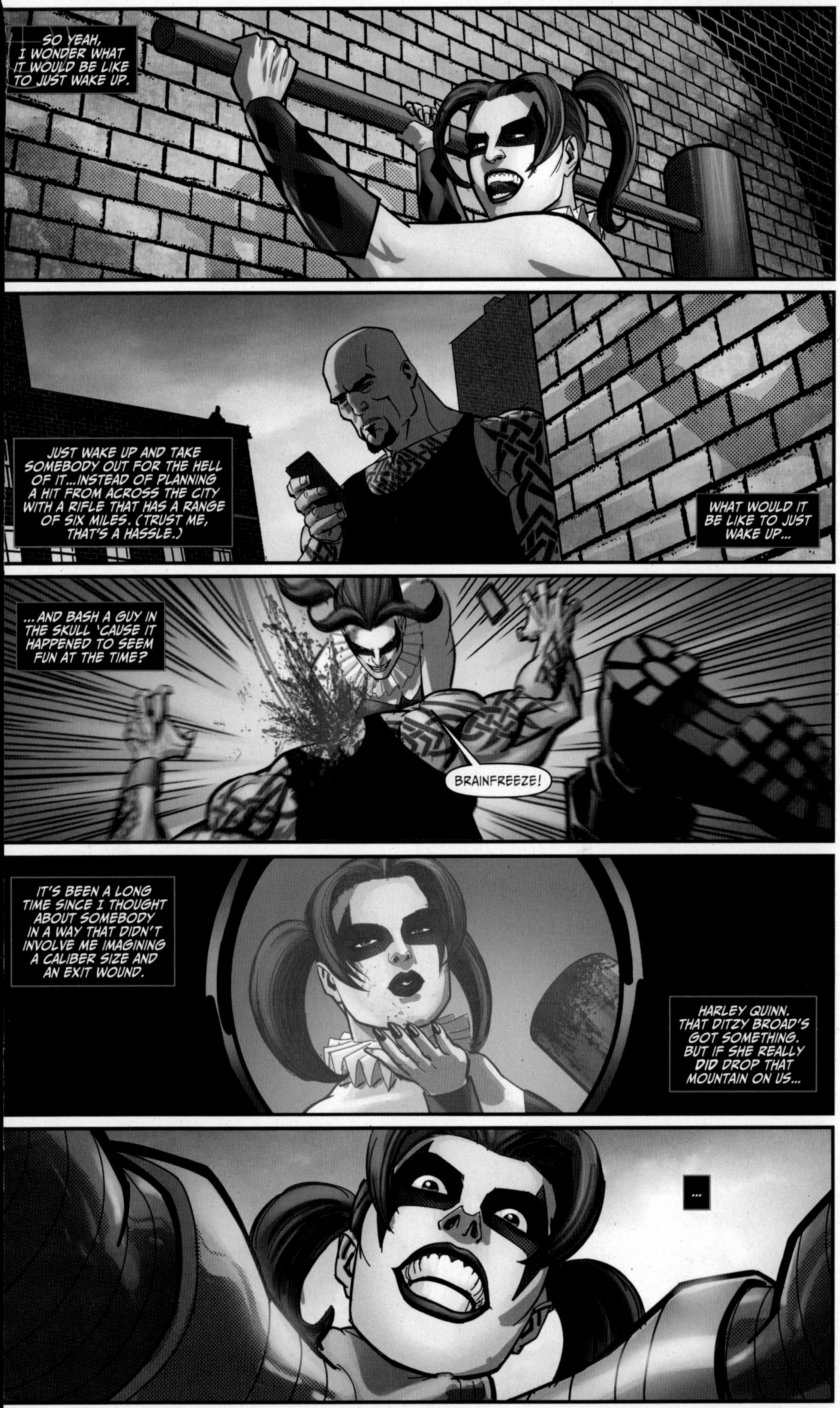
SO YEAH, I WONDER WHAT IT WOULD BE LIKE TO JUST WAKE UP.
JUST WAKE UP AND TAKE SOMEBODY OUT FOR THE HELL OF IT...INSTEAD OF PLANNING A HIT FROM ACROSS THE CITY WITH A RIFLE THAT HAS A RANGE OF SIX MILES. (TRUST ME, THAT'S A HASSLE.)
WHAT WOULD IT BE LIKE TO JUST WAKE UP...
...AND BASH A GUY IN THE SKULL 'CAUSE IT HAPPENED TO SEEM FUN AT THE TIME?
BRAINFREEZE!
IT'S BEEN A LONG TIME SINCE I THOUGHT ABOUT SOMEBODY IN A WAY THAT DIDN'T INVOLVE ME IMAGINING A CALIBER SIZE AND AN EXIT WOUND.
HARLEY QUINN. THAT DITZY BROAD'S GOT SOMETHING. BUT IF SHE REALLY DID DROP THAT MOUNTAIN ON US...
...

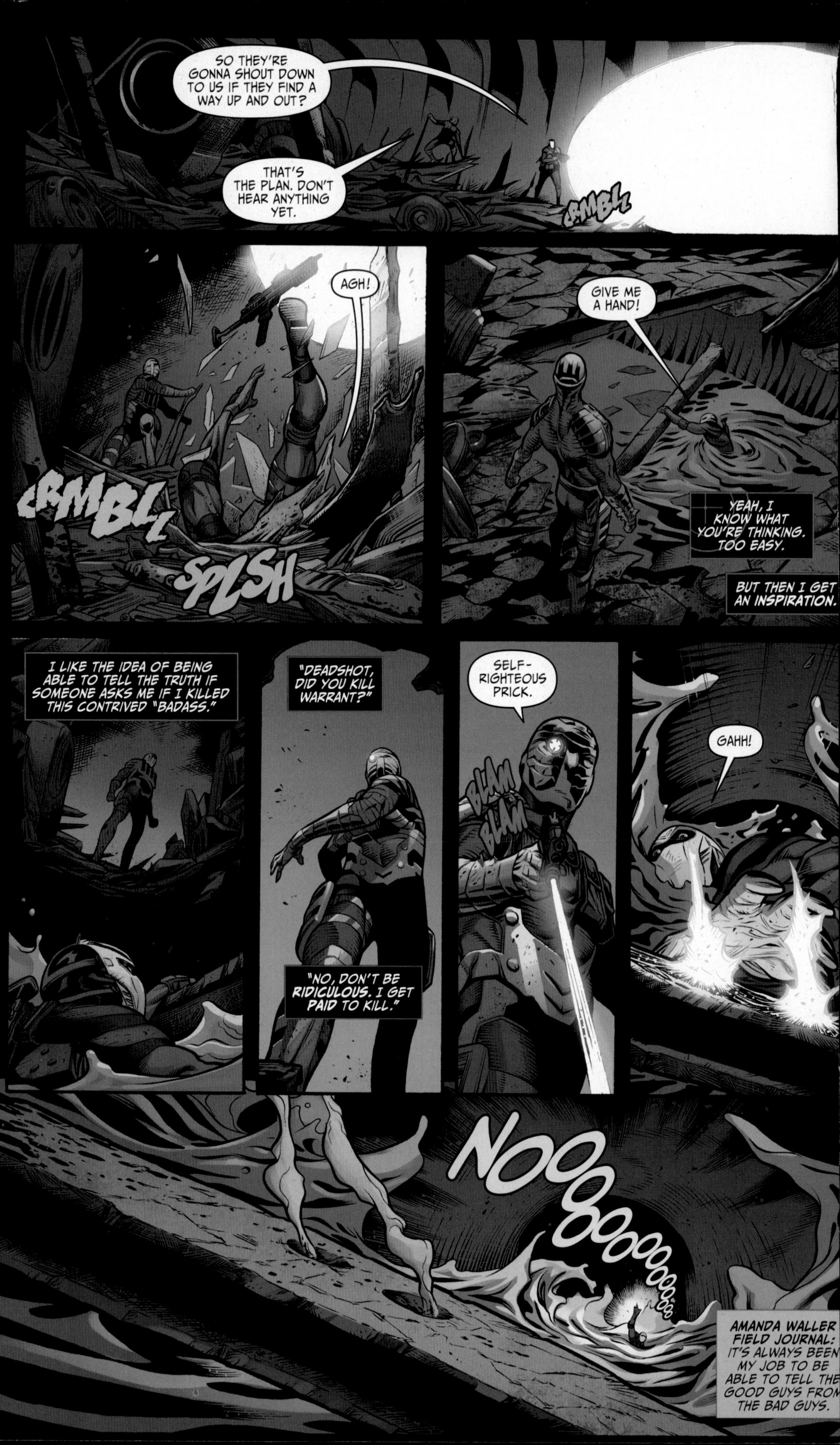

SO THEY'RE GONNA SHOUT DOWN TO US IF THEY FIND A WAY UP AND OUT?
THAT'S THE PLAN. DON'T HEAR ANYTHING YET.
CRMBLL
AGH!
CRMBLL
SPLSH
GIVE ME A HAND!
YEAH, I KNOW WHAT YOU'RE THINKING. TOO EASY.
BUT THEN I GET AN INSPIRATION.
I LIKE THE IDEA OF BEING ABLE TO TELL THE TRUTH IF SOMEONE ASKS ME IF I KILLED THIS CONTRIVED "BADASS."
"DEADSHOT, DID YOU KILL WARRANT?"
"NO, DON'T BE RIDICULOUS. I GET PAID TO KILL."
SELF-RIGHTEOUS PRICK.
BLAM
BLAM
GAHH!
NOOOOOOOOOOOOO
AMANDA WALLER FIELD JOURNAL: IT'S ALWAYS BEEN MY JOB TO BE ABLE TO TELL THE GOOD GUYS FROM THE BAD GUYS.

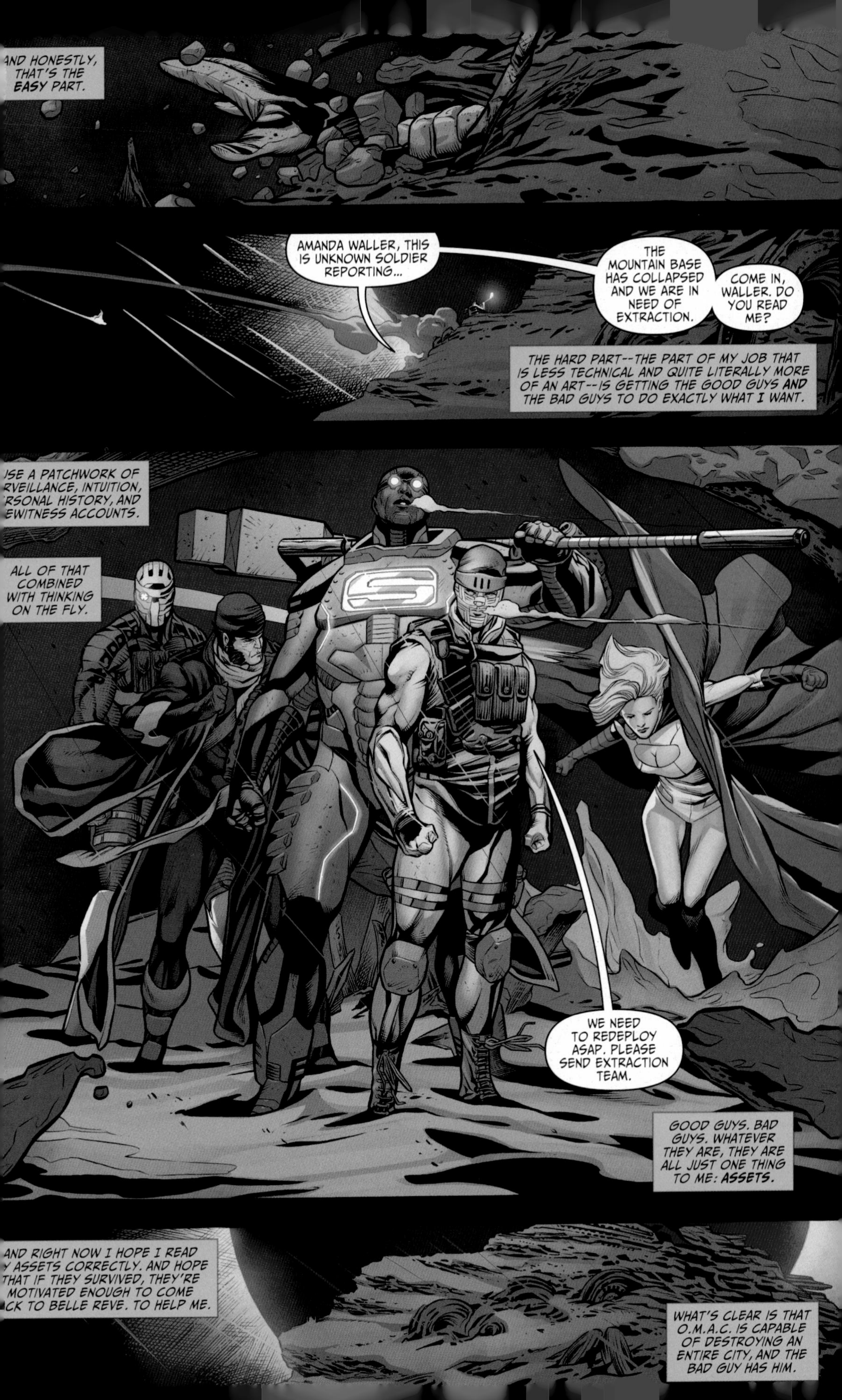
AND HONESTLY, THAT'S THE EASY PART.
AMANDA WALLER, THIS IS UNKNOWN SOLDIER REPORTING...
THE MOUNTAIN BASE HAS COLLAPSED AND WE ARE IN NEED OF EXTRACTION.
COME IN, WALLER. DO YOU READ ME?
THE HARD PART--THE PART OF MY JOB THAT IS LESS TECHNICAL AND QUITE LITERALLY MORE OF AN ART--IS GETTING THE GOOD GUYS AND THE BAD GUYS TO DO EXACTLY WHAT I WANT.
USE A PATCHWORK OF RVEILLANCE, INTUITION, RSONAL HISTORY, AND EWITNESS ACCOUNTS.
ALL OF THAT COMBINED WITH THINKING ON THE FLY.
WE NEED TO REDEPLOY ASAP. PLEASE SEND EXTRACTION TEAM.
GOOD GUYS. BAD GUYS. WHATEVER THEY ARE, THEY ARE ALL JUST ONE THING TO ME: ASSETS.
AND RIGHT NOW I HOPE I READ Y ASSETS CORRECTLY. AND HOPE THAT IF THEY SURVIVED, THEY'RE MOTIVATED ENOUGH TO COME CK TO BELLE REVE. TO HELP ME.
WHAT'S CLEAR IS THAT O.M.A.C. IS CAPABLE OF DESTROYING AN ENTIRE CITY, AND THE BAD GUY HAS HIM.

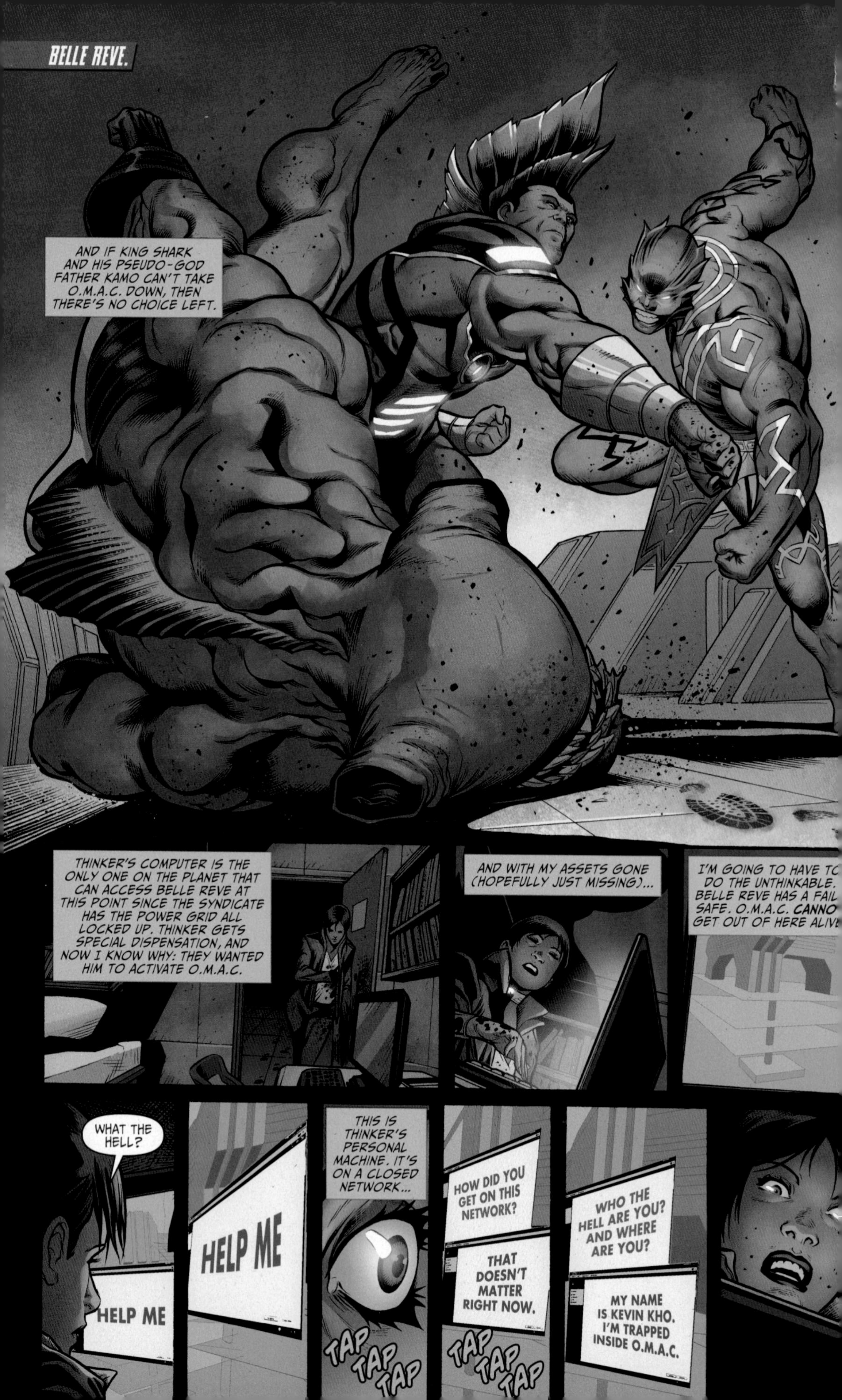
BELLE REVE.
AND IF KING SHARK AND HIS PSEUDO-GOD FATHER KAMO CAN'T TAKE O.M.A.C. DOWN, THEN THERE'S NO CHOICE LEFT.
THINKER'S COMPUTER IS THE ONLY ONE ON THE PLANET THAT CAN ACCESS BELLE REVE AT THIS POINT SINCE THE SYNDICATE HAS THE POWER GRID ALL LOCKED UP. THINKER GETS SPECIAL DISPENSATION, AND NOW I KNOW WHY: THEY WANTED HIM TO ACTIVATE O.M.A.C.
AND WITH MY ASSETS GONE (HOPEFULLY JUST MISSING)...
I'M GOING TO HAVE TO DO THE UNTHINKABLE. BELLE REVE HAS A FAIL SAFE. O.M.A.C. CANNO GET OUT OF HERE ALIV
WHAT THE HELL?
HELP ME
HELP ME
THIS IS THINKER'S PERSONAL MACHINE. IT'S ON A CLOSED NETWORK...
TAP TAP TAP
HOW DID YOU GET ON THIS NETWORK?
THAT DOESN'T MATTER RIGHT NOW.
TAP TAP TAP
WHO THE HELL ARE YOU? AND WHERE ARE YOU?
MY NAME IS KEVIN KHO. I'M TRAPPED INSIDE O.M.A.C.

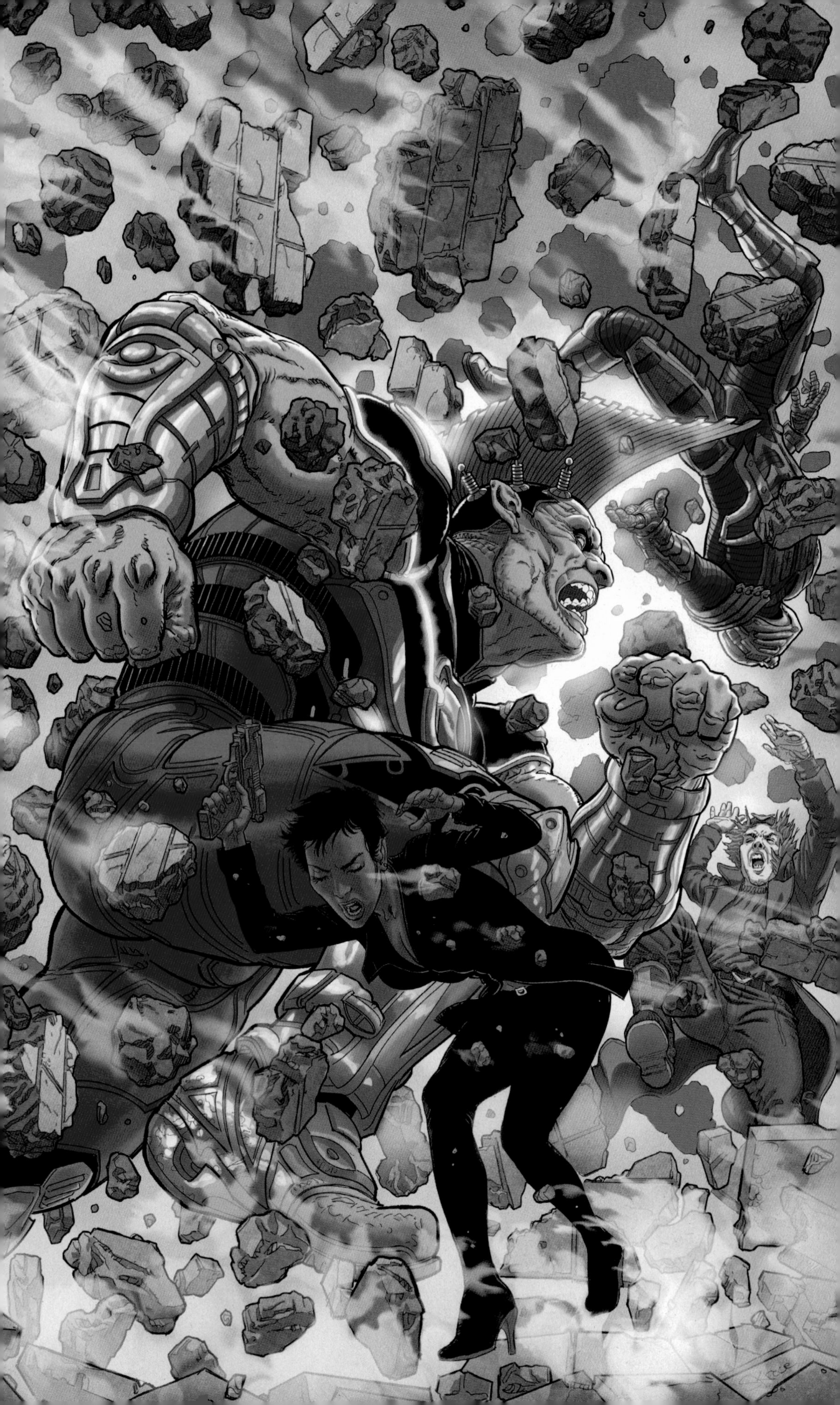

MAGIC BULLET

MATT KINDT writer **JASON MASTERS CARLOS RODRIGUEZ** artists **BRETT SMITH** colorist **JARED K. FLETCHER** letterer

cover by **STEVE SKROCE**

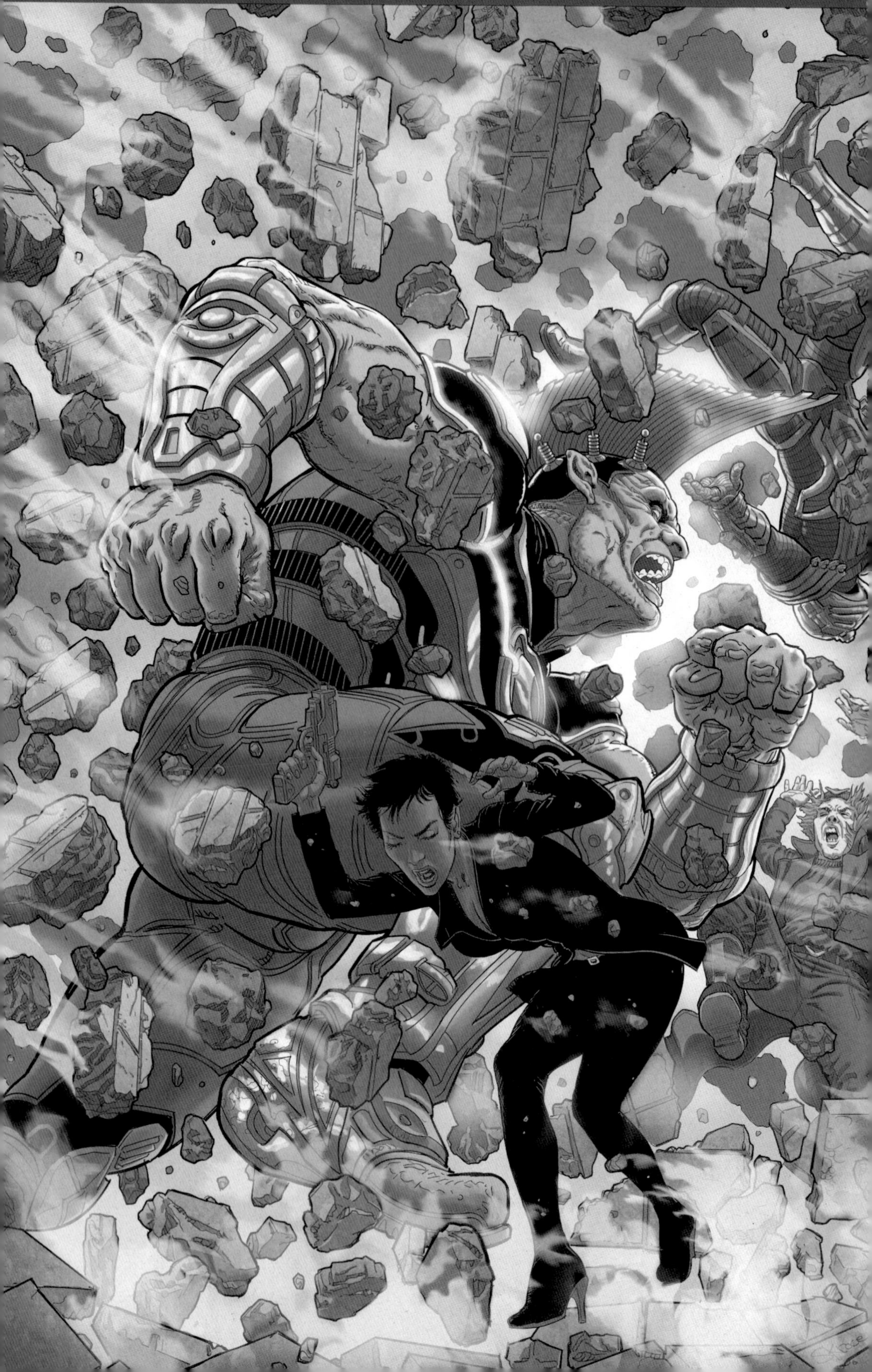

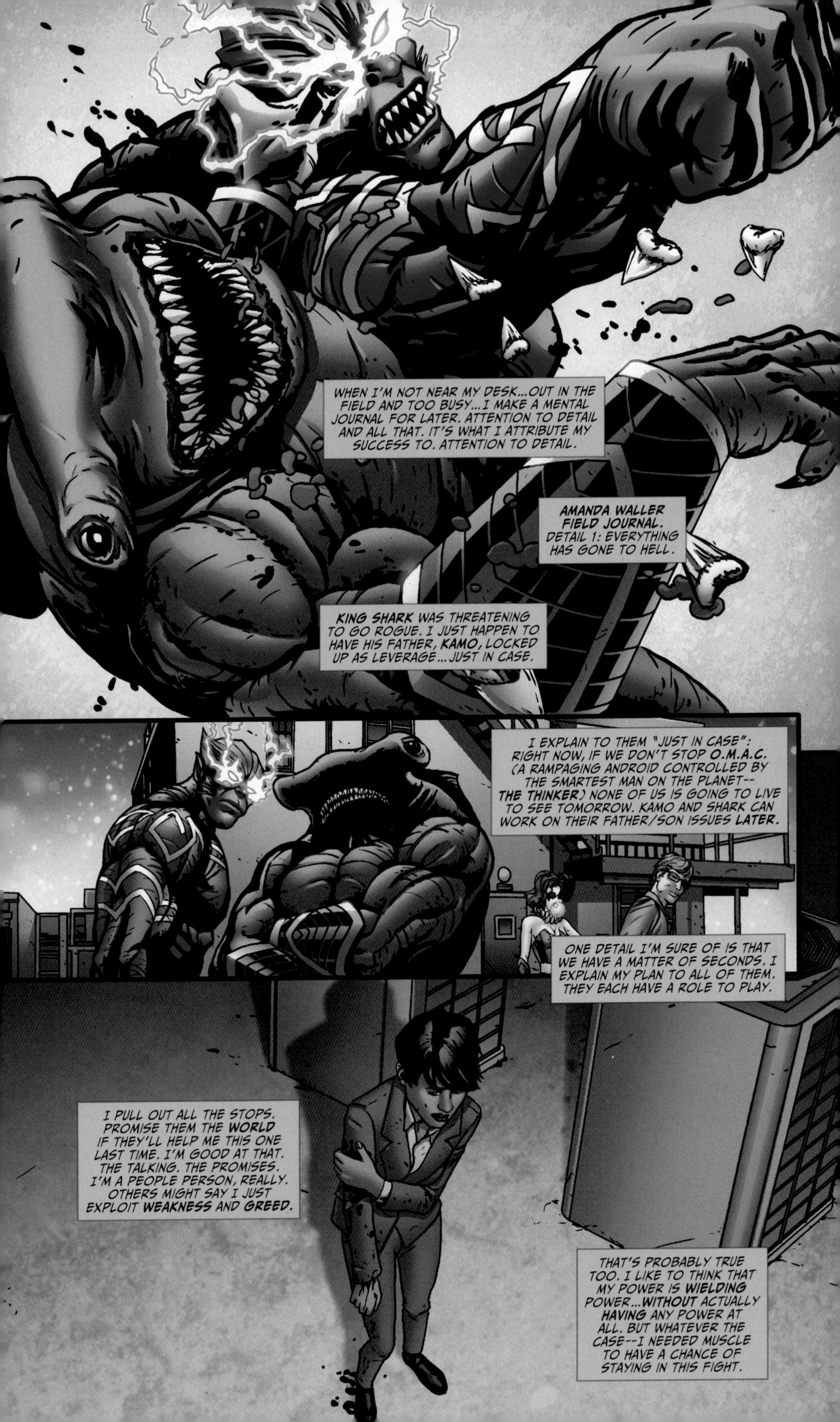

WHEN I'M NOT NEAR MY DESK...OUT IN THE FIELD AND TOO BUSY...I MAKE A MENTAL JOURNAL FOR LATER. ATTENTION TO DETAIL AND ALL THAT. IT'S WHAT I ATTRIBUTE MY SUCCESS TO. ATTENTION TO DETAIL.
AMANDA WALLER FIELD JOURNAL. DETAIL 1: EVERYTHING HAS GONE TO HELL.
KING SHARK WAS THREATENING TO GO ROGUE. I JUST HAPPEN TO HAVE HIS FATHER, KAMO, LOCKED UP AS LEVERAGE...JUST IN CASE.
I EXPLAIN TO THEM "JUST IN CASE": RIGHT NOW, IF WE DON'T STOP O.M.A.C. (A RAMPAGING ANDROID CONTROLLED BY THE SMARTEST MAN ON THE PLANET-- THE THINKER) NONE OF US IS GOING TO LIVE TO SEE TOMORROW. KAMO AND SHARK CAN WORK ON THEIR FATHER/SON ISSUES LATER.
ONE DETAIL I'M SURE OF IS THAT WE HAVE A MATTER OF SECONDS. I EXPLAIN MY PLAN TO ALL OF THEM. THEY EACH HAVE A ROLE TO PLAY.
I PULL OUT ALL THE STOPS. PROMISE THEM THE WORLD IF THEY'LL HELP ME THIS ONE LAST TIME. I'M GOOD AT THAT. THE TALKING. THE PROMISES. I'M A PEOPLE PERSON, REALLY. OTHERS MIGHT SAY I JUST EXPLOIT WEAKNESS AND GREED.
THAT'S PROBABLY TRUE TOO. I LIKE TO THINK THAT MY POWER IS WIELDING POWER...WITHOUT ACTUALLY HAVING ANY POWER AT ALL. BUT WHATEVER THE CASE--I NEEDED MUSCLE TO HAVE A CHANCE OF STAYING IN THIS FIGHT.

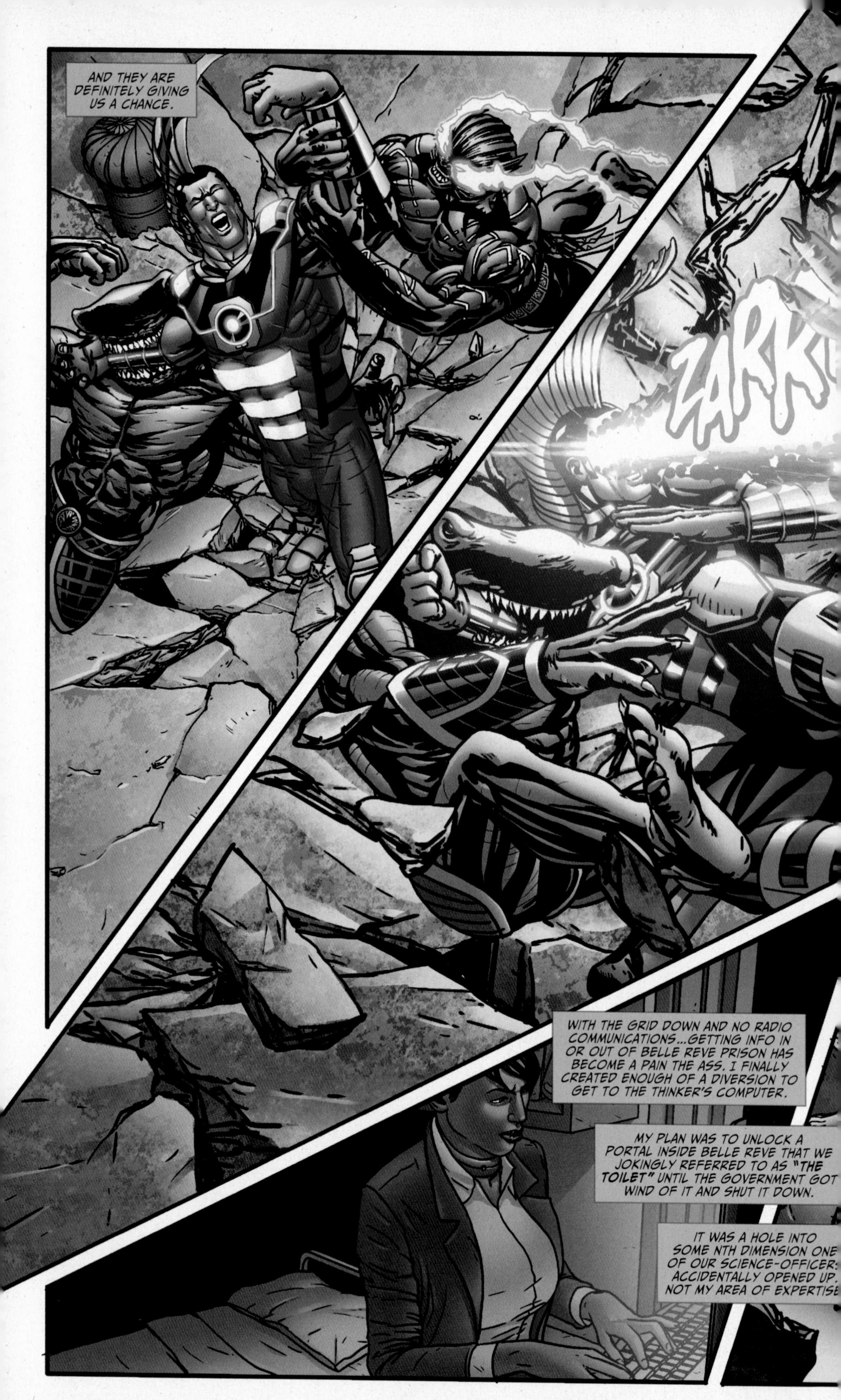
AND THEY ARE DEFINITELY GIVING US A CHANCE.
ZARK
WITH THE GRID DOWN AND NO RADIO COMMUNICATIONS...GETTING INFO IN OR OUT OF BELLE REVE PRISON HAS BECOME A PAIN THE ASS. I FINALLY CREATED ENOUGH OF A DIVERSION TO GET TO THE THINKER'S COMPUTER.
MY PLAN WAS TO UNLOCK A PORTAL INSIDE BELLE REVE THAT WE JOKINGLY REFERRED TO AS **"THE TOILET"** UNTIL THE GOVERNMENT GOT WIND OF IT AND SHUT IT DOWN.
IT WAS A HOLE INTO SOME NTH DIMENSION ONE OF OUR SCIENCE-OFFICER ACCIDENTALLY OPENED UP. NOT MY AREA OF EXPERTISE

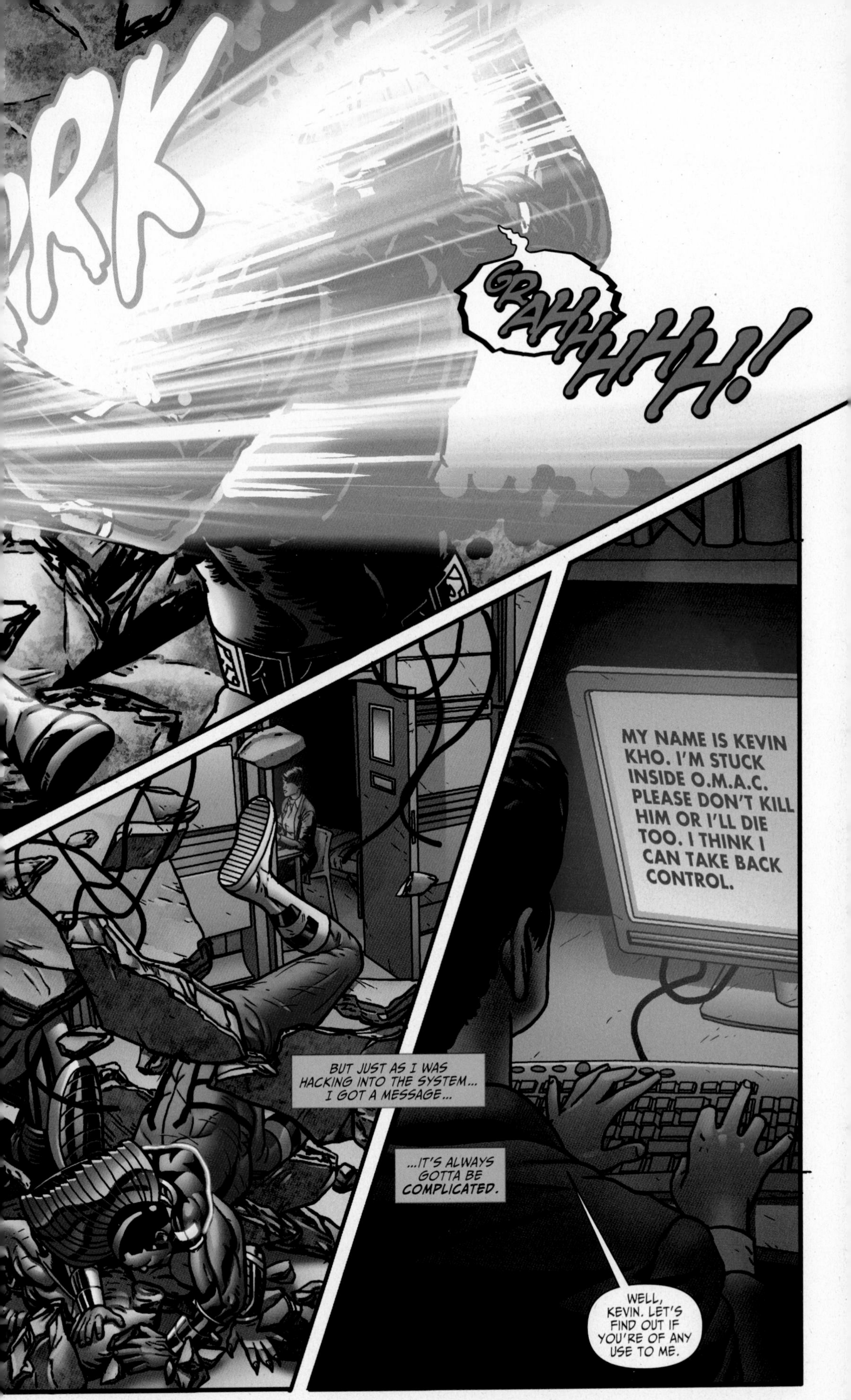
...RK
GRAHHHHHH!
BUT JUST AS I WAS HACKING INTO THE SYSTEM... I GOT A MESSAGE...
MY NAME IS KEVIN KHO. I'M STUCK INSIDE O.M.A.C. PLEASE DON'T KILL HIM OR I'LL DIE TOO. I THINK I CAN TAKE BACK CONTROL.
...IT'S ALWAYS GOTTA BE COMPLICATED.
WELL, KEVIN. LET'S FIND OUT IF YOU'RE OF ANY USE TO ME.

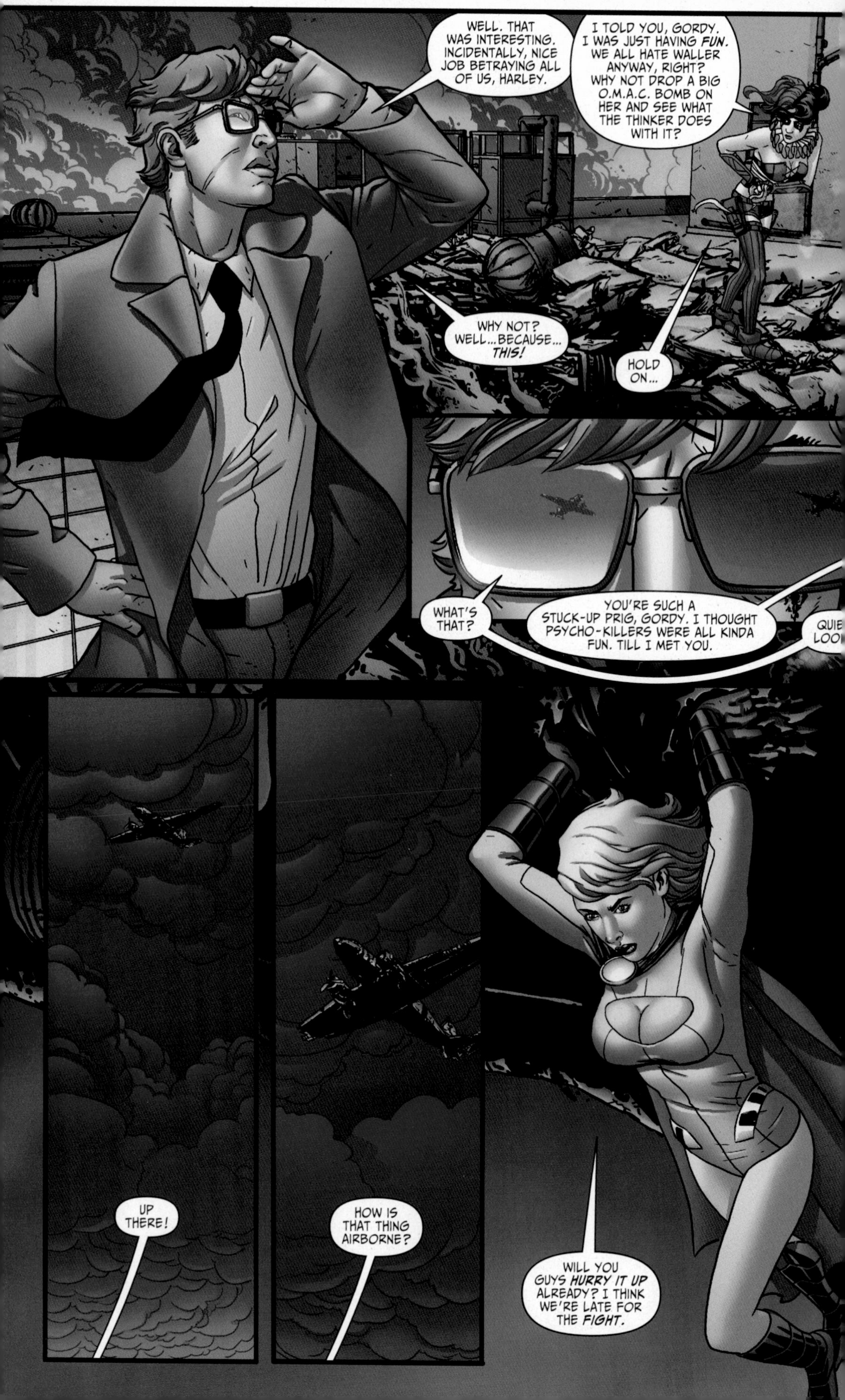

WELL. THAT WAS INTERESTING. INCIDENTALLY, NICE JOB BETRAYING ALL OF US, HARLEY.
I TOLD YOU, GORDY. I WAS JUST HAVING FUN. WE ALL HATE WALLER ANYWAY, RIGHT? WHY NOT DROP A BIG O.M.A.C. BOMB ON HER AND SEE WHAT THE THINKER DOES WITH IT?
WHY NOT? WELL...BECAUSE... THIS!
HOLD ON...
WHAT'S THAT?
YOU'RE SUCH A STUCK-UP PRIG, GORDY. I THOUGHT PSYCHO-KILLERS WERE ALL KINDA FUN. TILL I MET YOU.
UP THERE!
HOW IS THAT THING AIRBORNE?
WILL YOU GUYS HURRY IT UP ALREADY? I THINK WE'RE LATE FOR THE FIGHT.

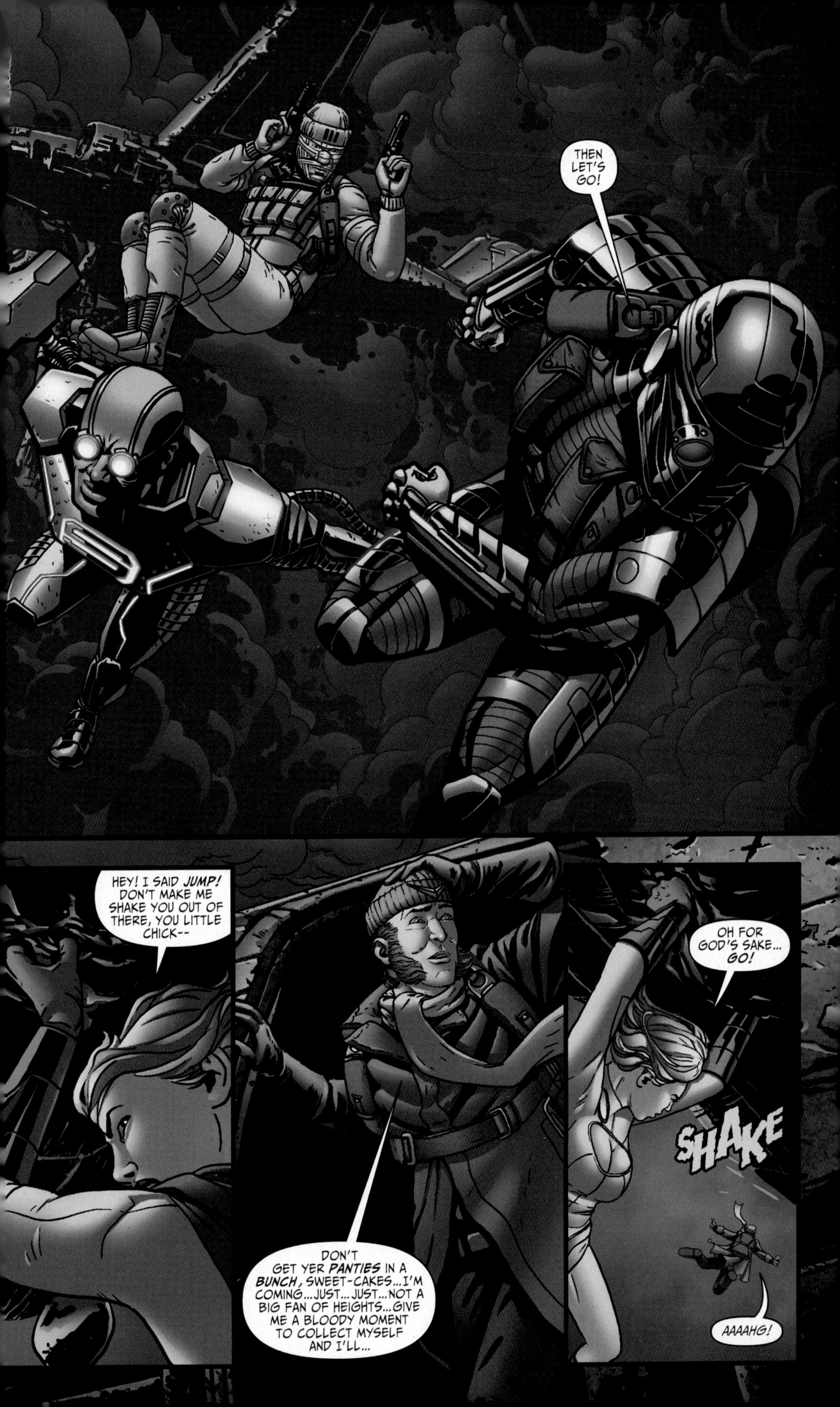
THEN LET'S GO!
HEY! I SAID JUMP! DON'T MAKE ME SHAKE YOU OUT OF THERE, YOU LITTLE CHICK--
DON'T GET YER PANTIES IN A BUNCH, SWEET-CAKES...I'M COMING...JUST...JUST...NOT A BIG FAN OF HEIGHTS...GIVE ME A BLOODY MOMENT TO COLLECT MYSELF AND I'LL...
OH FOR GOD'S SAKE... GO!
SHAKE
AAAAHG!

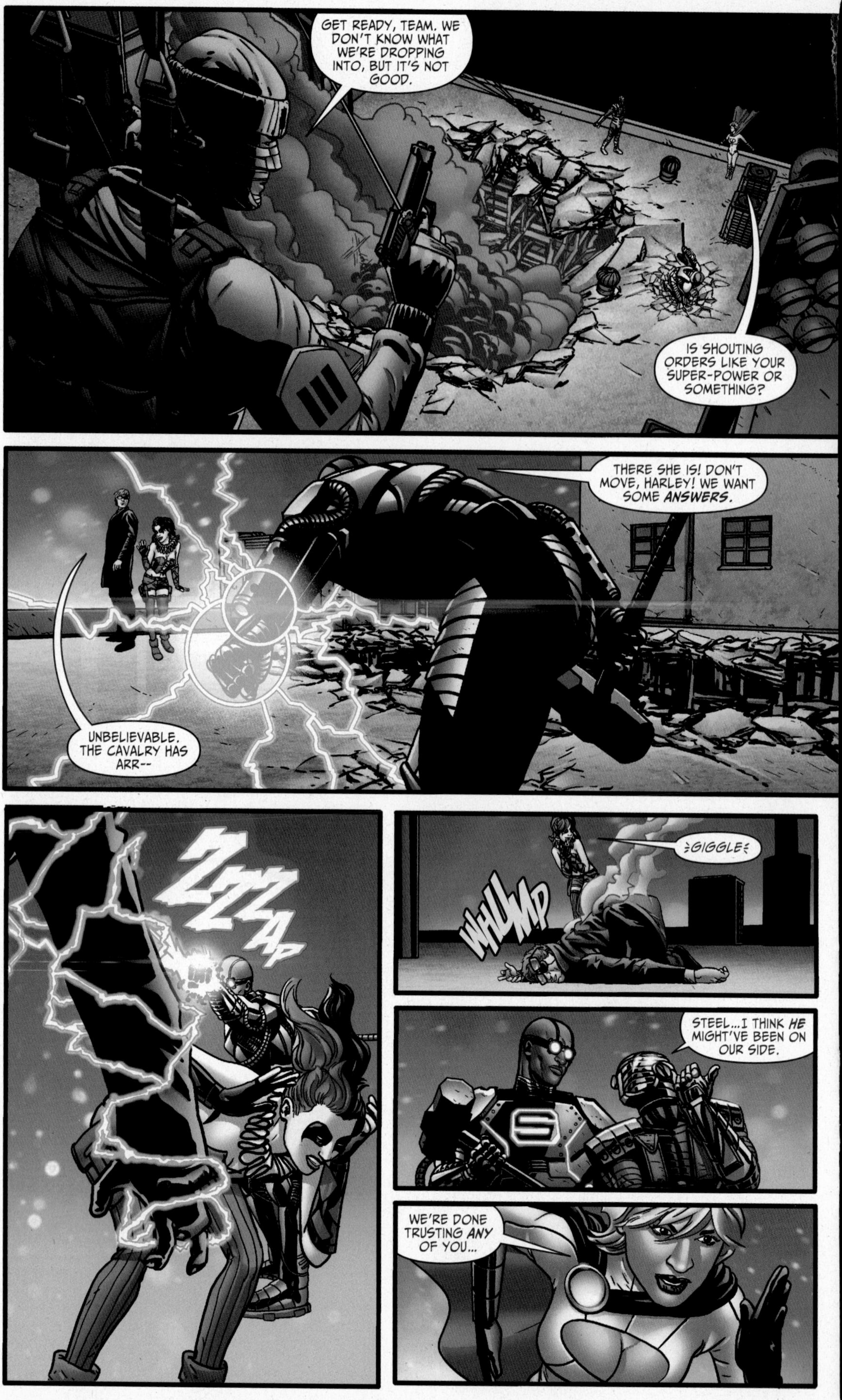
GET READY, TEAM. WE DON'T KNOW WHAT WE'RE DROPPING INTO, BUT IT'S NOT GOOD.
IS SHOUTING ORDERS LIKE YOUR SUPER-POWER OR SOMETHING?
THERE SHE IS! DON'T MOVE, HARLEY! WE WANT SOME ANSWERS.
UNBELIEVABLE. THE CAVALRY HAS ARR--
ZZZAP
WHUMP
GIGGLE
STEEL...I THINK HE MIGHT'VE BEEN ON OUR SIDE.
WE'RE DONE TRUSTING ANY OF YOU...

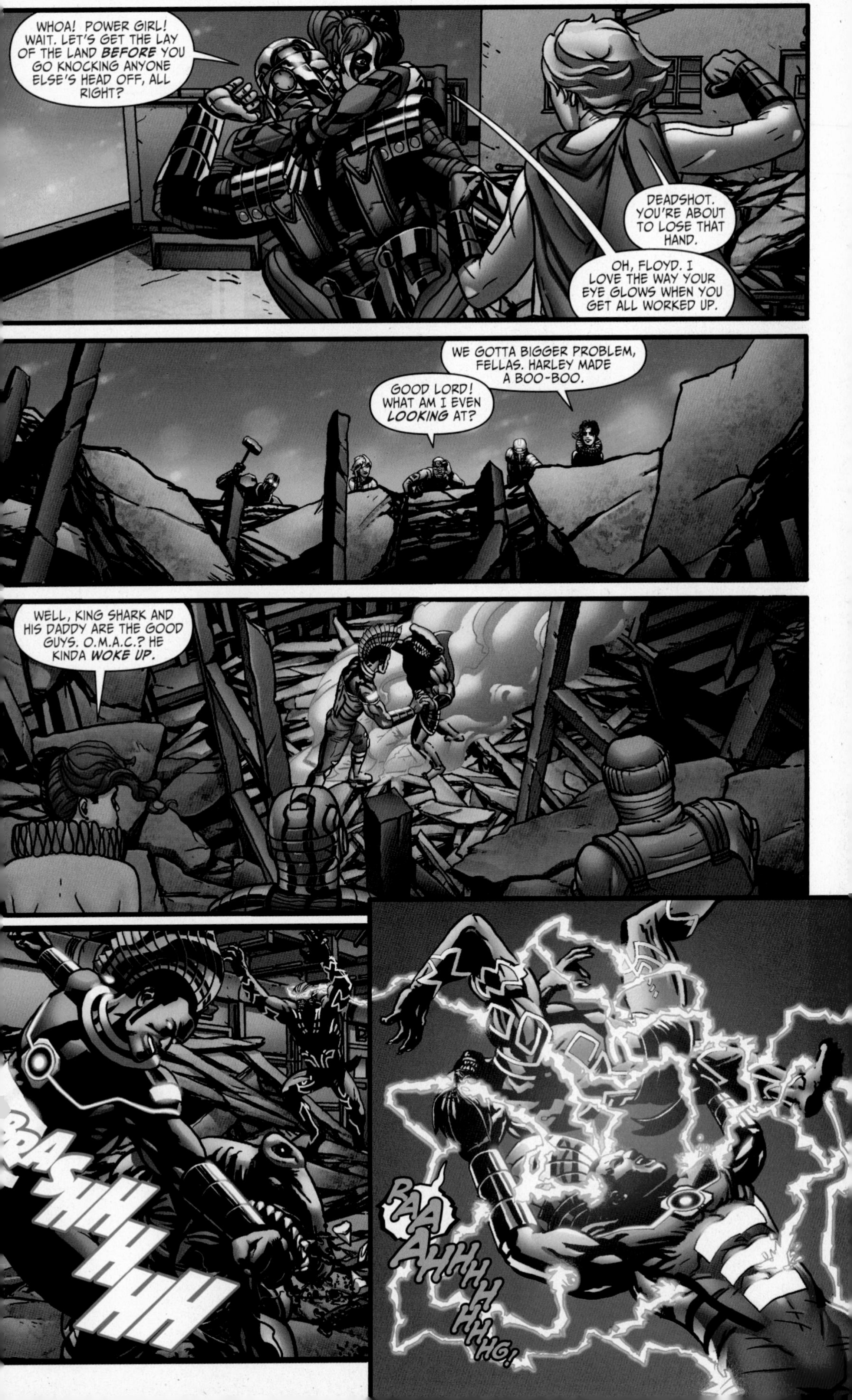
WHOA! POWER GIRL! WAIT. LET'S GET THE LAY OF THE LAND **BEFORE** YOU GO KNOCKING ANYONE ELSE'S HEAD OFF, ALL RIGHT?
DEADSHOT. YOU'RE ABOUT TO LOSE THAT HAND.
OH, FLOYD. I LOVE THE WAY YOUR EYE GLOWS WHEN YOU GET ALL WORKED UP.
WE GOTTA BIGGER PROBLEM, FELLAS. HARLEY MADE A BOO-BOO.
GOOD LORD! WHAT AM I EVEN **LOOKING** AT?
WELL, KING SHARK AND HIS DADDY ARE THE GOOD GUYS. O.M.A.C.? HE KINDA **WOKE UP**.
BRASHHHHHH
RAAAHHHHHHHG!

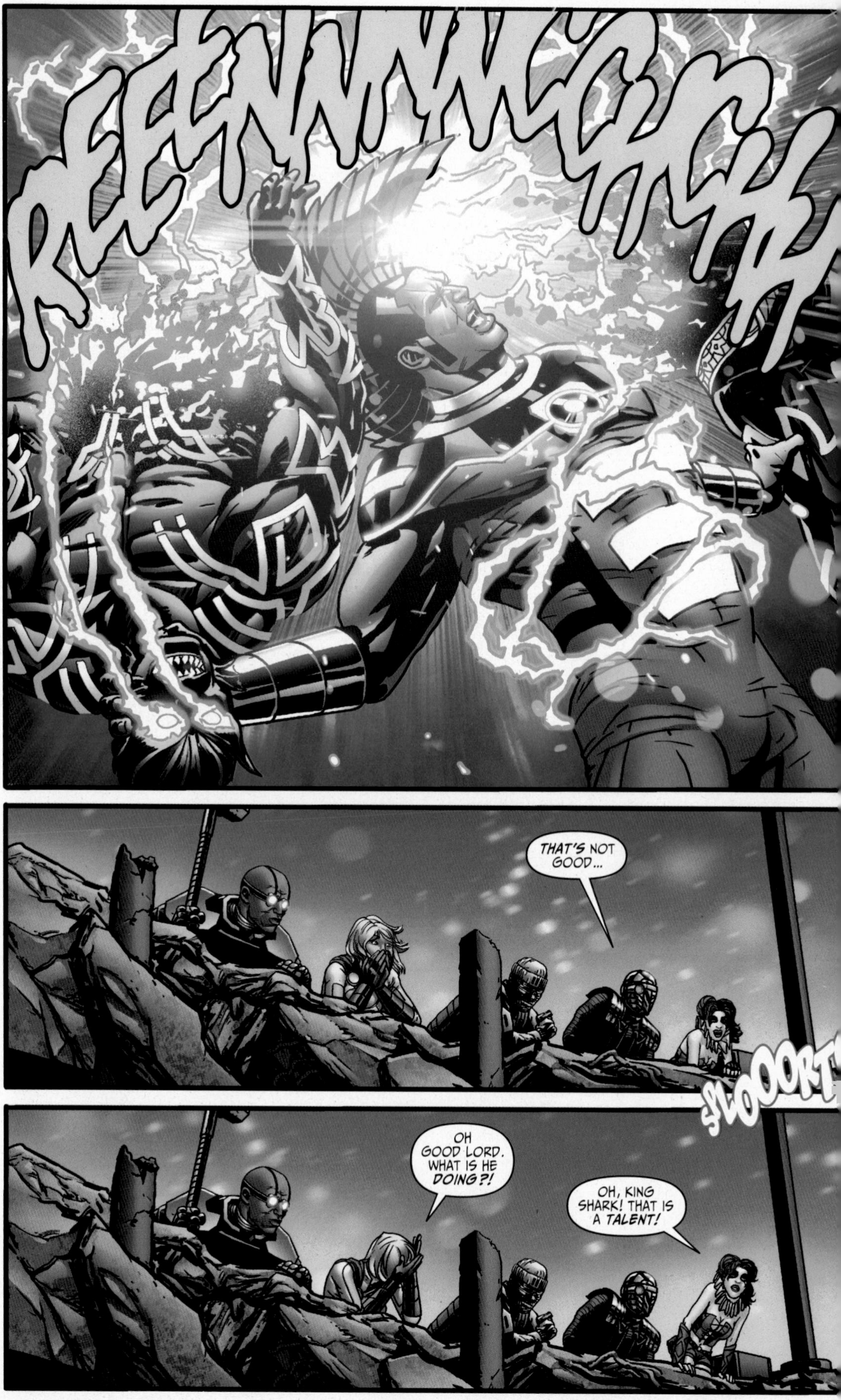
THAT'S NOT GOOD...
OH GOOD LORD. WHAT IS HE DOING?!
OH, KING SHARK! THAT IS A TALENT!

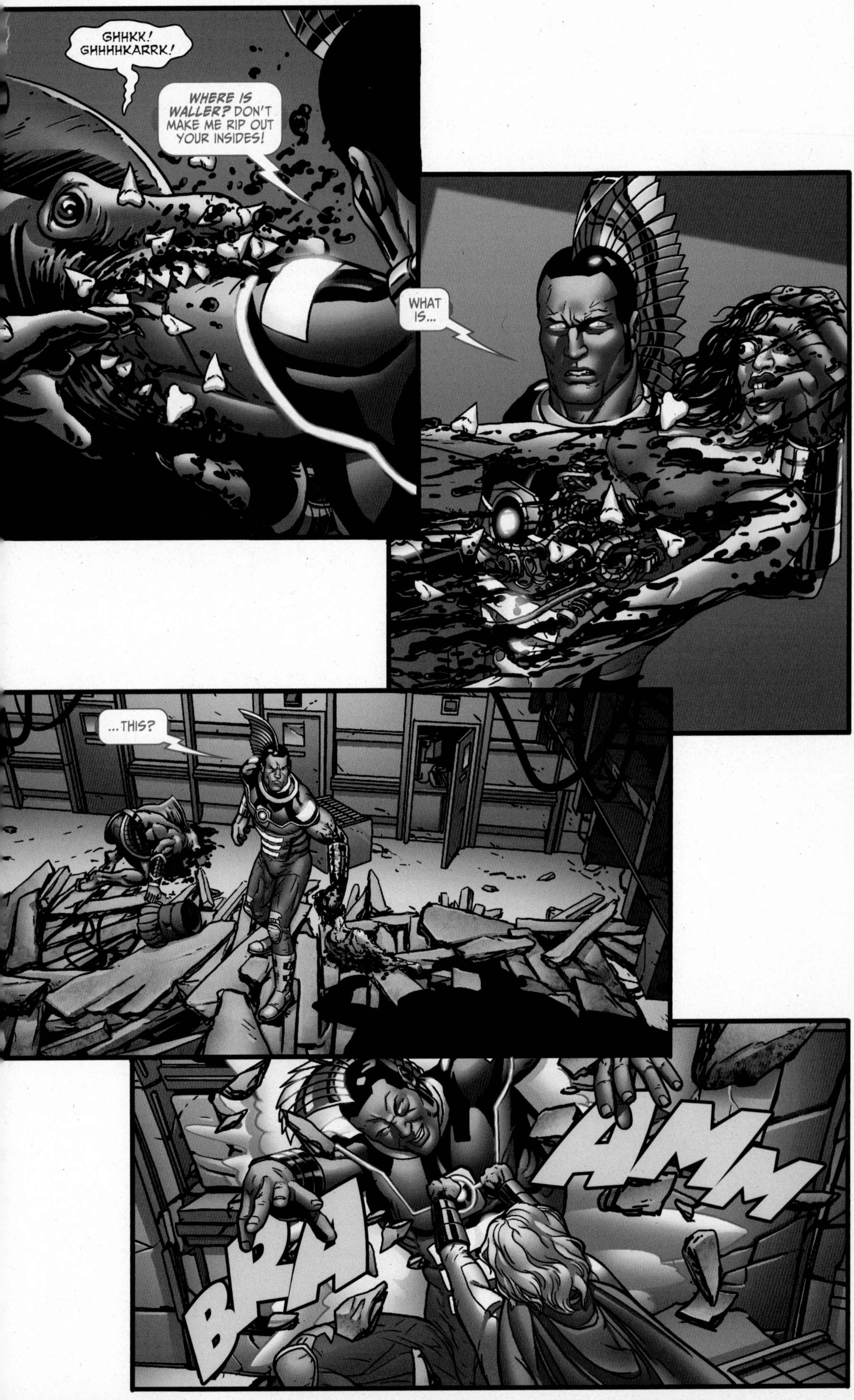
GHHKK! GHHHHKARRK!
WHERE IS WALLER? DON'T MAKE ME RIP OUT YOUR INSIDES!
WHAT IS...
...THIS?
BHAMM

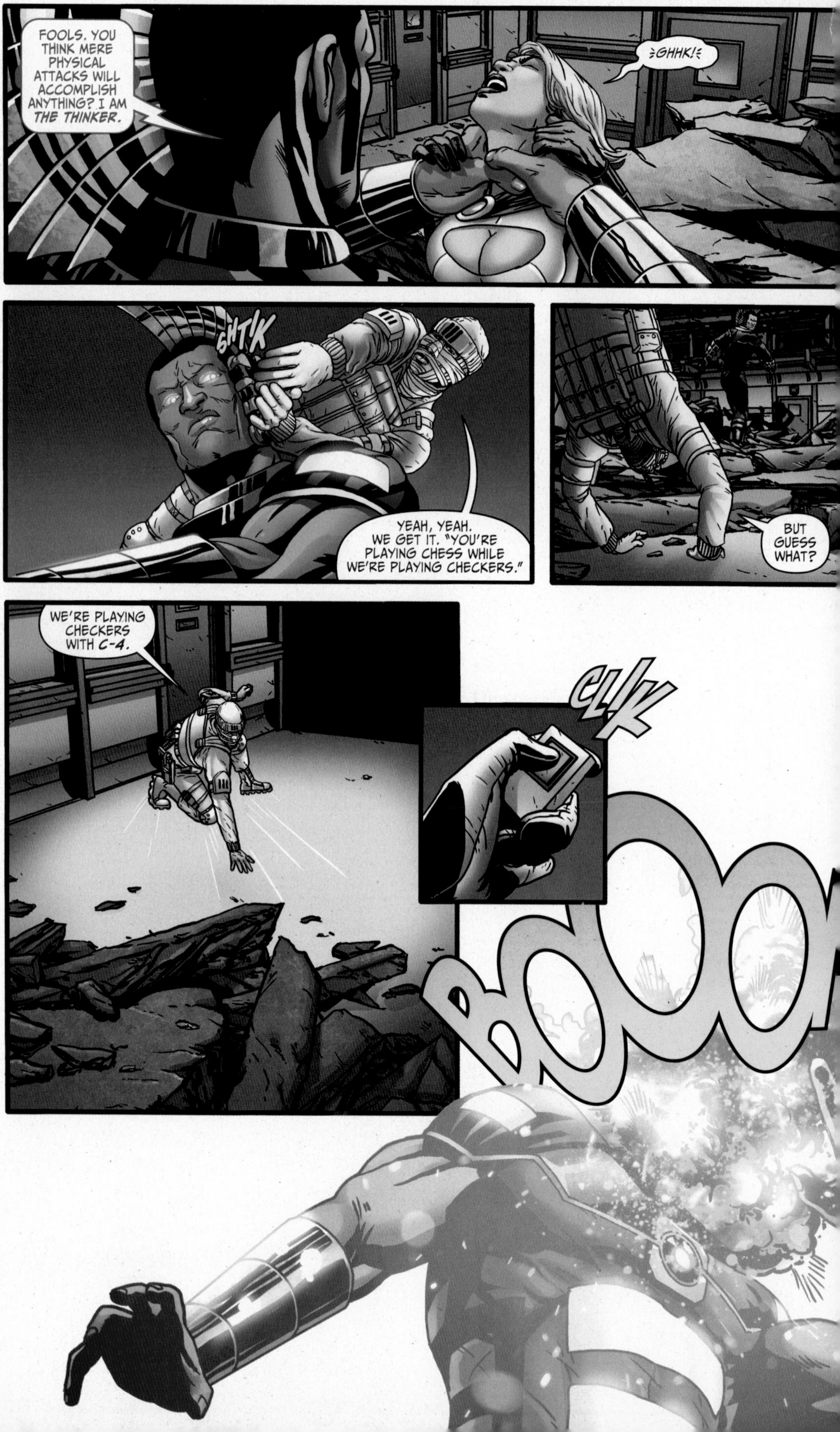
FOOLS. YOU THINK MERE PHYSICAL ATTACKS WILL ACCOMPLISH ANYTHING? I AM THE THINKER.
GHHK!
SHTIK
YEAH, YEAH. WE GET IT. "YOU'RE PLAYING CHESS WHILE WE'RE PLAYING CHECKERS."
BUT GUESS WHAT?
WE'RE PLAYING CHECKERS WITH C-4.
CLIK
BOOO

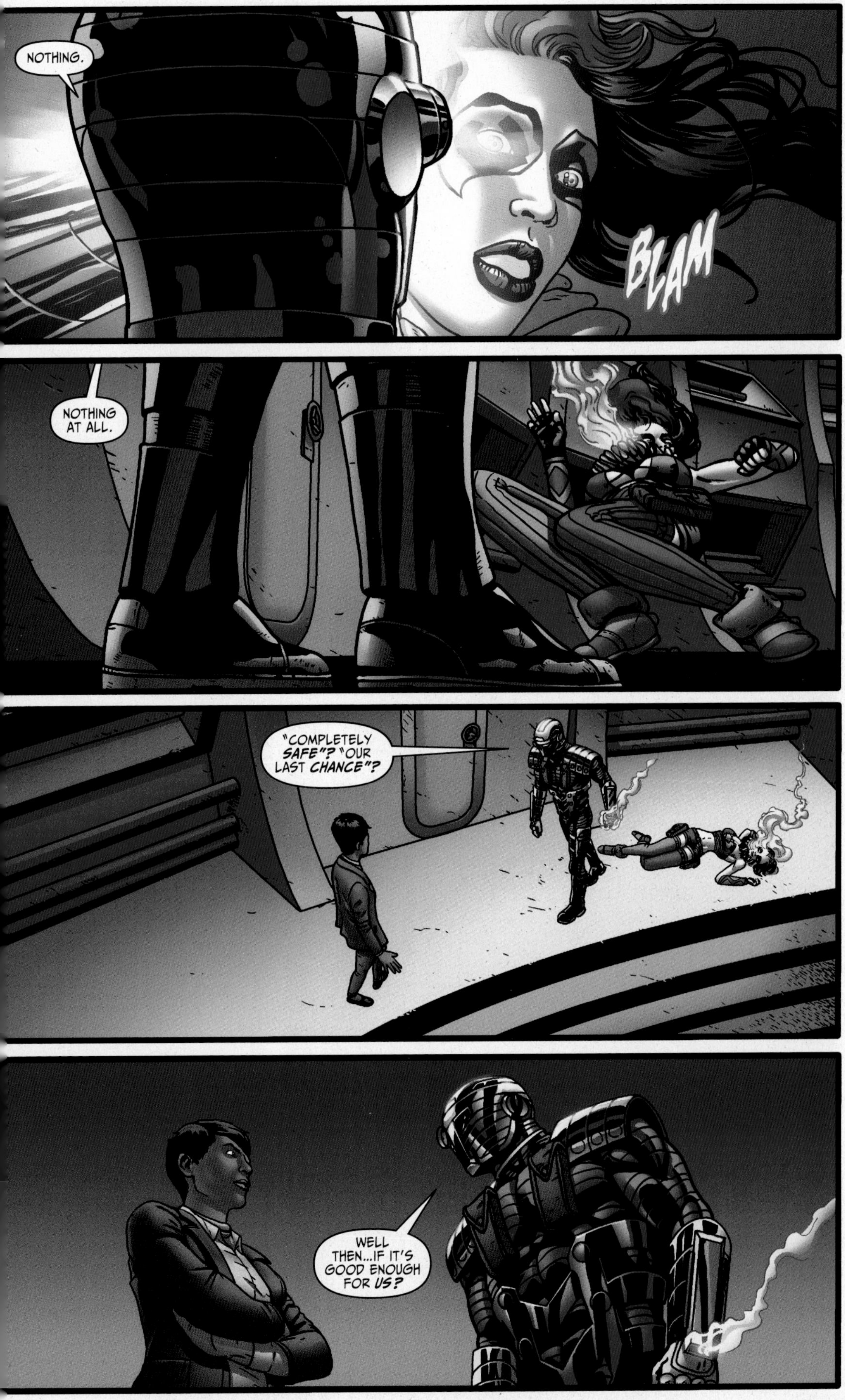
NOTHING.
BLAM
NOTHING AT ALL.
"COMPLETELY SAFE"? "OUR LAST CHANCE"?
WELL THEN...IF IT'S GOOD ENOUGH FOR US?

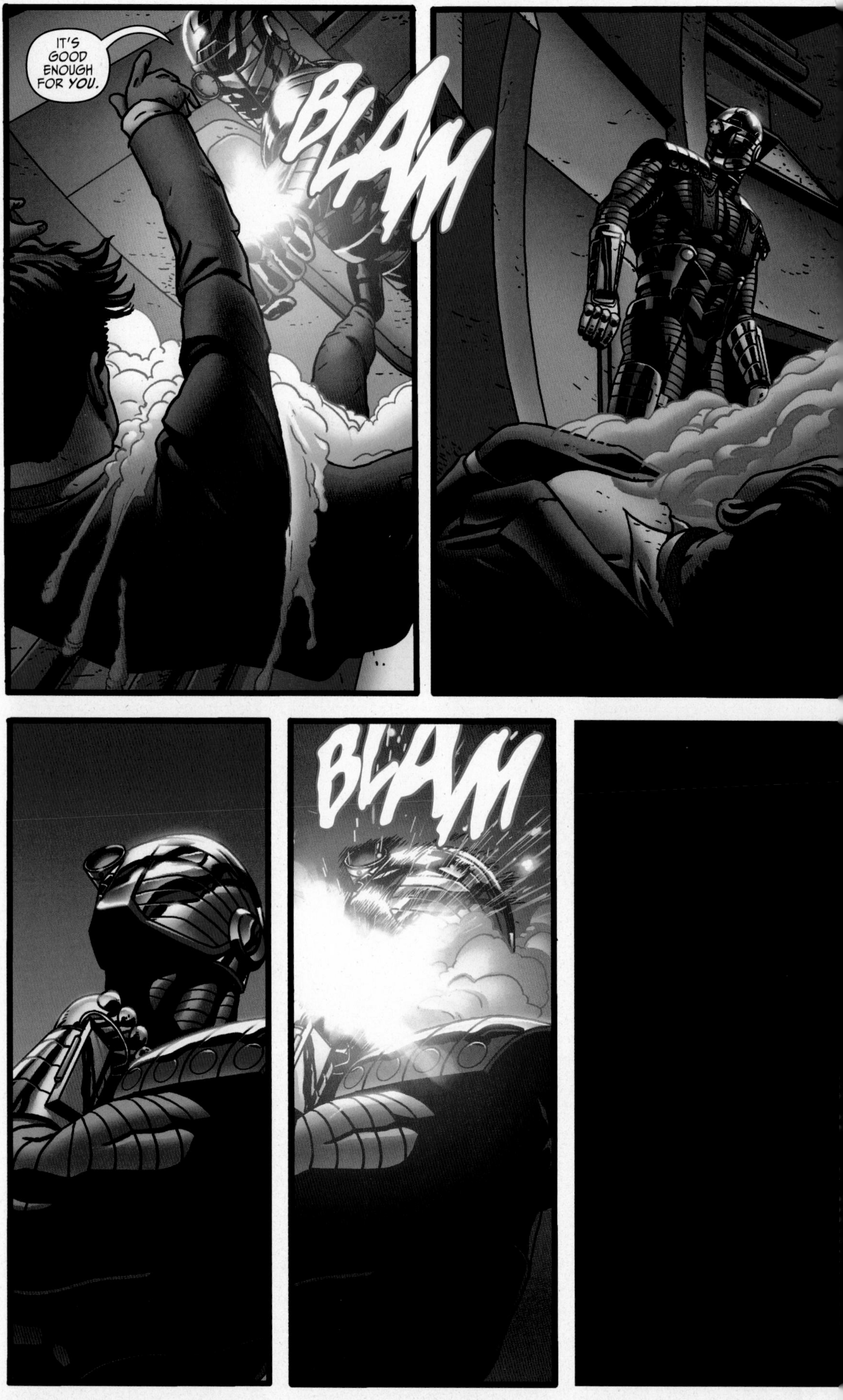
IT'S GOOD ENOUGH FOR YOU.
BLAM
BLAM

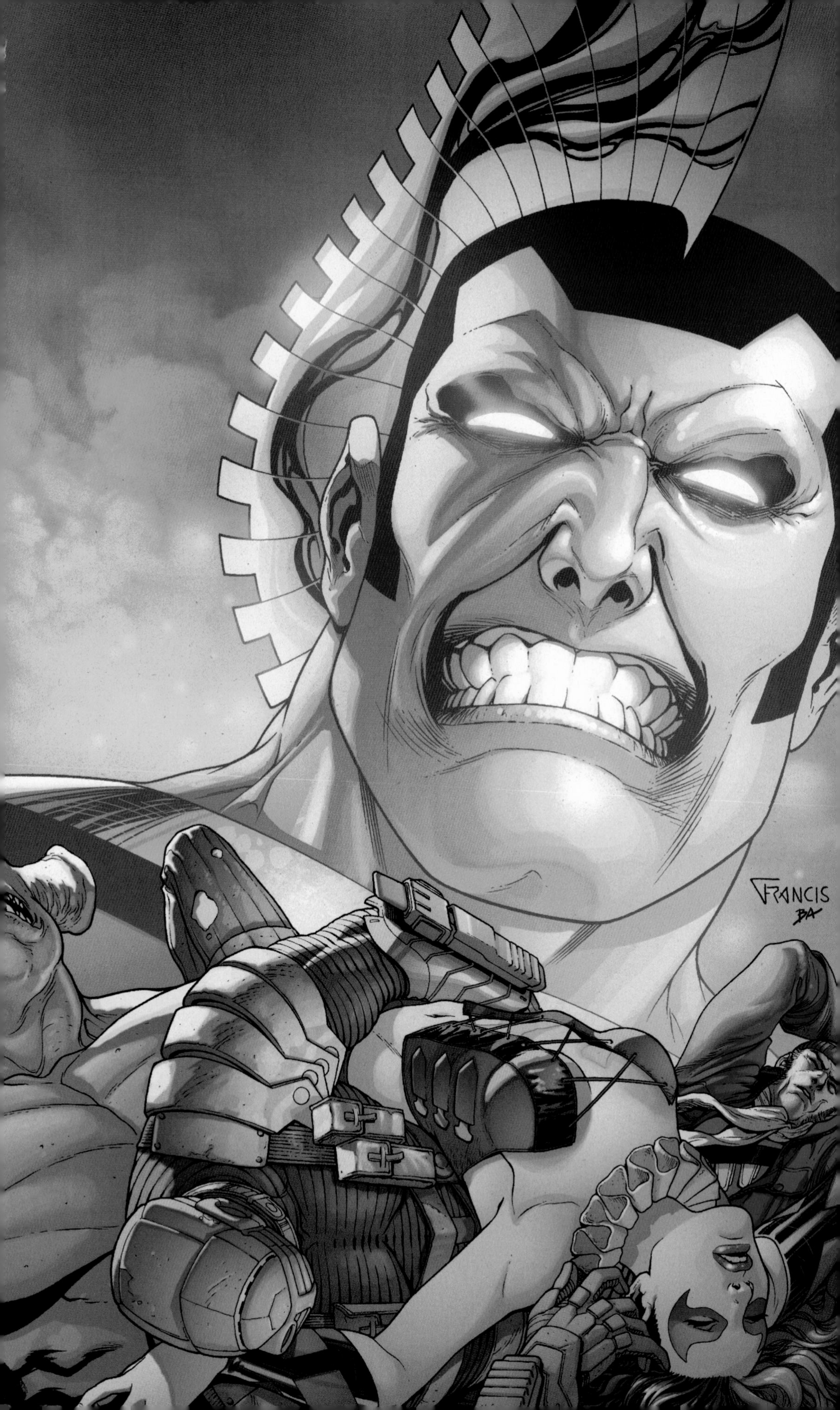
FRANCIS
BA

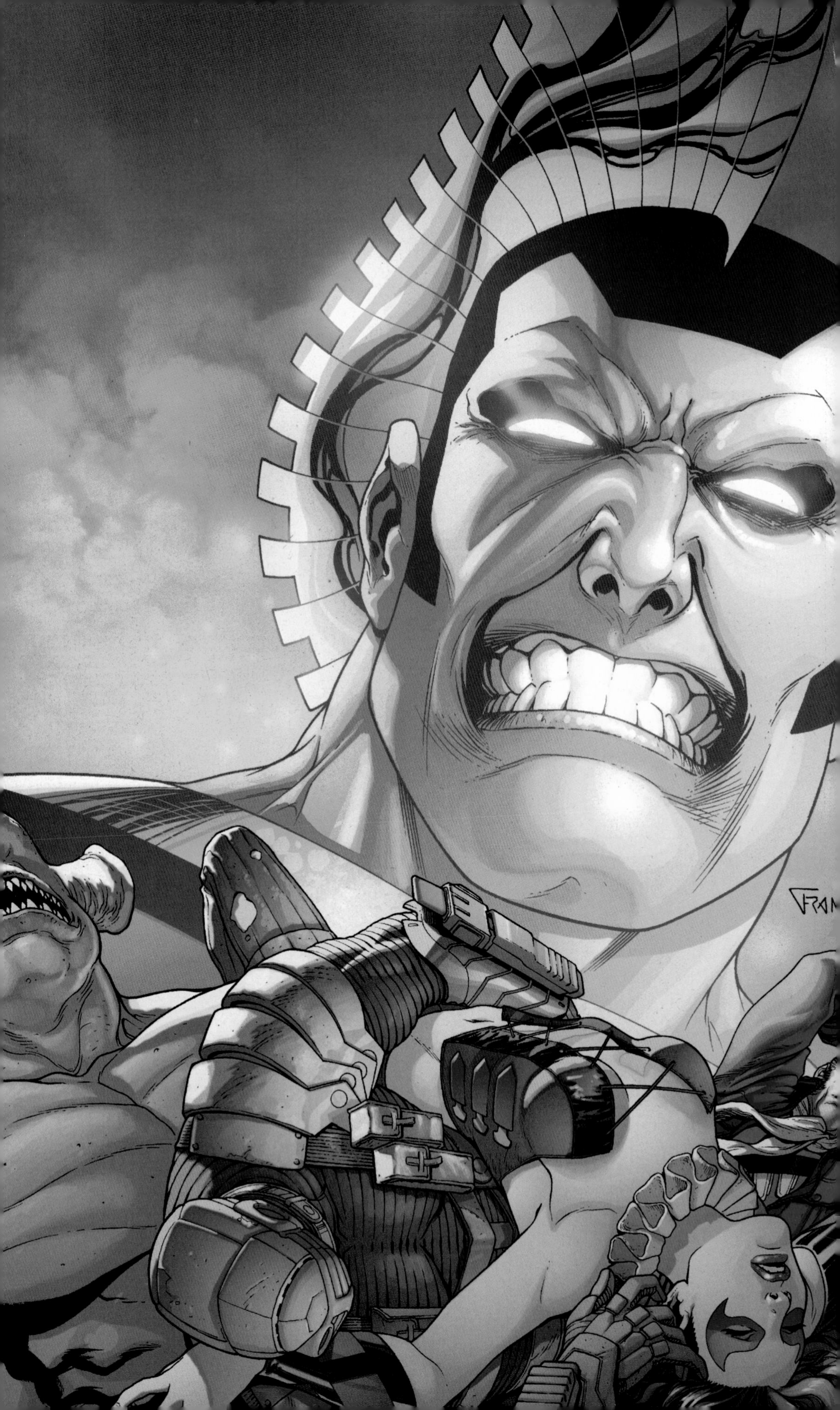

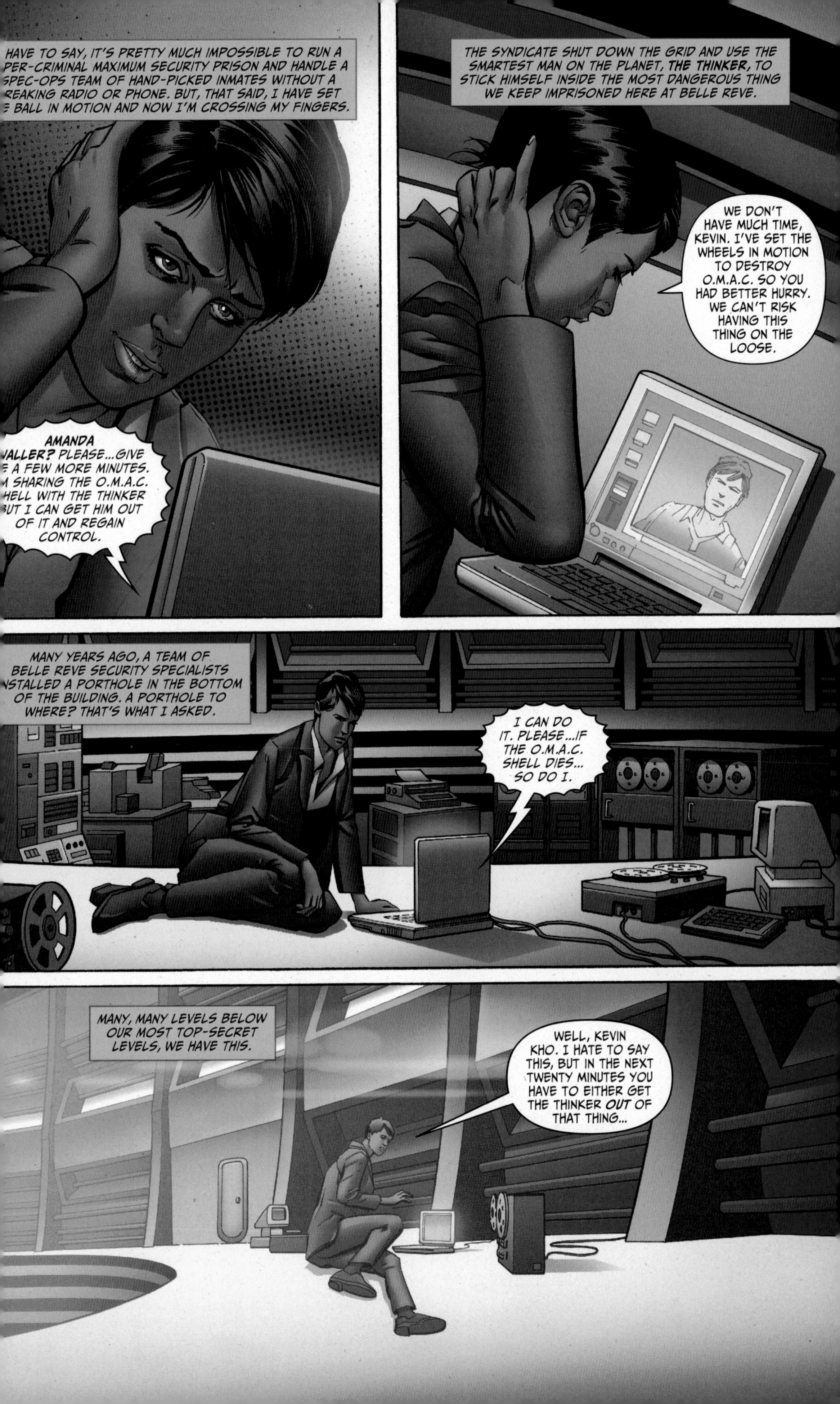

HAVE TO SAY, IT'S PRETTY MUCH IMPOSSIBLE TO RUN A PER-CRIMINAL MAXIMUM SECURITY PRISON AND HANDLE A SPEC-OPS TEAM OF HAND-PICKED INMATES WITHOUT A REAKING RADIO OR PHONE. BUT, THAT SAID, I HAVE SET BALL IN MOTION AND NOW I'M CROSSING MY FINGERS.
AMANDA WALLER? PLEASE...GIVE A FEW MORE MINUTES. M SHARING THE O.M.A.C. HELL WITH THE THINKER UT I CAN GET HIM OUT OF IT AND REGAIN CONTROL.
THE SYNDICATE SHUT DOWN THE GRID AND USE THE SMARTEST MAN ON THE PLANET, THE THINKER, TO STICK HIMSELF INSIDE THE MOST DANGEROUS THING WE KEEP IMPRISONED HERE AT BELLE REVE.
WE DON'T HAVE MUCH TIME, KEVIN. I'VE SET THE WHEELS IN MOTION TO DESTROY O.M.A.C. SO YOU HAD BETTER HURRY. WE CAN'T RISK HAVING THIS THING ON THE LOOSE.
MANY YEARS AGO, A TEAM OF BELLE REVE SECURITY SPECIALISTS NSTALLED A PORTHOLE IN THE BOTTOM OF THE BUILDING. A PORTHOLE TO WHERE? THAT'S WHAT I ASKED.
I CAN DO IT. PLEASE...IF THE O.M.A.C. SHELL DIES... SO DO I.
MANY, MANY LEVELS BELOW OUR MOST TOP-SECRET LEVELS, WE HAVE THIS.
WELL, KEVIN KHO. I HATE TO SAY THIS, BUT IN THE NEXT TWENTY MINUTES YOU HAVE TO EITHER GET THE THINKER OUT OF THAT THING...

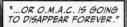

"...OR O.M.A.C. IS GOING TO DISAPPEAR FOREVER."

A PORTHOLE TO NOWHERE. YOU SHOVE SOMETHING IN THIS PORTHOLE AND IT NEVER COMES BACK. THERE WERE DESCRIPTIONS OF "NETHER DIMENSIONS" AND "FICTIONAL TIME STREAMS" BUT THE SHORT OF IT IS...IF IT CAN'T BE EXECUTED OR IMPRISONED, YOU STICK IT IN THIS THING AND NEVER SEE IT AGAIN.

THE SCIENTISTS GAVE IT SOME FANCY-SCHMANCY SCIENCE-Y NAME THAT I CAN'T PRONOUNCE. WE NICKNAMED IT...THE TOILET.

IT WAS SHUT DOWN ALMOST IMMEDIATELY FOR FEAR THAT WE WERE DUMPING OUR MOST DANGEROUS PROBLEMS INTO SOME OTHER UNIVERSE'S LAP.

BUT AT THIS POINT? ANOTHER UNIVERSE IS THE LEAST OF MY WORRIES.

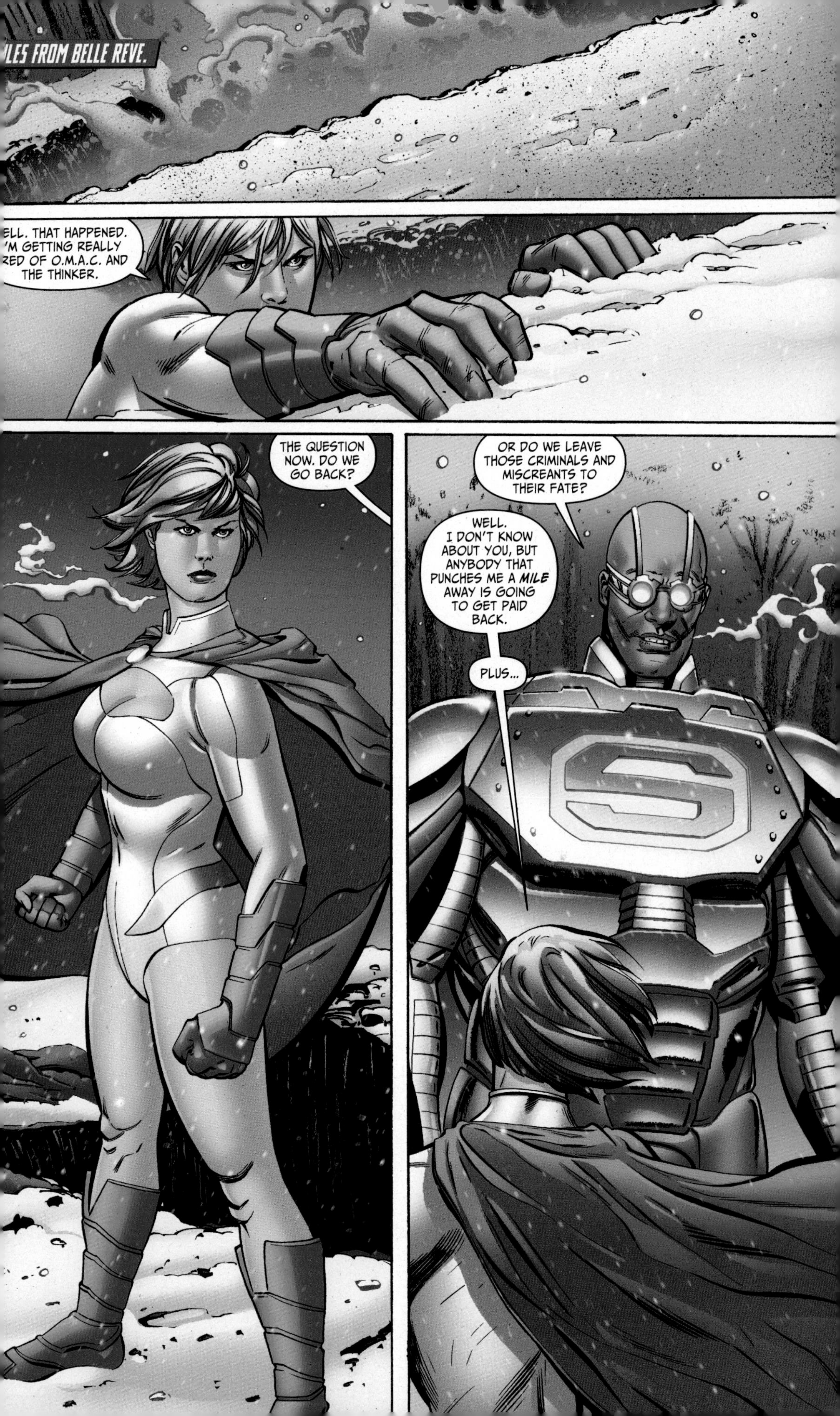

...ILES FROM BELLE REVE.
...ELL. THAT HAPPENED. ...'M GETTING REALLY ...RED OF O.M.A.C. AND THE THINKER.
THE QUESTION NOW. DO WE GO BACK?
OR DO WE LEAVE THOSE CRIMINALS AND MISCREANTS TO THEIR FATE?
WELL. I DON'T KNOW ABOUT YOU, BUT ANYBODY THAT PUNCHES ME A *MILE* AWAY IS GOING TO GET PAID BACK.
PLUS...

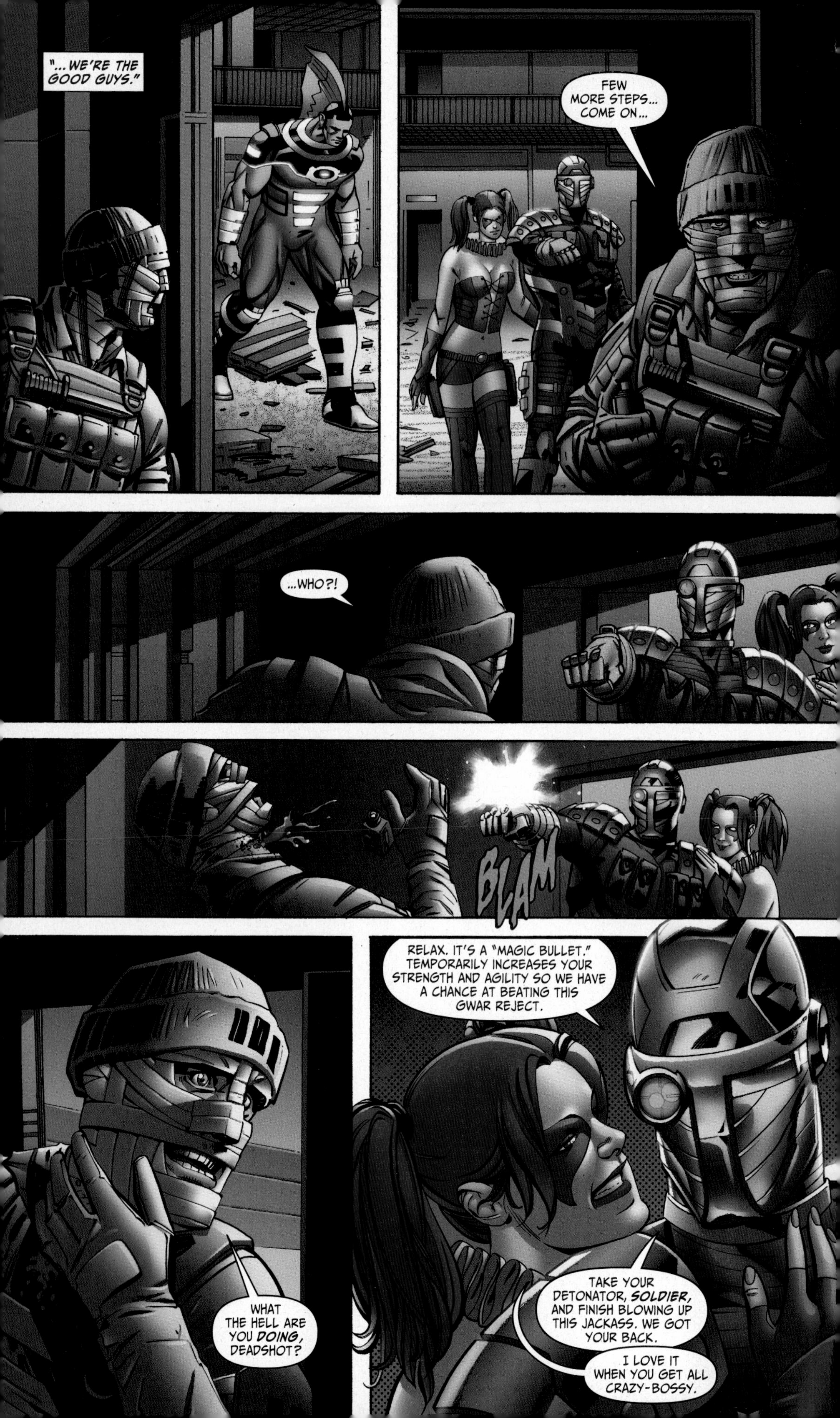
"...WE'RE THE GOOD GUYS."
FEW MORE STEPS... COME ON...
...WHO?!
BLAM
RELAX. IT'S A "MAGIC BULLET." TEMPORARILY INCREASES YOUR STRENGTH AND AGILITY SO WE HAVE A CHANCE AT BEATING THIS GWAR REJECT.
WHAT THE HELL ARE YOU DOING, DEADSHOT?
TAKE YOUR DETONATOR, SOLDIER, AND FINISH BLOWING UP THIS JACKASS. WE GOT YOUR BACK.
I LOVE IT WHEN YOU GET ALL CRAZY-BOSSY.

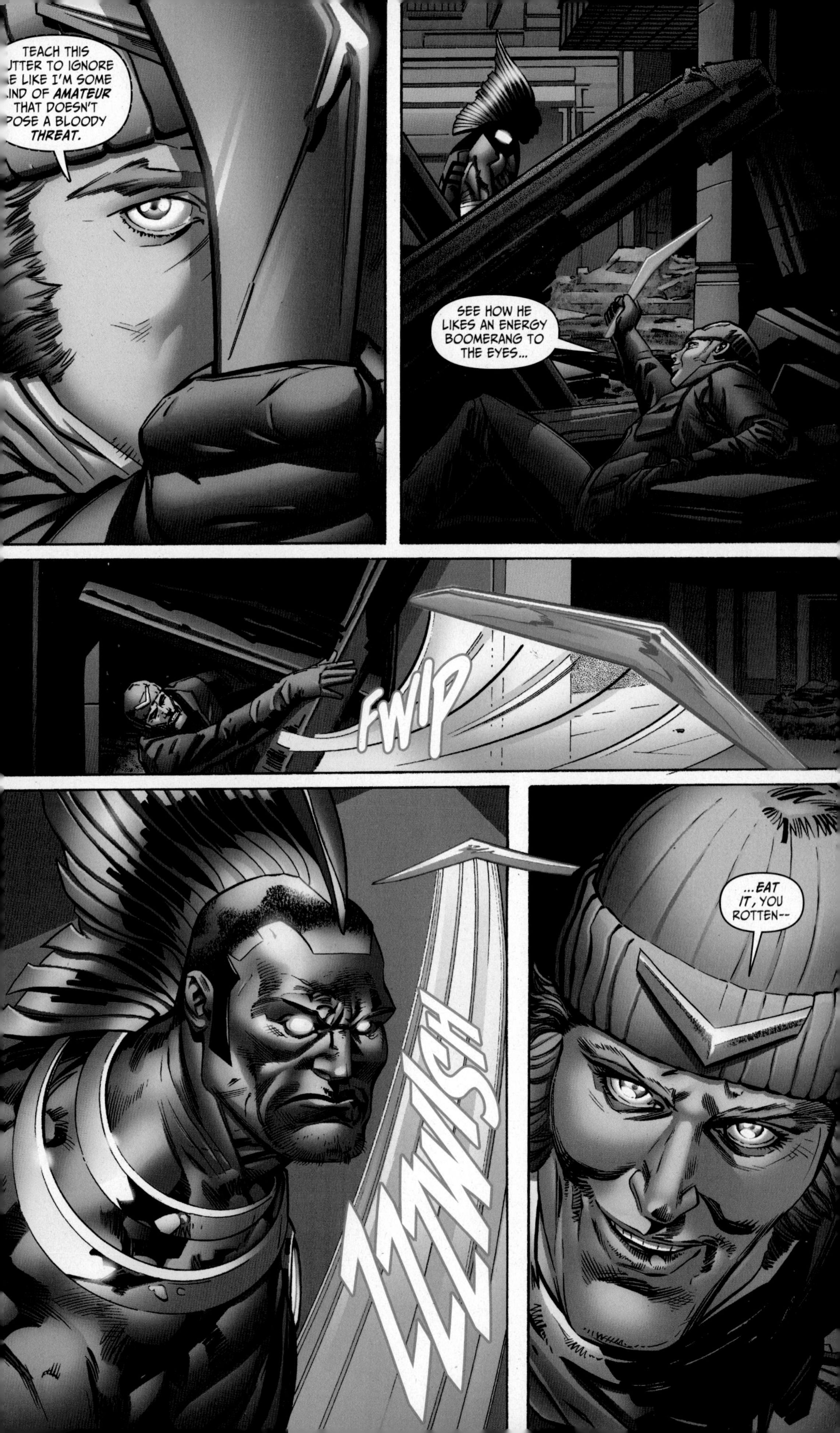

TEACH THIS UTTER TO IGNORE E LIKE I'M SOME IND OF *AMATEUR* THAT DOESN'T OSE A BLOODY *THREAT.*
SEE HOW HE LIKES AN ENERGY BOOMERANG TO THE EYES...
FWIP
...*EAT IT,* YOU ROTTEN--
ZZWISH

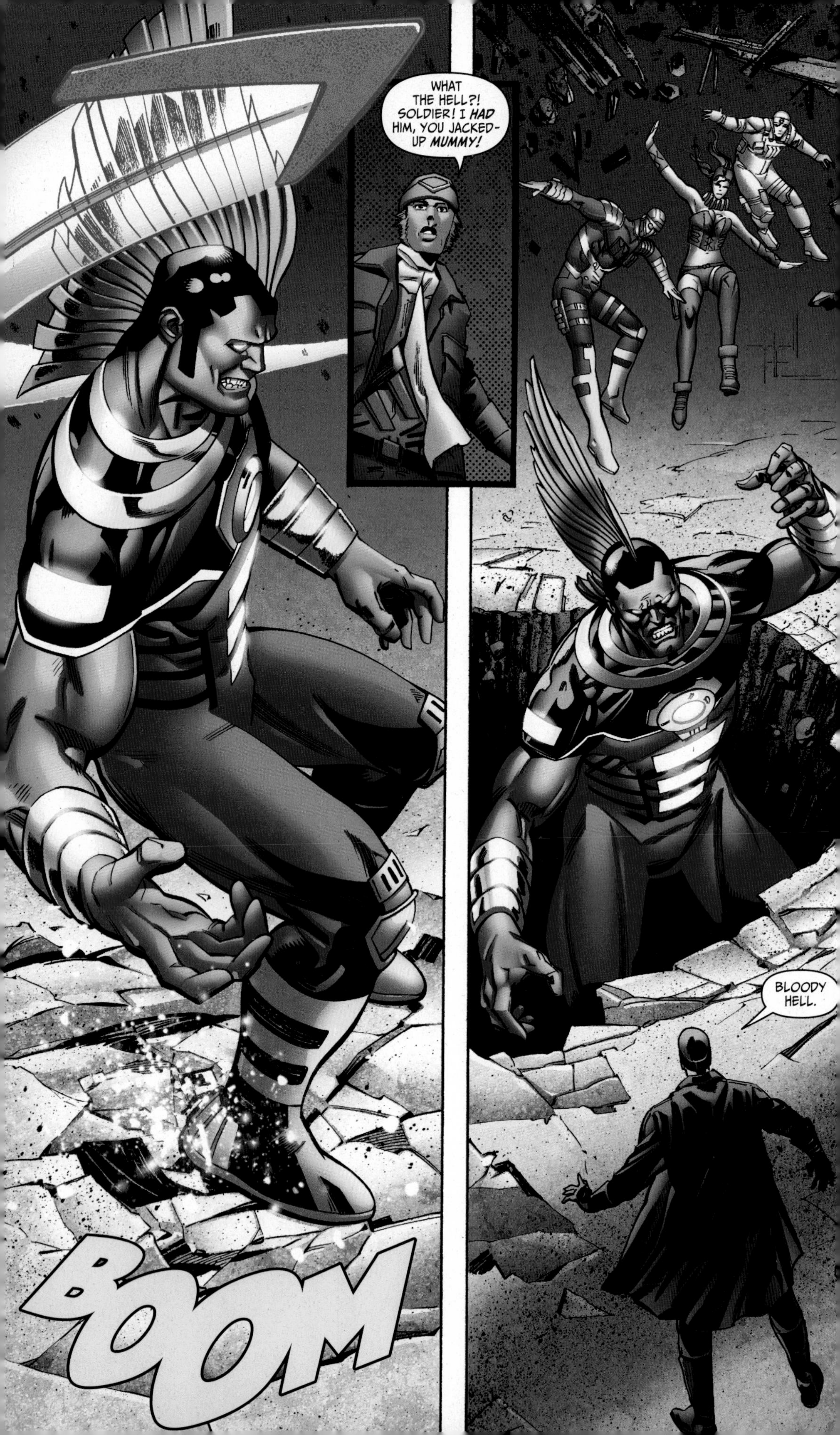
WHAT THE HELL?! SOLDIER! I HAD HIM, YOU JACKED-UP MUMMY!
BOOM
BLOODY HELL.

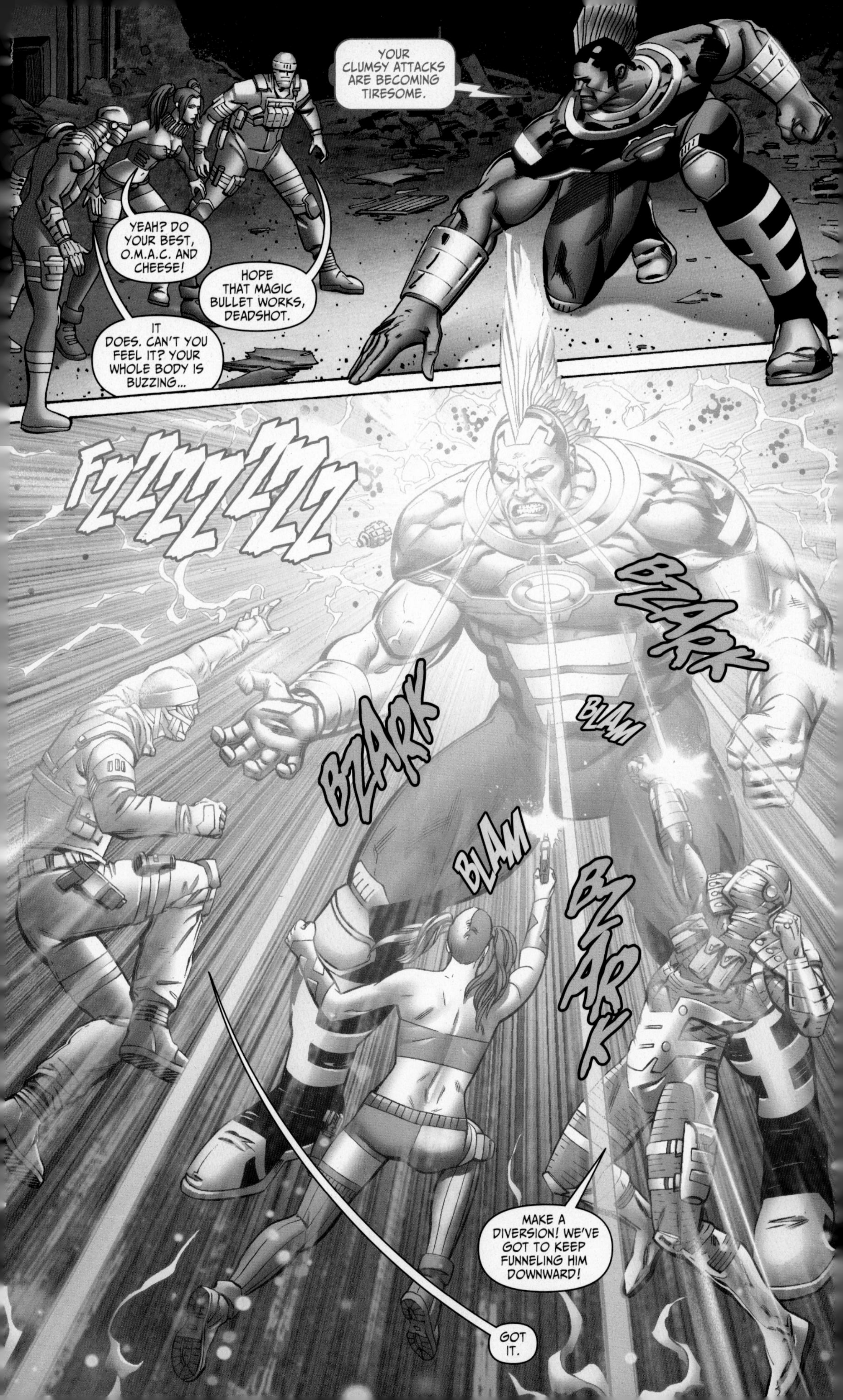
YOUR CLUMSY ATTACKS ARE BECOMING TIRESOME.
YEAH? DO YOUR BEST, O.M.A.C. AND CHEESE!
HOPE THAT MAGIC BULLET WORKS, DEADSHOT.
IT DOES. CAN'T YOU FEEL IT? YOUR WHOLE BODY IS BUZZING...
FZZZZZZZZ
BZARK
BLAM
BZARK
BLAM
BZARK
MAKE A DIVERSION! WE'VE GOT TO KEEP FUNNELING HIM DOWNWARD!
GOT IT.

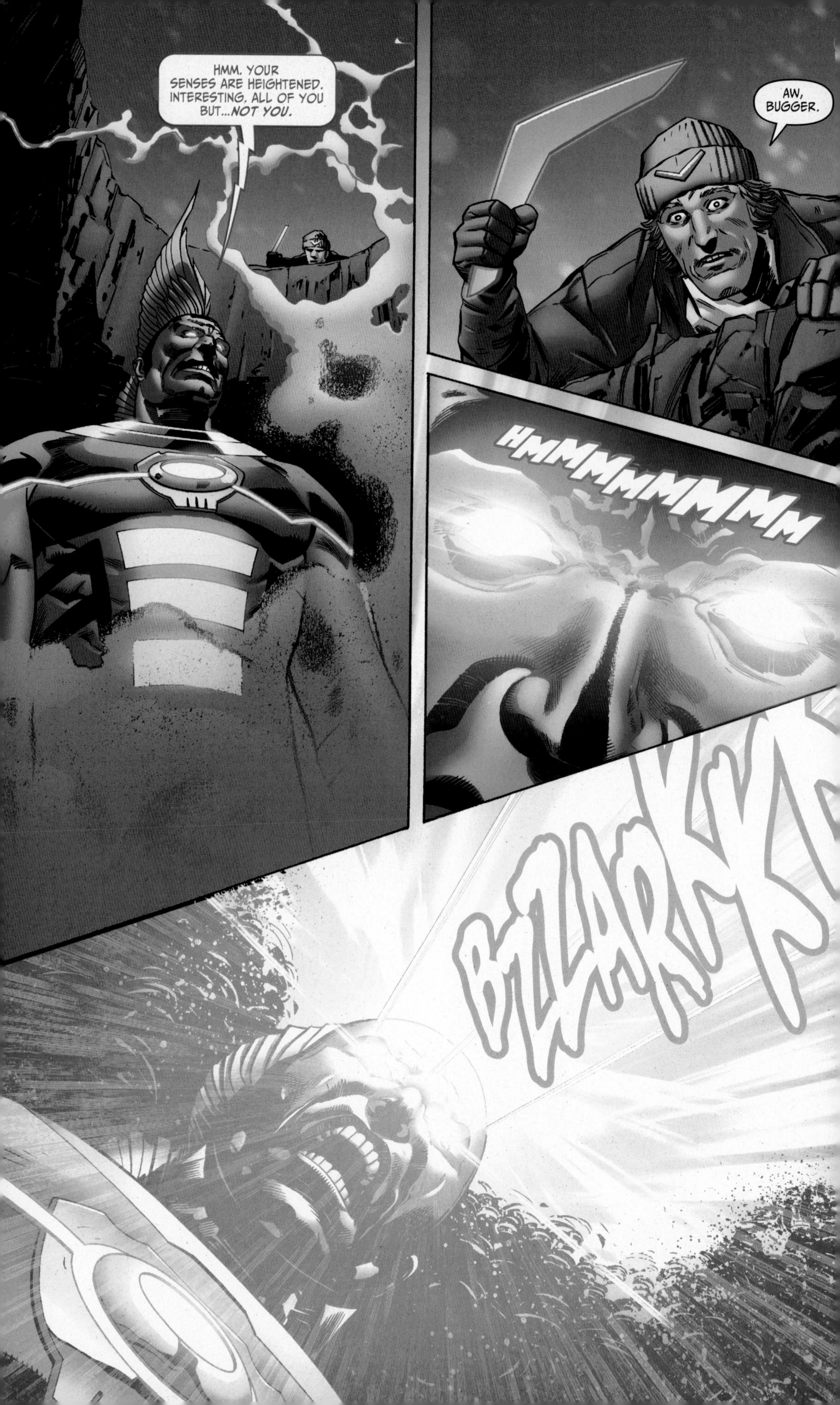

HMM. YOUR SENSES ARE HEIGHTENED. INTERESTING. ALL OF YOU BUT...NOT YOU.
AW, BUGGER.
HMMMMMMMMMM
BZZARK

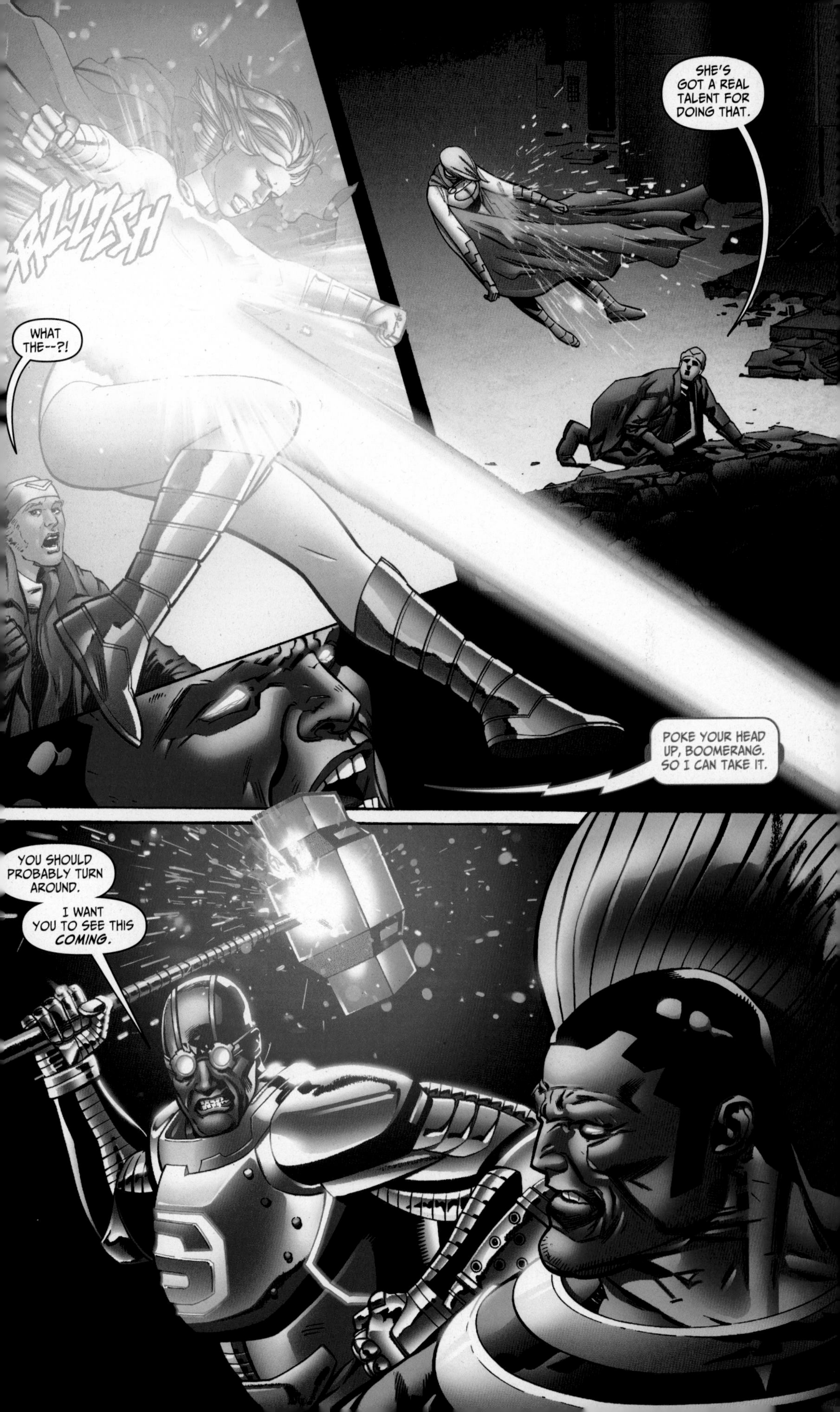
WHAT THE--?!
SHE'S GOT A REAL TALENT FOR DOING THAT.
POKE YOUR HEAD UP, BOOMERANG. SO I CAN TAKE IT.
YOU SHOULD PROBABLY TURN AROUND.
I WANT YOU TO SEE THIS *COMING*.

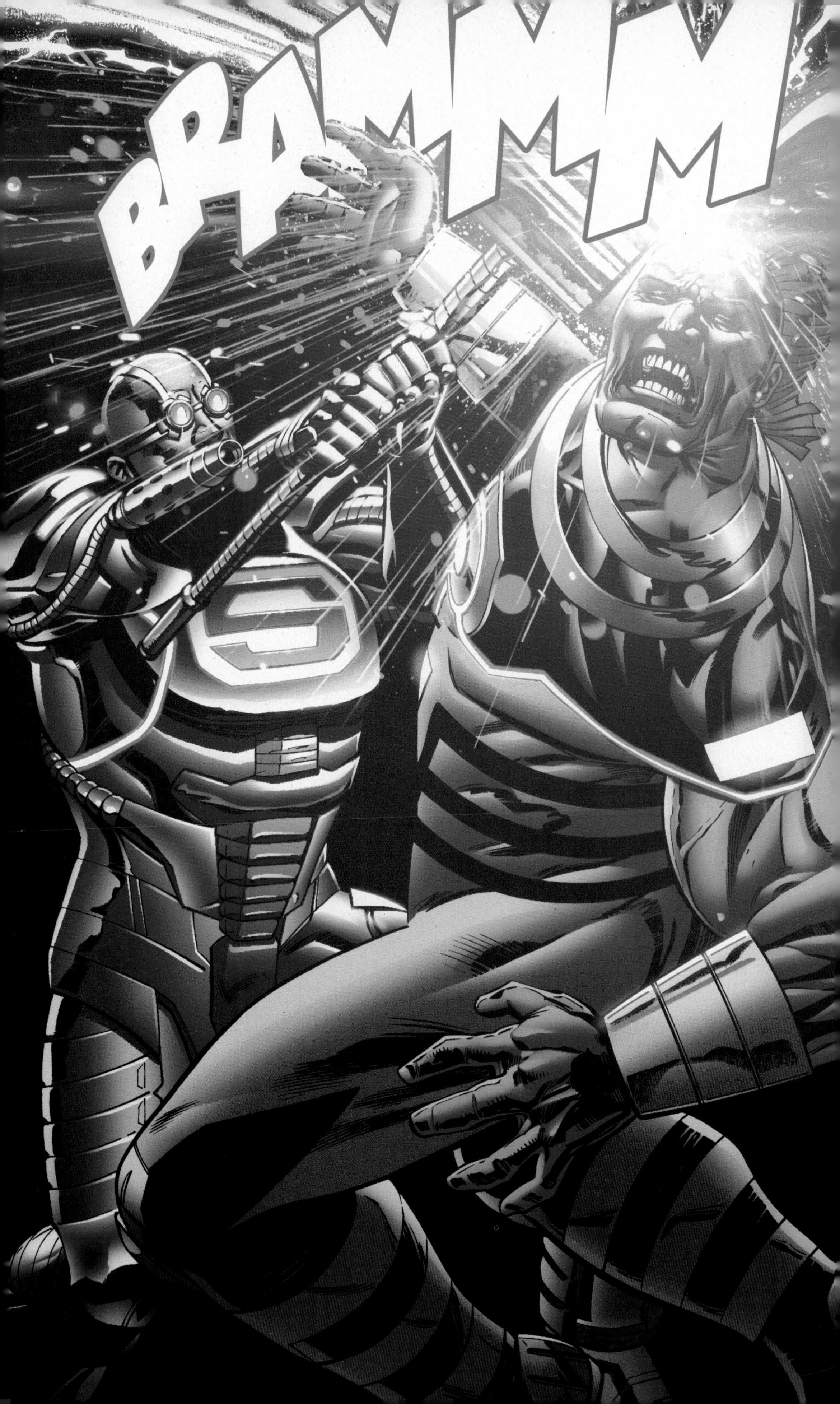
BRAMMM

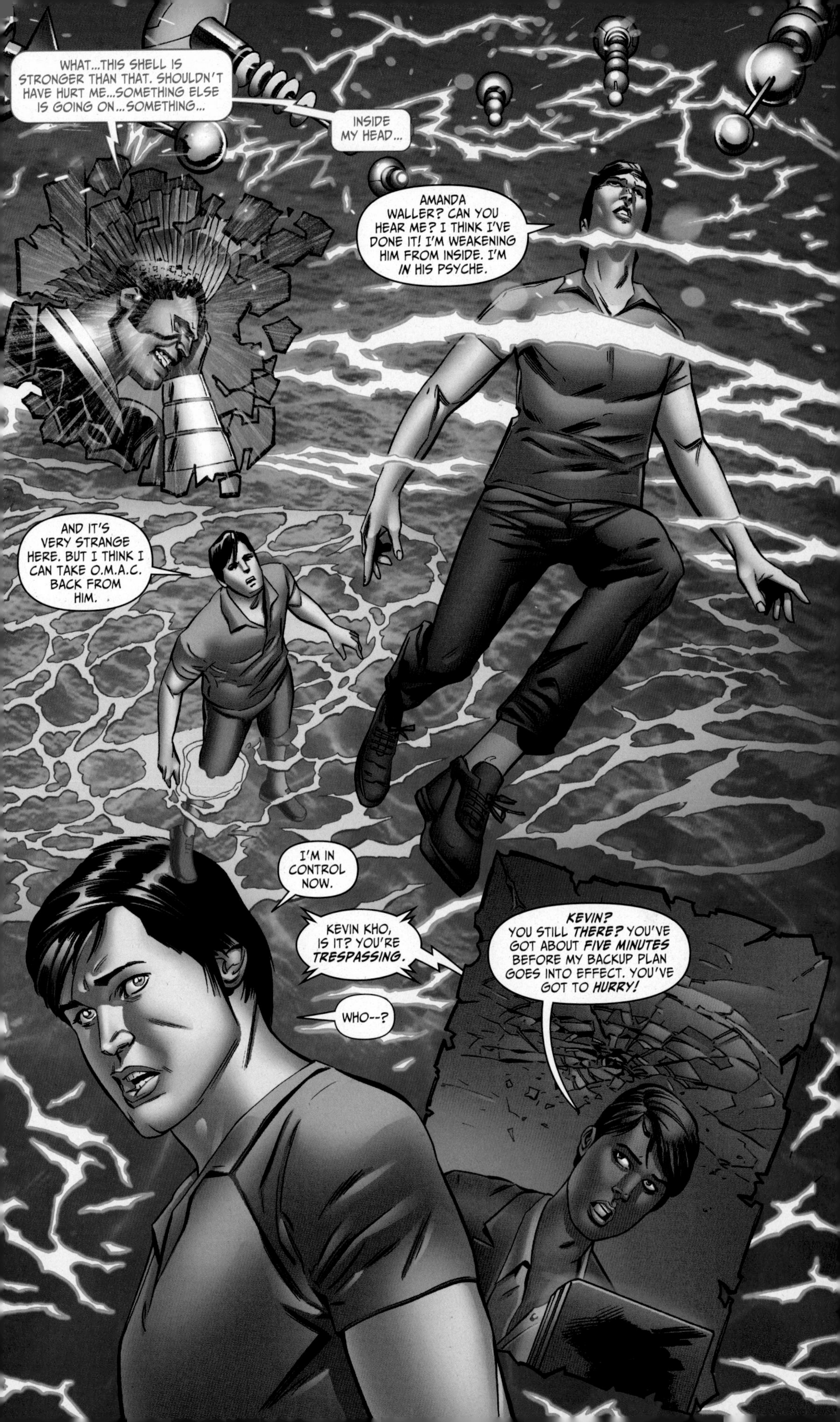
WHAT...THIS SHELL IS STRONGER THAN THAT. SHOULDN'T HAVE HURT ME...SOMETHING ELSE IS GOING ON...SOMETHING...
INSIDE MY HEAD...
AMANDA WALLER? CAN YOU HEAR ME? I THINK I'VE DONE IT! I'M WEAKENING HIM FROM INSIDE. I'M *IN* HIS PSYCHE.
AND IT'S VERY STRANGE HERE. BUT I THINK I CAN TAKE O.M.A.C. BACK FROM HIM.
I'M IN CONTROL NOW.
KEVIN KHO, IS IT? YOU'RE ***TRESPASSING.***
WHO--?
KEVIN? YOU STILL ***THERE?*** YOU'VE GOT ABOUT ***FIVE MINUTES*** BEFORE MY BACKUP PLAN GOES INTO EFFECT. YOU'VE GOT TO ***HURRY!***

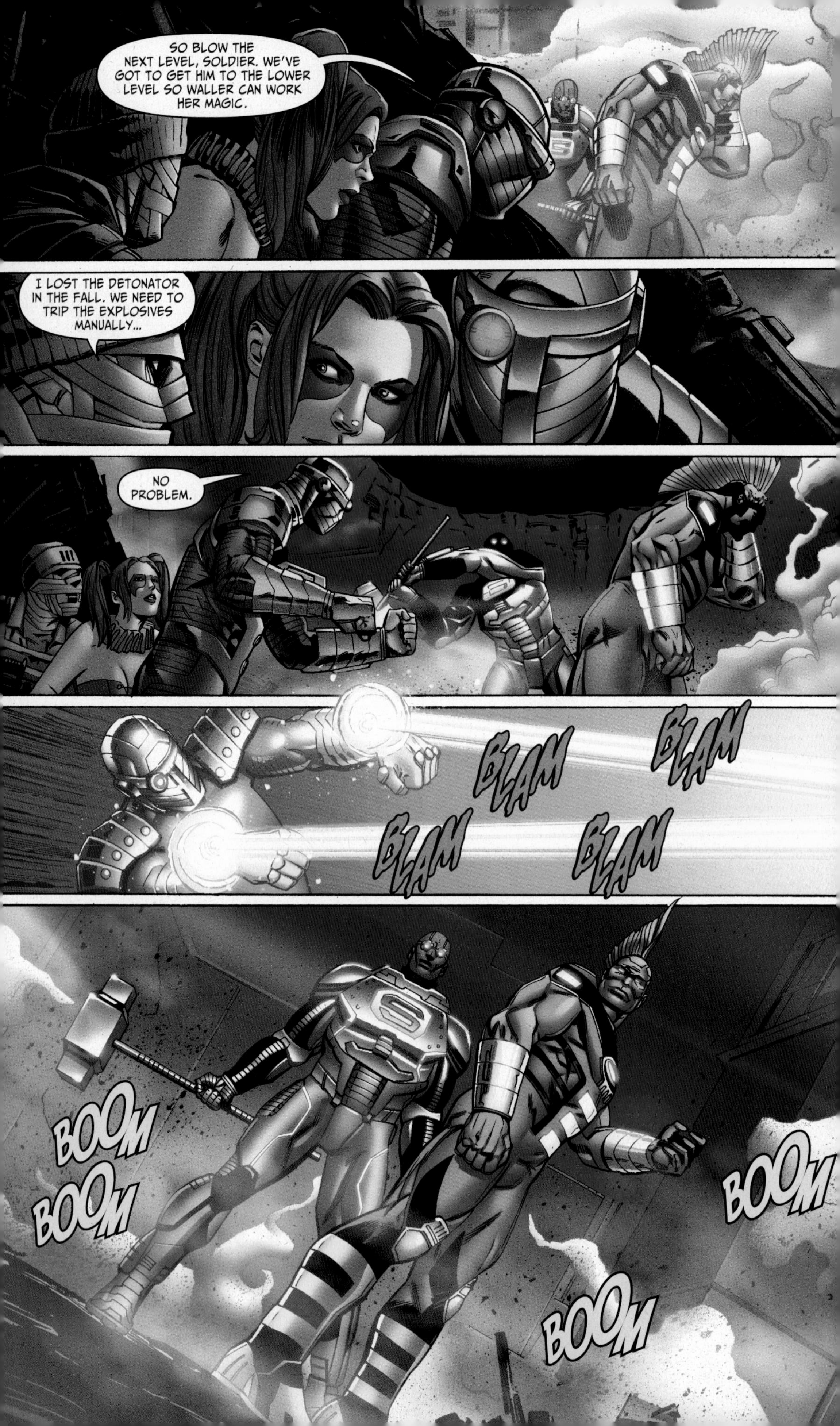
SO BLOW THE NEXT LEVEL, SOLDIER. WE'VE GOT TO GET HIM TO THE LOWER LEVEL SO WALLER CAN WORK HER MAGIC.
I LOST THE DETONATOR IN THE FALL. WE NEED TO TRIP THE EXPLOSIVES MANUALLY...
NO PROBLEM.
BLAM
BLAM
BLAM
BLAM
BOOM
BOOM
BOOM
BOOM

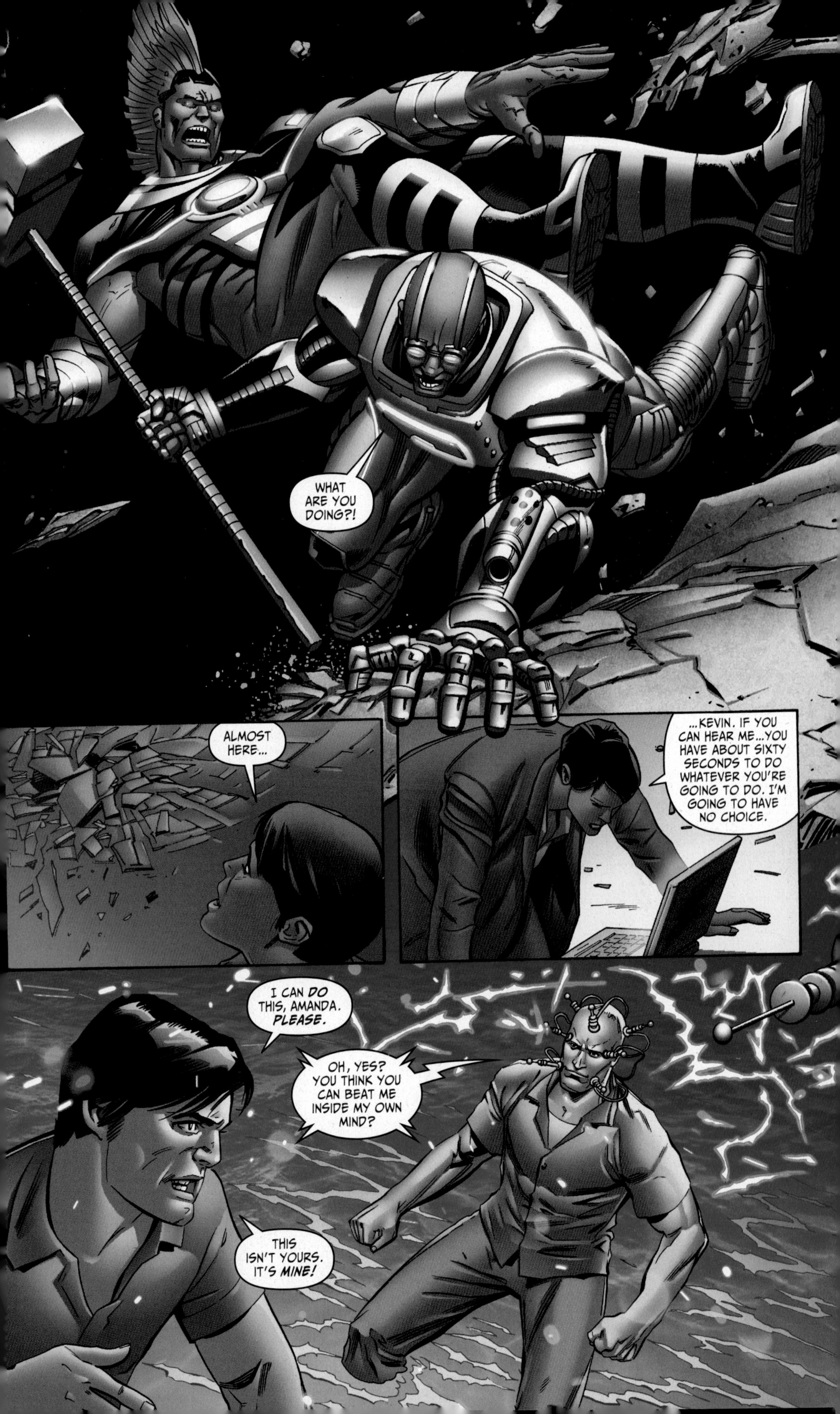
WHAT ARE YOU DOING?!
ALMOST HERE...
...KEVIN. IF YOU CAN HEAR ME...YOU HAVE ABOUT SIXTY SECONDS TO DO WHATEVER YOU'RE GOING TO DO. I'M GOING TO HAVE NO CHOICE.
I CAN *DO* THIS, AMANDA. ***PLEASE.***
OH, YES? YOU THINK YOU CAN BEAT ME INSIDE MY OWN MIND?
THIS ISN'T YOURS. IT'S *MINE!*

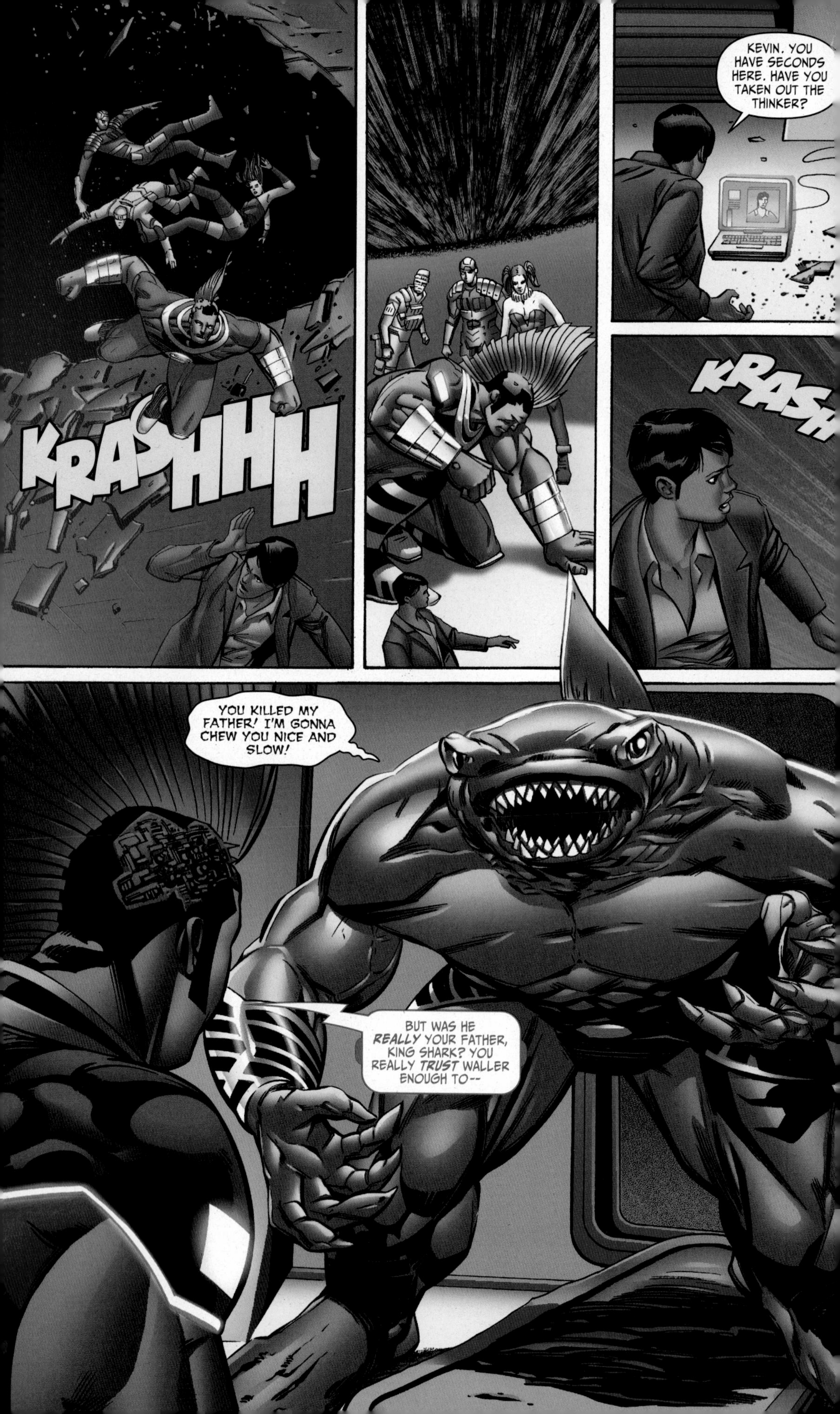
KRASHHHH
KEVIN. YOU HAVE SECONDS HERE. HAVE YOU TAKEN OUT THE THINKER?
KRASH
YOU KILLED MY FATHER! I'M GONNA CHEW YOU NICE AND SLOW!
BUT WAS HE *REALLY* YOUR FATHER, KING SHARK? YOU REALLY *TRUST* WALLER ENOUGH TO--

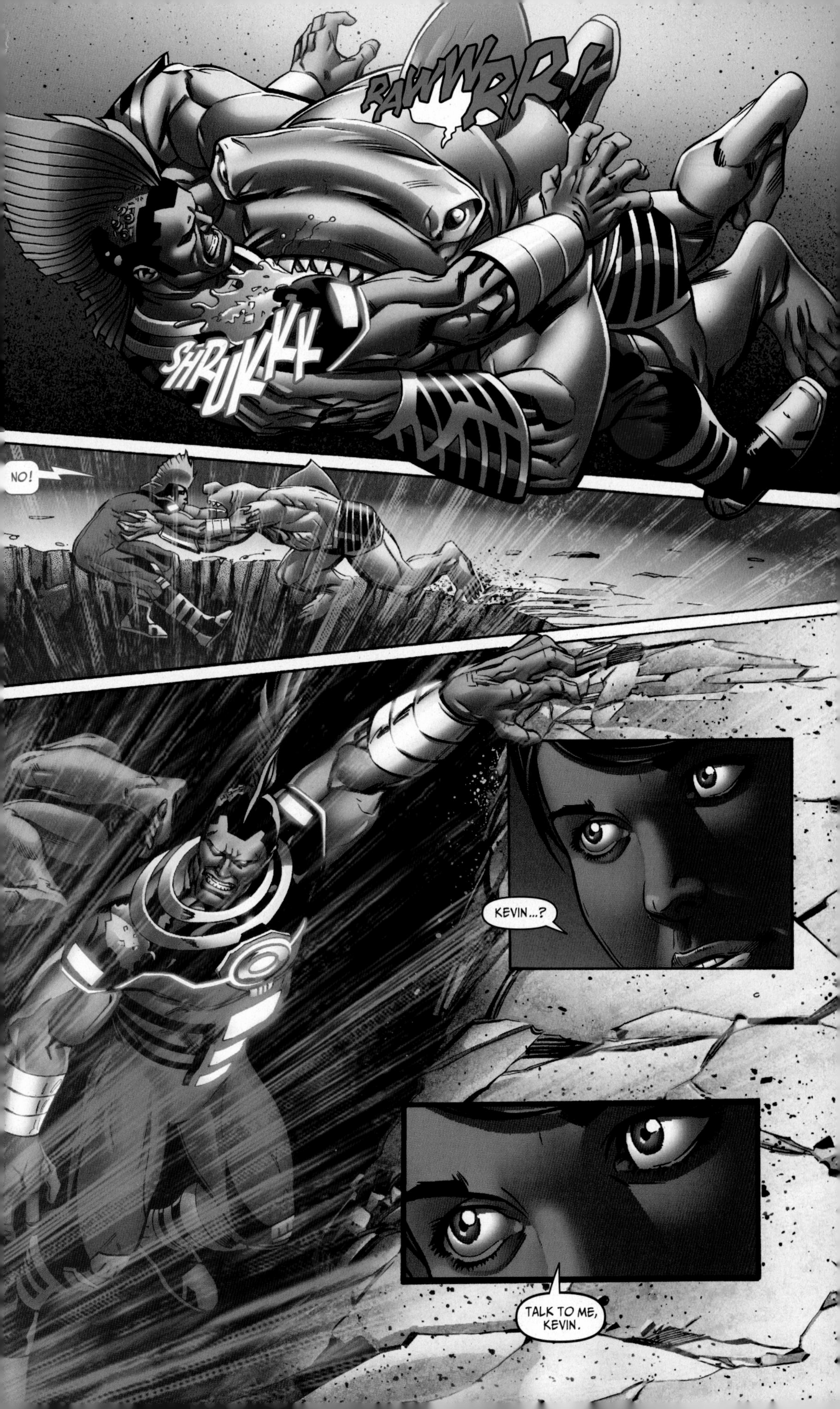
RAWWRR!
SHRUKKK
NO!
KEVIN...?
TALK TO ME, KEVIN.

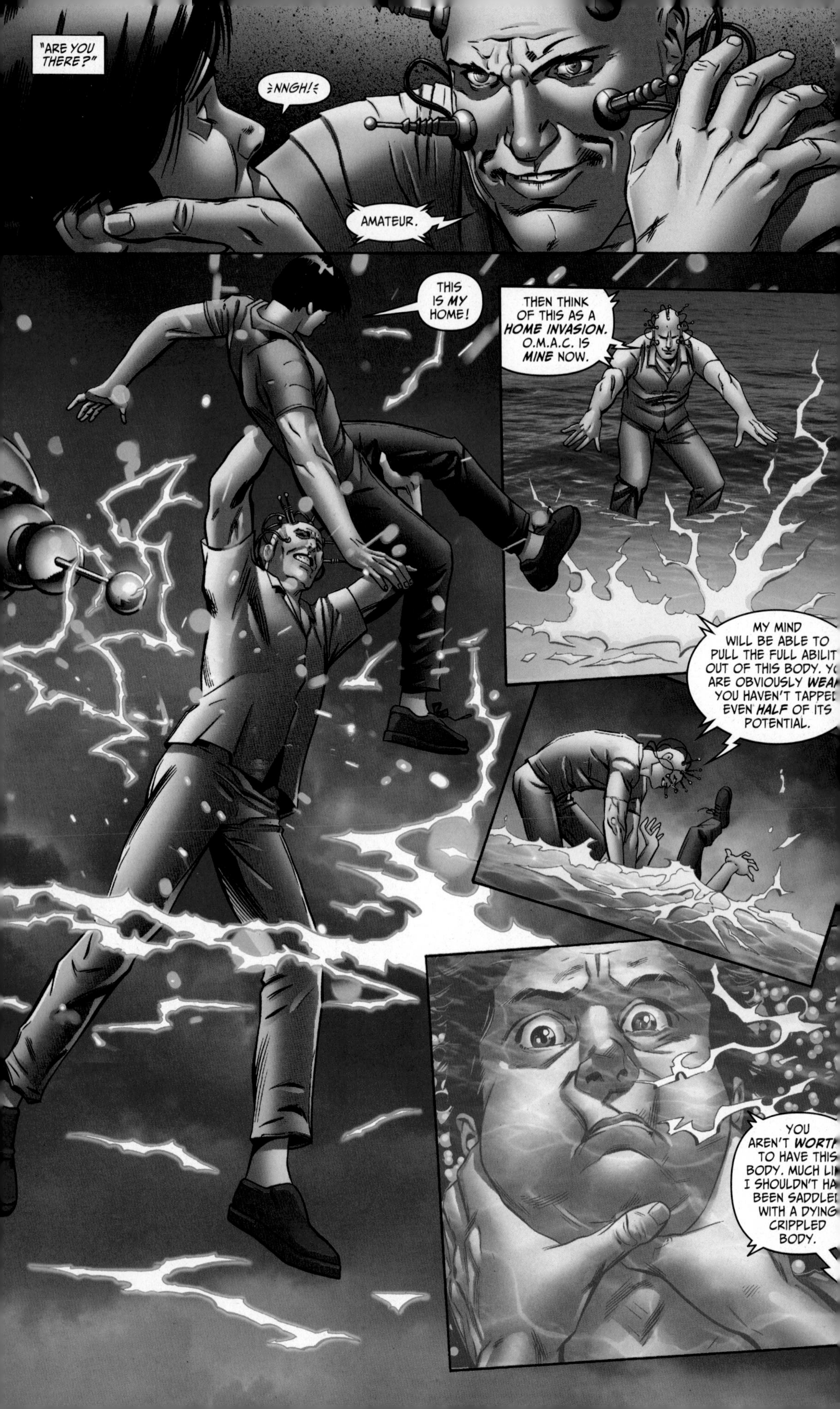

"ARE YOU THERE?"
NNGH!
AMATEUR.
THIS IS MY HOME!
THEN THINK OF THIS AS A HOME INVASION. O.M.A.C. IS MINE NOW.
MY MIND WILL BE ABLE TO PULL THE FULL ABILIT OUT OF THIS BODY. YO ARE OBVIOUSLY WEA YOU HAVEN'T TAPPE EVEN HALF OF ITS POTENTIAL.
YOU AREN'T WORT TO HAVE THIS BODY. MUCH LI I SHOULDN'T HA BEEN SADDLE WITH A DYING CRIPPLED BODY.

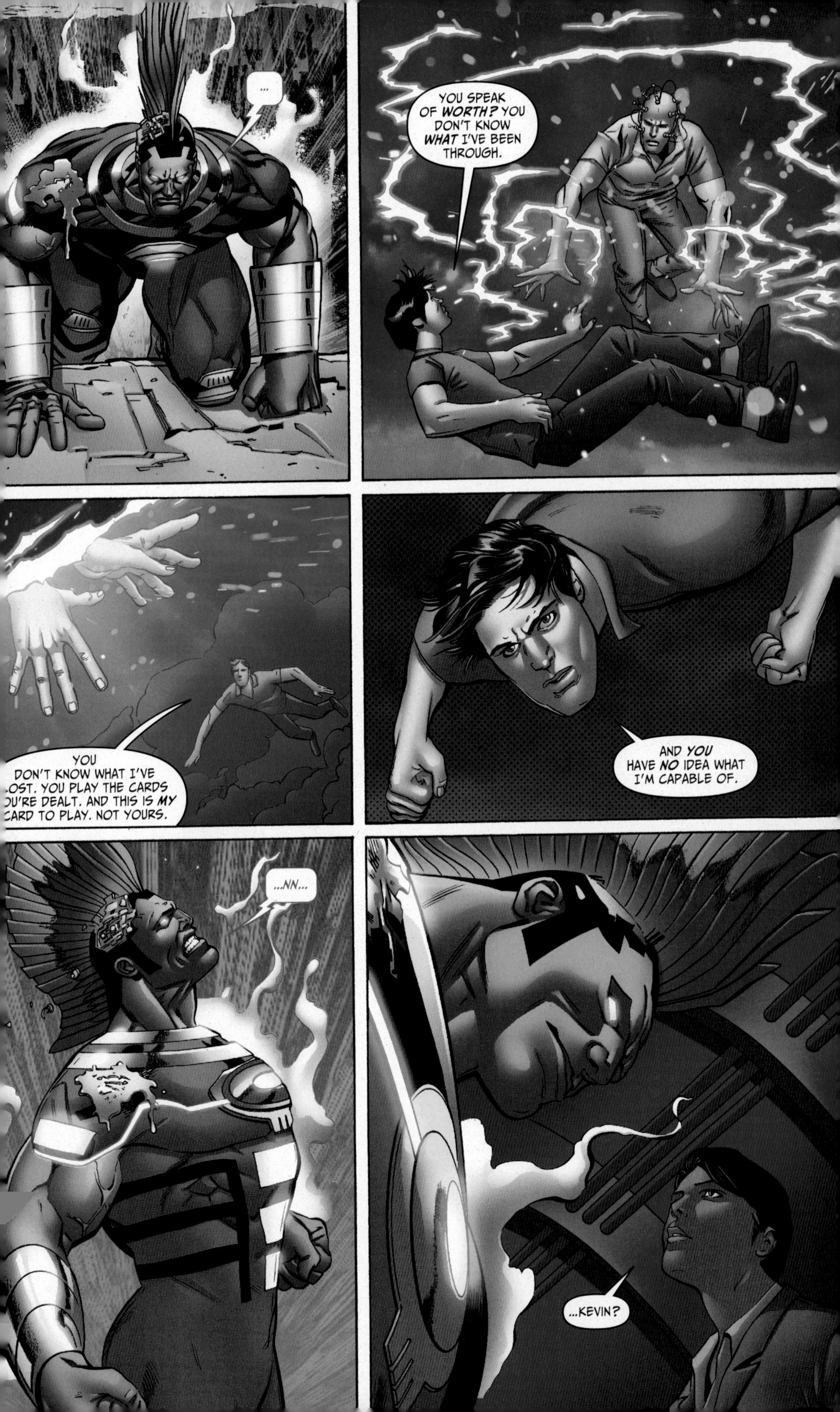
...
YOU SPEAK OF WORTH? YOU DON'T KNOW WHAT I'VE BEEN THROUGH.
YOU DON'T KNOW WHAT I'VE LOST. YOU PLAY THE CARDS YOU'RE DEALT. AND THIS IS MY CARD TO PLAY. NOT YOURS.
AND YOU HAVE NO IDEA WHAT I'M CAPABLE OF.
...NN...
...KEVIN?

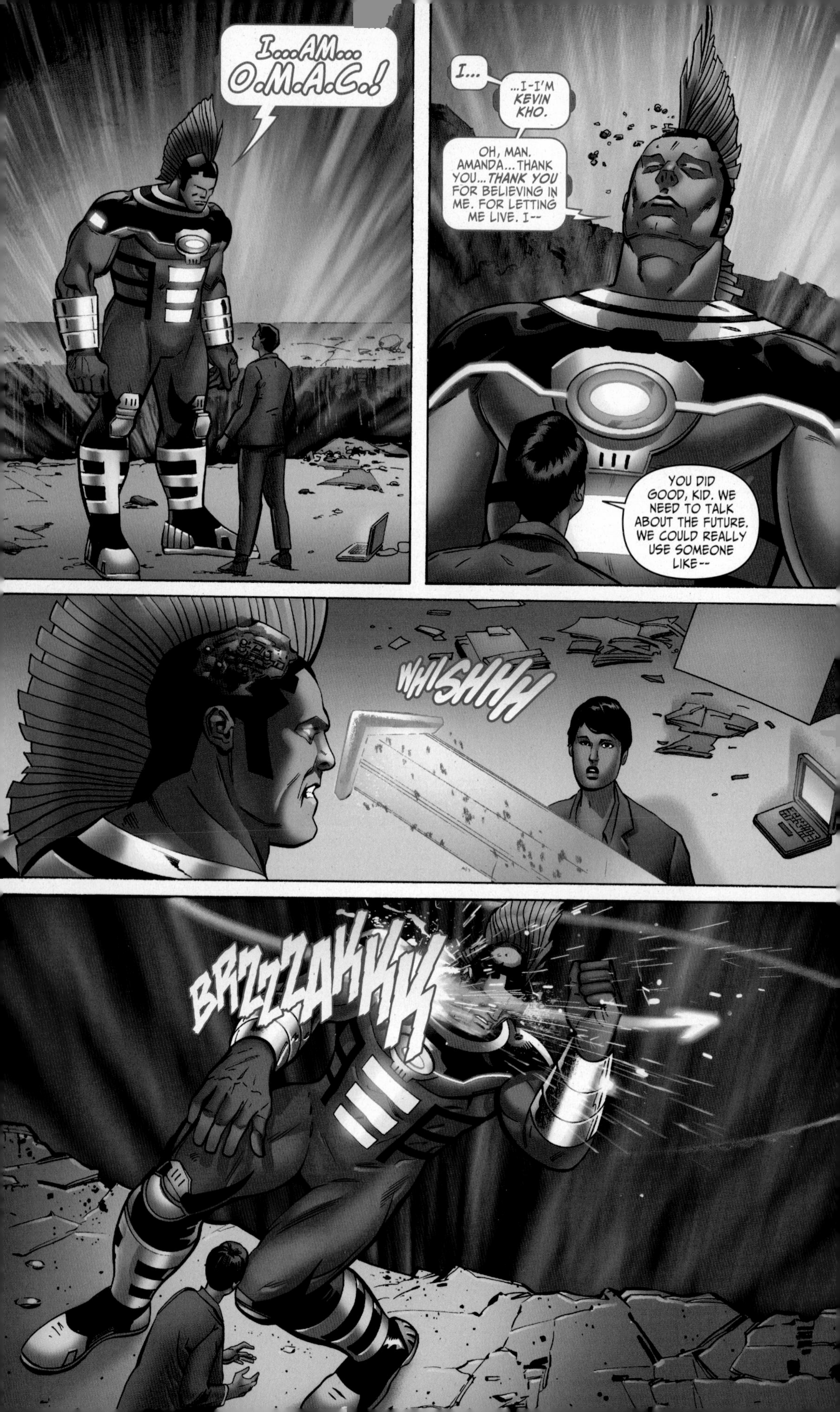
I...AM... O.M.A.C.!
I...
...I-I'M KEVIN KHO.
OH, MAN. AMANDA...THANK YOU...THANK YOU FOR BELIEVING IN ME. FOR LETTING ME LIVE. I--
YOU DID GOOD, KID. WE NEED TO TALK ABOUT THE FUTURE. WE COULD REALLY USE SOMEONE LIKE--
WHISHHH
BRZZZAKKKK

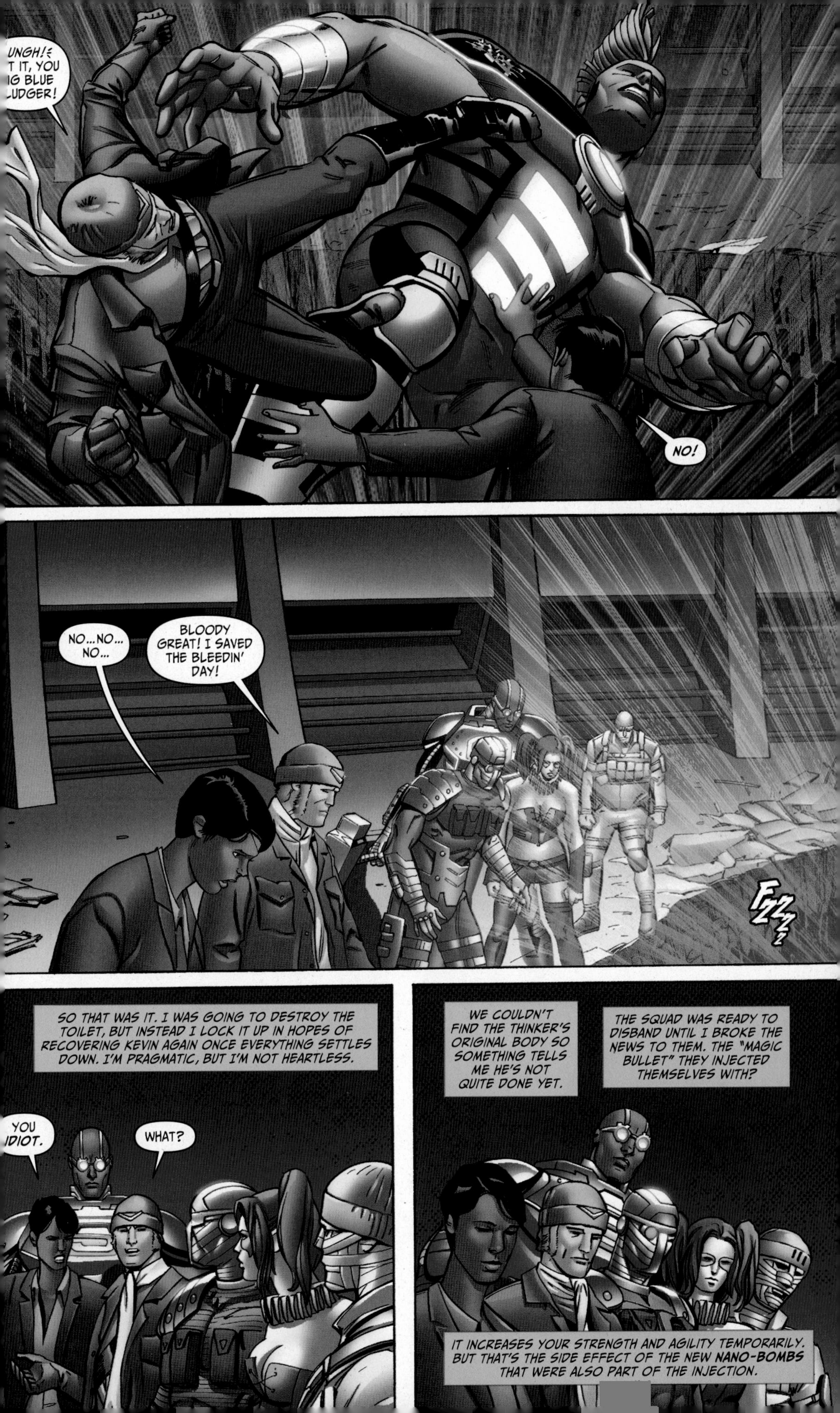
UNGH! ...T IT, YOU ...G BLUE ...UDGER!
NO!
NO...NO... NO...
BLOODY GREAT! I SAVED THE BLEEDIN' DAY!
FZZZZ
SO THAT WAS IT. I WAS GOING TO DESTROY THE TOILET, BUT INSTEAD I LOCK IT UP IN HOPES OF RECOVERING KEVIN AGAIN ONCE EVERYTHING SETTLES DOWN. I'M PRAGMATIC, BUT I'M NOT HEARTLESS.
YOU IDIOT.
WHAT?
WE COULDN'T FIND THE THINKER'S ORIGINAL BODY SO SOMETHING TELLS ME HE'S NOT QUITE DONE YET.
THE SQUAD WAS READY TO DISBAND UNTIL I BROKE THE NEWS TO THEM. THE "MAGIC BULLET" THEY INJECTED THEMSELVES WITH?
IT INCREASES YOUR STRENGTH AND AGILITY TEMPORARILY. BUT THAT'S THE SIDE EFFECT OF THE NEW NANO-BOMBS THAT WERE ALSO PART OF THE INJECTION.

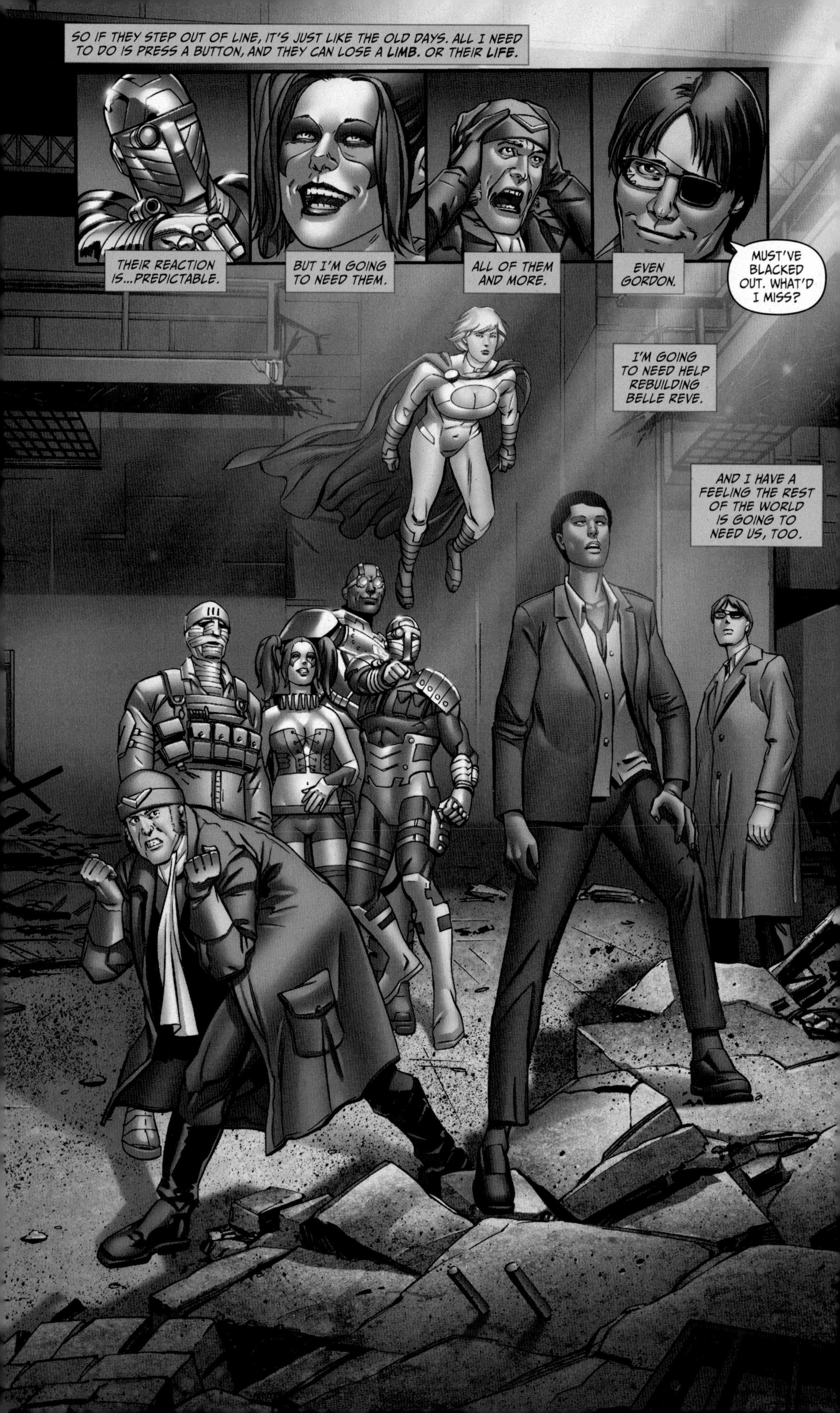
SO IF THEY STEP OUT OF LINE, IT'S JUST LIKE THE OLD DAYS. ALL I NEED TO DO IS PRESS A BUTTON, AND THEY CAN LOSE A **LIMB**. OR THEIR **LIFE**.
THEIR REACTION IS...PREDICTABLE.
BUT I'M GOING TO NEED THEM.
ALL OF THEM AND MORE.
EVEN GORDON.
MUST'VE BLACKED OUT. WHAT'D I MISS?
I'M GOING TO NEED HELP REBUILDING BELLE REVE.
AND I HAVE A FEELING THE REST OF THE WORLD IS GOING TO NEED US, TOO.

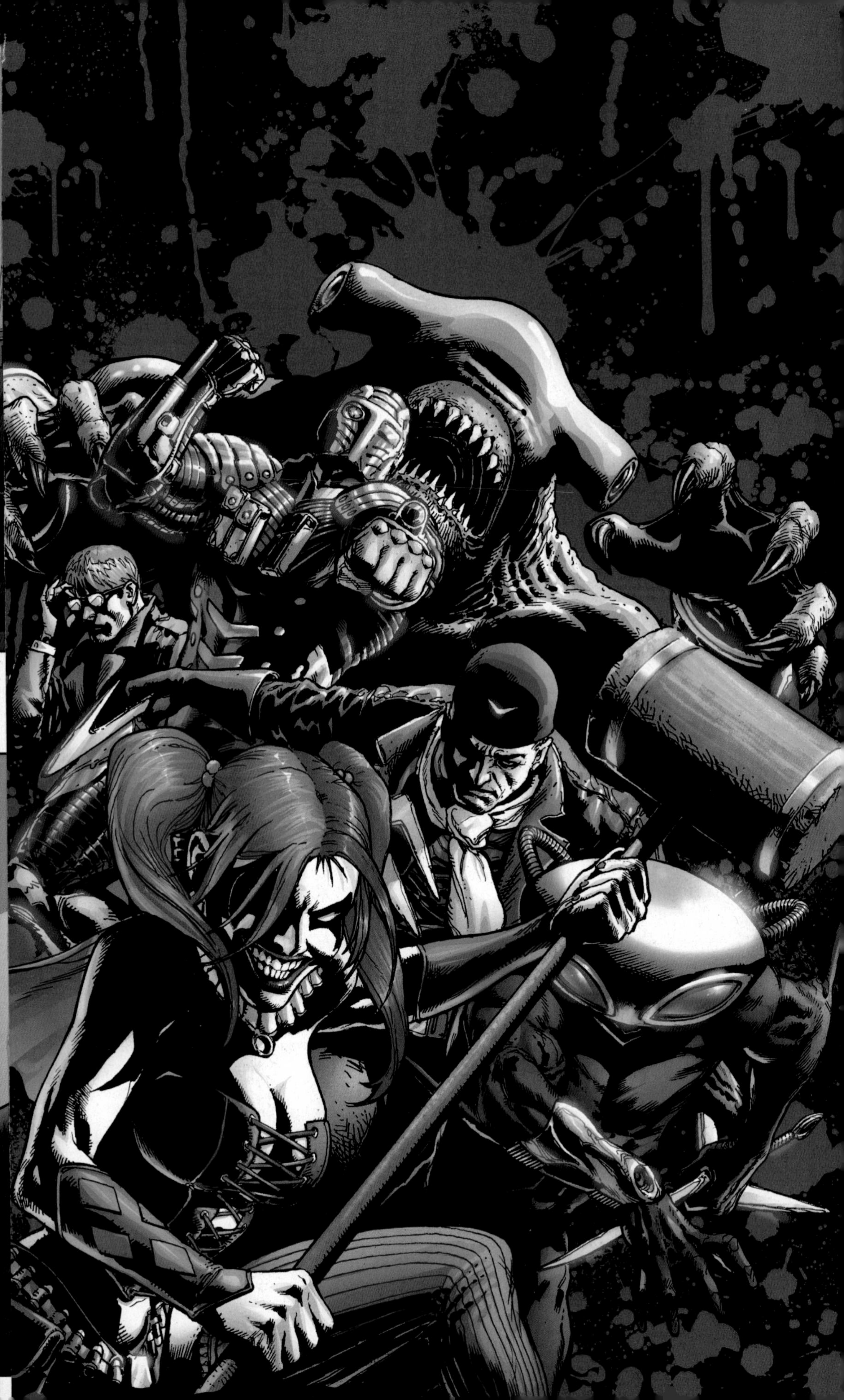

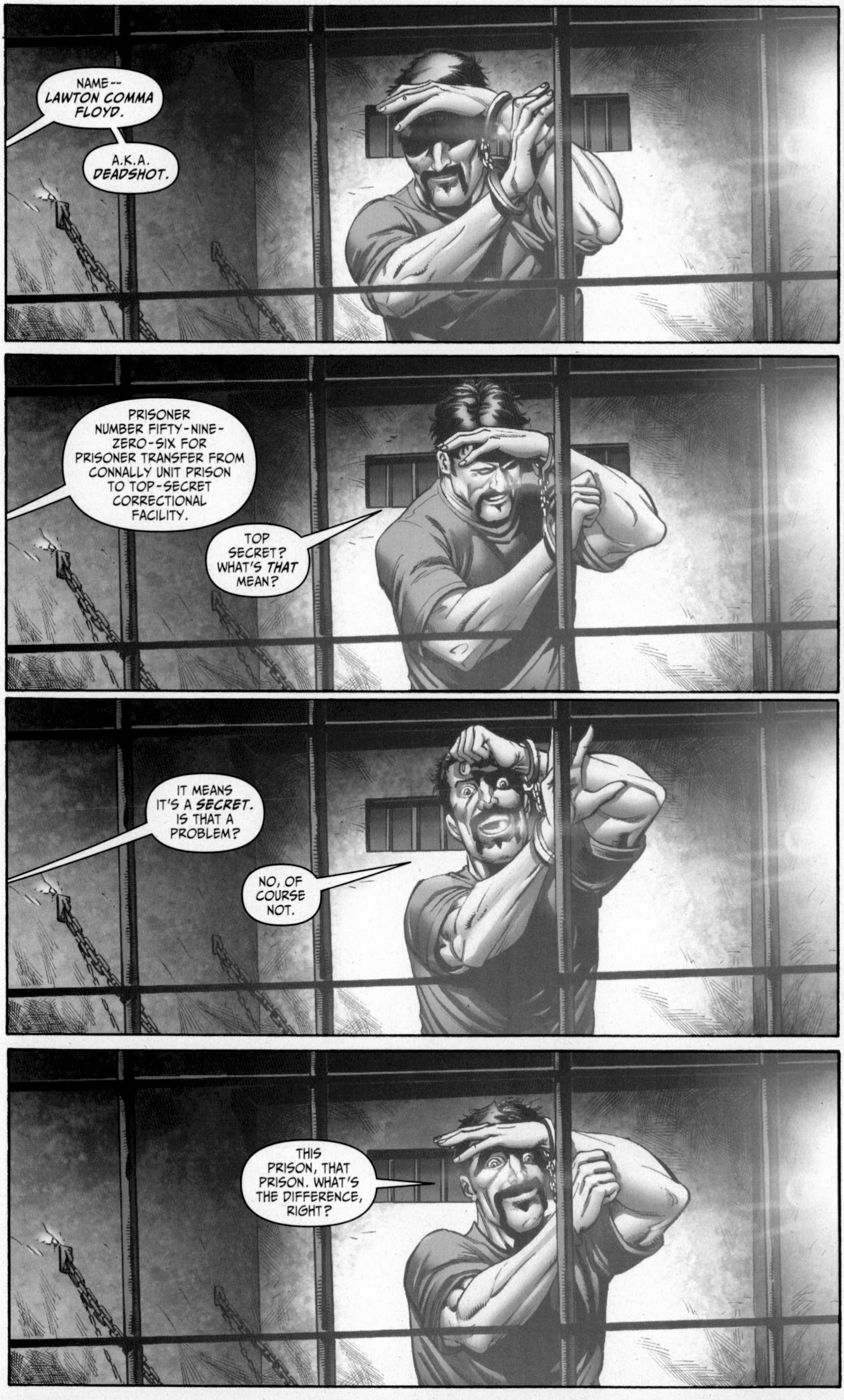
NAME-- LAWTON COMMA FLOYD.
A.K.A. DEADSHOT.
PRISONER NUMBER FIFTY-NINE-ZERO-SIX FOR PRISONER TRANSFER FROM CONNALLY UNIT PRISON TO TOP-SECRET CORRECTIONAL FACILITY.
TOP SECRET? WHAT'S THAT MEAN?
IT MEANS IT'S A SECRET. IS THAT A PROBLEM?
NO, OF COURSE NOT.
THIS PRISON, THAT PRISON. WHAT'S THE DIFFERENCE, RIGHT?

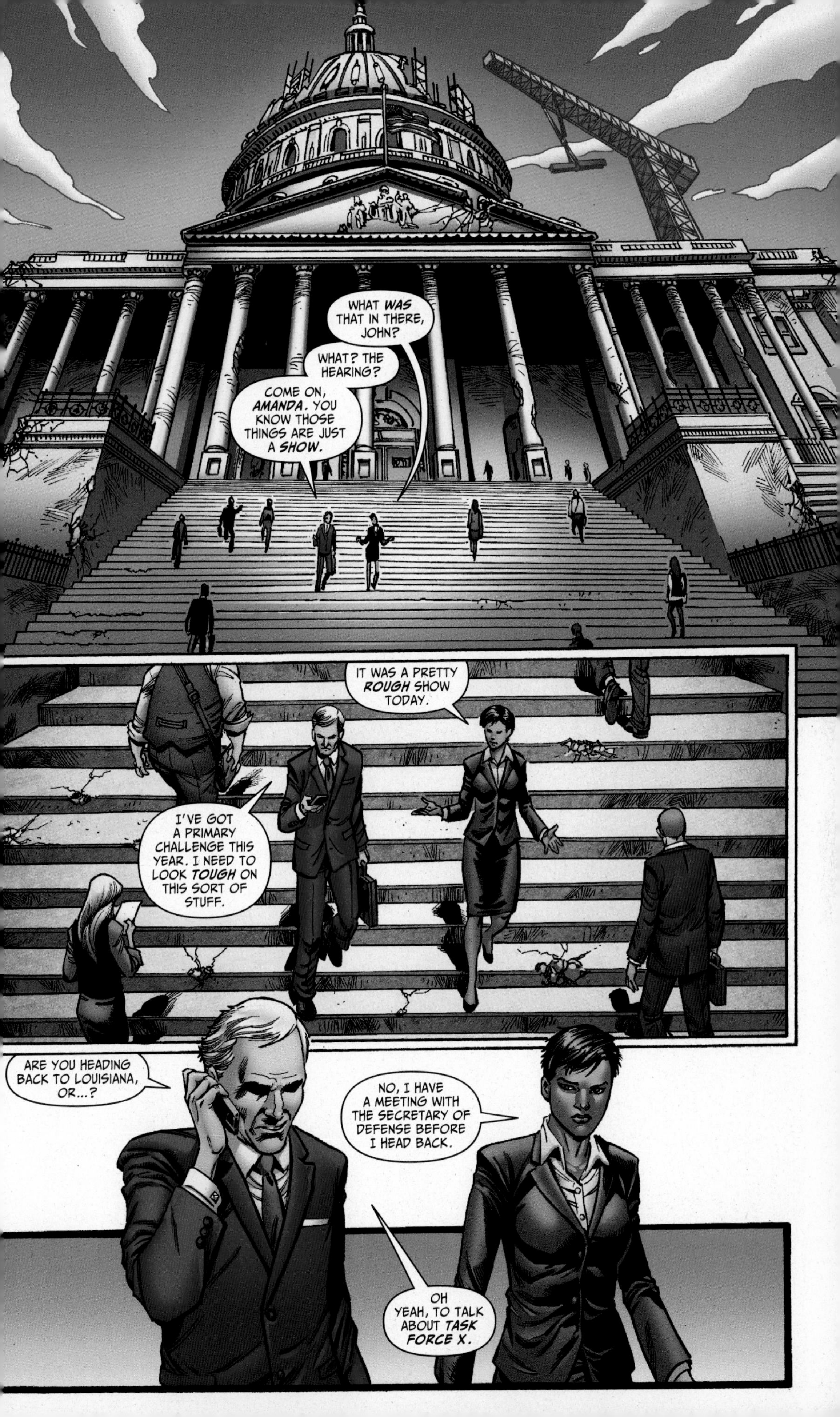
WHAT WAS THAT IN THERE, JOHN?
WHAT? THE HEARING?
COME ON, AMANDA. YOU KNOW THOSE THINGS ARE JUST A SHOW.
IT WAS A PRETTY ROUGH SHOW TODAY.
I'VE GOT A PRIMARY CHALLENGE THIS YEAR. I NEED TO LOOK TOUGH ON THIS SORT OF STUFF.
ARE YOU HEADING BACK TO LOUISIANA, OR...?
NO, I HAVE A MEETING WITH THE SECRETARY OF DEFENSE BEFORE I HEAD BACK.
OH YEAH, TO TALK ABOUT TASK FORCE X.

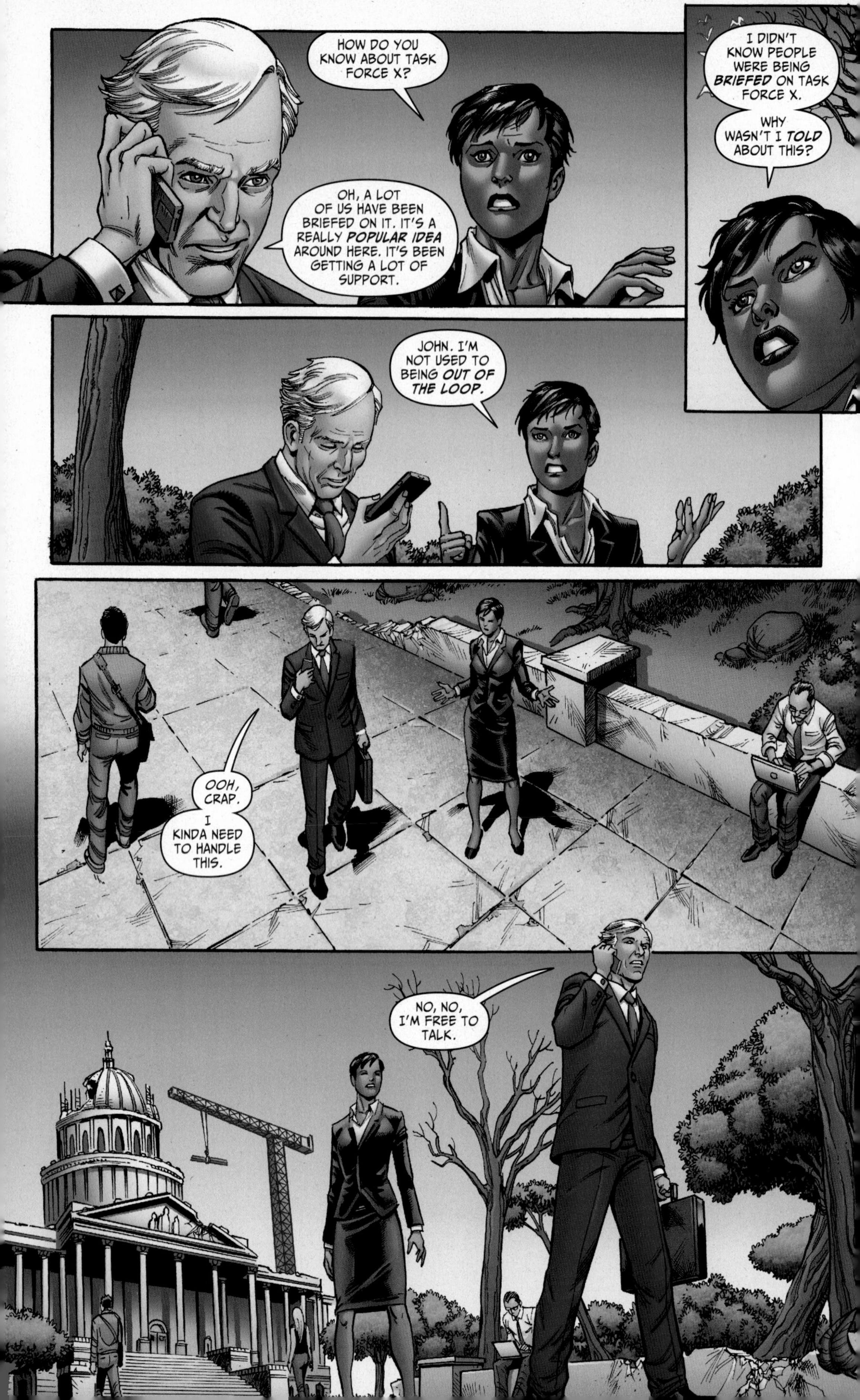
HOW DO YOU KNOW ABOUT TASK FORCE X?
OH, A LOT OF US HAVE BEEN BRIEFED ON IT. IT'S A REALLY POPULAR IDEA AROUND HERE. IT'S BEEN GETTING A LOT OF SUPPORT.
I DIDN'T KNOW PEOPLE WERE BEING BRIEFED ON TASK FORCE X.
WHY WASN'T I TOLD ABOUT THIS?
JOHN. I'M NOT USED TO BEING OUT OF THE LOOP.
OOH, CRAP.
I KINDA NEED TO HANDLE THIS.
NO, NO, I'M FREE TO TALK.

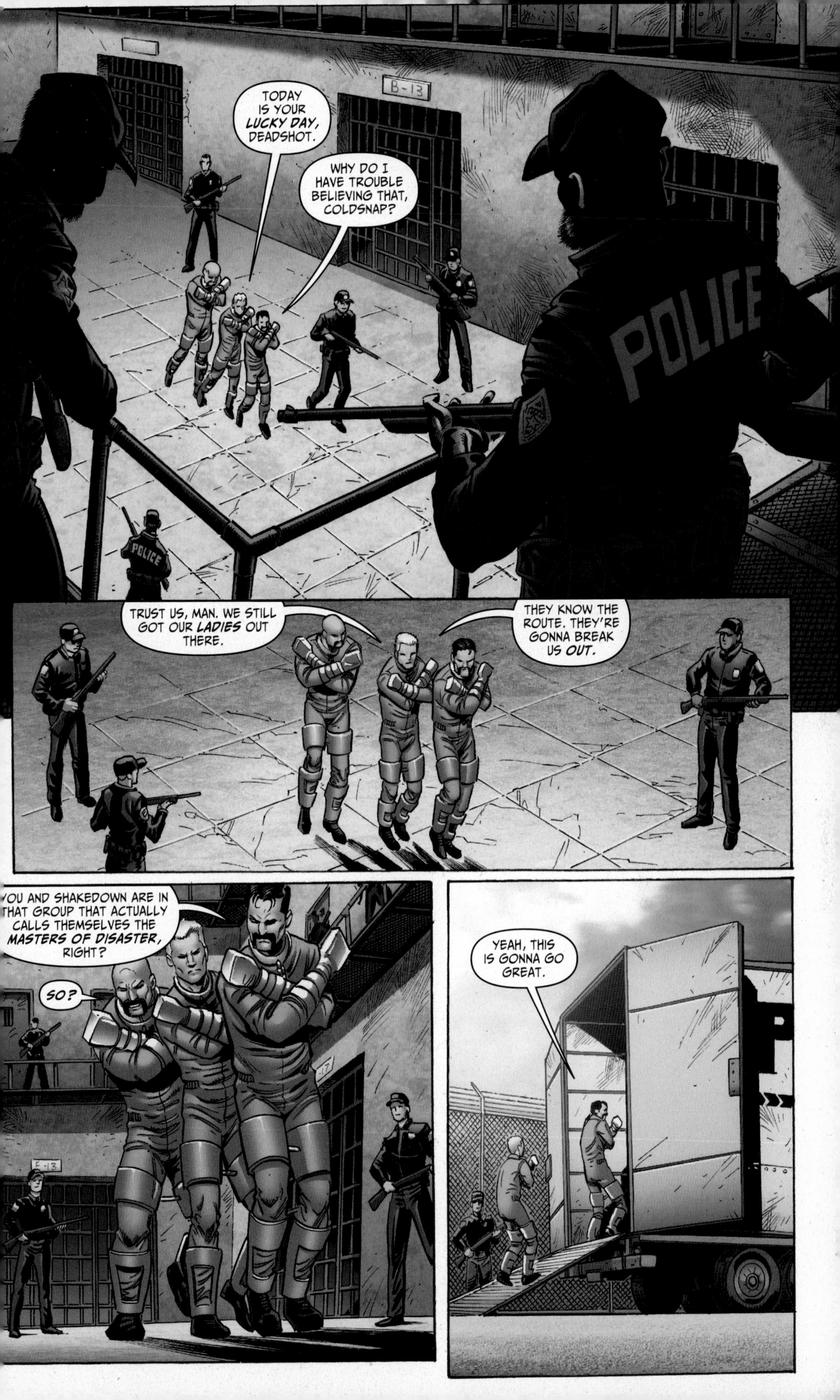
B-13
TODAY IS YOUR LUCKY DAY, DEADSHOT.
WHY DO I HAVE TROUBLE BELIEVING THAT, COLDSNAP?
POLICE
POLICE
TRUST US, MAN. WE STILL GOT OUR LADIES OUT THERE.
THEY KNOW THE ROUTE. THEY'RE GONNA BREAK US OUT.
YOU AND SHAKEDOWN ARE IN THAT GROUP THAT ACTUALLY CALLS THEMSELVES THE MASTERS OF DISASTER, RIGHT?
SO?
YEAH, THIS IS GONNA GO GREAT.

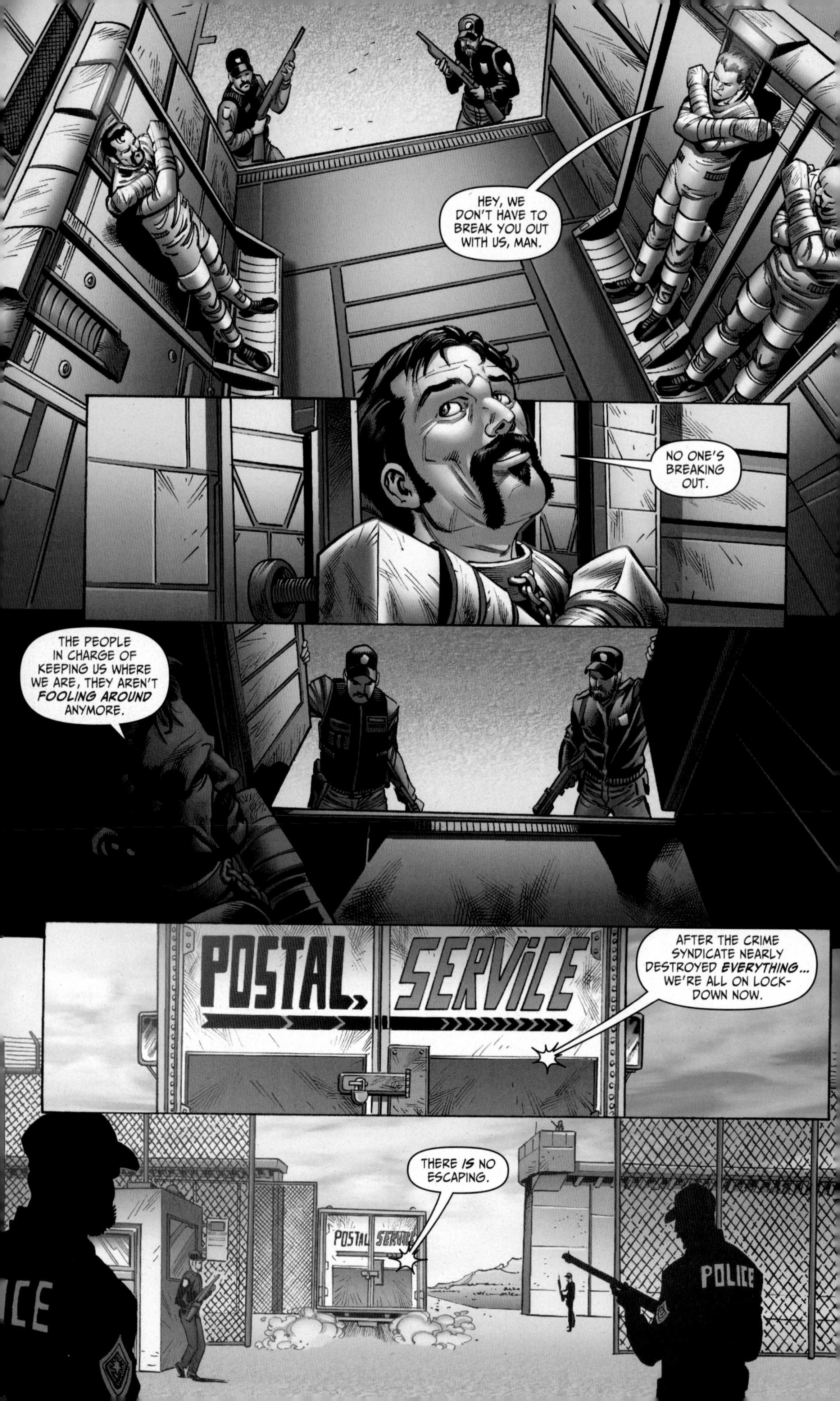
HEY, WE DON'T HAVE TO BREAK YOU OUT WITH US, MAN.
NO ONE'S BREAKING OUT.
THE PEOPLE IN CHARGE OF KEEPING US WHERE WE ARE, THEY AREN'T *FOOLING AROUND* ANYMORE.
POSTAL SERVICE
AFTER THE CRIME SYNDICATE NEARLY DESTROYED *EVERYTHING*... WE'RE ALL ON LOCK-DOWN NOW.
THERE *IS* NO ESCAPING.
POSTAL SERVICE
POLICE
ICE

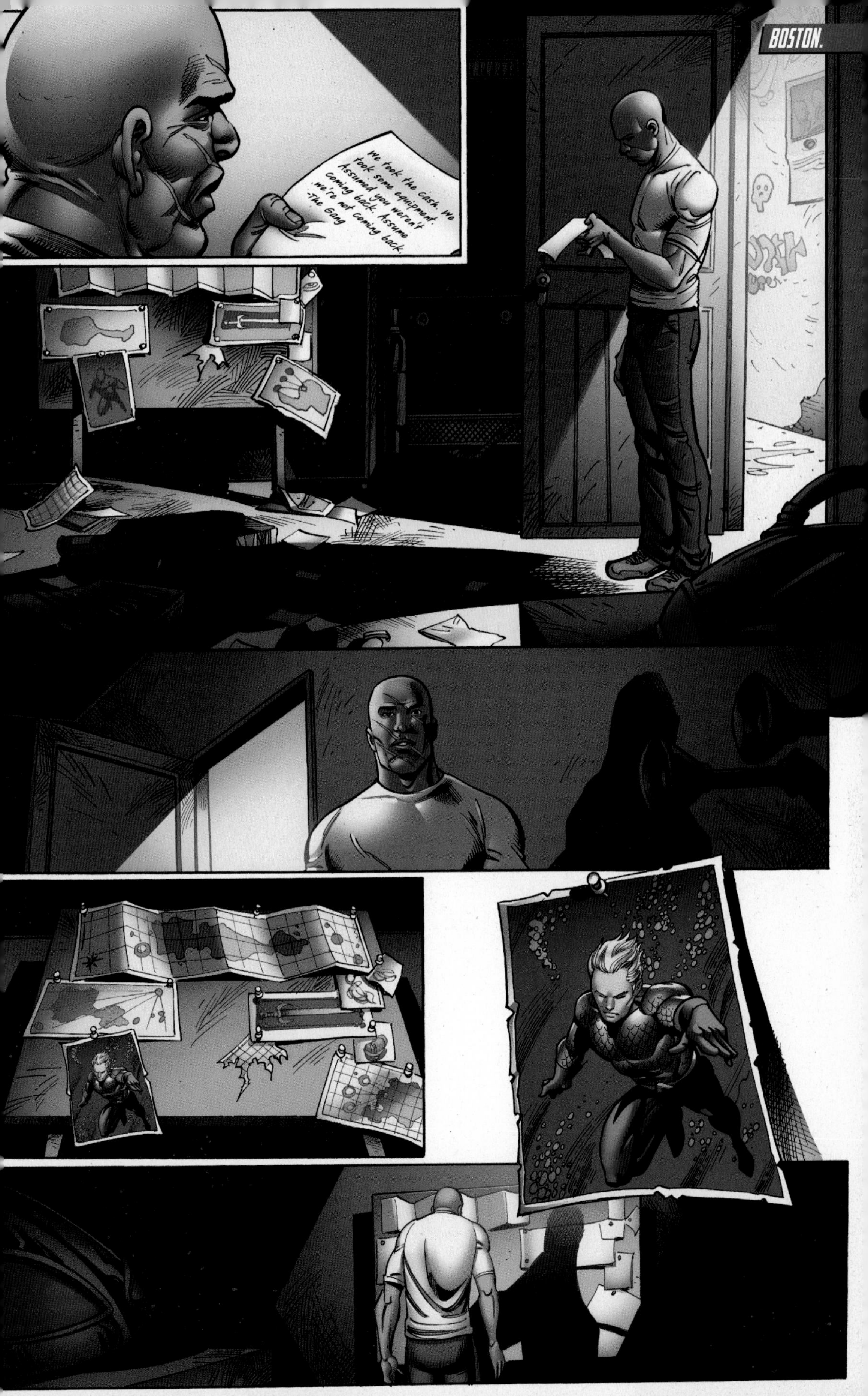
BOSTON.
We took the cash. We took some equipment. Assumed you weren't coming back. Assume we're not coming back.
-The Gang

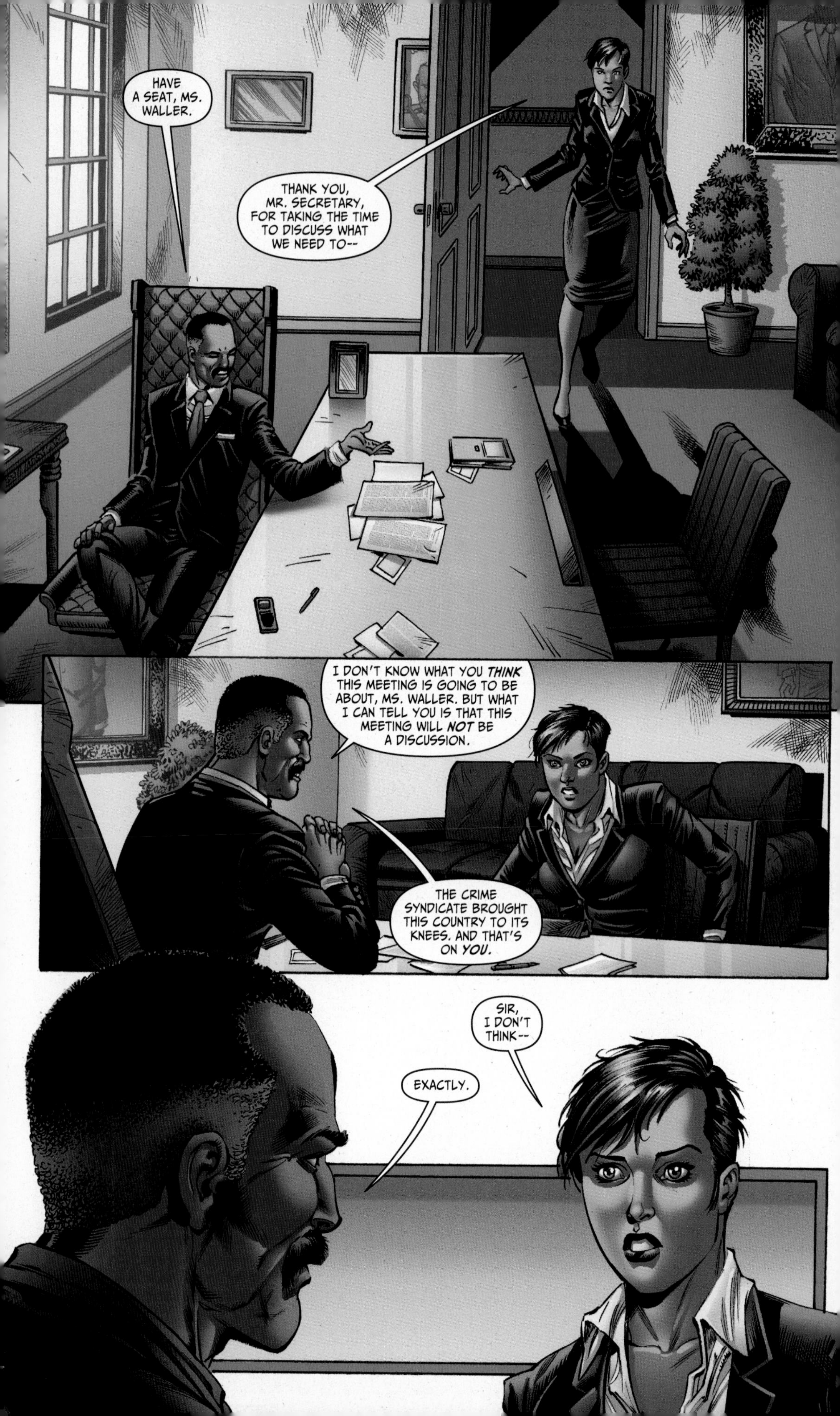
HAVE A SEAT, MS. WALLER.
THANK YOU, MR. SECRETARY, FOR TAKING THE TIME TO DISCUSS WHAT WE NEED TO--
I DON'T KNOW WHAT YOU *THINK* THIS MEETING IS GOING TO BE ABOUT, MS. WALLER. BUT WHAT I CAN TELL YOU IS THAT THIS MEETING WILL *NOT* BE A DISCUSSION.
THE CRIME SYNDICATE BROUGHT THIS COUNTRY TO ITS KNEES. AND THAT'S ON *YOU*.
SIR, I DON'T THINK--
EXACTLY.

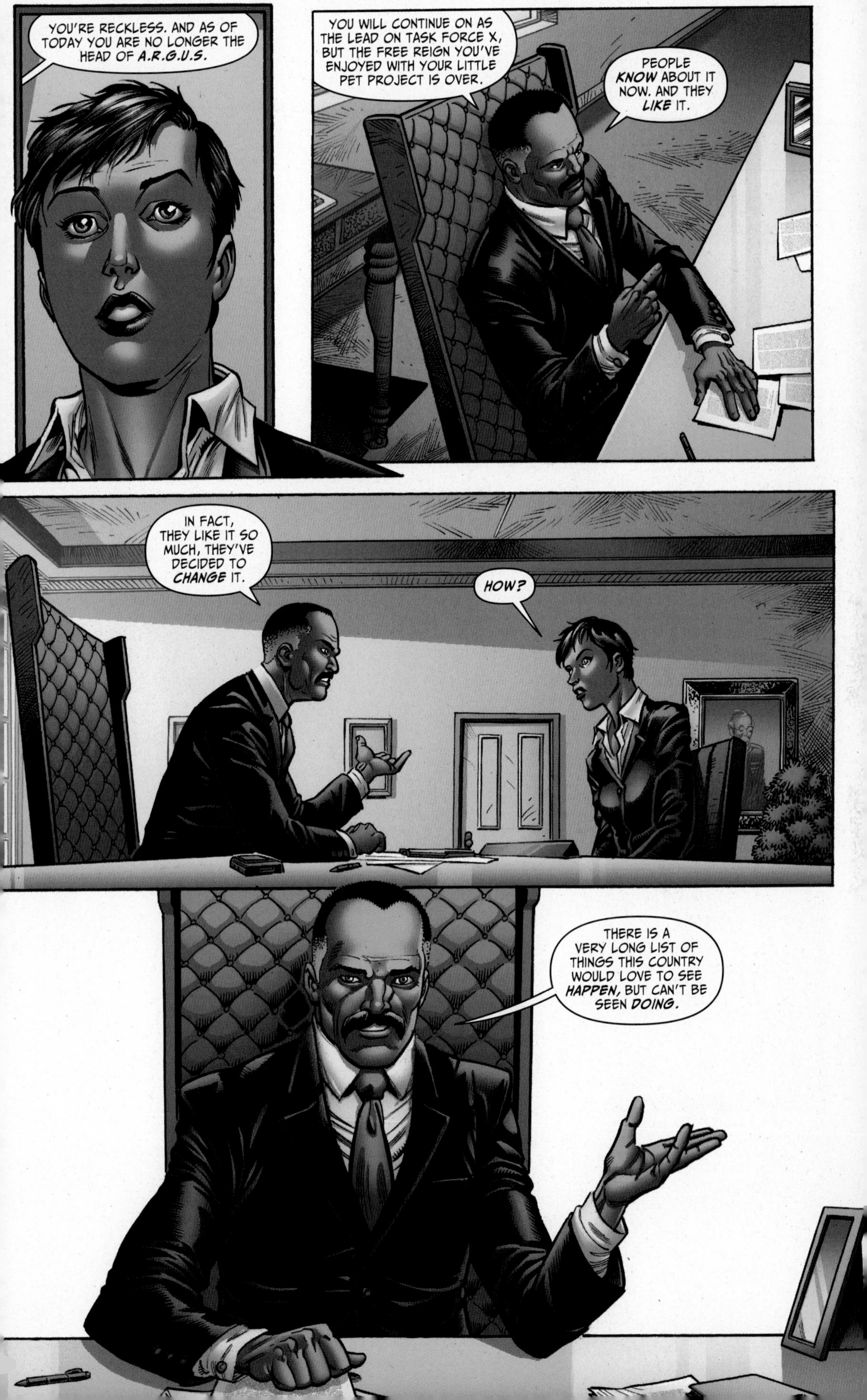
YOU'RE RECKLESS. AND AS OF TODAY YOU ARE NO LONGER THE HEAD OF A.R.G.U.S.
YOU WILL CONTINUE ON AS THE LEAD ON TASK FORCE X, BUT THE FREE REIGN YOU'VE ENJOYED WITH YOUR LITTLE PET PROJECT IS OVER.
PEOPLE KNOW ABOUT IT NOW. AND THEY LIKE IT.
IN FACT, THEY LIKE IT SO MUCH, THEY'VE DECIDED TO CHANGE IT.
HOW?
THERE IS A VERY LONG LIST OF THINGS THIS COUNTRY WOULD LOVE TO SEE HAPPEN, BUT CAN'T BE SEEN DOING.

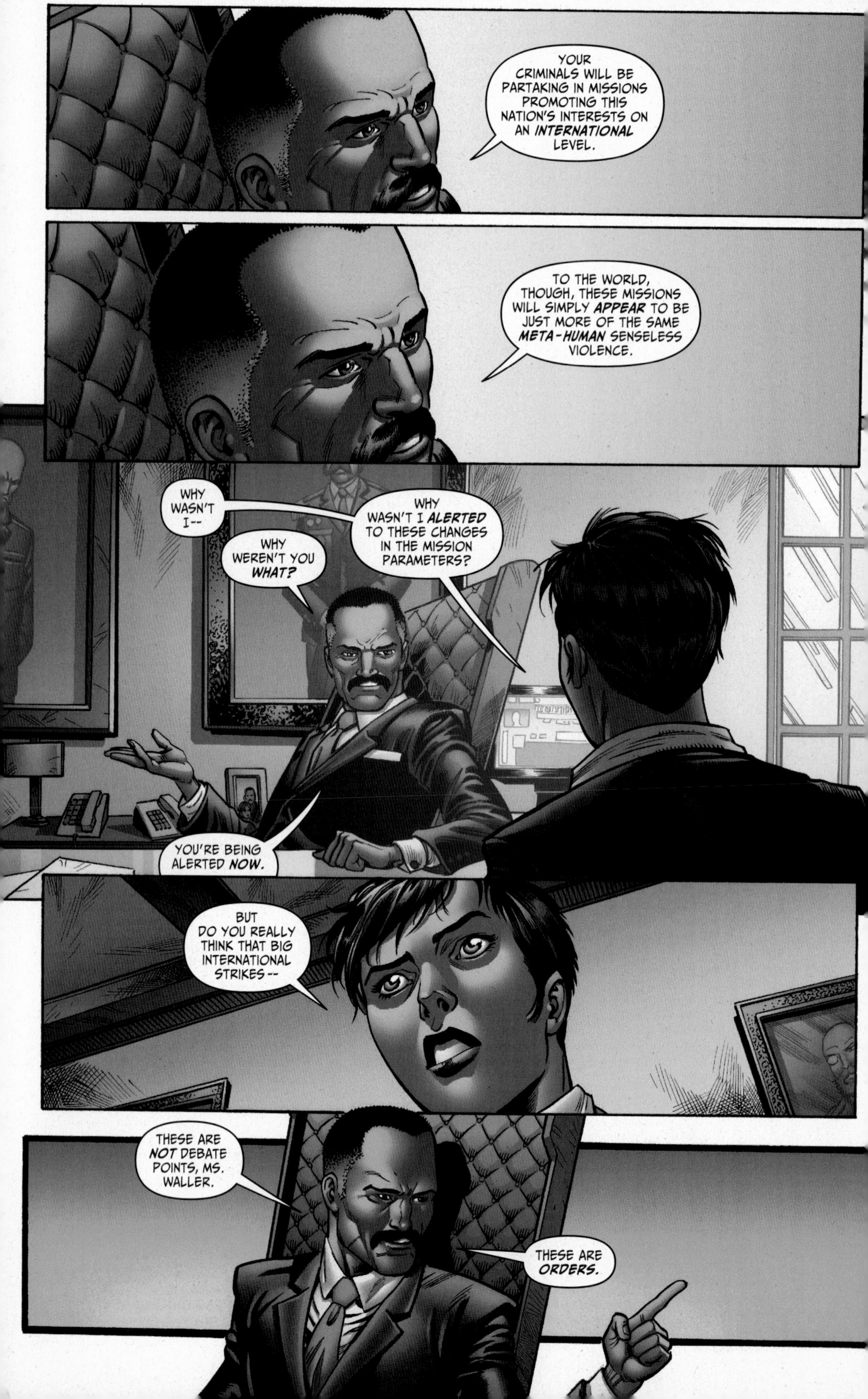
YOUR CRIMINALS WILL BE PARTAKING IN MISSIONS PROMOTING THIS NATION'S INTERESTS ON AN INTERNATIONAL LEVEL.
TO THE WORLD, THOUGH, THESE MISSIONS WILL SIMPLY APPEAR TO BE JUST MORE OF THE SAME META-HUMAN SENSELESS VIOLENCE.
WHY WASN'T I--
WHY WEREN'T YOU WHAT?
WHY WASN'T I ALERTED TO THESE CHANGES IN THE MISSION PARAMETERS?
YOU'RE BEING ALERTED NOW.
BUT DO YOU REALLY THINK THAT BIG INTERNATIONAL STRIKES--
THESE ARE NOT DEBATE POINTS, MS. WALLER.
THESE ARE ORDERS.

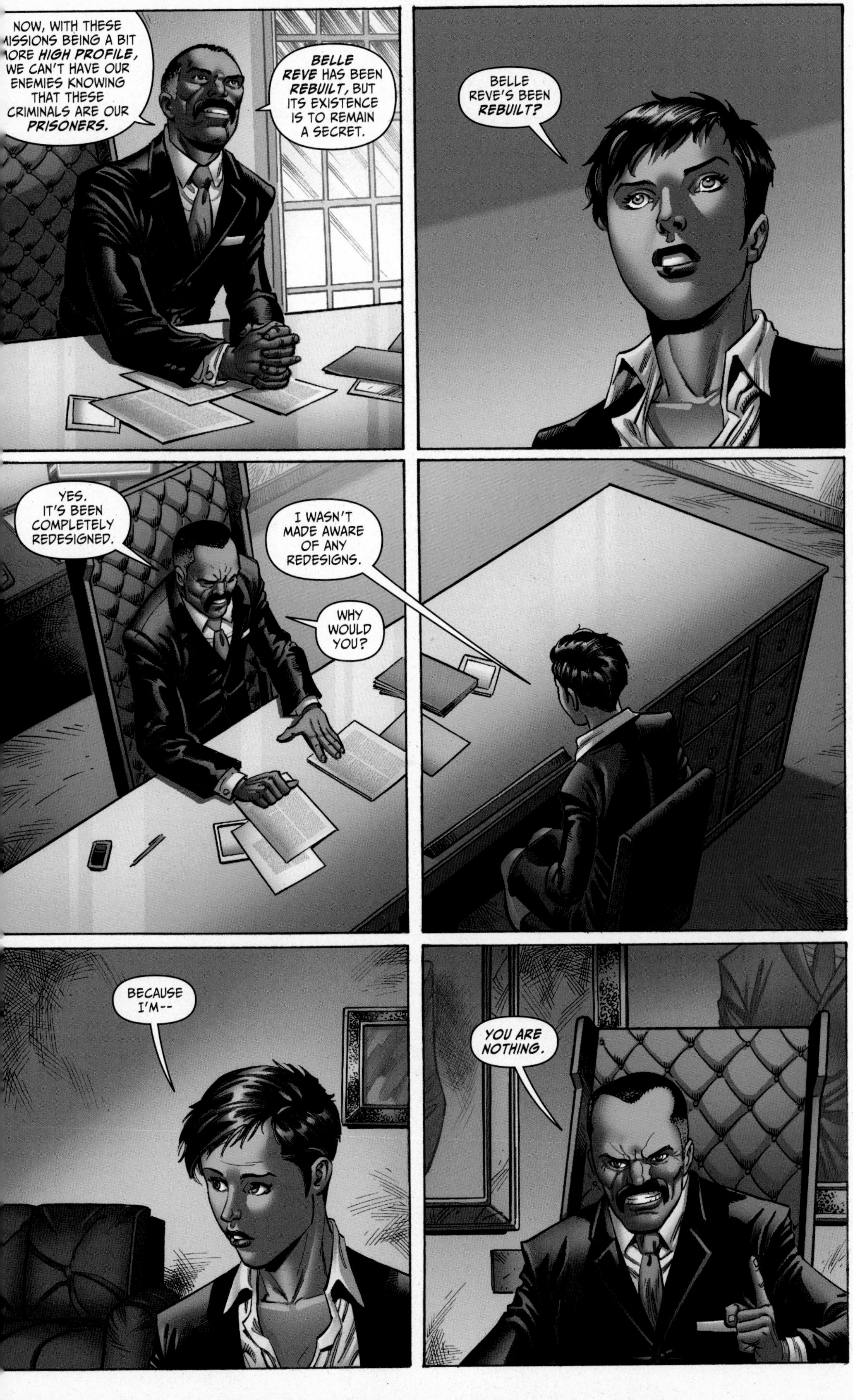
NOW, WITH THESE MISSIONS BEING A BIT MORE HIGH PROFILE, WE CAN'T HAVE OUR ENEMIES KNOWING THAT THESE CRIMINALS ARE OUR PRISONERS.
BELLE REVE HAS BEEN REBUILT, BUT ITS EXISTENCE IS TO REMAIN A SECRET.
BELLE REVE'S BEEN REBUILT?
YES. IT'S BEEN COMPLETELY REDESIGNED.
I WASN'T MADE AWARE OF ANY REDESIGNS.
WHY WOULD YOU?
BECAUSE I'M--
YOU ARE NOTHING.

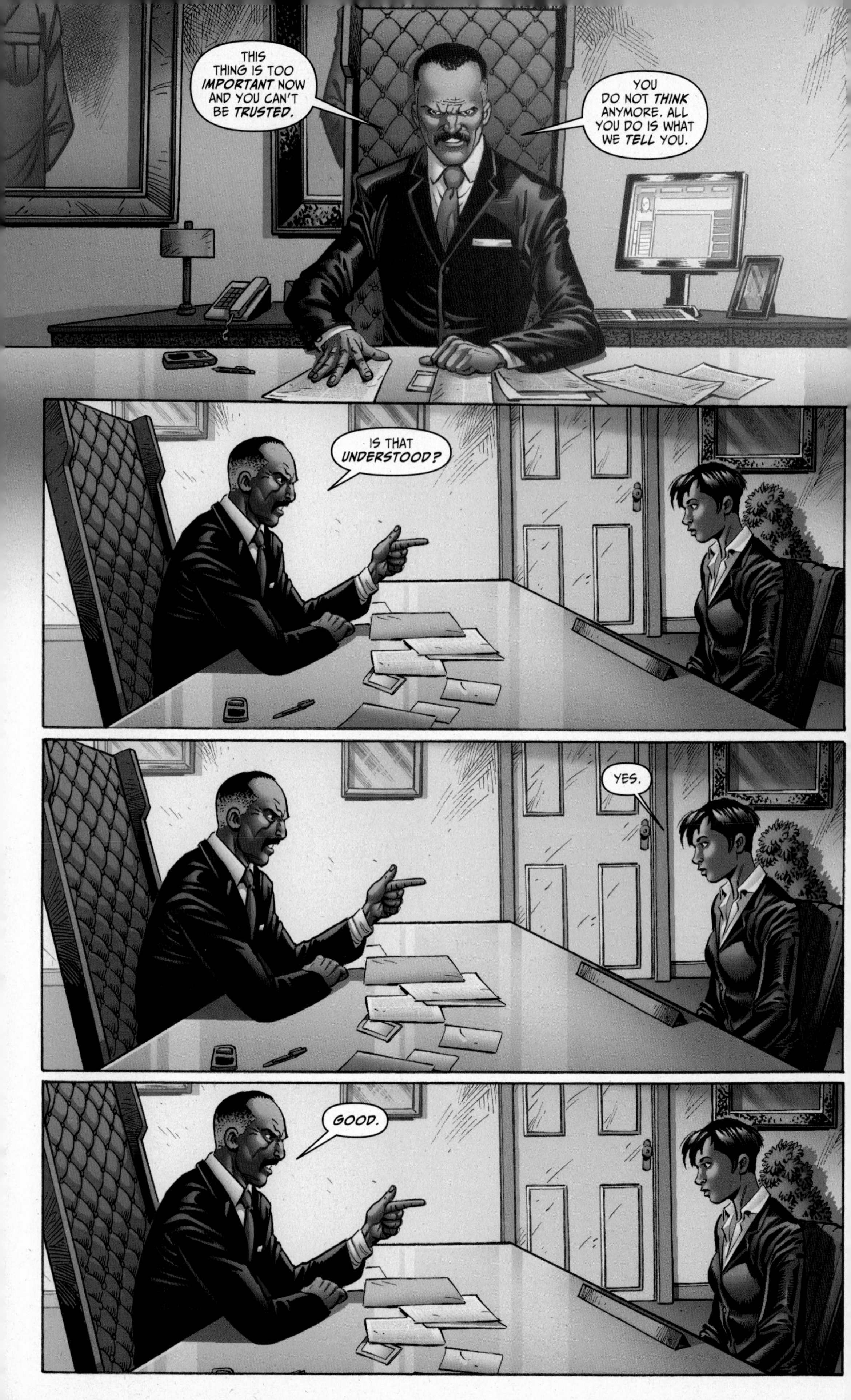
THIS THING IS TOO IMPORTANT NOW AND YOU CAN'T BE TRUSTED.
YOU DO NOT THINK ANYMORE. ALL YOU DO IS WHAT WE TELL YOU.
IS THAT UNDERSTOOD?
YES.
GOOD.

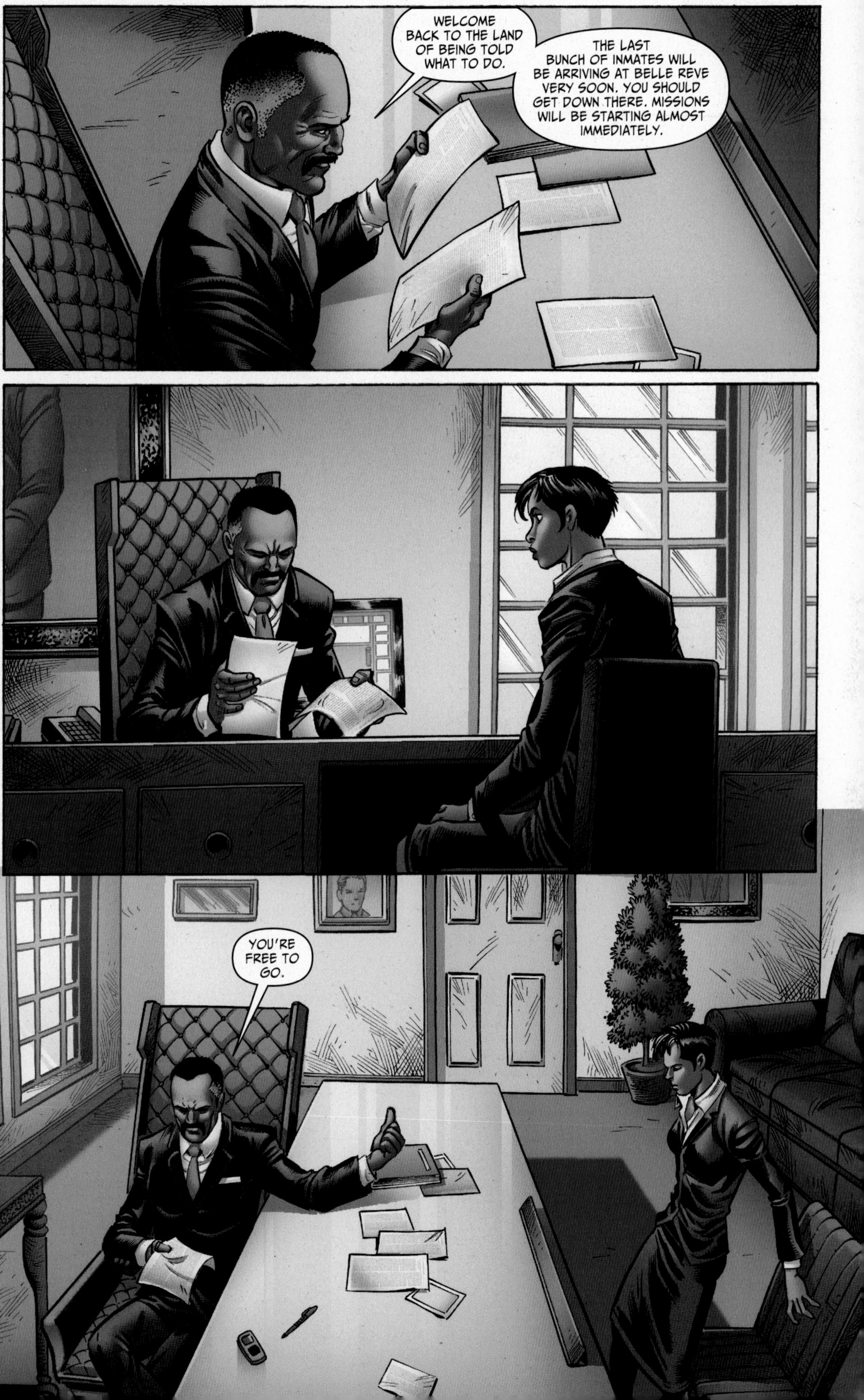
WELCOME BACK TO THE LAND OF BEING TOLD WHAT TO DO.
THE LAST BUNCH OF INMATES WILL BE ARRIVING AT BELLE REVE VERY SOON. YOU SHOULD GET DOWN THERE. MISSIONS WILL BE STARTING ALMOST IMMEDIATELY.
YOU'RE FREE TO GO.

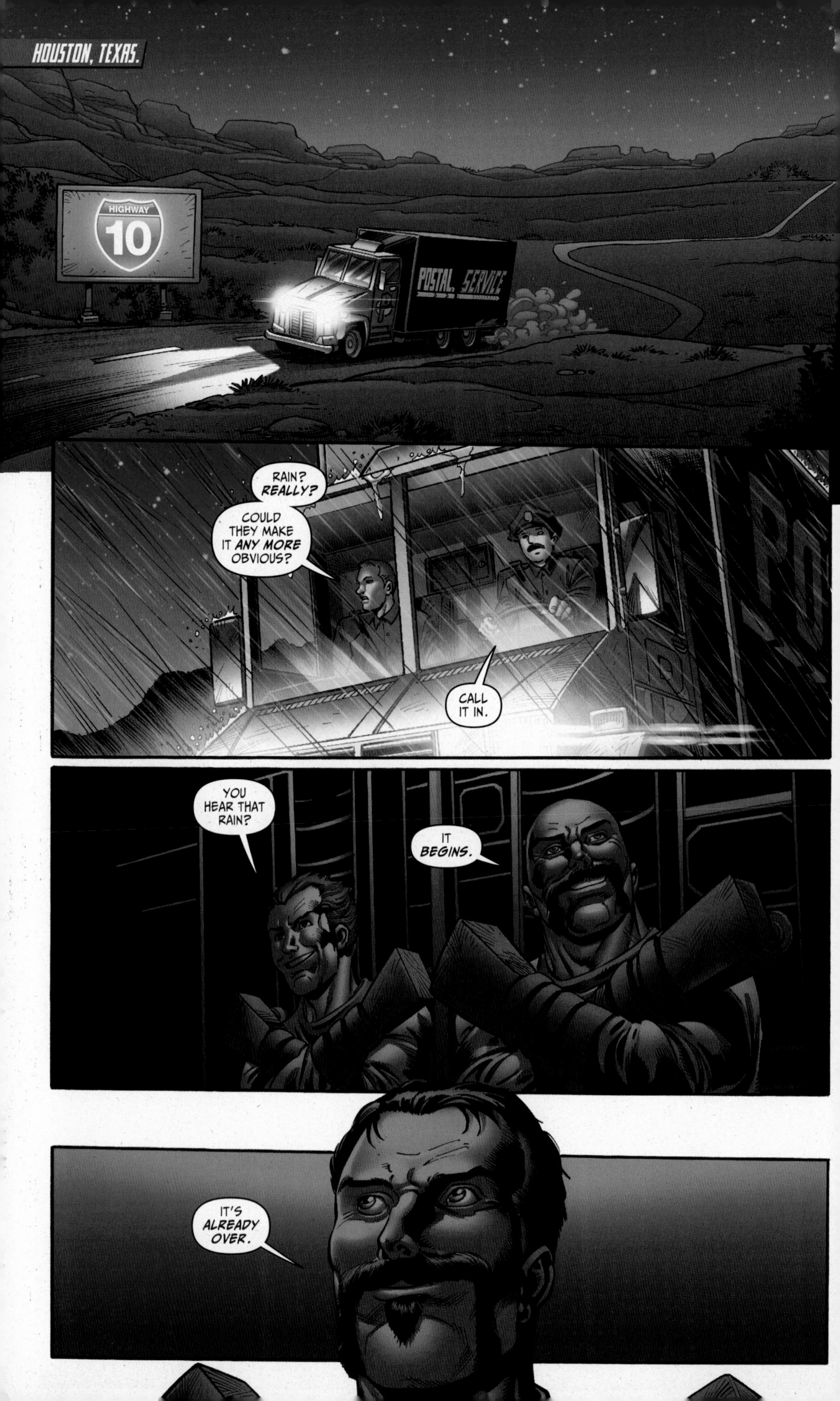
HOUSTON, TEXAS.
HIGHWAY
10
POSTAL SERVICE
RAIN? REALLY?
COULD THEY MAKE IT ANY MORE OBVIOUS?
CALL IT IN.
YOU HEAR THAT RAIN?
IT BEGINS.
IT'S ALREADY OVER.

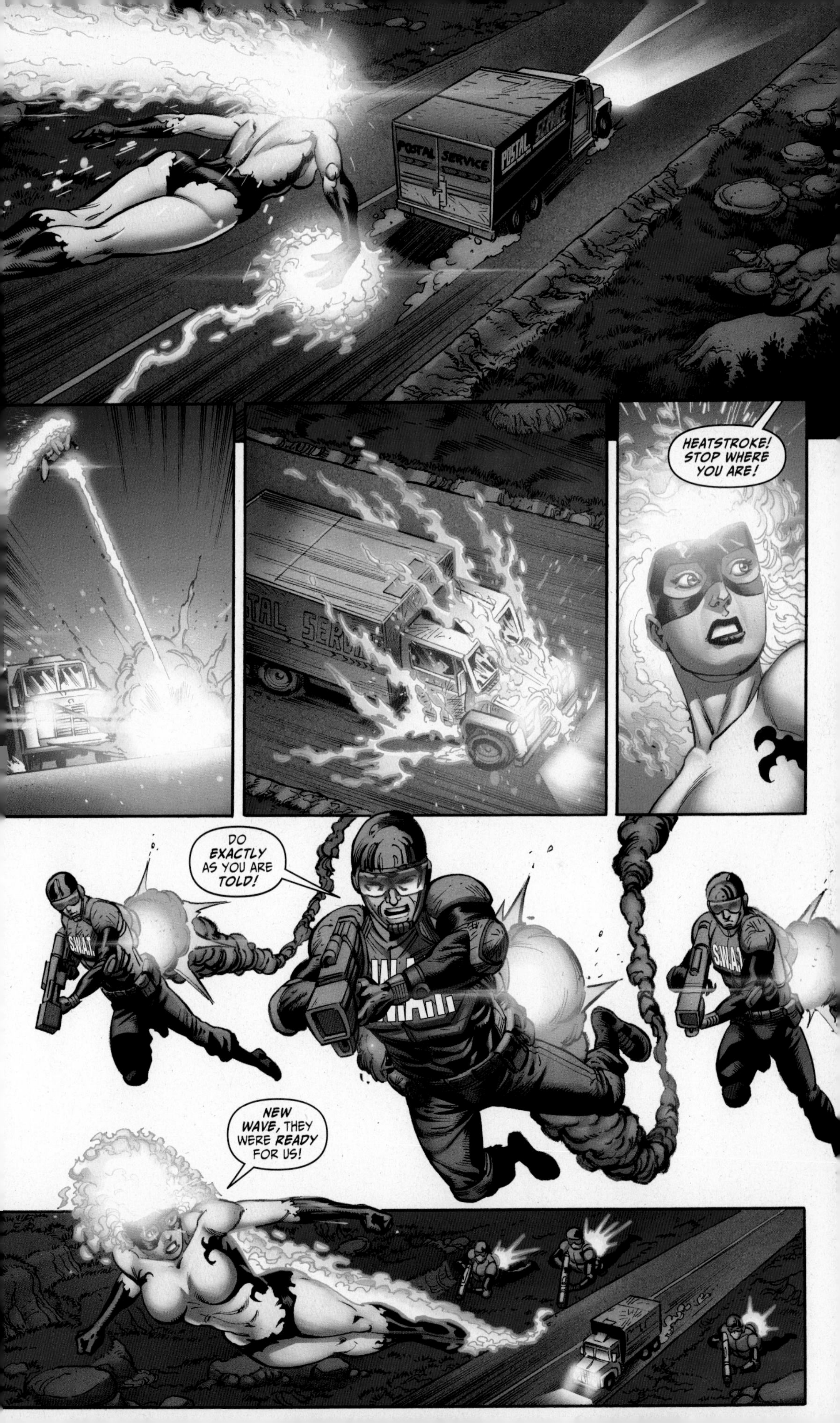
POSTAL SERVICE
POSTAL SERVICE
HEATSTROKE! STOP WHERE YOU ARE!
DO EXACTLY AS YOU ARE TOLD!
S.W.A.T.
S.W.A.T.
NEW WAVE, THEY WERE READY FOR US!

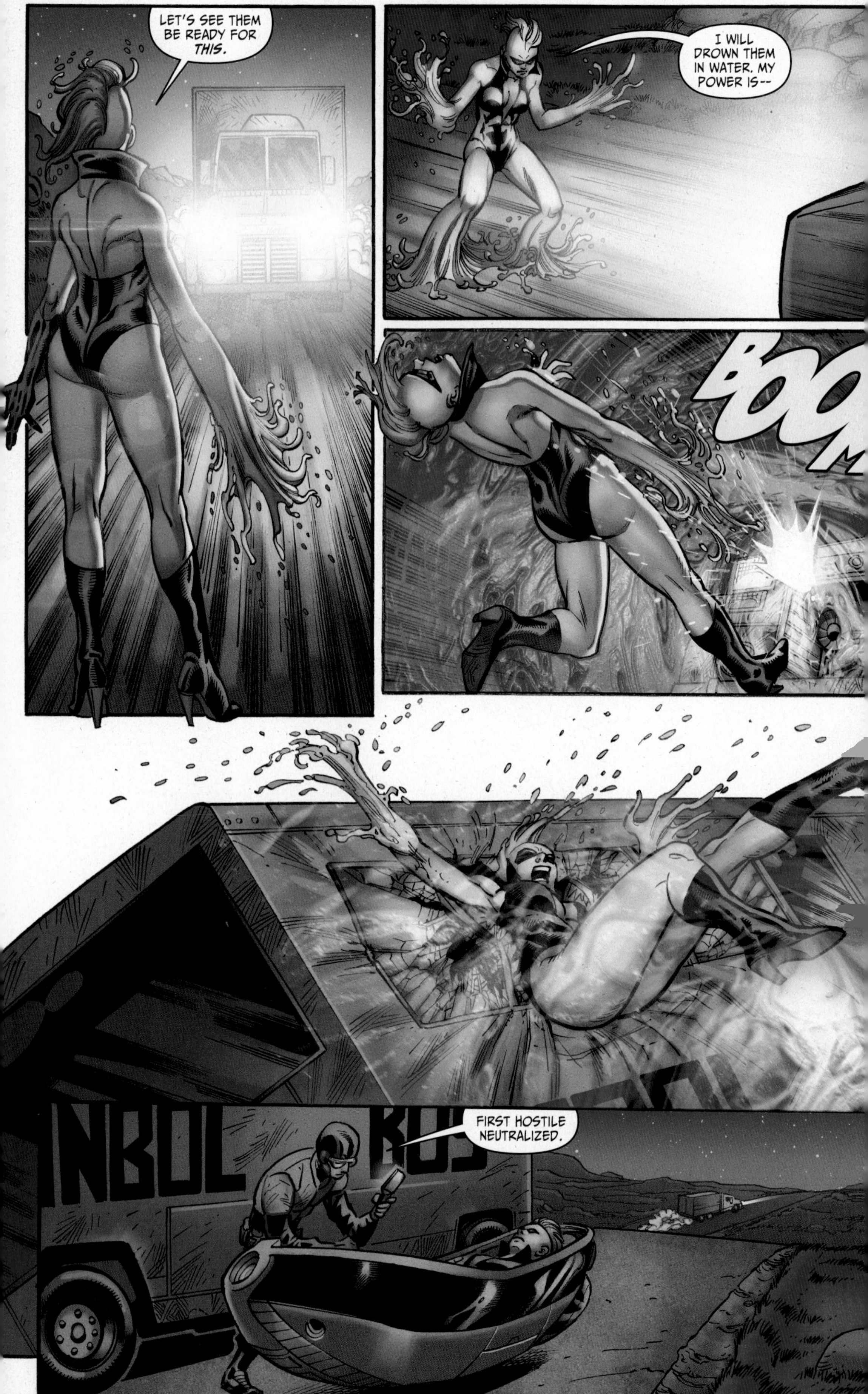
LET'S SEE THEM BE READY FOR *THIS.*
I WILL DROWN THEM IN WATER. MY POWER IS--
BOOOM
FIRST HOSTILE NEUTRALIZED.

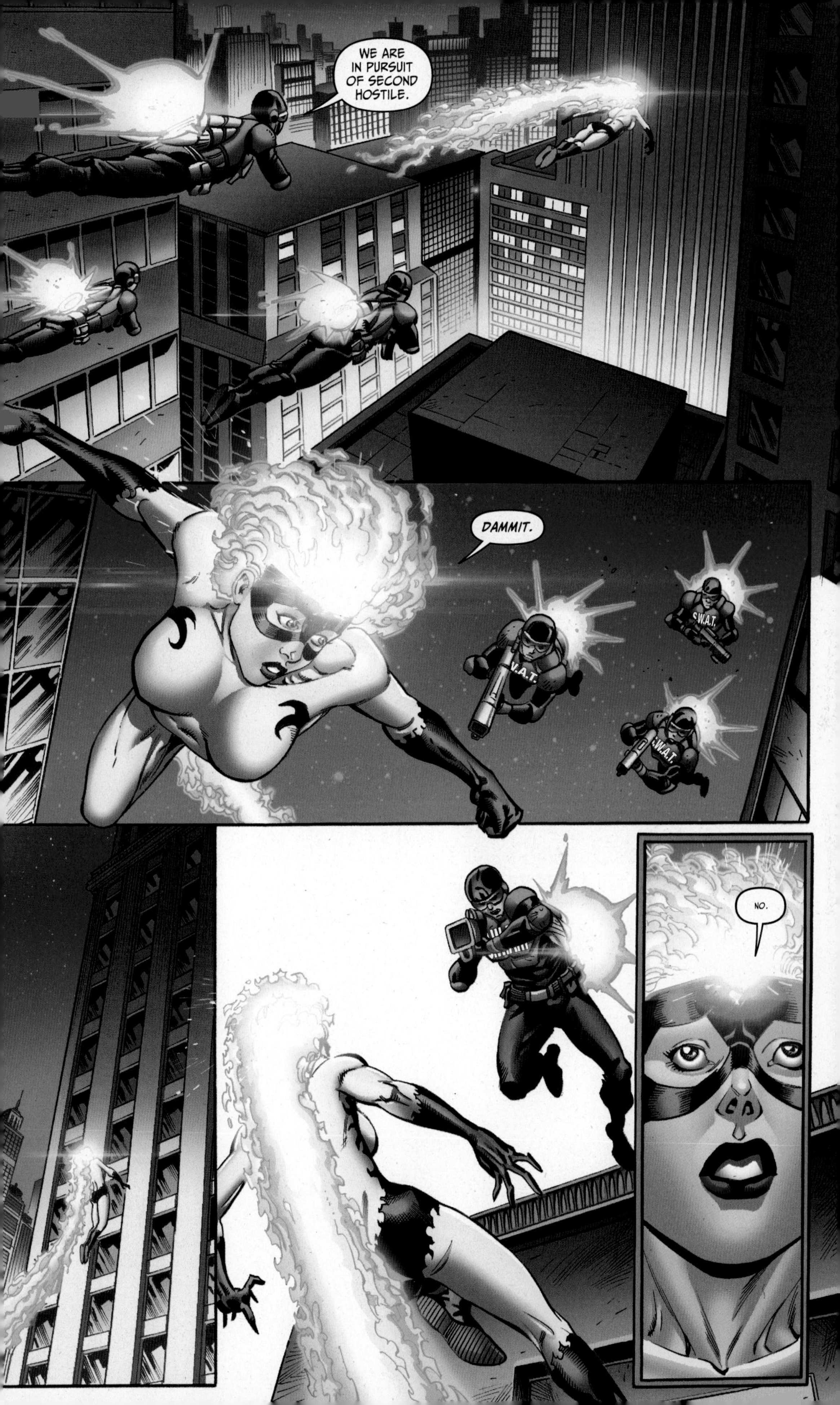
WE ARE IN PURSUIT OF SECOND HOSTILE.
DAMMIT.
NO.

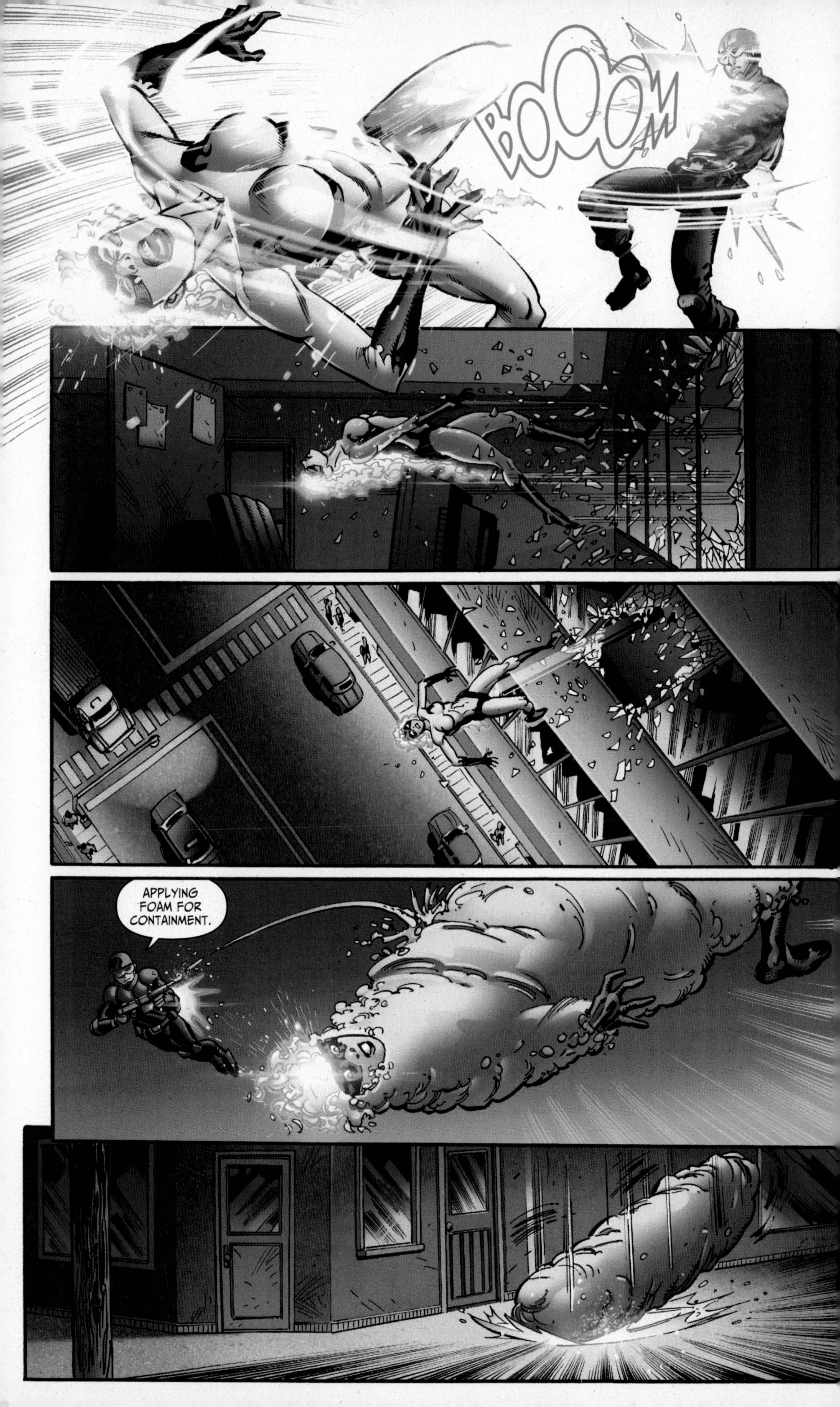
BOOOOM
APPLYING FOAM FOR CONTAINMENT.

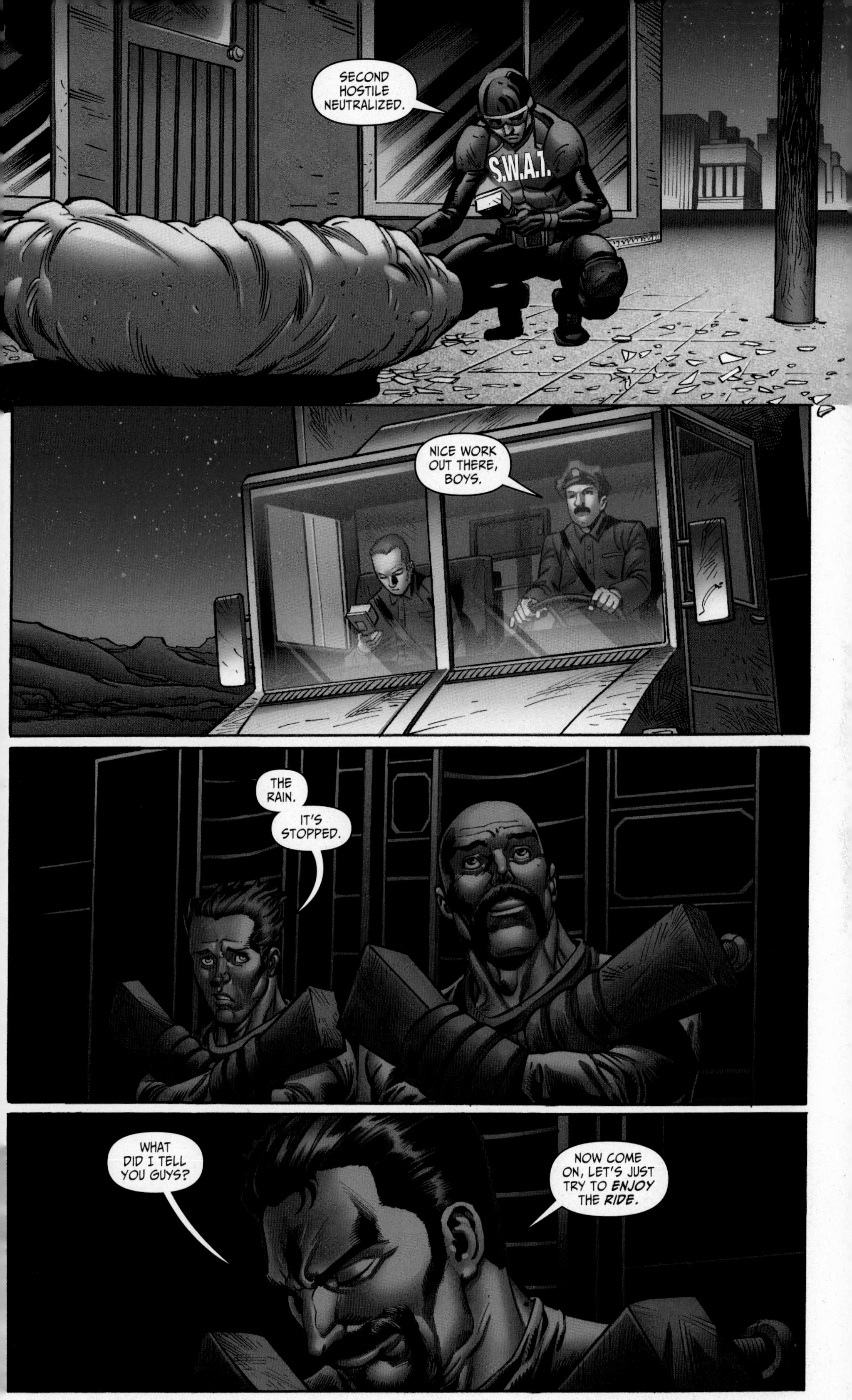
SECOND HOSTILE NEUTRALIZED.
S.W.A.T.
NICE WORK OUT THERE, BOYS.
THE RAIN.
IT'S STOPPED.
WHAT DID I TELL YOU GUYS?
NOW COME ON, LET'S JUST TRY TO *ENJOY* THE *RIDE*.

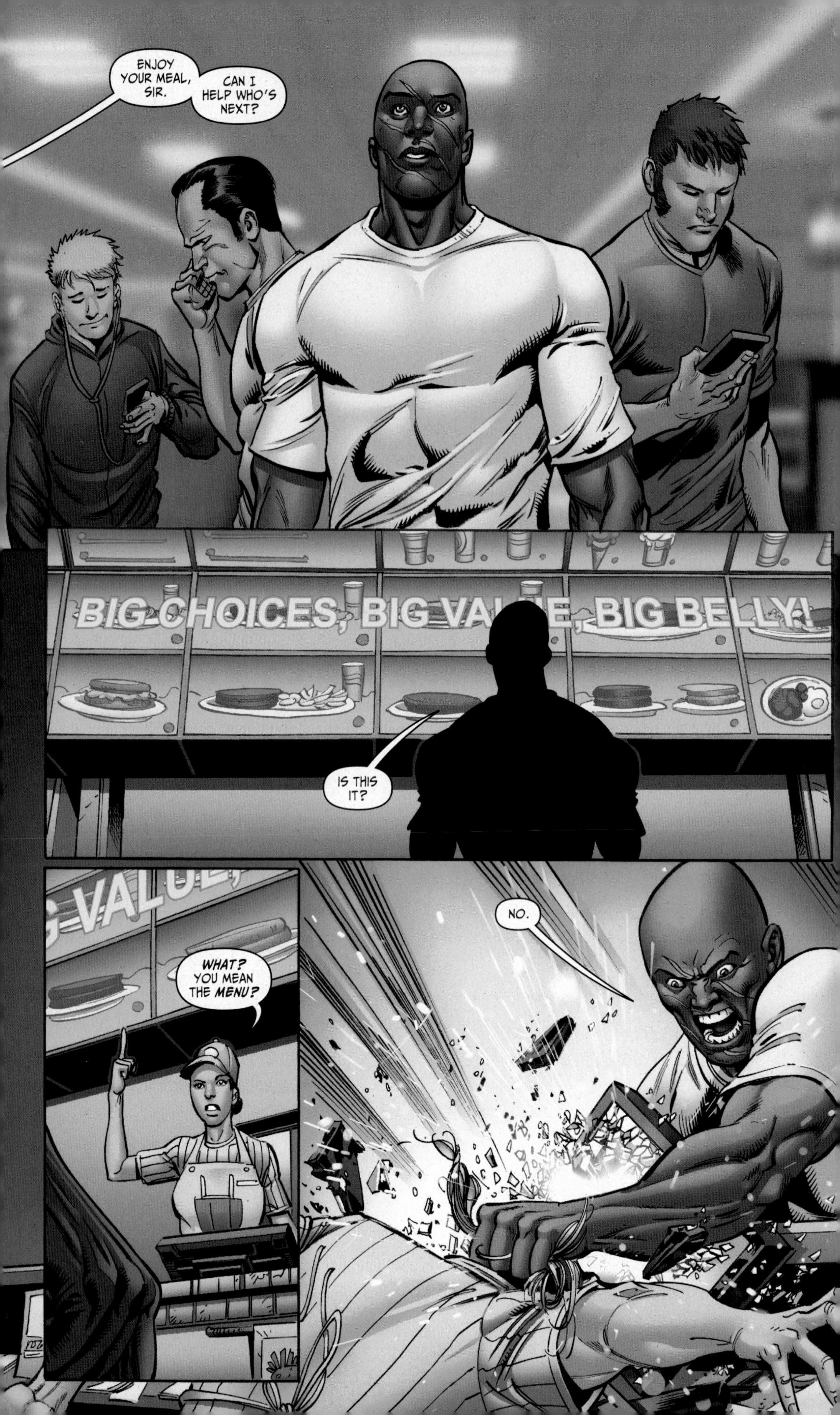
ENJOY YOUR MEAL, SIR.
CAN I HELP WHO'S NEXT?
BIG CHOICES, BIG VALUE, BIG BELLY!
IS THIS IT?
WHAT? YOU MEAN THE MENU?
NO.

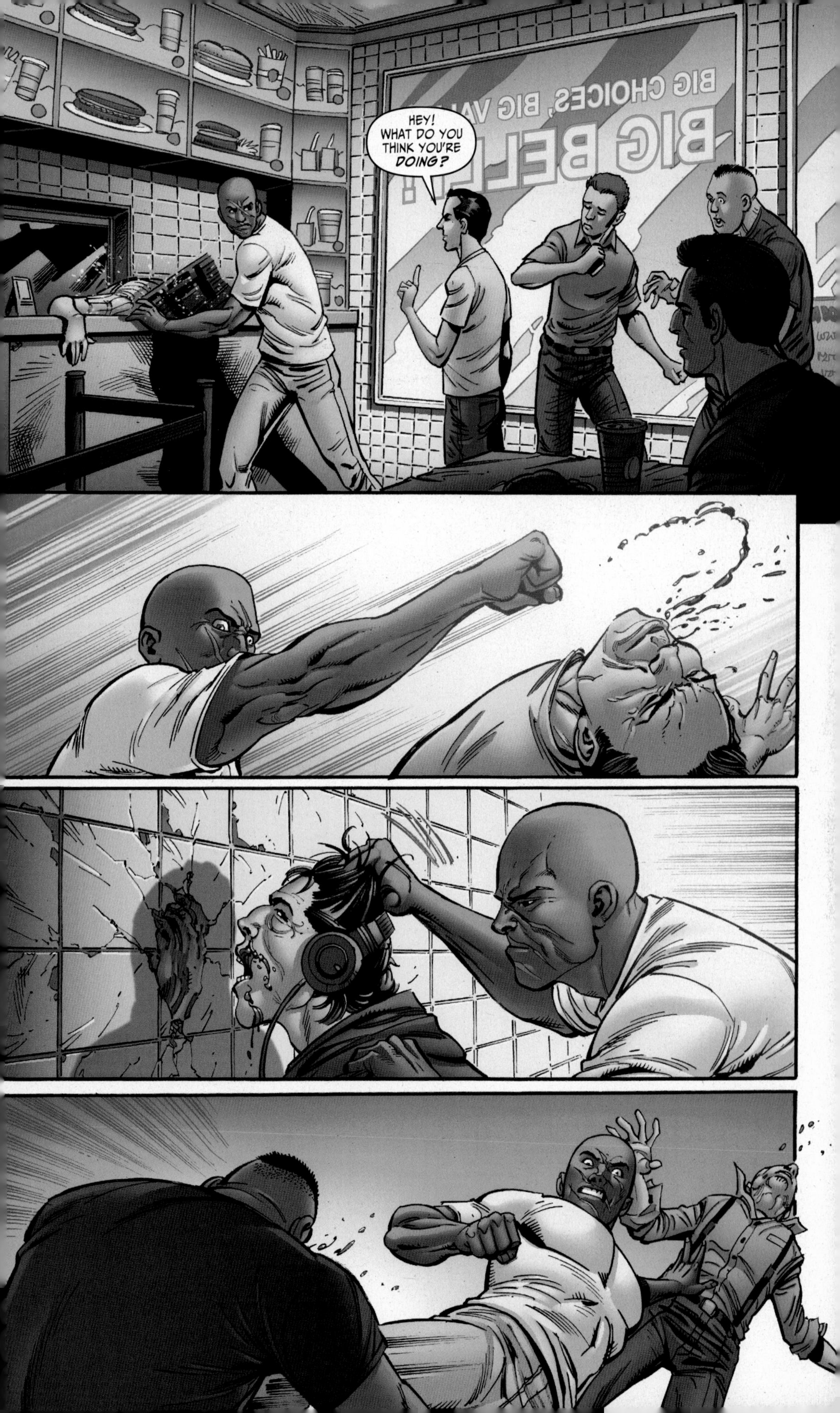
HEY! WHAT DO YOU THINK YOU'RE DOING?

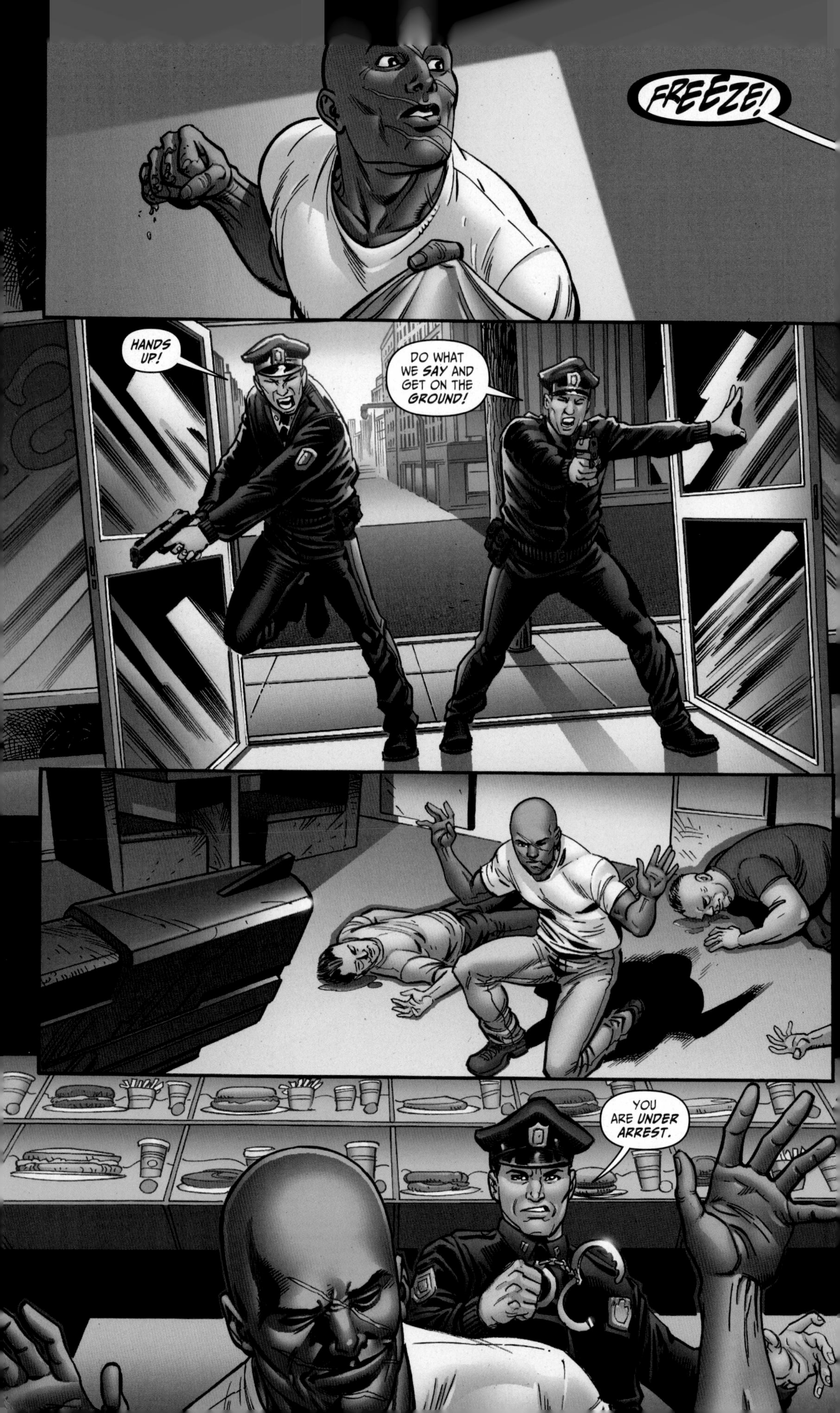
FREEZE!
HANDS UP!
DO WHAT WE SAY AND GET ON THE GROUND!
YOU ARE UNDER ARREST.

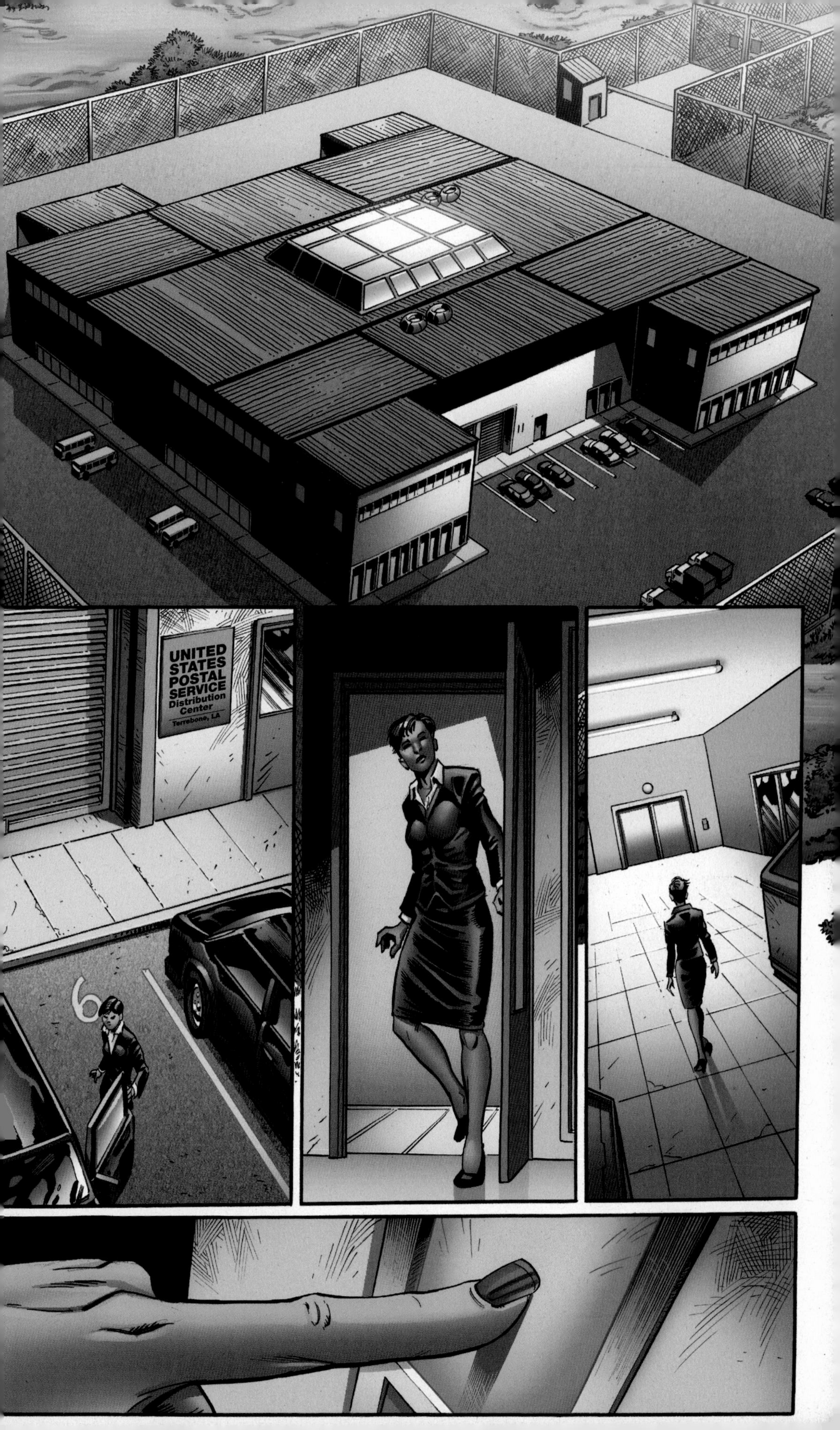
UNITED STATES POSTAL SERVICE Distribution Center
Terrebone, LA

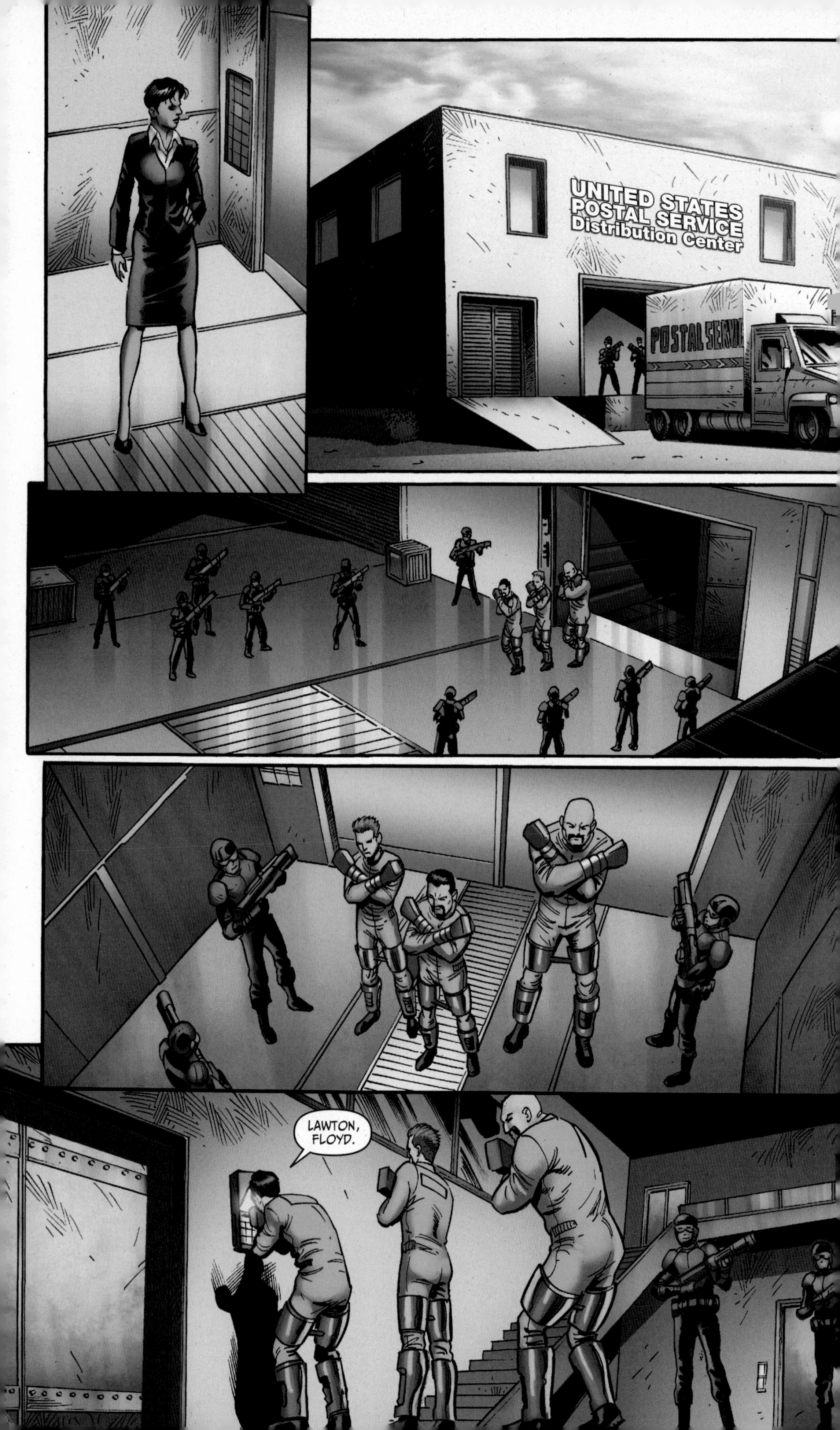
UNITED STATES
POSTAL SERVICE
Distribution Center
POSTAL SERVICE
LAWTON, FLOYD.

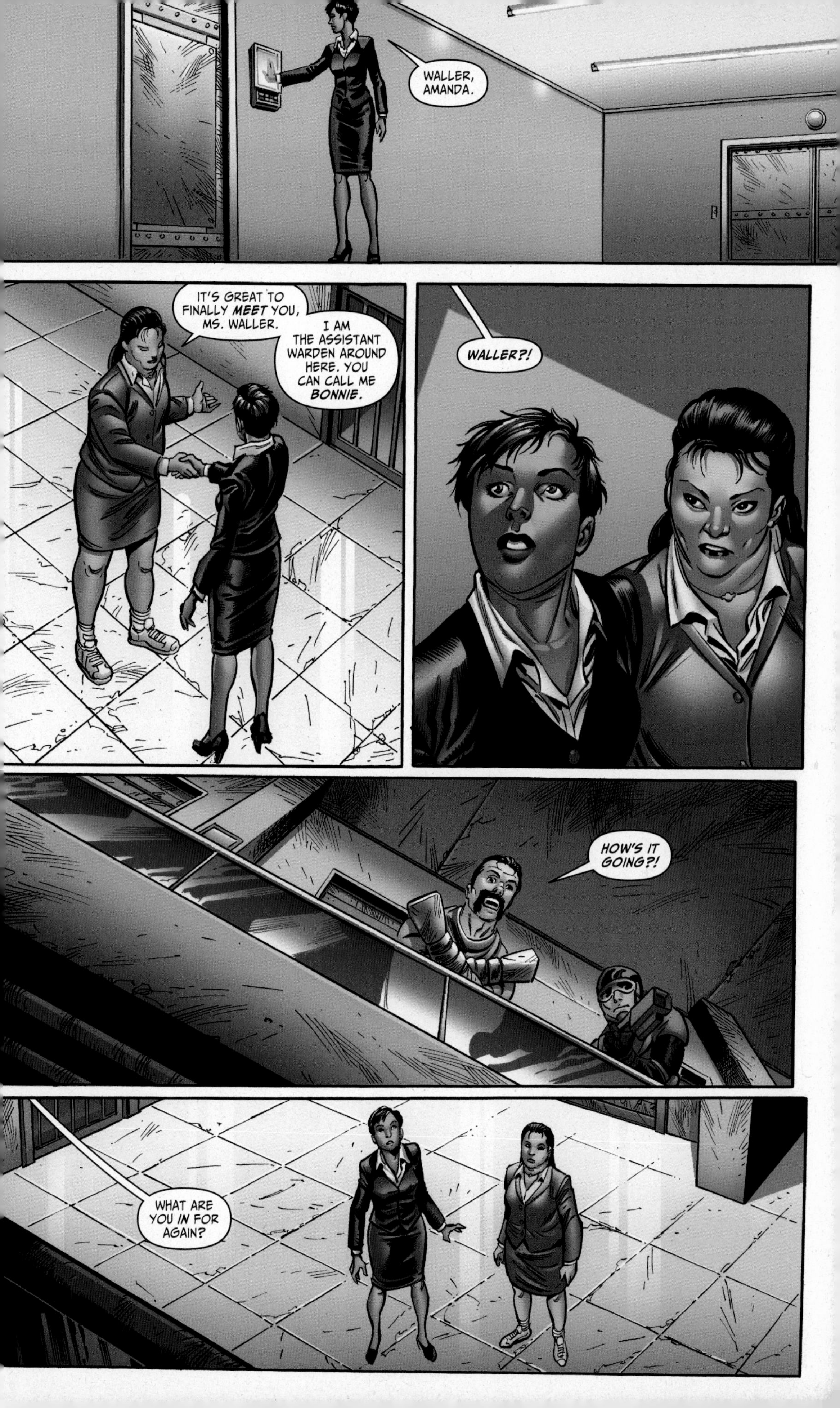
WALLER, AMANDA.
IT'S GREAT TO FINALLY MEET YOU, MS. WALLER.
I AM THE ASSISTANT WARDEN AROUND HERE. YOU CAN CALL ME BONNIE.
WALLER?!
HOW'S IT GOING?!
WHAT ARE YOU IN FOR AGAIN?

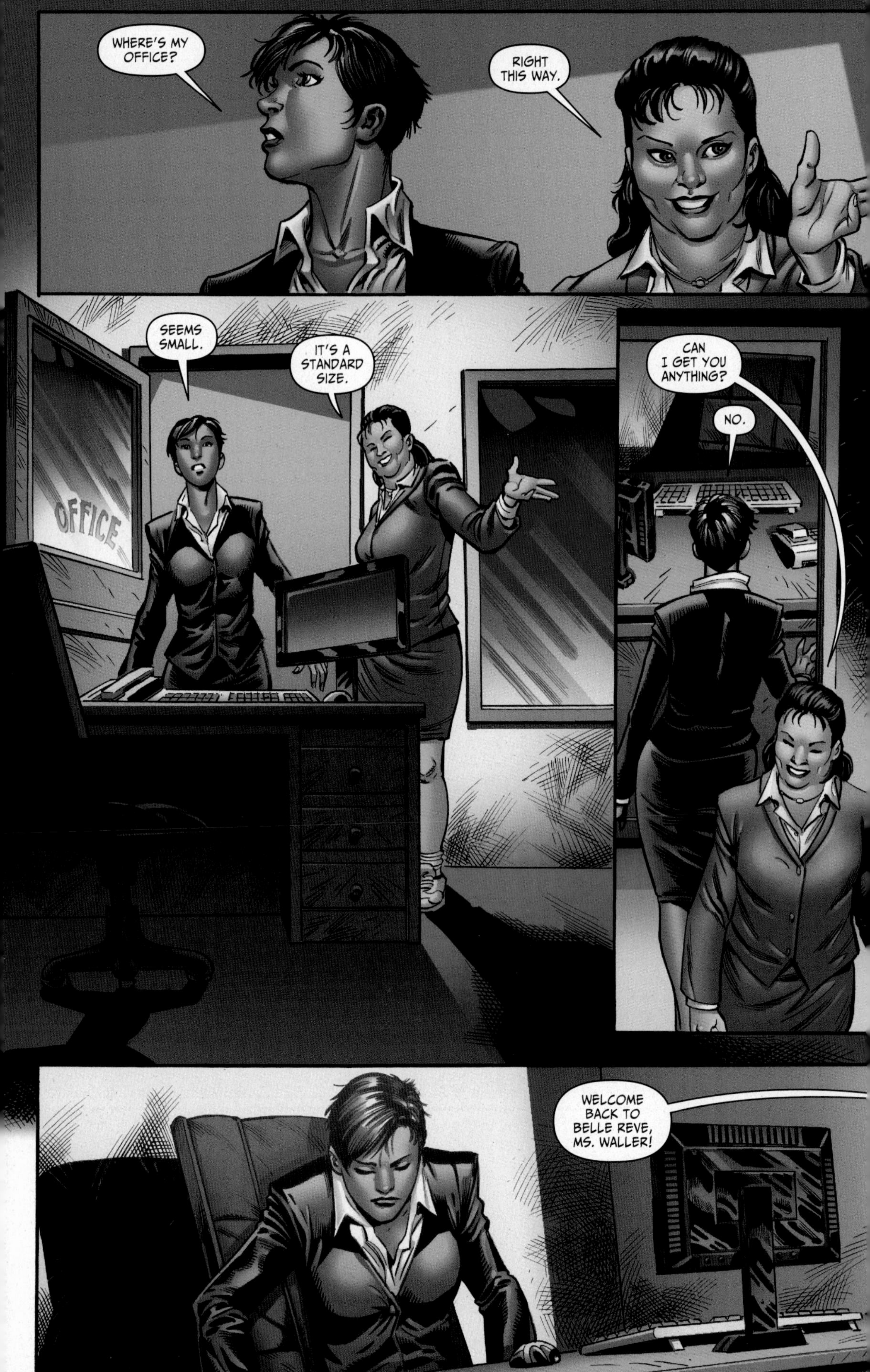
WHERE'S MY OFFICE?
RIGHT THIS WAY.
SEEMS SMALL.
IT'S A STANDARD SIZE.
OFFICE
CAN I GET YOU ANYTHING?
NO.
WELCOME BACK TO BELLE REVE, MS. WALLER!

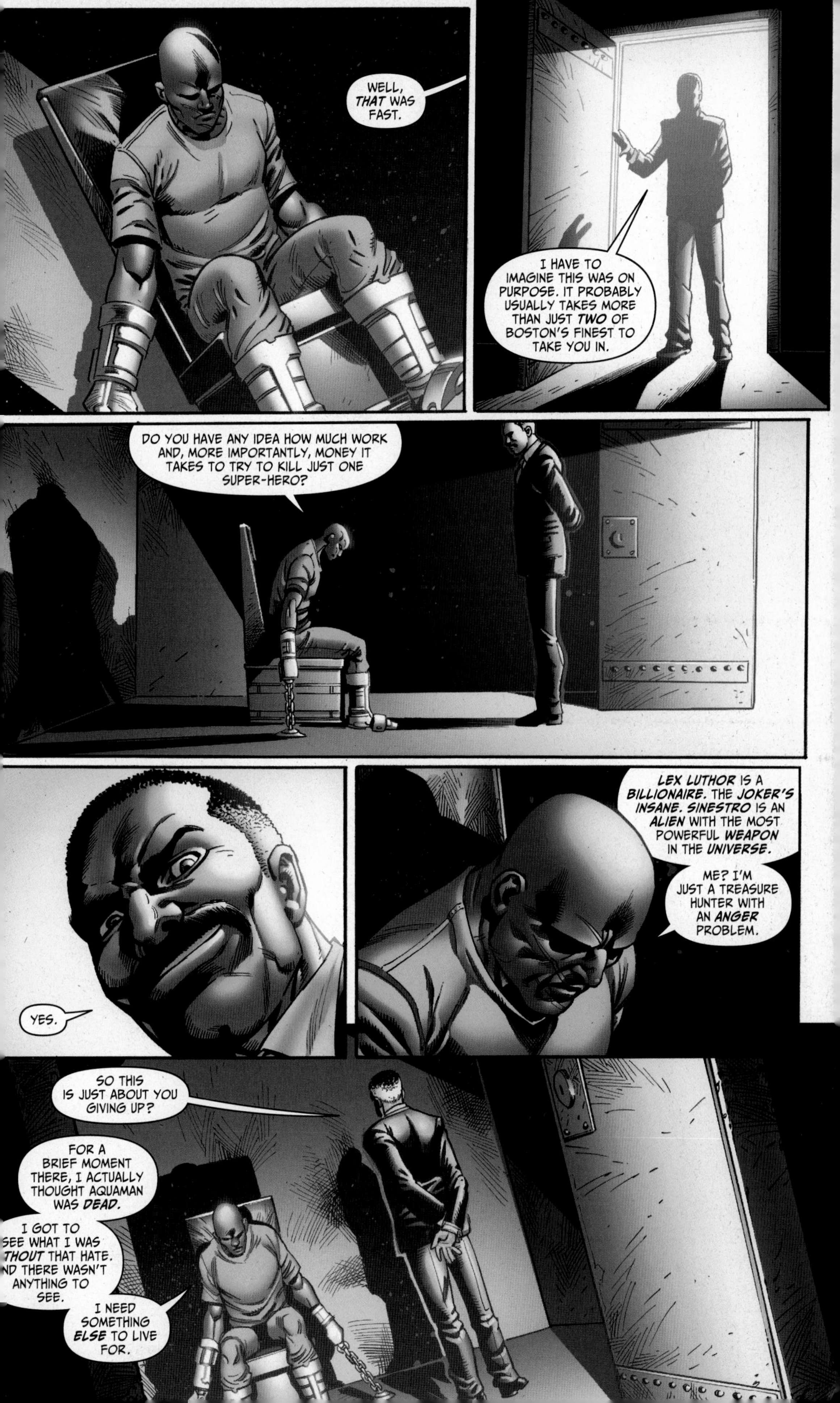
WELL, THAT WAS FAST.
I HAVE TO IMAGINE THIS WAS ON PURPOSE. IT PROBABLY USUALLY TAKES MORE THAN JUST TWO OF BOSTON'S FINEST TO TAKE YOU IN.
DO YOU HAVE ANY IDEA HOW MUCH WORK AND, MORE IMPORTANTLY, MONEY IT TAKES TO TRY TO KILL JUST ONE SUPER-HERO?
YES.
LEX LUTHOR IS A BILLIONAIRE. THE JOKER'S INSANE. SINESTRO IS AN ALIEN WITH THE MOST POWERFUL WEAPON IN THE UNIVERSE.
ME? I'M JUST A TREASURE HUNTER WITH AN ANGER PROBLEM.
SO THIS IS JUST ABOUT YOU GIVING UP?
FOR A BRIEF MOMENT THERE, I ACTUALLY THOUGHT AQUAMAN WAS DEAD.
I GOT TO SEE WHAT I WAS THOUT THAT HATE. ND THERE WASN'T ANYTHING TO SEE.
I NEED SOMETHING ELSE TO LIVE FOR.

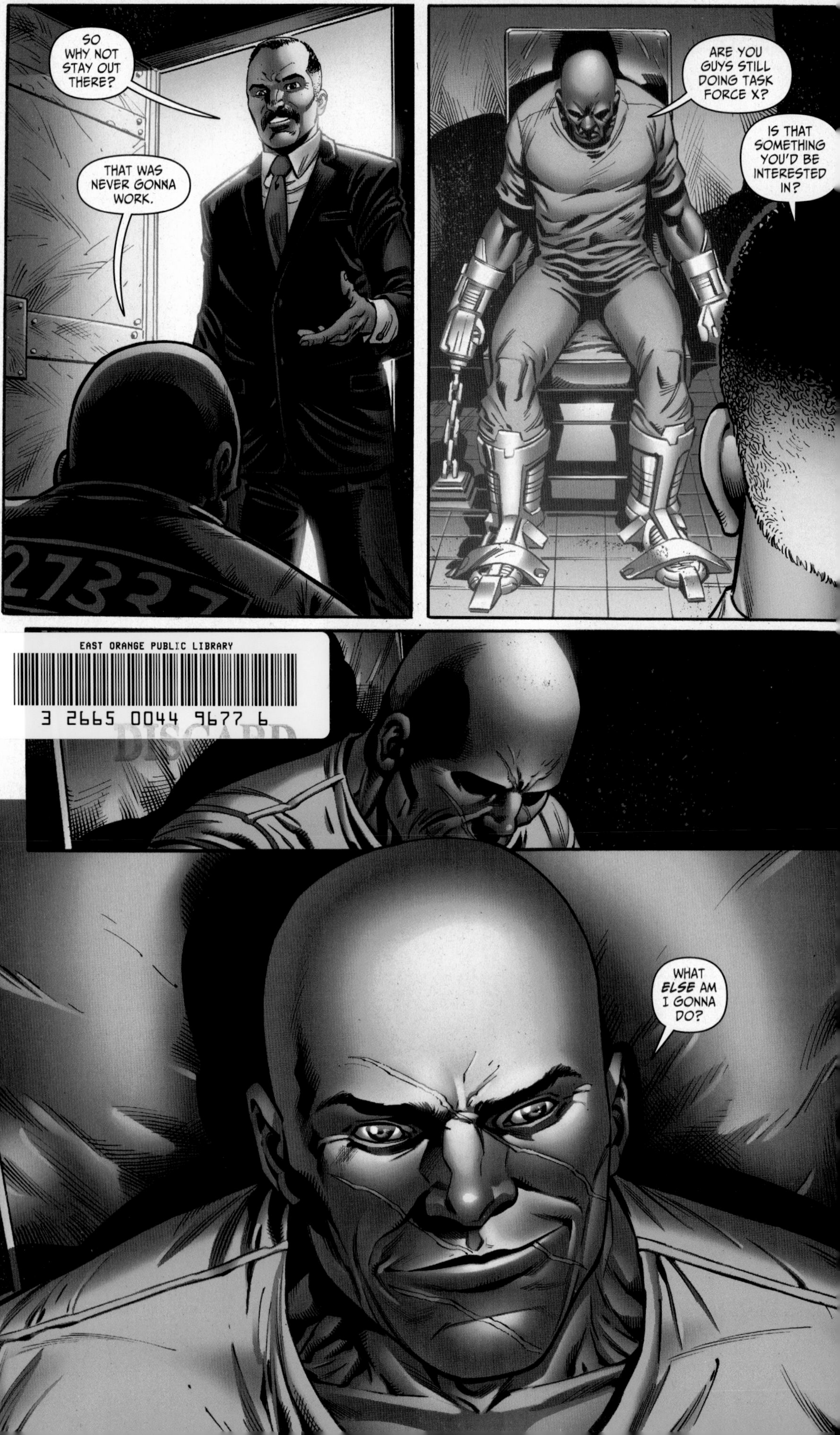

SO WHY NOT STAY OUT THERE?
THAT WAS NEVER GONNA WORK.
27337
ARE YOU GUYS STILL DOING TASK FORCE X?
IS THAT SOMETHING YOU'D BE INTERESTED IN?
WHAT *ELSE* AM I GONNA DO?